THE WILDCATS

A Story of Kentucky Football

THE WILDCATS

A Story of Kentucky Football

by
Russell Rice

THE STRODE PUBLISHERS, INC.
HUNTSVILLE, ALABAMA 35802

All Photographs Courtesy Of
University Of Kentucky
Department Of Athletics

Copyright 1975
By Russell Rice
All Rights In This Book
Reserved Including The Right
To Reproduce This Book Or Parts
Thereof In Any Form—Printed In U.S.A.
Library Of Congress Catalog Number 75-26071
Standard Book Number 87397-075-6

Contents

Introduction
 1. The First Game 11
 2. Prof. A. M. Miller 18
 3. Time Out: D. D. Slade 27
 4. The "Immortals Of '98" 30
 5. Era Of Professionalism 35
 6. Time Out: "Tommie" Bryant 41
 7. A Period Of Transition 47
 8. Long Journey For A Pigskin 54
 9. An All-Time Team 58
10. The Dutch Influence 66
11. "Injun Bill," "J. J.," And "Murph" 75
12. Curtis M. Sanders 84
13. Roll Out The Barrel 88
14. "Gloomy" Harry 94
15. Time Out: Shipwreck Kelly 103
16. Ralph Kercheval 112

17.	"The Chetter"	119
18.	The Thoroughbred Connection	126
19.	A. D. Kirwan	134
20.	Time Out: Ermal Allen	146
21.	Time Out: Bernie Shively	152
22.	The System	159
23.	The Salesman	169
24.	The Blanda Years	177
25.	Time Out: "Cholly Mac"	187
26.	A Minority Opinion	192
27.	"Sweet Kentucky Babe"	197
28.	Time Out: Steve Meilinger	207
29.	Bear Goes Bowl-ing	216
30.	Seeing Orange	224
31.	Bear Says Goodbye	228
32.	Blanton Collier	233
33.	Time Out: Bob Hardy	242
34.	The Actors	251
35.	Time Out: Lou Michaels	256
36.	All In The Family	263
37.	Charlie Bradshaw	270
38.	The Thin Thirty	276
39.	The Die Is Cast	282
40.	Run For The Roses	291
41.	Time Out: Dicky Lyons	298
42.	The Black Cloud	306
43.	Ray Of Sunshine	312
44.	Close Doesn't Count	322
45.	Super Sonny	330
46.	Time Out: Fran Curci	336
47.	Rupp: "The Way I Saw It"	344
	Appendix	359

Introduction

The razing of the University of Kentucky's McLean Stadium on historic Stoll Field in the summer and fall of 1974 was prime cause for nostalgia, but few Kentuckians regretted the passing. Oh, there were some former letter winners and longtime holders of season tickets who came around to say goodbye to the hallowed sod, but they shed no tears. Some even purchased the seats for a modest fee, but they also felt it was just as well that the old had given way to the new.

In Kentucky's case, that "new" was Commonwealth Stadium, a handsome, cantilevered concrete and steel structure located on an 86-acre tract that once was part of the UK Agricultural Experimental Station Farm on the south campus. Seating approximately 58,000 persons, it has parking spaces for more than 5,000 vehicles in four lots immediately surrounding the stadium, with two lots blacktopped and the other two in grass and gravel, to facilitate drainage in periods of heavy rainfall. The lower section is all precast concrete, the upper part structural steel columns, beams, and risers. Each section is independent of the other.

The press box, from 30 to 30 yard lines, is serviced by two elevators and has twin VIP booths on each end, six booths for radio, scoreboard, timekeeper, coaches-to-field setup, two food service lounges, regular working space with approximately 105 seats, two telecopier service areas, stats room, darkroom, and a photo deck that stretches across the entire front of the box.

The stadium became the new home of the Wildcats on September 15, 1973, and they christened it in grand style by defeating honored foe Virginia Tech, 31-26. Many spectators did not realize that occupancy of the facility was an uncertainty until the week of the game. In fact, the athletic ticket office had printed tickets for both the old and new stadiums just in case, and some people were wondering how it expected to get all those people in 37,500-seat McLean Stadium if the 50,000-plus Commonwealth was not ready in time.

Games that season were played before the stadium was completed, and the formal dedication did not take place until the first home game of 1974. During the rush-rush job of constructing the stadium in a period of 14 months (ground was broken July 23, 1972) priorities went to the playing field, seats, locker rooms, rest rooms, parking area, press box, scoreboard, and other areas vital to the playing of a game. The field was to be sprigged with Bermuda in the spring, but frequent rains kept the field wet until past the July 1 deadline. Bluegrass sod, befitting the state, was brought in as a temporary measure. It was beautiful but not the best playing surface for football since its blades grow singularly, it gets slick when it rains, and it does not replenish the cleated "divots" as does the creeping Bermuda.

One set of end zone bleachers was transferred from Stoll Field that first fall and erected in the west end zone of the new stadium. The other set was moved the following year, bringing the total seating capacity to just under 58,000. The stadium was constructed so that the seating can be continued around each end zone to make it a bowl-shaped facility seating 70,000 if and when the need arises. The bluegrass was replaced with Bermuda, modern offices were completed for the football staff in late August, and the constructing firm finally turned control of the facility over to the university.

To say the new stadium and Curci's brand of football—his team led mighty Alabama, 14-0, at half time of the second game played there—caught the state's fancy is putting it mildly. On a football game Saturday all Kentucky highways lead to Lexington, resulting in some traffic and parking problems that were ironed out when the 1974 season rolled around. With ample parking only the distance of a kickoff from the stadium, Wildcat fans suddenly caught up with the times and learned about tailgating. They came early and stayed late, picnicking, socializing, and just plain enjoying themselves.

It was with more than a tinge of pride that everyone rejoiced when the ABC-TV cameras beamed the Wildcat-Vanderbilt game to a regional audience on the afternoon of

November 9, 1974, and who could believe it when Bill Flemming and crew were right back the following weekend to telecast the UK-Florida game? The Wildcats defeated both the Peach Bowl-bound Commodores and the Sugar Bowl-bound Gators and then lost a bowl bid themselves when Tennessee defeated them the following Saturday in Knoxville.

The Wildcats drew a total of 328,515 fans for six home games in 1974, an average of 54,752 per game, good for 15th in the nation. And when the season ended, Curci had given them their first winning slate in nine years, winning six of 11 games. It was truly a cause for rejoicing, and for the first time in the memory of veteran UK fans Kentuckians were still talking football long into the basketball season.

I hereby express my sincere appreciation to all those former Wildcat players and coaches who accepted this venture so graciously and who gave so freely of their time. Special thanks also to Charles Atcher and his staff at the Archives of the Margaret I. King (UK) Library, and to chief editorial (and moral) supporter Doris Rice, my wife.

The First Game

The first intercollegiate football game ever played in the South and perhaps the first to take place west of the Alleghenies was played April 9, 1880, in Lexington on what later became known as Stoll Field, home of the University of Kentucky football team until 1973.

It is ironic that the UK campus boasts the distinction of serving as the birthplace of Dixie football but the forerunners of the present-day Wildcats were not involved in that early grid contest.

The facts pertaining to the origin of football in Kentucky are pretty well documented, and there seems no better place to start than with a letter written by Miles M. Dawson in the spring of 1916:

Miss Mae Cornelison, Editor-in-Chief
Crimson Rambler; Transylvania College,
Lexington, Kentucky

My Dear Madam:

The interest which the Rambler very naturally takes in the athletics of the college impels me to write you briefly concerning the origin of the football team.

During the sessions of 1878-79, which was my first year at Lexington, an Australian boy, C. L. Thurgood—afterwards pastor of a church in Pittsburgh, Pa., but now I think again in Australia, who had come with Mark Collis, having played on a football team in Ballarat, just outside of Melbourne, using the regulation football and Rugby rules. Like most college boys, I had read 'Tom Jones at Rugby', and I was much interested in his account.

Accordingly, in the spring, he and I clubbed together and sent for balls, rules, etc. To the best of my recollection he had to import them, or at least did import them, but of that I am not certain.

In any event, practice games were instituted in the spring of 1879. The next autumn my boyhood chum, Albon Lindeman, came down from Wisconsin to be my roommate. He joined the club which consisted among others, I remember, of John Fox, Jr., of Bassett, now president of a leading Lexington bank, and of Duncan, who has since been very prominent in Lexington.

While I played in practice games, I never 'made the team,' though the boys did utilize me in directing the training and also as one of the umpires in all the match games. Our match games were with Centre College which took it up, I think, at our suggestion soon after we did, and during the 1879-1880 season, we were uniformly successful in all contests. My boyhood chum Lindeman was quite an important factor in the game, and his prowess, I am sure, is well remembered by Joe Porter, Bassett, Duncan and the rest of the Lexington boys who were on the team and who are still there.

It may interest the undergraduates more in attendance to know that in a conversation with Professor Bacon, of the Yale Theological School, a few years ago, I learned that he was in the earliest Yale team and that this antedated our team by only about two years.

Yours very sincerely,

Miles M. Dawson.

After receiving a football from London, Thurgood, a student at the College of the Bible, assembled the students on the school campus at Third and Broadway in Lexington, selected two teams, and started teaching them the game.

Thurgood probably just divided the crowd because everyone present played in the game. John C. Taylor, who played, said in a letter to Prof. Ezra R. Gillis, dated February 23, 1940, "The ball was round and the game was quite different from the game called football today. The principle difference was they kicked the ball and were not allowed to run with it."

The aforementioned first intercollegiate game ever played in the South resulted from a challenge issued to Centre College by KU. Centre College promptly accepted. The game was played at City Park, also known as the baseball park, only 11 years after Princeton and Rutgers played the first intercollegiate football game.

The *Lexington Daily Transcript* reported the game as follows:

13 3/4 to 0

The above is the result of the match game of football played yesterday afternoon at the City Park between Centre College and Kentucky University teams. As the Danville boys had the reputation of being a splendid club, our boys expected to be beaten. The visiting club was composed of tall, athletic men, while the University Club was mostly made up of short but muscular boys, whose style of physique is considered best for such a game.

A large crowd of ladies and gentlemen, estimated at five hundred, witnessed the game. The ladies seemed to take especial interest in the fun, and it was pronounced that foot-ball had decidedly the advantage of base-ball as a means of amusement to the spectators. The collisions between players at various times were almost equal to the coming together of two Spanish bulls, and provoked much laughter. The game lasted two hours, commencing at 4 and ending at 6 o'clock. It was played according to the Princeton rules.

The Danville team was composed of the following young men: Fulton, Dunlap, Vaughan, Clark, McCartney, Cowan, Moore, Cowles, Barbour, Ernst, Taylor, January, Skinner, Webster, Read, Barrett and McKee.

The University Club of Fox, Allen, Logan, Shelby, King, Craig, Overstreet, Graves, Patterson, Hoopman, Garvey, Johnson, Lauderman, Langsford and Thurgood.

Ernst was Captain of the Danville Club and Patterson of the University. January, of the Danville Club acted as umpire. During the progress of the game, one of the Danville boys had his hand badly cut by falling on a piece of glass, the grounds having previously been used for glass ball shooting. We hope that another contest will come off soon between these clubs. Having played together for the first time, and knowing each others style, we have no doubt the Centre College boys will have better luck in future.

KU students continued to play the game on the Morrison Campus that year and the next year. In 1878 the state legislature withdrew the Agricultural and Mechanical College from KU. The new school was moved to South Limestone Street in 1882. By then A&M College was becoming known as Kentucky State College. It would become known as Kentucky State University in 1908 and the University of Kentucky in 1917.

City Park was located on a large tract deeded to A&M College by the city and later became the practice area next to what was known as Stoll Field. When that area was razed in 1974, the protective wall around the practice area also was demolished.

The A&M College did not play its first intercollegiate game until 1881, and football was not looked upon favorably by a majority of the people. That disfavor was expressed at times, as evidenced by the following story in the *Daily Press* of December 5, 1880:

> On Tuesday evening as some of the students of the A&M College were playing football, a man who afterwards gave his name as White, came riding by, and not liking the noise the students were making, commenced firing a pistol at them. They all ran and were followed by this man, who repeatedly loaded and fired whenever anyone appeared in sight. This continued for about an hour, when two or three of the more courageous approached near enough to knock the pistol from his hand, when they all pitched in and gave him a severe drubbing. They then took his cartridges from him and started him home.

It was almost a year later, on November 12, 1881, before A&M played in its first intercollegiate game, which was one in a series of three games with KU. KU issued the challenge and stipulated that all participants must be under 17 years of age. The game was played on Morrison Campus and was won, 7½ to 1, by KU. The second game, played one week later on the A&M grounds, was reported by the *Daily Transcript* as follows:

> In this exciting game between KU and A&M Saturday afternoon, KU carried off the honors beating the A&M 2 to 1. A good showing. A&M must wake up. The colleges play fifteen men on a side. The Eastern colleges play eleven. These contests develop muscle wonderfully, and if

Distant lake view of Kentucky State College, one of the most beautiful sites in the South.

not carried too far, are admirable accomplishment for hard study. Play a fair, gentlemanly game, my hearties, but work for all that's in you.

A&M lost the third and final match game to KU, 3¾ to 2¼.

The playing fields for those early games were about 110 yards long, but they were not marked off in 10-yard spaces. To start a game, the two teams lined up in the middle of the field, facing each other, and the referee stood on the side and threw the ball in between the two teams. It was legal to either kick the ball or run with it. When the runner was stopped, the teams would line up as before, and the referee would toss the ball in again. After one team succeeded in getting the ball across the opponent's goal line, the ball was placed on the 20 yard line, and the offensive team tried for goal.

Although numerical scoring had not yet been introduced in rugby football, persons in charge of those games obviously had arrived at some sort of agreement, assigning values to the various scoring plays. Noting the scores printed in newspaper accounts, it may be surmised that a touchdown perhaps counted ¼ point and that a goal or an end-kick (a punt into the modern end zone) counted one. Players were allowed a short rest period about midway into a contest. Admission was free, but there were no seats for spectators.

The *Lexington Leader* said the players wore a one-piece canvas suit, called a "smock," which was adopted from the Princeton pattern of a few years before. It laced up the front and was padded only on the shoulders. Players wore no headgear, hip pads or nose guards, but despite this lack of protective equipment few men were injured in early games.

There is no record of early games being played at A&M from 1882-1891. Football as we know it today got its beginning in Kentucky in 1891, when W. Durrant Berry, one of Amos Alonzo Stagg's "Christian Workers" squad members from the University of Chicago, was employed at Centre College and taught the students there to play the game. They promptly challenged State College. Old gray uniforms, cut off at the knee and stuffed with hay, together with stockings borrowed from sisters and others, constituted a part of the paraphernalia of battle. Centre won, 10-0, but State learned enough to hold Centre scoreless in the second half.

In April of that year, KSC had challenged the Georgetown College team to a game to be played at State. It resulted in an 8-2 victory for KSC. One week before the KSC-Centre game that fall, a contest between KSC and KU was terminated at the very beginning when Harrison, a State player, was knocked unconscious on the first play and was revived only after considerable difficulty. He was not hurt seriously, but the accident put an end to the game.

Prior to the game with Centre, State students held an ardent meeting for the purpose of choosing permanent college colors and a college yell. They decided on blue and light yellow, blue because it was typical of the bluegrass, and light yellow because it represented the richness of the land. Also adopted at that meeting was the following yell, chosen because of its brevity:

Rah! Rush! Ree! A! M!! C!!!

Neither the colors nor the yell stayed around very long. In a letter to Professor Gillis, R. C. Stoll, a member of the 1891-95 KSC teams, recalled:

"We had some other colors—I really don't recall what they were. But we had a meeting in the chapel in 1891 or 1892, my recollection is, to discuss the colors of the university."

After deciding on the now familiar blue and white, someone asked, "What color blue will it be?"

"I happened to have on a blue necktie and took it off and held it up," Stoll said. "That was the blue which was adopted."

After the turn of the century, State teams would be referred to often as the "Blue & White," with those colors being officially adopted in 1910. However, blue and yellow were the colors for that 1891 game with Centre, as noted in the following description from the *Lexington Daily Press*:

> The much talked of football game between the teams of State College and Centre College came off yesterday in the presence of over 500 people at the Baseball Park.
>
> The Danville team did not arrive until 2:40 in the afternoon, and it was past four when the game was called. Hundreds of people had been waiting over an hour. Ropes were stretched twenty feet away from the boundary line on either side and strips of board plank had been placed for people to stand on.
>
> The State College team went out about half past two o'clock. They created a good deal of enthusiasm with their band, and blue and yellow silk flag. Their suits were a white shirt, black stockings, and military trousers cut off at the knee.
>
> The Danville team were a formidable-looking set of fellows, and as they went out on the field they were generously cheered. It could be seen at a glance that they were in good training trim, and it must be confessed that the State College boys got a little 'skeered at the outset.'
>
> Danville scored after fifteen minutes of play on a pretty end run, scoring four points for Centre. The kick for goal was successful, scoring two points more for Centre. After thirty minutes of the game had passed, Centre, using splendid interference, scored on another end run from the five yard line. This made the score 10 to 0. The first half was 45 minutes—and at the half was a ten minute rest period. The second half was called at the end of twenty minutes because of darkness.
>
> It is said that the faculty, who have taken little interest in the game, are determined now to encourage the athletic feature of the college in every practical way they can.

From that point on, football would be a major interest of schools throughout the Bluegrass area.

Prof. A.M. Miller

The "daddy" of University of Kentucky football generally is conceded to have been Prof. A. M. Miller, whose scholarly appearance and position belied his enthusiastic interest in college athletics. A graduate of Princeton University with advanced degrees, he joined the staff of KSC in 1892. He later became dean of the College of Arts & Sciences and head of the Department of Geology.

His football knowledge apparently stemmed from sideline inspection of the game while a student at Princeton (there is no record of his playing the game) and experience of a sort gained while attempting to coach it at a girls' school in Pennsylvania. In the October, 1915, issue of the *Kentucky Alumnus,* he explained about coaching that team:

"I taught the girls to play the game in somewhat modified form. It was the theory of the president of the institution that all girls ought to understand how the different positions in the game were played so that they would better understand the fine points when they went down to Princeton or Yale to see the big game."

A delegation of students approached Professor Miller early in the fall of 1892 to urge him to coach the state team, and he consented to dispense his limited knowledge and talent.

Prior to 1892 State played its games in the City Park, which was also used as a pasture for President Patterson's cattle. President Patterson did not want football to interfere with his bovine herd, but Miller sold him on the idea that the pasture should be enclosed, a grandstand erected on it, and the field devoted exclusively to football. Miller formed a stock company

Prof. A. M. Miller.

to raise the money to finance the project, promising to set aside 10 percent of the gross gate receipts, from which he would pay dividends. The students did not buy the idea, but he did succeed in inducing members of the faculty, including Patterson and his brother, to take enough shares to defray the cost of the fence and to erect a grandstand costing $500 (a tidy sum in those days).

The professor later wrote in the *Kentucky Alumnus:*

When the grand stand was well on the road to completion at the place in the field best adapted for it, and two trees in front of it were partially dug up with a view of re-setting them in another part of the grounds, an order came from the President not to remove the trees.

Work on them was stopped immediately, but that night they were chopped down and removed, presumably by some of the students who were on the grounds at the time the order to stop work on them was received.

The President was very angry over the work of the midnight marauders and offered a reward for the detection

Jackie Thompson, coach 1892-93.

of the culprits. However, it was never disclosed at the time who constituted the tree cutting party.

The effect of this escapade was apparently to make the President still more suspicious of athletics, and though not openly opposing them from now on for several years, many obstacles were placed in the way of those who were endeavoring to put athletics somewhat on the plane that it was enjoying in other colleges.

After the KSC boys lost their next two games to Central and beat the Louisville Athletic Club by only four points, it became evident to Miller and everyone concerned that a more competent coach was needed. Paul Anderson, dean of the College of Engineering, saw Jack Thompson, a 145-pound halfback, playing for the great Purdue team and asked him to come to Lexington and help the State boys with their team. Thompson purchased a train ticket and arrived in Lexington the day before State was to play at Virginia Military Institute. He coached the boys on the train to Virginia and before the game. State played so raggedly that he stepped into a sweater and played the remainder of the afternoon, but, alas, the Kentuckians lost, 34-0.

When Thompson arrived at State, due partly to Miller's urging, Miller graciously accepted the position of manager of finances. This meant that Miller was to dig up the money for suits and other expenses, except shoes, which team members purchased individually. "If I couldn't make it out of gate receipts, it was my duty to foot the deficit," he said.

Since Miller was a member of the faculty, it is doubtful that he received extra compensation for his efforts in behalf of athletics. Thompson got no salary and was probably paid from the gate receipts by Miller and was hired for only the duration of the season. Fifty years later Thompson said all he got was a round trip ticket from Lafayette to Lexington.

"In those days we had to rely for officials very largely on persons who only knew the rules from having read them over in the book, and hence decisions were apt to be pretty raw," Miller said. "The first game of the season...was officially called a tie, 0-0, but really resulted in a victory for Kentucky State College, 2-0. Wallace of KSC clearly made a safety and it was only the ignorance of the officials in regard to the rules of the game that led him to call it a touchback."

In the 1893 season opener against Georgetown, the KSC

students, upon seeing the immaculate white suits of the visitors, exclaimed, "The Lord hath delivered them into our hands." After State won, 80-0, the *Daily Press* said, "The Georgetown team were a nice gentlemanly looking lot, but had not yet learned to play football."

John Bryan scored six touchdowns, John Redmon scored five, J. B. Jolly and George Scott scored two each, and M. T. Boswell had one for a total of 16 touchdowns. Bryan kicked five of eight goals, Scott three of eight. A touchdown counted four points, a goal two points.

In the next game, as recorded by the *Daily Press* of October 22, 1893, KSC defeated the University of Tennessee, 56-0, in the first football game played between these two institutions. The *Press* said the KSC boys gave UT "a superb lesson in almost faultless football playing. . . .The game was furious from start to finish. The 4,000 spectators, many of whom were ladies and in secret sympathy with the boys from the Blue Grass, witnessed just such a game of ball as they never have seen before or perhaps ever will see again."

The Centre game that year ended in confusion after Centre won, 6-4, and the teams attempted to arrange another game. Centre defended the right to play two ineligible players because State wished to use two former Centre players who were then enrolled in the Calhoun Business College in Lexington. State lost one other game, to Central, and tied Indiana, 24-24, in the first intersectional game in which State participated. It was described as the most stubbornly contested game seen in Kentucky in some time.

After the game it was decided that another game would be played the following day to break the scoreless deadlock. The *Leader* reported: "The visitors arrived in the city yesterday morning and are making the Hotel Reed their headquarters until the game Saturday, which will decide the game of yesterday. Quite a number of their supporters followed them from Indiana. . .to give their rather unusual and outlandish yell:

>Gloriana! Fransipani! Indiana!
>Kazoo, Kazah! Kazoo, Kazah!
>State University
>RAH! RAH! RAH!

The newspaper reported that the Thursday game was "unparalleled in Kentucky and yet it was due not to any intentionally rough playing, but rather to the unusual strength and

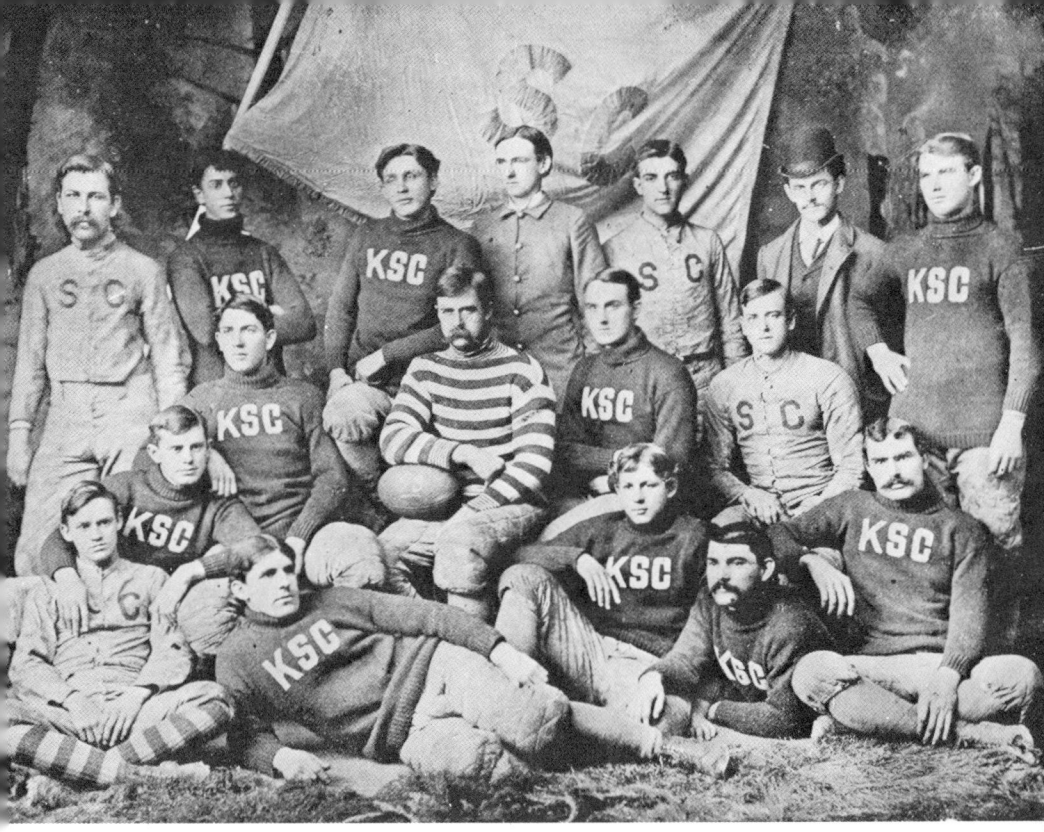

1893 Team. Standing: Rufus L. "Mudcat" Weaver, E. H. Hobdy, John Woods, Student Manager B. F. Van Meter, Tom Gunn, Herbert "Yankey" Hill, George Carey. Sitting: J. I. Lyle, Captain U. A. Garred, J. S. Steely, M. T. Boswell. Reclining: Harry Redmon, Harvey "Sandy" Gardner, John Bryan, R. C. Stoll, J. V. Faulkner, J. B. Jolly.

weight of the two teams." Those injuries took their toll, and the two teams decided not to play the tie-breaking game.

Captain of the 1894 State team was George Carey, who later said there were 15 men on the team and not one of them had seen a football game before entering KSC. They were able to secure some sweaters and trousers and felt themselves well equipped.

Hero of a 38-10 State victory over Central in 1894 was James W. Carnahan. Carnahan was called "ox" and "steer" because of his size, but he had played center with little success in 1892. Then, after VMI's small center outplayed him in a game in 1892 and he received a chafing by his teammates, Carnahan refused to play at all the following year. However, he indicated to Professor Miller in the fall of 1894 that, if given a suit, he would try football again. He was moved to tackle and played so well that near the end of the game the crowd would yell, "Give the ball to Carnahan!" One time he tore through the line for 15 yards with the entire CU team on his back.

A typical game of 1895 is described in a typewritten paper dated November 4, 1895, which was owned by the late S. A. Boles:

"The State College defeated Kentucky University by a score of 26 to 0 yesterday afternoon (Nov. 3, 1895). The KU team had disbanded a week ago, but consented to play the State College boys by making up a team composed of both Kentucky University and Lexington Athletic Club Players.

"The day was an ideal one for a football game, being clear and cool and having no wind. The game was very poorly attended, there being only about 150 present. The game was absolutely devoid of slugging and the utmost good humor prevailed throughout. Mr. Martin acted as referee and Mr. Mason (State's coach) as umpire. Capt. Alford won the toss and took the western end for State College, KU kicking off. State College got the ball and by steady work soon made a touchdown and missed a goal. The first half ended State College 4, KU 0.

"In the first half, the KSC team did not play as well as

From the 1894 Kentuckian.

usual, but livened up in the second half and made four touchdowns, kicking all but one goal and making the score 26 to 0 in favor of State College. The KU team was strengthened by Helm and Duncan, of the KSC team. The best playing for KU was done by Stoll, Coleman, and Lucas. Stoll played a great game and showed that he will be a great addition to the State College team. The State College manager is trying to arrange a game with Richmond for next Saturday, but it has not been definitely arranged as yet."

Eligibility apparently was not considered an important factor in this game since several KSC students played with KU. The team also included members of the LAC. The KU team was evidently very trusting since it permitted State coach Mason to act as umpire. But at least he did not play in the game.

The State team that year provided no special thrills, and the year was distinctive only because it marked first-time meetings with Purdue, DePauw, and Ohio State. Each defeated State, as did two other foes in a 4-5 season. Concerning the salary paid Coach Mason, Professor Miller wrote:

"There was a deficit at the close of the season and Mr. Mason never received the full amount of the salary promised him. However, in the judgment of the writer, he got all he was worth."

Professor Miller felt that William Ed Hobdy (1892-93) was probably the best athlete at State in those days. Hobdy won the 100-yard dash competition in 10.75 seconds in his baseball shoes and clothes. He also won the pole vault, hammer throw, and running broad jump in a track meet held on the campus.

"The most spectacular performances in the majority of the games was the work of William Martin and John Kehoe, the speediest ends State had in that era," Professor Miller said. "In the style of game permitted by the rules then, it was possible to run speedy ends to good advantage, and these two players were used to carry the ball fully as much, if not more than the backs."

Throughout the remainder of his years at the university, Miller was a friend of the athletic program, serving on various boards and committees. He performed an invaluable service in recording some of his memories for posterity in the *Kentucky Alumnus,* although some of his facts, gleaned from memory, were subject to question.

For instance, he reported that the 1900 Wildcat team

defeated Louisville YMCA, 12-6, without running an offensive play from scrimmage. The Wildcats would punt on first down every time they got the ball and won the game by recovering the other team's fumbles, he reported. However, newspaper accounts list the Wildcats as running several plays, but they did get their first touchdown by recovering a blocked kick in the end zone and the other by recovering a ball in the end zone after the Louisville punter had kicked it back over his head instead of forward.

Dr. Miller served as dean of the College of Arts & Sciences from 1909 to 1917 and was professor emeritus of geology at the time of his death in 1929. Old-time UK players remembered him as the man who took the greatest interest in getting a team together, securing a competent coach, and promoting new interest in football. A speaker at the dedication ceremony for Stoll Field in 1916 paid tribute to him for his part in the uphill struggle of the early days to establish athletics as something worthy of encouragement and support.

Time Out: D. D. Slade

By his own admission, D. D. Slade was a fine bicyclist but not much of a football player at Kentucky State College in 1897.

"I only played that one year," the 95-year-old retired poultry expert said in January, 1975. "I didn't play any at all in high school, but I was a regular at end every time they lined up at old Stoll Field. They played me because I could outrun all of them—the whole shebang."

Sitting in the living room of his apartment in Lexington's Hanover Towers, the oldest living "K-Man" searched the back roads of his memory and told of a time when football was a "minor issue." Teams played their own coaches and sometimes borrowed players from the other team to fill the quota for a game.

"We had only four or five more players than we needed to make a team," he said. "The students weren't satisfied with the coach they had the previous year, and they got a new coach named Lyman Eaton from Cincinnati. I don't remember that we had very many practices. We just got in and played the best way we could.

"It was kinda harem-scarem on defense, and I got to carry the ball once in a while when they would call on me to run it around the other end. We had nothing on our heads and no padding, just extra heavy cloth trousers. We called it pretty rough, but if you look at the way they play now, it wasn't rough at all. It's rougher today because the boys count on protection that is given them by all that equipment and pads, so they really ram.

"I remember we had a guy come down from Cincinnati to

play one game, but I don't remember if he helped us any. Your memory gets foggy as the devil when you're as old as I am, you know."

If ever a team needed help, it was that 1897 crew. It played so badly that rumors persisted that it would be disbanded. It defeated KU, 8-6, lost to Wesleyan, 4-0, and defeated Georgetown, 20-4, before losing to Vanderbilt, 50-0, Central, 18-0, and Centre, 36-0, for a 2-4 record.

The series with Vanderbilt was inaugurated the year before in Nashville, where the Commodores defeated State, 6-0.

"The game I remember most was the Vanderbilt game," Slade said. "They beat the tar out of us. They ran all over the top of us. They didn't hold back a thing."

That was without question the worst football team State

Team of 1897. Front, left to right: C. C. Clarke, L. W. Martin, Harvey, Captain Roscoe Severs, D. D. Slade. Middle: Samuel Hogg, Andrew Asher, James Campbell, Coach Lyman Eaton, Eugene Whane. Back: Charles Straus, J. M. Elliott, Mgr. W. T. Carpenter, Jack Johnson, T. S. Hamilton.

had produced up to that time. To make matters worse, the covered grandstand burned due to unslaked lime having been carelessly stored under it. A rain came up one night, the ground under the stand was flooded, the lime slaked, the barrels caught fire, and the stand was consumed before morning. A short while later, the fence fell to pieces, and the track was in bad condition. That was all a considerable loss. Although the grandstand and fence were modest structures, there were no funds to replace them. The students did not know what to do, and it became necessary for the faculty to assume a greater control of financial matters pertaining to athletics. That year the student management of athletics was vested in an athletic association, a consolidated organization formed by the union of three subdivisions known respectively as Football, Baseball and Track Athletic Associations. Faculty control of athletics was secured through its Committee on Athletics which acted in accordance with a special set of regulations adopted by the board of trustees and also by the faculty itself.

The *Minutes of the Senate*, December 3, 1897, recorded that a new athletic committee appointed by President Patterson that fall had taken disciplinary action against two of the players, Clarke and Slade. They were charged with violating a regulation that provided that a certain class standing must be maintained as a condition of eligibility. The faculty passed a resolution providing for the suspension of Clarke and Slade for two weeks from college duties and privileges, and they were forbidden to engage in athletics for the remainder of the year.

In essence, that was not much of a penalty as the season had ended and Slade played on no other athletic teams. After that school year he accepted a position with a coal company in Eastern Kentucky. He eventually returned to the university, became head of its poultry department, and then spent more than 40 years in the chicken hatchery business in Lexington before retiring in 1967 at the age of 88.

"I lost track of football for a while after leaving Lexington," he said, "but I caught back up with it. I went to a game in the new stadium when it was first opened here two years ago, but I haven't been back since—didn't like the seats.

"I watch football all the time on television. I never thought for a minute it would grow like it has."

The "Immortals Of '98"

The only undefeated, untied, and unscored upon football team at the University of Kentucky was a squad known as the "Immortals of '98." The team amassed a total of 180 points while holding opponents scoreless, but experts of that era refused to label it as the best State college team because it played during the Spanish-American War. Football was at a low ebb, and a great many athletes were in the armed services.

There were several military camps located in Kentucky, with an estimated 20,000 soldiers in the Lexington area. According to Professor Miller, it was considered creditable to defeat those teams because many ex-college football players could be found in their ranks.

The "Immortals" played only seven games. The Centre game was called off after 15 minutes of play because a cloudburst practically washed the field away, and the spectators all went home. With no one to cheer them on, the two teams decided to call it quits and State, ahead 6-0, was declared the winner. State also defeated KU (18-0), Georgetown (28-0), Company H of the 8th Massachusetts (59-0), a picked team of two divisions of soldiers (17-0), the Louisville Athletic Club (16-0), and the Newcastle Athletic Club (36-0).

W. R. Bass of the University of Cincinnati was the coach that year, and W. L. Bronaugh was team manager. The regular lineup was John Kehoe, LE; E. C. Whayne, LT; J. W. Graham, LG; C. C. Clarke, center; Charles L. Straus, RG; W. C. Wills, RT; Louis Martin, RE; Roscoe Severs, captain and quarterback; Milward Elliott, LH; A. S. Reese, RH; and James D. Turner, FB. The substitutes were Sidney Smith, Ernest Lyle, Herman

Scholtz, Dick Wilson, Roy Maddox, Sam Hogg, and Claude Humphreys.

Graham, who later became head of the UK College of Engineering, told the *Kentucky Kernel* in 1936 that the hardest game they played was with "that bunch of picked soldiers."

"They bet around $25,000 on the game and they weren't betting they would win," he said, "but that they could score on us. We managed to keep them from scoring though, and the next week we finished off the season without being scored on."

Professor Miller charged that KU used two soldiers who had matriculated from the Smith Business College, which had a nominal connection with that university. It was not uncommon then for athletes to matriculate in business schools and play with the local colleges. State objected to the use of these "ringers" and protested the game, but the matter was dropped after State won the game. The soldiers had registered at the school, played in the game, and then dropped out—all in one day. Eighteen years later Dr. John J. Tigert, then UK athletic director, said in a letter to Presley Atkins:

> This morning one Mr. Anderson, U. S. Pension Inspector, called on me to find out if I could give him any information about a certain man who played football at Kentucky University (Transylvania) in 1898. The man's name was Oren H. Kunce. He was at that time in a company which was camping around here, and when the KU-State game was played Kunce claimed that he played with KU under an assumed name against State. That he had his knee injured in the game and he is now applying to the Government for Pension on this ground. He says that he was ordered to play in the game by his superior officer, Col. Gunder. Kunce also alleges that a Sergeant by the name of Bloss played in the game under an assumed name. . . The game was played on Oct. 1, 1898, and resulted in a victory for State by the score of 18 to 0.

Colonel Graham said he played against a lineman named Hart in the game with the Louisville Athletic Club, and, "I later read that he had won the heavyweight championship of the world. I think he must have been in training that day."

No matter how and against whom they achieved their record, the "Immortals" were a hard-working, dedicated lot, as evidenced from the following statement by Graham:

"We would go out for practice at 3 o'clock in the afternoon and practice until dark. When the light got so bad that we couldn't see the ball, we would run around the field for a while to improve our wind. We adhered strictly to training rules, and scrimmage was a part of every practice except on Monday, when we rested up a little from the Saturday game."

The State team used the T-formation. Games were divided into two 35-minute halves. Only one official took care of the game, and the defense kept tackling until the player carrying the ball yelled "down."

"Not a man was hurt all year," Graham said, "and play was really rough. Why, if a man tackled above the waist he was disgraced. Tackles were usually made by diving 10 or 15 feet through the air to grab the ballcarrier's ankles.

"We ran about 130 plays a game while today they run only 50 or 60. And once we took the opening kickoff, ran four plays, and scored a touchdown—all in 51 seconds. I could run the 100 yards in 10 seconds, and the rest of the team wasn't much slower. I've lost track of the fellows, but they were all grand fellows and played the game because they liked it."

The all-winning season had the apparent effect of swaying the opinion of the anti-athletic element in the faculty and the board of trustees. An indication of this support was in the *Minutes of the Senate*, December 9, 1898:

"The record of the football team was excellent and by the continued supervision of the faculty over the details of athletic sports we believe that the present high standard will be maintained."

In 1899 a writer for the *Kentuckian* noted:

> For a long time I thought that college football was an invention of the devil, and I wondered why he did not take better care of his own, and guard them against such accidents as are sure to happen in the best regulated teams. It seemed to me that a gang of shock-headed lunatics, turned loose in padded bloomers, and gum noses, and leather ear-flaps, for the especial purpose of interfering with each other was likely to create pandemonium on earth. When I heard, or read, of their "half-backs," and "quarter-backs," I supposed that the acme of cruelty in mutilation had been attained; and when I read of a "full-back" I conceived the vision of a bushy-headed Frankenstein, very concave in the abdomen, and most artistically drunk.
>
> Such conceits governed my judgement until, once, I

Team of 1898. Front, left to right: Ernest Lyle, J. D. Turner, L. W. Martin, J. H. Kehoe, C. C. Clarke. Middle: James W. Graham, Charles Straus, Captain Roscoe F. Severs, Claude Wills, Eugene C. "Mad Anthony" Whayne. Back: S. J. Smith, John Willim, Coach "Billy" Bass, Student Manager W. L. Bronaugh, Claude Humphreys, Milward Elliott, Roy Maddox.

witnessed a game wherein our then post-master, McChesney, and myself were chasing down the side lines yelling as best two effete old "has-beens" could, and trying to overtake President Patterson, who was flying along on three legs in an effort to be in at the finish when a wild-eyed youth was about to make a touchdown....

The following article denotes the attitude of the students at KSC concerning football at their alma mater:

The Kentucky State College has the grittiest little team on the southern gridiron. Tho' the average weight is only one hundred and forty-seven pounds, they hung KU's hide on the fence when her team was much larger, and played Central a tie when the latter played a team averaging nearly twenty pounds more than that of K. C.

We are glad that the team of the State College is held in such high regard by the other colleges of Kentucky and the South....The State College has always put forth a *college* team—not a set of "ringers"....The blood of old Kentucky, the best in the world, that courses through the veins of our gridiron heroes, clearly manifests itself on all occasions, and though they may be beaten, that team does not exist that can conquer them....

This was the period during which the foundation for organized football was laid at the University of Kentucky. Coaches were secured to direct and teach the skills of the game, with students choosing the coaches and the salaries being paid by the manager from the gate receipts at the close of the season. It was not unusual for a coach to play with his team or officiate a game in which his team was not playing.

At the request of the president and the board of trustees, a faculty athletic committee was organized in 1893, but it had little control over athletics for several years. Having more control was an athletic association composed of student officers.

The Kentucky Intercollegiate Athletic Association was organized during that era, with a membership consisting of KSC, KU, Centre, Georgetown, and Central University. The association suspended Centre in 1894 because of disagreements between the Centre coach and other colleges.

The faculty established its control over football at KSC in 1897, giving first priority to control of finances, the second to eligibility. Its plea for funds was rejected in 1897, but after the successful season turned in by the "Immortals," the Board of Trustees appropriated $150 annually—beginning that year and continuing it for several years to come. Football was therefore established as a definite and integral part of the KSC program at the turn of the century.

Era Of Professionalism

"Football annihilates the society dude and the cigarette worm," the *Kentuckian* opined just before the turn of the century. "For this, if for nothing else, it deserves well of the state."

Kentucky State College president Patterson did not agree. He loathed football, baseball, and all other sports. "Almost as soon as college work begins, football teams are organized and begin training," he complained to the trustees. "Twenty or thirty men are withdrawn for athletic exercise almost every afternoon."

Calling this "an atmosphere uncongenial to study," he continued. "I do not speak of broken noses, legs and arms, but of the time wasted, idleness encouraged and a heritage of demoralization carried over to the succeeding year. This is a serious matter and deserves your careful attention."

The matter was so serious and injuries and deaths from the game so numerous that editors, ministers, educators, doctors, and other concerned persons cried out against the professionalism and mayhem of football as it was known then. The game had reached such a low state that some institutions discontinued it, and others threatened to follow suit if abuses did not end.

After the 1895 season, the trustees passed resolutions practically abolishing football, but Patterson realized that this was going too far and suggested to the students a plan by which they might get the game reinstated. They agreed, and he appointed a new committee on athletics which was responsible for the selection of a KSC alumnus as coach of the football team.

Dudley Short, former State athlete, was secured as coach, but he did not remain for the entire season and was succeeded by Smith Alford, who was captain of the 1895 team and a member of the 1896 team. The team won three of nine games that year and finished the following year with a 5-2-2 record under Coach W. R. Bass. However, the faculty athletic committee at one time thought seriously about disbanding the team when it behaved badly on a trip to Knoxville.

Many colleges were guilty of playing professionals, and State was one of the worst offenders, with a record of such practice dating back to the very beginning of the organized game in Kentucky. In 1894 State hired W. P. Finney, a tackle and captain of the 1893 Purdue team, as trainer for the express purpose of playing him in a scheduled game with Centre. The excitement over his impending arrival turned to disappointment when he hobbled out on crutches for that first practice session. He had broken his leg while playing in a game before coming to Lexington. However, State went ahead and arranged a game with Centre in which coaches were to play. Meanwhile Centre had secured Messler, a Yale man. After Centre won, 67-0, Professor Miller wrote, "Messler was a superb athlete, and Finney would have been no match for him, even had he (Finney) been at his best."

In 1900, Cincinnati refused to pay expenses after State failed to finish a game. State objected strongly to Cincinnati's best athlete, who was not a matriculate of that institution and who left immediately after the game to join the team of the Pittsburgh Athletic Club. Cincinnati was ahead, 20-6, when State walked off the field. In Centre's game with Cincinnati that year, sworn deputies had to escort the Cincinnati players to the railway station to protect them from bodily harm.

Jackie Thompson, who succeeded Miller as coach midway through the 1892 season, loved the game so much that when he was not playing for State, he filled in by playing for an Indianapolis athletic club or any other outfit that could use a good player. When State played him against Central in a game in 1892, the visitors protested vehemently; however, Centre's coach complained the following year that State was the only school in Kentucky that objected to the playing of coaches.

The most flagrant violation involving the forerunner of the University of Kentucky occurred in 1903. State did not want to play KU on Thanksgiving since that team allegedly was composed almost exclusively of "ringers." However, the public demanded that the game be played, and the athletic council realized that if once State could beat KU, it could feel justified in the severance of all athletic relations. There seemed, however, no prospect in defeating KU under existing conditions, although State, like KU, was undefeated at the time.

The committee finally gave a free hand to a delegation of alumni and supporters with the understanding that they should raise the necessary funds to secure an outside team to play KU. A delegation went East and made the arrangements. Most of the players, including a fullback named Smith who was listed on Walter Camp's All-American team, came from Columbia University's team, and a few were from athletic clubs in or about New York.

The State team that trotted out on the field on Thanksgiving Day contained only a few State college students, while

1903 team.

KU started and finished with its own players. However, there were some "strangers" on the sideline, apparently being held in reserve in case of need. The crack Eastern players in State uniforms showed up poorly, especially on offense. The only State gains were made near the end of the game when, with defeat almost a certainty, the State coach began putting in his real students.

The game attracted more attention than any played in Kentucky up to that time. The crowd was estimated at 3,500, and a total of approximately $12,000 was bet on the outcome. Outclassed from the start, State lost, 17-0, with Smith (alias Dixon) gaining only 28 yards. Hogan Yancey gained 169 yards and scored two of KU's touchdowns. Worth Yancey gained 49 yards.

Captain F. M. Maddox of State took the loss philosophically—"I have nothing to say; when I am beat, I am beat"—but the board of trustees took a different view of the situation and condemned the action of the athletic committee. An investigating committee reported, "It has a bad effect on the student body, tending to encourage insubordination which seems to be rampant in the college and has brought reproach to the institution."

The following year State, under Dr. F. E. Schact, an All-American tackle at Minnesota, had what was probably its best team of that era, winning nine of 10 games. After an opening 28-0 thumping of Paris Athletic Club, it met Indiana at Bloomington. According to Dr. Tigert, halfback C. W. Haynes "made the big Indiana line look like shredded wheat biscuits and eye witnesses claim that the like was never seen before or since." Manager Dan Bryant telegraphed Prof. Paul Anderson: "Twelve to nothing. Old State wins. We eat chicken tonight."

The message set off what Tigert described as "a negligee parade, bonfires, and other student frivolities that sometimes prove such a nuisance to unsympathetic citizens."

Later that season State overwhelmed Centre, 81-0, which set a scoring record in Kentucky at the time. State scored 14 touchdowns and 11 goals in the game, for the largest total made by a UK team since the 1893 team scored 16 touchdowns (counting four points each) and eight goals (at two points each) in an 80-0 win over Georgetown. By 1904, a touchdown counted five points and a goal one point. UK would defeat Wilmington, 87-0, in 1916, and North Dakota, 83-0, in 1950, when a touchdown would count six points and a goal one point.

The only State players who did not score a touchdown in that game were the center and the quarterback. Presley Atkins, the quarterback, apparently modestly let his teammates capture the glory.

The final game was the traditional meeting with KU. Prof. A. Fairhurst, chairman of the faculty athletic committee at KU, remembered the wide assortment of players brought in by State the preceding year. He wrote to A. St. Clair MacKenzie, of the KSC Athletic Committee, and said, in part:

"Whatever may be the composition of your team. . .KU will play you. You may bring your team as you did last year from the four quarters of the earth, and from the fifth quarter, if you can find it—bring Hottentots, Flat-Headed Indians, Patagonans, native Australians, Esquimaux, New Yorkers, Danvillans, Whatnots, Topknots—gather them from all the tribes and kindreds of the earth—the more motley the conglomeration the merrier it will be—and we will play you..."

State won, 21-4, in what was described as "a hard-fought, clean, and high-toned example of pigskin science."

The experience of 1903 had its effect on State policy, but there still was some relaxing of the rules, as evidenced by the fact that J. White Guyn earned a fifth varsity football letter after he graduated and while he was working as an engineer for the city of Lexington. During a visit to Lexington in October, 1946, he explained that after his collegiate career ended (officially, that is) in 1904, he accepted an engineering position with the city. When he entered Stoll Field on the afternoon of a football game during the 1905 season, he became a participant again when his former teammates pressed him into service.

"While they huddled around me, I hastily donned a substitute's jersey and played the second half," he said. "Sure, the other team griped, but nothing came of it. However, President Patterson said I'd have to register to play, though, and I did that just before the team started on a trip to West Virginia. I refereed their game at Marshall, but then I came on home while they went to Morgantown."

Dissatisfaction resulting from such laxness of eligibility rules, professionalism, and degradation of the game itself brought about measures to regulate football. The biggest changes in the rules in 1906 were ones in which the pushing and pulling of all types of mass plays was done away with; the forward pass was legalized; seven men were required on the line of scrimmage when the ball was centered; and the offensive team was given three downs to make 10 yards and a first down, instead of five yards. Under these rules the style of play became more open, and there was a definite increase in the amount of punting. The more open type of game enabled light, fast teams to compete with the heavy, plunging teams. Kentucky threw its first forward pass that year, but it took some time before the potential of that new offensive weapon was realized.

Time Out: "Tommie" Bryant

In January, 1975, Thomson R. "Tommie" Bryant was apparently the oldest living person to have won varsity letters in both football and basketball at the University of Kentucky, having received his basketball "K" as a player in 1905-06-07 and his football letter as team manager in 1907.

Sitting in his office in the Agricultural Experimental Station on the UK campus just before his 90th birthday, the tall, former athlete remembered the infamous 1903 game with KU and a couple other unique situations that occurred during his six years as a prep and undergraduate student at the university.

"The alumni and some other boosters brought in those 'ringers' for the Thanksgiving Day game with KU," he said. "The coach got them together on the eve of the game and ran a few signals on the dirt floor in the drill hall of Buell Armory, and they just weren't ready. We recovered a fumble right after the kickoff and carried the ball inside their 20, but that was the only time we played in their territory all afternoon.

"I saw my first lateral pass in that game. Just as they were getting ready to tackle Worth Yancey, he threw to Hogan Yanccy, who made a good gain. I can still see that play in my mind. The Yancey boys were great, and they beat us. We were heartbroken. That was our first defeat of the season. The only guy who played any good for us was one of our own guys, and he didn't get in until the second half."

The other two games Bryant spoke of were played in 1905. One was conducted under order of law, and the other involved a scrub team and the worst loss ever suffered by a UK football team.

Here is how the *Herald* explained what must rank as one of the most unusual situations ever to have occurred in the history of college football:

As will be remembered the Kentucky State College football team left Lexington last Wednesday morning for Huntington, W. Va., to meet the Marshall College eleven on the gridiron Thursday afternoon. Friday afternoon, KSC was scheduled to play the Catlettsburg Athletic Association. During the summer KSC had scheduled a game with the University of West Virginia for Nov. 4th. This game with West Virginia was cancelled a few days before the team left and nothing was said regarding the forfeit of $225, if either team cancelled.

While the game with Marshall was in progress at Huntington, the West Virginia manager came and attached the gate receipts for the game and had three officers waiting at the hotel to confiscate the football material of the KSC boys when they came in from the game. Things were lively for a while. . . the boys trying to hide their clothes or get them out of the hands of the officers.

The KSC authorities with the team. . .employed counsel to defend the team. After consultation. . .the team and authorities were ordered to appear in court.

The situation of the KSC boys was rather embarrassing; the money from Marshall College could not be collected; their clothes at police headquarters; a game of football the following day with Catlettsburg. . . .Every different phase of the situation was discussed. . .and a conclusion was finally reached that the KSC team accompany the West Virginia manager to Morgantown and play the University of West Virginia eleven.

State was overwhelmingly defeated, 45-0, by the Mountaineers.

"I don't remember much about the game," Bryant said, "but I do remember Dr. Schact (the coach). They called him 'Germany,' and he still had an accent. We had chapel every morning, and sometimes President Patterson would invite others to speak. Dr. Schact got up one day and said, 'If you don't play, you can rut.'"

Schact was not around to "rut" (root) when his team suffered their most disastrous loss, to St. Louis on November 18, 1905. With a hard game coming up against Centre the following week, he had decided to conserve himself and his regulars for the Danville boys. He asked a friend, Dr. Pryor, to accompany the team, assuring him that he would send along a representative team. When the train left Lexington, every starting player, Schact, and the team manager were missing. St. Louis defeated State, 82-0, and threatened not to pay the guarantee because Schact had not sent his team. Dr. Pryor talked them into paying off.

Schact was succeeded by J. White Guyn, who got excused from his job with the city to attend practice sessions each afternoon. His first State team had some difficulty mastering the new rules, but they learned quickly and played well at the end. They lost the opening game to Vanderbilt, 28-0, simply because of their lack of confidence in the rules, along with Vanderbilt's superior play. It was said the Commodores gave them a good indoctrination into the forward pass and other innovations of the game. In the next contest, with the Eminence Athletic Club, the first pass ever thrown by a Kentucky team was attempted.

With State leading, 12-0, Eminence kicked and George Brockman advanced the ball to the 35. Earl Stone threw UK's first forward pass, completing it to Stanley Baer for 35 yards; however, the play was called back because the ball was not pitched five yards from center. State was leading, 28-0, when Stone completed a 22-yard pass to Baer for UK's first completion. He later hit Brockman for 15 and Baer for 32 and had one intercepted. In the opening game with Vanderbilt, one newspaper said neither team threw a pass while another account said Vandy scored one of its touchdowns on a delayed pass. UK definitely did not throw one until the Eminence game.

State defeated KMI, 16-11, by scoring in the last 10 seconds. Then the team lost to Marietta and Centre but defeated Georgetown and Tennessee, for a 4-3 record. Guyn's best season was in 1907, the year Bryant was team manager. State won nine games that year, losing only to Vanderbilt, 40-0, and tying Tennessee, 0-0, at Knoxville. The only team beside Vanderbilt to score on State was Maryville, in a game played two days after the Tennessee game.

"We arranged the schedule so both games could be played on the same trip, which wasn't an unusual thing," Bryant said. "I was appointed head linesman for the Tennessee game, and despite my efforts in favor of the home team, I don't think either team made a first down. It had been raining for three

Team of 1907. Front row, left to right: Jefferson Elgin, Peter Rodes, Ralph Routt, Neville Stone, James Wilson, Richard Barbee. Middle row: J. H. Paine, William Clark, George Adair, George Dunlap, George Hendrickson, J. White Guyn, Coach. Back row: T. R. Bryant, manager, George Brockman, Horace Walker, Albert Mathers, Richard Stoffer, J. D. Brewer.

weeks, and it was rough going. Each team would make two efforts and then punt. That process went on until the clock mercifully put an end to it.

"Earlier that year, the Winchester Athletic Club forfeited a game with us, and we arranged a game with the Louisville Manual Training School on that same date, beating them, 30-0. Sometimes you played games two weeks apart, sometimes two or three days apart. Scheduling was kinda loose."

In 1899, Washington & Lee lost to Central of Richmond at Louisville on Thursday and then came directly to Lexington to play State. After the Friday contest ended in a scoreless tie, managers of the two teams decided on a playoff the following day. The time of each game was 45 minutes, and it looked as if the second game might end as had the first until State Capt. A. S. Reese scored on a 10-yard plunge and again carried the ball to the 10 yard line on what was called a guards-back formation. One of the squabbles so frequent in those days arose, and it got dark before matters could be adjusted. The Generals lost to

Tennessee the following day at Knoxville.

"We only made two trips out of state—both into Tennessee—the year I managed," Bryant said. "It was after that year that they started going to Michigan, Indiana, Illinois, North Carolina, and some of the southern schools on a more or less regular basis. Travel took a long time, and it was just a matter of not having enough funds to pay expenses for a lot of trips."

A financial report prepared by treasurer H. E. Curtis and submitted to the Faculty Committee on Athletics by Prof. A. M. Miller, its chairman, showed that Bryant did a pretty good job as manager. Bryant personally sold $1,015 worth of season tickets and ran his operation in an efficient manner. Total receipts were $3,149.84, compared to expenditures of $2,464.93.

With the football program finally on a sound financial basis, Guyn visited the Indian school at Carlisle, Pennsylvania, in the fall of 1908 and studied the style and character of football as taught by Coach Glenn L. Warner at Carlisle Institute. Guyn returned to KSU with new plays and formations.

The first official action of the athletic association that fall was to name the gridiron "Stoll Field" in honor of Mr. R. C. Stoll, a member of the board of trustees, a member of the 1891-95 State football teams, and an ardent supporter of his alma mater. State defeated Berea, Maryville, Rose Polytechnic Institute, and Centre and lost to Tennessee, Sewanee, and Michigan.

Bryant always maintained that one of the most extraordinary features of football in his era was the arbitrary time limit in each game. There were no quarters, not even a definite number of minutes in each half. The best example of this came in 1908. Guyn took his team to Ann Arbor for a game with Michigan's "point a minute" team, which needed a workout before meeting the University of Pennsylvania.

The rules stated that a player could not return to the game when he was taken out in a half, but Fielding Yost agreed to let Guyn substitute freely if he would consent to a long game. They started playing at 2:00 p.m. and continued until dark. State fumbled seven kicks—which resulted in 42 points for Michigan. A "four-cornered" pass failed to materialize in a desperate State attempt to score. Michigan won, 62-0.

Throughout that season, State used the tactics apparently approved by the best eastern coaches. It gained chiefly by split interferences and old style football and resorted to forward passes only when the opponents had closed up their defenses to resist line plays. Everything considered, it was a successful season, but State was not content to be champion of Kentucky. It wanted to be a more important factor in southern football.

Guyn resigned as head coach that year, but continued to serve as an assistant to his successor, E. R. Sweetland. Bryant had a long and honored career with the UK College of Agriculture.

A Period Of Transition

The first experienced and fully qualified person to hold the position of head football coach at the University of Kentucky was E. R. Sweetland, a big, square-built man who compiled the best record (23-5) of any coach who led the Wildcats for more than one year.

A graduate of both Cornell and Syracuse universities, he was quite an itinerant coach, whose portfolio included a total of eight years at such places as Hamilton College, Colgate, and the Ohio State University.

Immediately after assuming his new duties at KSU in the spring of 1909, he inaugurated spring football practice, a training table for athletes, and class teams from which he could develop varsity material. He abolished all nose guards, shin guards, and other unnecessary paraphernalia because of the excess weight which made the players considerably slower. He apparently was a hard taskmaster because immediately after an opening 18-0 win over Wesleyan, he held an hour's practice for the entire squad.

The team defeated Berea, 28-0, and then gained wide recognition by defeating Illinois, 6-2, at Champaign-Urbana, for Kentucky's most important victory up to that time. Dr. John J. Tigert, giving Sweetland credit for pulling a shrewd move that sealed the Illini's doom, wrote a quarter-century later:

"By an artifice which no one had ever understood he succeeded in getting it into the contract that 15-minute halves would be played. After the Illinois people discovered how brief the game was to be they sent someone to Lexington to try to get the halves lengthened. Sweetland told them that his men

Action during the Kentucky-Illinois game at Champaign-Urbana, October 9, 1909. The Wildcats won, 6-2.

were very small and that on account of the excessive heat in the far South they were scarcely able to play longer than that. However, he promised that when the 30 minutes were up he would consider going on with the game if the men were able to stand it. The Illini management advertised a game between the varsity and freshmen to follow the game with Kentucky, so that the crowd could get their money's worth."

Sweetland was not kidding when he said State had a small team. The backfield, smallest in the school's history, did not average over 140 pounds. Tigert said the squad entered the arena amid the strains of "My Old Kentucky Home" and "Dixie," and the entire team went into the game "sobbing like orphan children with cramp colic."

State struck early, with Capt. Richard Barbee skirting end for 30 yards and a touchdown. Illinois scored a safety on a blocked punt, but when the 30 minutes were up, State had the ball on the Illini five yard line and was proceeding for another touchdown. Illinois did not ask for a further extension of time, and the game was ended.

Prior to that game, State teams had been known by such

names as "Cadets," "Colonels," "Corn-Crackers," and "Thoroughbreds." In chapel the morning after the game, Commandant Corbusier, who had accompanied the team to Champaign-Urbana, said the boys "fought like Wildcats." The cognomen caught on the following year and was officially adopted by the football team in 1911.

"The Wildcat, when undisturbed, is most peaceful and unobtrusive," the *Kentuckian* noted. "Yet of battle he is not afraid, from difficulty he does not turn aside, and when aroused, other beasts hold no terror for him."

That 1909 team lost only to North Carolina A&M and won nine games for a record that in 1974 still stood as the third best in UK football history. The important victories included the Illinois game, a 17-0 blanking of Tennessee, and a win over Centre for the state championship.

Following that season, football rules underwent two major changes: the halves were divided into quarters, with each quarter 15 minutes long; and the teams were allowed four downs in which to make 10 yards for a first down. The length of the playing field was shortened from 110 yards to 100 yards, also. Important changes the following year would increase the value of a touchdown from five to six points, put a touchback in play from the 20 yard line, and change the kickoff to the 40 instead of the 50.

After his 1910 UK team won its first seven games and lost to St. Louis and Centre, Sweetland coached one year at Miami University (Ohio) and then returned to coach the 1912 team at UK. P. P. Douglass coached the Wildcats to a 7-3 record in 1911, and the record included a 12-0 victory over Sweetland's Miami team. The Wildcats also blanked Maryville, Morris-Harvey, and Lexington High School before losing to Cincinnati, 6-0. Other losses were to Vanderbilt and Transylvania. They defeated Centre and shut out Tennessee, 12-0.

Halfback Jake Gaiser turned in his greatest game when he scored both touchdowns to lead the Wildcats in blanking the Vols. "Stoll Field held about 3,000 people and was for both the football and baseball games," Gaiser recalled in a letter written in February, 1975, from his home in New York. "When it rained, we would have a coating of mud to contend with. I woke up the morning of that Tennessee game on Thanksgiving Day 1911 and there was a big snow on the ground. Up to the last 10 minutes, it was 0-0. Our mountaineer tackle (Harrison) turned to me—I was the left half and supposed to carry the ball—and said he had his man licked and for me to carry over, which I did for 10 yards and the first touchdown.

"They were kicking to us, and I told 'Doc' Rodes, the right halfback, that I would tear off and block for him. I didn't watch the ball. I had my eyes on the oncoming tacklers and when the ball hit the snow, it took a funny bounce and landed in my arms. I avoided the two tacklers for our second touchdown.

"We did not have much in the way of equipment, no noseguards (nose broken three times) and footballs would get in bad shape. During one of the scrimmages and after a big pile-up, the ball carrier was feeling around for the ball. It had exploded during the scramble."

Leslie L. Guyn, starting quarterback whose 35-yard field goal produced the victory over Centre that year, also was a standout against the Vols.

Centre canceled the 1912 Thanksgiving Day game because of a KIAA ruling which suspended the Wildcats that year for using ineligible baseball players. The Wildcats played only one Kentucky team that year, defeating the University of Louisville, 41-0, and then claimed the state championship since Louisville had beaten both Centre and Transylvania. They lost only two games, the first to Miami and the second to VMI in a thrilling encounter. State led, 2-0, with two minutes left when a VMI man kicked a field goal and the game ended, 3-2. Sweetland resigned to coach the boat crew at the University of Wisconsin.

Sweetland had become the first person to be named UK athletic director in 1910. The position was created to lend prestige and distinction to the athletic program and perhaps to entice him to remain in Lexington. When Sweetland went to Miami University in 1911, Dr. Tigert had agreed to fill the position of athletic director for one year, returning fulltime to his chair of philosophy when Sweetland returned. When Sweetland again resigned, at the end of the 1912 season, the athletic committee obtained Alpha Brumage as head coach of football, basketball, and baseball. Brumage was a Kansas University graduate with five years of experience as director of athletics and football coach at Nevada State Normal School and two years of experience in the same capacity at VMI. He was assisted by Tigert.

One of those ineligible baseball players in 1912 was Jim

Park, who would letter in football, basketball, and baseball and put on the UK gridiron ledger some records which would stand the test of time. He was such a good passer that in a 21-6 loss to Illinois in 1913, he took advantage of a rule which, on a forward pass out of bounds, gave the ball to the opposition at the point where it left the field. Park would fire the ball out of bounds 50 or more yards down field. The rule was changed the following year.

State lost only one other game that year, falling to Tennessee. As in the previous year, the Wildcats played only one team from Kentucky. They beat Louisville and claimed the state championship. As a preliminary attraction to a victory over Wilmington, the Lexington High School team defeated Louisville High School, 15-0. This was one of the earliest high school games played in Lexington.

Brumage and Tigert again coached the 1914 team. They arranged two training tables, one for the varsity and one for the freshmen, who were also coached by Tigert. That freshman team became known as the "point-a-minute" squad and established Tigert as a fine coach.

Several innovations took place at KSU that year. One of the first was the appearance of "No Loafing" signs at conspicuous points on Stoll Field. As a result, practice sessions were fast and furious. Another more serious innovation was the "rushing" of the fence by irksome culprits. Several guards were stoned as they approached the fence-crashers, and several students and spectators were injured by the hurling missiles.

In the opening game Park returned a kickoff 75 yards for a touchdown and threw touchdown passes of 15 and 30 yards to lead an 87-0 romp over Wilmington, which did not make a first down. He scored three touchdowns the following week as the Wildcats swamped Maryville, 80-0. The *Kentuckian* described the Maryville game as "a parade of blue jerseys across the goal line."

In the Maryville game teammate Bill Tuttle scored six touchdowns and kicked seven extra points, a school scoring record that still stands.

State players accused Mississippi A&M players of greasing their moleskin pants with axle grease. The visitors changed trousers at half time. Despite this obvious handicap, the Wildcats scored first on a pass from Park to C. C. Schrader and a second time on a "double pass" carried over by Tuttle from the two, after being set up by a 30-yard pass from Park to Schrader.

With nine minutes remaining and the Aggies leading, 13-12, Park tried a 34-yard field goal. He had missed an earlier attempt from the 25, but this one was good. He came through with another three-pointer later, this one good for 40 yards, to make the final score 19-13. He rushed for 75 yards, averaged 30.6 yards on punts, and threw the touchdown pass for what he considered his best game. His lot was to call signals, run with the ball from scrimmage, punt, run back punts and kickoffs, and come up with key plays on defense. His most sensational day came on October 24, 1914, when he led the Wildcats in an 81-3 romp over Earlham. He scored five touchdowns and completed 19 of 29 passes. Five of the passes were for touchdowns—four of them going to Floyd Wright. Two were lost by interceptions.

Earlham was a big team which was not regarded as a cripple on the UK schedule, having held the Wildcats to a 28-10 margin the previous season. The Wildcat lineup also was spotted with substitutes, and it was largely for that reason that so much passing was attempted. The results were described by some as "bewildering."

That 1914 team finished with a 328-93 margin over its combined foes. The 41.0 average per game was still a UK record 60 years later. Park went on to gain fame of a sort by pitching the first home run ball to the immortal Babe Ruth. That was in Park's first year with the old St. Louis Browns. He was leading Boston, 3-0, with two men on base in the seventh inning when the Red Sox manager sent in his ace pitcher Ruth to pinch-hit. Ruth hit the ball out of the park. Park played three seasons with the Browns and was with Columbus, Kansas City, and Columbus again. In 1915 he was an assistant to Dr. Tigert, who was chosen athletic director that year in charge of all sports at the university.

Tigert was one of the most unique persons ever to coach UK athletic teams. Born on the Vanderbilt University campus, he was the son of a bishop and the grandson of a bishop. He entered VU in 1900 when he took the entrance prize of $50 for standing highest in examinations in Latin and Greek. After he won fame for himself as an athlete, the faculty selected him for another honor—delivering an oration at commencement. In the same year he was chosen Rhodes Scholar from Tennessee.

With his unquestioned ability as an educator, he combined

S. A. Boles, John J. Tigert, and William Tuttle.

a practical nature that made him a successful athletic coach. He had a keenness that was equalled by few of the coaches in the South and an interest in the game that meant much to his teams. His droll wit, sometimes sarcasm, made him a general favorite in the classroom, and his distinctive gait and height (well over six feet) attracted attention to him. He was a keen student of the Bible and an earnest worker in Christian affairs. He later became U. S. Commissioner of Education and president of the University of Florida.

His 1915 team opened with victories over Butler, 33-0, and Earlham, 54-13, and a loss to Mississippi A&M, 12-0, under a torrid sun at Starkville. The big game with Sewanee was considered a moral victory after the Wildcats "won" a 7-7 tie. They defeated Cincinnati, Louisville, Purdue, and Tennessee for a fine 6-1-1 season.

Tigert's second and last Wildcat team opened the 1916 campaign by brushing Butler, 39-3, and polishing off Centre, 68-0. Then came a 45-0 setback by Vanderbilt, followed by a scoreless deadlock with Sewanee. Wins over Cincinnati, 32-0, and Mississippi A&M, 13-3, and a scoreless duel with Tennessee were the last entries on the ledger.

Long Journey For A Pigskin

Occupying a place of honor in the archives of the University of Kentucky Athletics Association is a battered football which traveled the usual yardage in the course of a fall afternoon in 1912 in the fair city of Knoxville, Tennessee, where it was kicked, thrown, carried up and down, pounced upon, and rolled out of bounds. But that is only part of the story. The football traveled to the other side of the equator and then at last came to Lexington for safe and quiet repose among other trophies and memorabilia of days gone by.

The ball was the one with which W. C. Harrison, a Wildcat grid great of that long time ago, registered the only touchdown he ever scored. Until 1939 when he sent the ball back from South America to his alma mater, it had remained in the possession of the six-foot-four Kentuckian, who earned his football letters in 1910-12 and was called by many old-timers one of the greatest tackles in the history of Wildcat football.

Not only was he a starting tackle on the 1912 team, but he was the "iron man" of the squad, playing every minute of all 10 games. As a postgraduate student he captained both the UK football and basketball teams. That year his outstanding performance was eight-for-eight point-after touchdown kicking in a 56-0 rout of YMI of Cincinnati.

In 1939 the story of Harrison's touchdown was told to Larry Shropshire of the *Lexington Leader* by Dr. J. S. "Brick" Chambers, then director of the UK Health Service (1928-57) and a starting center on the 1911 and 1912 Wildcat teams.

During the train ride to Knoxville, it seemed that the popular Harrison complained to the other Wildcats that in all the time he had played football, he had never made a touchdown. Several teammates, in a kidding manner, decided that when the team took the field the next day against the Vols, that situation would be remedied.

Perhaps their frivolity was enhanced by the fact that Coach E. R. Sweetland was sick at the time, and Dr. John J. Tigert was in charge of the team. Anyway, in mock seriousness the players made their plans. They decided that the best way for Harrison, the left tackle, to make a touchdown would be to block a kick. Leaders in the plotting were Chambers and "Red Doc" Rodes, who played defensive end alongside Harrison.

They mapped it out so that Harrison would open a hole in the Tennessee line while Chambers, from his position backing up the line, would go through and get the Vol back protecting the kicker. Rodes' job was to cut through and block the punt, with Harrison there to pick up the ball and scoot for a touchdown.

After receiving the opening kickoff the Vols failed to gain and lined up in punt formation on about their own 30 yard line. "Now is the time, now's the time," the conspirators whispered. "We'll do it now."

It could not have been carried out better. Chambers took out the protecting back, Rodes thrust his chest in the way of the punted ball, and Harrison grabbed up the bounding leather and galloped some 20 yards for the first UK touchdown, to help the Wildcats win, 13-6.

The game ball was given to Harrison, and it became one of his prized possessions.

After completing his work at the university, he returned to his home near Bagdad in Shelby County, purchased a farm adjoining his father's property, married, and settled down there. He was successful as a farmer and also prospered, along with his father, in a roller mill they bought near their home. But after the death of his wife and three of their four children, he lost interest in his work and suddenly decided to enter the ministry.

He entered the Louisville Baptist Seminary, received his master's degree in 1924, and went to South America. There he taught Latin and Greek in a Spanish Baptist College in Rio de Janeiro and pursued his hobby of studying archaeology of the Holy Land, a subject in which he had become intensely interested.

On a visit to Lexington in 1935, he renewed acquaintances

W. C. Harrison.

on the UK campus; then, in 1939, in response to circular letters Prof. Ezra Gillis was sending out to former UK students in a football research project, he sent his prized football back to his alma mater. Gillis turned it over to Dr. Chambers, and the latter passed it on to the athletic department.

There were other interesting players of that era. One was German-born A. A. Bablitz, who played at the age of 35 and was the father of five children. He also participated in boxing and wrestling and later became a lawyer and labor leader in Lexington.

Jake Gaiser, starting halfback, turned in his greatest game against arch-rival Tennessee when he scored both touchdowns to lead the Wildcats in a 12-0 blanking of the Vols on Stoll Field. Also a basketball standout, he captained the 1911 cage squad and starred as a guard on the undefeated 1912 team (9-0). He became a farmer and rancher in Alberta, Canada.

Leslie L. Guyn was a quarterback starter on the 1911 team and a dropkicker supreme. His 35-yard field goal produced an 8-5 victory in the 1911 game with Centre. He also was a standout in the 12-0 Thanksgiving Day defeat of Tennessee.

J. E. C. Johnson, a starting tackle, did not miss a minute of 1912 action. An outstanding track man, he once captured the state 440 run and won medals in the discus, shot put, and hammer throw. He also was a collegiate heavyweight boxer and wrestler. He was the first person from Lee County, Kentucky, to earn a degree from the university.

W. P. Tuttle was the third member of the group to make his home outside the continental United States, serving as vice president of the Maui Pineapple Co. of Maui, Hawaii. He was also a member of the basketball team.

George Clark "Possum" Watkins was a halfback starter in 1911 and also one of the school's top track men of that era. His top effort of that season came in the Georgetown game, when he scored one of three Wildcat touchdowns.

Other teammates were James Park, Harry M. Woodson, H. C. Galloway, captain Tom Earle, Gibson Downing, William Rodes, William Collins, Howell Spears, G. F. Meadors, Delan Williams, and Carl Brandstetner.

An All-Time Team

When the foresighted Dr. J. J. Tigert called together a group of football experts-in-residence, and they selected an All-Kentucky State University football team from players of the years 1892 to 1915, the family of Rodes got more than its share of honors.

First, there was J. Waller "Boots" Rodes (1902, '04, and '06). He was a back on the 1904 team which finished with a 9-1 record and was generally conceded to be one of the best, if not *the* best, in its era.

Boots was followed by his brother Pete, who was a halfback on the 1907 team. That team also won nine games, losing only to Vanderbilt and playing Tennessee to a scoreless tie at Knoxville. At the end of the season Pete entered the U. S. Naval Academy and was captain of the 1912 Middies team.

The first of the two famous William Rodes lettered at UK in 1909, '11, and '12. He was known as "Red Doc" (to distinguish him from his cousin "Black Doc") and was a popular 140-pound halfback, very compactly built, very fast, and full of pep. In spite of his diminutive stature, he always played end on defense and broke interference with the same ease and certainty as a big, heavy man.

His cousin "Black Doc," a brother to J. W. and Pete, played quarterback on the 1915 and 1916 teams and was considered the greatest open-field runner and place-kicker who had ever played on a State eleven. "He is so well known that it is hardly worth while to dwell here upon his ability," Dr. Tigert wrote in 1916, "and his spectacular feats of the past season are still fresh in the minds of all followers of the gridiron game."

In a tie game with Sewanee that season, "Black Doc" had dislocated a shoulder early in the first quarter, but he played well into the second period before he fainted and was taken from the game. However, the shoulder healed in time for him to kick two field goals of 45 and 43 yards, to defeat Tennessee, 6-0, on "Homecoming Day." This was probably the first Homecoming ever held at KSU, and in the game he personally gained 150 yards.

It was during the 1915 season that the Wildcats scored one of their biggest victories—a 7-0 upset of Purdue. Here, in part, is how the *Kentuckian* described that game:

"A misunderstood signal at the beginning of the second quarter resulted in Quarterback Olmstead passing the ball, but the three backs were charging the line, and the oval rolled upon the sod. (Howard) Kinne, ever on the alert, picked up the ball on the 42-yard line and stopped running only after he had placed it between the goal posts. Schrader kicked the perfect

William "Black Doc" Rodes lugs the leather in UK's 6-0 victory over Tennessee in Lexington in 1915. Other Wildcats, left to right, are Howard Kinne, who would be killed in action in World War I; Emmett Kelly; Jim Server; Ernest McIlvaine; and John Brittain.

A shoulder injury fails to keep "Black Doc" Rodes from entering Kentucky's 7-0 victory over Purdue in 1915.

goal, and the scoring ended.

"The game was a beautiful exhibition of football, a breathless struggle throughout. Varsity was outweighed ten pounds to the man, but in the pink of condition. Official information shows that 'State' advanced the ball 6.9 yards a play, and Purdue, 4.8 yards. State's kicks were longer, and they returned punts further. Shortly after the beginning of the game, Doc Rodes, who had been out of the game for some time on account of injuries, was sent in at quarter. After several unsuccessful attempts to score a field goal, he was removed, following an injury to his shoulder.

"Throughout the game, Varsity showed All-American form—in fact, to such an extent that brilliant individual playing gave way to team work, which was beautiful to behold. In the last quarter Purdue rallied in a vain attempt to score. Within 20 yards of their goal a series of forward passes were attempted, which kept Kentucky followers in suspense until the final whistle, when the stands poured forth a mighty multitude of fans thrilled with the joy of one of the greatest victories ever won by a Kentucky team."

With rumblings of war emitting from overseas, Rodes began the 1916 season by scoring three touchdowns and kicking three extra points against Butler. He scored three touchdowns and kicked seven extra points in a 68-0 rout of Centre, with one of his touchdowns coming on a 70-yard kickoff return. Vanderbilt inflicted the only defeat on the Wildcats, blanking them, 45-0, and mopping up on everything but Rodes. His heroics included a 50-yard nonscoring kickoff return.

He was the offensive star of a 0-0 tie with Sewanee and scored two touchdowns in a victory over Cincinnati. After defeating Mississippi A&M, 13-3, with Rodes scoring the touchdown, the Wildcats went into their long-awaited battle with heavily favored Tennessee. Rodes picked up an apparent fumble and scooted 60 yards for a score, but an official called the play an incomplete pass. The Wildcats had to settle for a scoreless tie.

During Rodes' two years as quarterback, State teams had a combined 10-2-3 record. He scored 64 points in 1916, but his story cannot be told in cold figures. It was his all-around playing that made him a legendary figure. He could run, punt, pass, and place-kick—all with equal ability. His affability, good nature, and humor fired a team with renewed vigor when it

Howard Kinne, left, and William "Black Doc" Rodes.

might otherwise be spent. Tigert said those qualities resulted in "Black Doc" being placed at the head of the list of all-time KSU players of his era.

Richard Barbee (LE in 1907, RH in 1908, and LH in 1909) was selected captain of the all-time team. His work was conspicuous in the success of three state championship teams. Although he did not weigh more than 150 pounds, he was a power on offense and a vicious tackler. He was a star in the famous 1909 victory over Illinois and played a remarkable game on Thanksgiving that year against Centre. In the Centre game he scored all of State's 15 points, making a touchdown and three goals from the field.

George Hendrickson lettered four years and was left tackle on the famous 1909 team. "Mad Anthony" Whayne, left guard in 1897 and left tackle for the "Immortals," was the first man selected for guard. He was big, strong, and aggressive, and he played in the days of the old "guards-back" formation, when the guard was a tremendous factor in the offense as well as on defense.

R. S. "Dick" Webb, Jr., played center on the teams of

1908, '09, and '10. He was captain of the 1910 team and an assistant coach in 1911 and 1912. Tigert described him as "the most active big man at KSU, on occasions jumping flat-footed over the line into the backfield, scattering men like straws."

Claude Humphreys (1897, '98, and '99) was given the right guard spot over Joe Coons simply because he had played two more years.

Cravens was the right tackle in 1901, '02, and '03. He was a regular giant for those days, being considerably over six feet and weighing 196 pounds, and was one of two members of the 1903 team allowed to play against KU in the year in which such a large number of "ringers" were used by KSU. He played throughout that game.

Lewis Winn Martin played right end on the 1898 and 1899 teams and was right halfback in 1901. He was fast, nervy and steady, and he was a good ground gainer, tackler, and overall defensive man. In his time, the ends played behind the line of scrimmage, alongside the halfback, and were relied upon in advancing the ball much more than nowadays.

William P. Tuttle (1911, '12, '13, and '14) was one of the best all-around athletes turned out by State, also starring in basketball and as a baseball pitcher. He weighed 160 pounds, was very sturdy and exceedingly fast, and made an ideal halfback.

Haynes, right halfback on the strong 1904 team, played only that year, but impressed the all-star panel with his great driving power. Those who saw him play said no other player who had worn the State colors could compare with him as a line plunger. It was largely due to his constant gains through the line that State was able to defeat Indiana at Bloomington in

A Wildcat offensive formation in 1915.

1904.

If the football "experts" had chosen an all-time KSU coach in that era, Dr. Tigert certainly would have ranked high on the list. Bart Peak of Lexington, who was an end and substitute quarterback for the 1915 team, remembered him as a person who was always figuring out how to outguess the other team.

"He used the 'Statue of Liberty' play and taught us a system of calling plays in sequence beforehand, so we didn't have to call signals in certain situations," the retired YMCA director and former county judge recalled in early 1975. "Sometimes, we would go back to punt on third down, and practically the whole team would run around one end with the kicker behind them.

"We had a lot of tough players. 'Black Doc' Rodes could make any football team today. None of us were good on receiving except him. I remember muffing a punt once, and it bounced right into a Cincinnati man's hands. He scored on the play, but we beat them, 27-6. I couldn't raise my head on campus for a week.

"Dutch Schrader was one of the best punters of our time, and John Brittain, our left guard, seemed to get his nose broken all the time. We had no nose guards or face masks. We did have shoulder pads, and hip pads that fitted into our pants."

Peak noted that it was during those years just before World War I that football at UK experienced a period of expansion, increased emphasis, and growth. "We were climbing in the ranks of Southern competition and withdrawing from playing the colleges within the state," he said. "After the war, UK would be ready to go all-out for an expanded football program."

The Dutch Influence

Take one athletically inclined violin player; let him save the life of a roving, football playing fellow musician; add a former schoolmate who wants to spend a one-year vacation in college—you have the unlikely circumstances that led John Heber to the University of Kentucky in the fall of 1916.

Better known to old-time UK football fans as "The Flying Dutchman," Heber visited the UK athletic department in January, 1975, the winter of his 80th year, to talk about that happening.

"C. C. 'Dutch' Schrader and I were raised in the same neighborhood and attended the same high school together in North Philadelphia," he said. "Neither of us played football there. I tried it for three days, but the field was twenty-two blocks from the school, and that was too far to walk. However, we did play some sandlot ball in a lot across from my house.

"C. C. was playing in a band in Philly with a fellow named F. A. Schilling, who had played football one year in Virginia and one year in Vermont and was going to play the next year at Kentucky. They became pretty good friends after C. C. saved his life, and C. C. decided to go to UK with him."

University records show that F. A. Schilling earned a varsity letter in 1912, while C. C. "Dutch" Schrader lettered in 1912, '13, '14, and '15. Schrader was team captain and earned a berth on the All-Southern team his senior year.

While Schrader was starring at UK, the German-born Heber worked a couple of years, played some football at a prep school, and worked two more years at a mill in Philadelphia.

"I had saved up some money and decided to take a vacation," he said. "When I heard Dutch talking about UK and Lexington, I decided to spend a year there, just for kicks.

"I arrived in Lexington on the first day of school. The football coach, Dr. Tigert, had just brought his players back from an encampment on the Kentucky River. When I asked for a uniform, he just shook his head and refused to issue me one."

The small, persistent, and speedy Heber finally got that uniform. He watched on the sideline as UK opened with a 39-3 victory over Butler and finally saw action in a 68-0 massacre of Centre, as the two schools renewed their rivalry. After a 45-0 loss to Vanderbilt and a scoreless tie with Sewanee, the *Ken-*

F. A. Schilling.   C. C. "Dutch" Schrader.

tuckian said Heber, "displayed wonderful feats of daring at end and won himself a permanent berth."

The 1916 season had been successful enough to make $1,400 profit for the State Athletic Association. However, the association had a deficit of $3,800 due to financial losses on basketball, baseball, and track and due to the previous debt of $5,000 for expenditures on Stoll Field. The athletic committee faced two alternatives: drop basketball, baseball, and track for the remainder of the year or have the university increase the student incidental fee from $15 to $17.50 (this would provide $7.50 instead of $5 for athletics). The students approved the latter alternative.

It was also in 1917 that Dr. Frank L. McVey, an enthusiastic supporter of athletics, was elected as president of the univer-

Team of 1915. Front, left to right: George Gumbert, Howard Kinne, Earl Grabfelder, Dutch Schrader, J. J. Tigert, Jr., mascot, Charles Haydon, William Rodes, M. J. Crutcher. Second row: R. S. Clayton, Clay Simpson, J. P. Ricketts, F. M. Dempsey, James Server, J. A. Brittain, Karl Zerfoss. Third row: Ernest McIlvaine, Frank M. "Shorty" Heick, Bart Peak, E. E. Kelly, J. W. Thompson, Fay Townes, mgr. Fourth row: William Tuttle, asst. coach, John J. Tigert, head coach, James Park, asst. coach.

sity to succeed Henry S. Barker. McVey would do much in later years to improve facilities and coaching at State.

Dr. Tigert returned to full time duties in philosophy and education and was succeeded by S. A. Boles, who became both director of athletics and football coach. James Park, former UK athlete and assistant to Dr. Tigert, remained as an assistant to Boles. Bill Tuttle also was an assistant.

UK expected to have its finest football team in 1917, one that would make a strong bid for the SIAA championship. Only captain Maury Crutcher had been lost from the 1916 team, and some fine young players were moving up in the ranks. But World War I came that year. All spring sports were canceled because many of the finest athletes on campus were among the first students to leave school. Before the season ended, almost 400 UK students had entered the armed services. That included more than half of the baseball and track teams.

"We lost our entire starting backfield of 1916," Heber said. "That included 'Black Doc' Rodes, Earl Grabfelder, Ernest McIlvaine, and Charles Haydon—all very talented performers. The linemen entering the service included C. F. Dempsey, the regular center; Broadus Hickerson; 'Shorty' Heick; Howard Kinne; Clay Downing and Earle Clements, a substitute."

Kinne was shot down over France on October 1, 1918, becoming the first Kentucky aviator killed in action. It was he who picked up a Purdue fumble and returned it 48 yards for a touchdown in the memorable 1915 upset of the Boilermakers. Clements was to return from the war and later become governor of the state and a member of the U. S. Senate.

Meanwhile, State continued to play football—but without much success.

"I thought a lot of 'Daddy' Boles personally, but he was inexperienced in coaching and it showed," Heber said. "We couldn't fight our way out of a paper bag. We beat Butler (33-0) and Maryville (19-0), but Miami tied us (0-0), and then we lost to Vanderbilt (5-0), Sewanee (7-0), Centre (3-0), Mississippi A&M (14-0), and Alabama (27-0) without scoring a point. Then we turned loose for 52 points and shut out Florida in the final game.

"Centre beat us when 'Bo' McMillin dropkicked a field goal, something he hadn't tried in college. They were cussin' and cussin' all through the first half, and then they got to praying in the second half. I always figured that's where they got the name of 'Praying Colonels.'"

John Y. Brown, Sr., in his book, *Legend of the Praying Colonels*, said the nickname came about by an incident that occurred in the dressing room as the Colonels were preparing to go out on the field to play UK that day.

"Mind you, the University of Kentucky had beaten us 66-0 (68-0) the year before and in fact, had beaten us for a number of years. There had been a long rivalry between Centre and the University and there had been a time in our early history when we had rather methodically beaten them, but that was not the case in the few years preceding 1917.

"As Chief (Myers) addressed the boys in his customary prep talk before a game, he suggested that there was a power higher than that of mere humans and he thought it might be well if we bowed our heads and asked guidance from that superior power, to guide our conduct through that game. I recall that it was Hunk Mathias who, in a burst of enthusiasm, said 'Let me lead that damned prayer.'"

The "entire game was played on Kentucky's ten-yard line, or practically the entire game," Brown recalled. "We had a sweeping end run, where the guards came out to join in the interference and, although we had as many as five and six men in our interference as we swept down the field time after time to Kentucky's ten-yard line, we never could put the ball across. Kentucky had an end named John George Heber. . .who stopped Bo (McMillin) on every play and we never could get across the goal line. Bo finally decided that the only way to win was to try a drop-kick. Now, believe me, he had never drop-kicked a goal in his life, but we got down to the ten-yard line, he dropped back and tried one. He missed it. When we found ourselves down near the goal line the next time, Bo dropped back again and tried a drop-kick. This time he made it and, except for one other lone exception that I shall tell you about later on, that's the only drop kick that Bo ever made in his life. And it was necessary that he do that to win the game against Kentucky and, of course, we went on the balance of the way undefeated."

Heber was called the "ferret" of the Wildcats because of his proclivity for picking up fumbles or staying the progress of a blocked punt. He recovered five fumbles in that Centre game. "Either I or John Brittain blocked that first drop-kick by McMillin," he recalled. "I don't remember which. But I recovered it and had a wide open field, and nobody was going to catch me. Then my shoe split right across the cap. It dangled and made me stumble, and they caught me."

Against Mississippi A&M in Starkville that year, he had wide open field when the ball suddenly squirted out of his hands. "I don't know what happened," he said. "I just fumbled it." The 'Cats lost, 14-0.

During the following year Boles was appointed athletic director for the 400 drafted men involved in the Student Army Training Corps program at UK. The War Department that year encouraged athletics in its training corps provided that the com-

John G. Heber.

manding officer of the school was in charge of athletics and that no extensive trips or specialized training interfere with military duties. With much of his time taken up in organizing army and navy football teams from the sections of the SACT, supervising practices three days a week, and conducting intersquad games, Boles had little time to devote to coaching Wildcat football. However, he assisted the new coach, T. A. Gill, when possible. Gill, a graduate of the University of Indiana, had played professional baseball with the Chicago White Sox and was employed as football and baseball coach at the University of North Dakota before coming to UK.

"We didn't get along too well, although Andy was a fraternity buddy of mine," Heber said. "He didn't like my playing, and I didn't like his coaching. His idea of coaching was to get out there and run back punts and have us try to tackle him. He also liked to scrimmage with us. He was a fine athlete, but he didn't teach us much.

"He sent me up to scout Miami one of the few times we scouted anybody, but about all I found out was what color jerseys they wore. It didn't matter because our game with them was canceled because of a flu epidemic in Oxford. Centre canceled its game with Indiana that year because of an order restricting teams from being away from home more than 24 hours in succession. We had not received the order yet, and we traveled to Bloomington in place of Centre and won, 24-7."

But the Wildcats were weakened by the virus. They lost to Vanderbilt, 33-0, in Nashville; defeated Georgetown, 21-3; canceled a game with Centre; and called it quits because flu had reached epidemic proportions in Lexington.

"Eger Murphree, the captain, and I didn't start either game because Andy was mad at us," Heber said, "but he put us in mighty quick. I remember Josh Cody beat the hell out of me in the Vandy game. When he charged, he always found my mouth with the heel of his hand. It was perfectly legal.

"It was a poor season all around. We played no home games, and those we played away from home weren't much fun."

Due to a ruling, the war year of 1918 was not considered against them, so both Heber and Murphree would earn their fifth football "K" letters in 1920. (Only one other State football player earned a fifth letter—J. White Guyn, in 1906.) The *Kentuckian* reported about Murphree that "nobody saw him studying, yet his record shows almost all A's." He became president of Esso Research and Engineering Company, largest firm of its kind in the world.

Gill coached the team again in 1919, compiling a 3-4-1 record that included losses to Indiana (24-0), Ohio State (49-0), Cincinnati (7-0), and Centre (56-0). The lone saving graces were a 13-0 victory over Tennessee and a scoreless tie with Vanderbilt. A victory over Sewanee was the first for UK in the rivalry and the tie with Vanderbilt was considered quite an accomplishment. John Y. Brown, Sr., remembered the Centre-UK game because Centre boosters had to give 50 points in order to secure a bet. "Kentucky put up a spirited fight and we found ourselves in great difficulty trying to amass the number of points which we had given," he wrote in his book. "With only ten seconds left to play, the score was 49-0 and we were on our own 40-yard line, sixty yards away from pay dirt. Again, as he did in the Indiana game and a great many other games when we faced great stress, Bo called time out.

"All week long, we had been working on a play where Lefty Whitnell lined up wide on the sideline. Bo faded back to pass. Lefty raced down the sideline and, at the proper moment, Bo would turn the pass loose and Lefty would be under it. It would be a fingertip catch, but he would make it and he would go the rest of the way. If we had tried that once the following week before we had tried it 50 to 100 times and always it clicked."

Centre lined up and McMillin called the play. "Lefty is wide to the right sideline and the ball is snapped by Red Weaver," Brown recalled. "Bo fades back to pass, dodges three or four would-be tacklers, lets the proper amount of time pass while Lefty is racing down the sideline, he turns that pass loose and it's literally a bomb. While the ball is high in the air, Bo hollers over to the ones of us on the sideline and says, 'Tell the boys to go on downtown and collect their money.' Well, Lefty was under the pass, he caught it and went on for a touchdown. Red Weaver kicked the goal and the final score was 56-0 and we who had been willing to take the long gamble doubled our money on that game."

The nationally famous Centre team defeated the Wildcats before 5,000 persons. UK students complained they were defeated by a "gang of imported players under the leadership of a Texas ranger" and that they would rather support a team of

Kentucky boys than a "band of Texas cowboys imported to represent the school."

The student attitude toward that season was pointed up by an editorial in the *Kernel*:

> The season as a whole has not been unsuccessful although more games have been lost than won. The Wildcats had an unusually hard schedule. Notwithstanding, there has been an undercurrent of dissatisfaction and dissention among players of the team. . .and an attitude of disappointment among students and alumni. They are offering no censure for any one defeat or any one individual but are seeking an explanation for the play and results of the entire season. The *Kernel* wants a winning team and asks that every possible step be taken to get one.

A group of alumni who had won letters at UK met with Boles for the purpose of advancing clean athletics and elevating the alma mater to her proper place in the realm of collegiate sports.

Demands from that group and from students and alumni—all wanting a winning team—found a sympathetic ear at the university. Consequently, there was a reorganization of athletics in 1920, with stress laid on a winning team.

"Injun Bill," "J.J.," And "Murph"

William J. "Injun" Bill Juneau came to Lexington in the fall of 1920. He boasted an illustrious past which included coaching stints at the universities of Wisconsin and Texas. But in the long run he proved to be just another in a long series of well-qualified persons who tried to make the best of what was not an all-out effort by the University of Kentucky to win football championships.

"He has the appreciation and faith of the entire Blue Grass State," the *Kentuckian* said, "and time will bring his reward—a championship team for old Kentucky."

But "Injun Bill" never won that championship. In fact, his overall record of 13-10-2 fell almost a percentage point short of the combined percentage of the 18 coaches who had preceded him at UK. He was 3-4-1 in 1920, 4-3-1 in 1921, and 6-3 in 1922.

There were few redeeming features of the 1920 season other than a 6-6 tie with Sewanee and a 7-6 victory over Cincinnati. The Wildcats opened with a 62-0 victory over Southern Presbyterian University of Memphis in UK's first encounter with that institution. Then the Wildcats defeated Maryville, 31-0, but they dropped four games to stiffer competition, with Centre beating them, 49-0.

During a banquet given for the team that season by R. S. Webb, someone suggested that a real, honest-to-goodness, wild wildcat would be a good mascot for UK. Webb immediately began a search that extended from Montana to Pennsylvania and from Florida to Arizona.

Shortly before Christmas he purchased a cat through J.

"Injun Bill" Juneau.

McNeeson of Yardstown, Pennsylvania, who had obtained it from a Texan. The beautifully pointed brindle yearling was expressed to Lexington from San Antonio, but it died quickly in captivity. It was succeeded the following year by a cat called "TNT," which also died some months later. A tamer cat, "Whiskers," died during the Georgia Tech basketball game February 23, 1924, and was replaced by a cat obtained from New Mexico.

An interesting story centers around a live cat presented to Coach Harry Gamage at half time of the 1928 UK-Tennessee game in Lexington. Fifteen-year-old John Hall, of Rowan County, Kentucky, traced the feline to its den, grabbed it by the nape of the neck, and brought it home. A Morehead businessman presented it to Gamage before 20,000 snow-drenched fans. There would be other live mascots, all passing from the scene due to death or being turned loose in the mountains because they did not thrive out of their native habitats.

"Colonel" would stay around the longest. Acquired somewhere around Williamsburg, Kentucky, he came to UK during the 1947 grid campaign and stayed on the scene until 1954, when he was taken to the State's wildlife farm beyond Frankfort. But he was not used to the elements and died shortly of pneumonia. He was mounted and returned to the Department of Biological Sciences.

SuKy, the student pep organization, obtained a stuffed Wildcat from a Brooklyn taxidermist in 1958, named it "Tucky," and displayed it at football and basketball games. The cat lasted about 10 years. The final attempt to have a live mascot was in 1969, when Lexington newspaperman John Alexander had his pet cat "Baby" on the sidelines for the first two games of that season. A kind old lady complained about the manner in which the cat was handled, and that ended Baby's career as a mascot.

Back when the first cat—"Tom"—arrived on the scene in 1920, the *Leader* reported, "If the University of Kentucky Wildcats of next year get imbued with the spirit of their mascot and act as ferocious on the gridiron as the mascot in his cage, their opponents will be a dilapidated, cat-pawed, battered and man-handled aggregation at the end of each encounter."

Those 1921 Wildcats got off to a growling start, rolling over Wesleyan (68-0), Marshall (28-0), Georgetown (33-0), and VMI (14-7). They lost by *only* seven points to Vanderbilt (21-14) and tied Tennessee (0-0). It was considered a moral vic-

First live mascot.

tory when they scored on Vanderbilt. Vanderbilt had scored twice in the first half. Then Pribble went over for a touchdown after a long drive by State. Next, Lavin scored on a pass from Fuller. However, the Commodores also scored again, to take a 21-14 half-time lead—and this was the final score.

The only real embarrassment of that year came at Danville. Centre used an "avalanche of passes" and end runs to subdue State, 55-0. The *Kentuckian* said, "Bo and his gang of Texas steers were too much for the plucky Kentuckians." That was the year Centre upset mighty Harvard, 6-0.

William H. "Cave Man" Rice, who was on the freshman squad in 1921 and then played varsity football in 1922, '23, '24, and '25, recalled that Bo McMillin was a master in all phases of the game. "He was a great passer, and he could run longer without being tackled than any man I've seen," Rice said. "I've seen him take the ball from center on the 20, run all the way back to his own goal line, and then go for a touchdown.

"We did very little passing because we had nobody who could catch it and nobody who could pass it except when Ab Kirwan came along and threw some. We ran out of the single wing or double wing, and the quarterback always got the direct snap from center. There were seven men on the line and four in the backfield, which was the way we also lined up on defense. We had a brute of a back on defense in Curt Sanders. He was undoubtedly one of the best defensive backs I ever saw.

"The first football game I ever saw was when we beat Kentucky Wesleyan, 68-0, in 1921. I felt kinda bad about not getting in the game, but I couldn't have done anything anyway. When we led Centre, 3-0, at half time in 1922, we thought we were doing pretty good, but they scored 27 points in the second half. They had just been playing with us. I think maybe they got some bets up at half time."

With the Wildcats holding that half-time lead, the UK band struck up "The Old Gray Mare Ain't What She Used To Be," substituting "Old Red Roberts Ain't What He Used To Be." Roberts apparently was all he used to be, leading interference superbly for Hump Tanner, who scored three touchdowns in the Colonel victory.

The Wildcats began the 1922 season with consecutive victories over Marshall, Cincinnati, Louisville, Georgetown, and Sewanee—outscoring those opponents 151-6. (Georgetown got a touchdown in a 40-6 game.) But then Centre ended the streak, and Vanderbilt blanked them, 9-0, in Nashville. They beat Alabama, 6-0, for what was still on the books a half-century later as the only Wildcat victory over the Tide.

After Tennessee beat them, 14-7, in Knoxville, Juneau stepped down as head coach, having compiled a 473-264 edge over 25 opponents. He was succeeded by J. J. Winn, a Princeton man.

The 1923 season brought tragedy when one of the players died after the second game, a 14-0 victory over Cincinnati in the Queen City. Price Innes McLean, a 20-year-old UK engineering junior, received a head injury in a pile-up and died the following night in a Lexington hospital. The new concrete stands on Stoll Field were later named in his honor.

One of the big games that year was against Georgia Tech in

Atlanta. "It was a long way from home for a lot of us," W. H. Rice said, "and we were surprised that they didn't have good facilities. We dressed at the hotel. We got lucky and held them to a field goal in the first half. At half time, we got in the shade of a big tree. That was maybe the first or second year that UK emphasized its band and called it the 'Best Band in Dixie.' I guess that was because we didn't have very good football teams. They came out there at half time and played 'My Old Kentucky Home,' and it was the first time I realized what it meant to me, since I was so far from home. We went out there and kicked them all over the place. We should have beat them instead of a 3-3 tie."

Charles "Turkey" Hughes, a halfback who would win 13 letters before graduating from the university in 1925, always felt that "they tied us—we didn't tie them. We went down there for practice on Friday and the papers came out the next morning proclaiming that Tech was playing a practice game with Kentucky," the retired athletic director of Eastern Kentucky University recalled in April, 1975. "They were getting ready for Alabama the next week. We decided to make it the toughest practice game they ever had. We missed a field goal in the last two minutes by a yard.

"I thought Jack Winn was a good coach. Alabama only beat us 16-8, and I believe if Chuck Rice hadn't got his knee hurt, we would have beat them. We didn't have anybody but Rice who could catch a pass. Of course, you didn't pass much in those days, since the ball was like a pumpkin."

When Chuck Rice left the game in the second half, Kirwan moved from backfield to the vacant end position, and Len Tracy filled Kirwan's backfield spot. A few minutes later Tracy carried the ball around left end, cut across to the opposite sideline, and scored a 60-yard touchdown. The final UK points came on a safety shortly before the game ended.

After the tie game with Tech, UK lost, 18-0, in the final quarter to Tennessee. "There was no score and Kirwan started off tackle when somebody tackled him, and the sloppy ball squirted right into the hands of the fastest boy Tennessee had," Hughes said. "He had a straight line for the touchdown. They kicked off and we thought the ball would go into the end zone, and we let it die on the two or three. They blocked a punt for a touchdown and pulled a trick play for another."

Coach Winn was succeeded by Fred J. Murphy, a former

Yale quarterback who would compile a 12-14-1 record in three seasons with the Wildcats. His first UK squad dedicated the new stands in Stoll Field in grand style, beating Louisville, 29-0, and then defeating Georgetown, 42-0. The Wildcats lost, 10-7, to Washington & Lee. Then they defeated Sewanee, 7-0, but lost by an identical score to Centre.

They were trailing Alabama, 14-0, at Tuscaloosa when Hughes intercepted a Tide pass near the UK goal line and returned it for a touchdown. (Birmingham and Lexington newspapers said Hughes intercepted the pass on the three-yard line, but he was credited with a 98-yard return.) On the ensuing kickoff, Alabama's Johnny Mack Brown (later to become a famous western movie actor) caught the ball in the shadow of his goal posts and returned it 98 yards for a touchdown. These two plays were the longest plays of this type in the nation that year. "I guess I made him mad," Hughes said a half-century later.

Although they were 4-4 for the season, the Wildcats accepted an invitation to play West Virginia Wesleyan in a game dedicating a new stadium at Charleston. They lost, 24-7, to a team that apparently included some noncollegiate players.

They won six of nine games the following year, losing only to Chicago (9-0), Washington & Lee (25-0), and Alabama (31-0), while beating Maryville, Clemson, Sewanee, Centre, VMI, and Tennessee.

"We were staying at the Hotel Del Prado, and Chicago

Curtis M. Sanders kicks a field goal in the first game played in the new Stoll Field stadium on October 4, 1924.

coach A. A. Stagg came by and talked to our team," W. H. Rice recalled. "I didn't pay much attention to him. All I remember is that he talked about what a great team he had.

"A guy from Northwestern, where Murphy coached, had scouted Chicago all year, and he came by the night before the game and gave us a scouting report. He said, 'Five yards! Three yards! Five yards! Three yards! That's the way they'll beat you. They'll ram it right down your throat.'

"I nearly blocked a field goal, and I looked around and didn't think it went through, but the official signaled that it was good. Ab Kirwan was playing next to me at left end, and he had a knee that sometimes would go out. A Chicago play came toward us, and I took out the interference. As Ab started to tackle the ballcarrier, that knee went out and he (Chicago ballcarrier) scored a touchdown. They beat us, 9-0."

Murphy's 1926 team defeated only Maryville and Florida and tied VPI while losing six games, including the last four in a row. There was a fine passer in Paul Jenkins and capable receivers in Gayle Mohney, Ellis Smith, and Al Portwood, but other phases of the game were not quite so spectacular. In the opening game against Indiana, Jenkins received the snap from center, stumbled, almost fell, but completed a 40-yard aerial to Mohney, who stumbled over the goal line. But the Hoosiers won, 14-6.

The Wildcats' best game that year was a 14-13 loss to powerful Washington & Lee, which had tied Princeton, 7-7, the preceding Saturday. Jenkins completed 11 of 22 passes for 209 yards in that game, setting up two scoring thrusts by captain Frank Smith. Norris Royden of the *Herald-Leader* called it "the greatest passing attack ever seen in the state." There were three interceptions of UK aerials, however. One was returned 60 yards for a TD by W&L.

Kentucky was trailing Florida in 90 degree weather on a hard clay field in Gainesville when Jenkins threw a 59-yard pass to Mohney on a fourth and 20 situation. Mohney gathered it in for the winning score. Centre beat the Cats on what was described as a "peculiar spread formation," completing a two-yard scoring pass on third and goal. En route to that 2-6-1 season, the Wildcats also lost to Alabama, VMI, and Tennessee. The UK president, pressured by some alumni members of the athletics board, called a meeting of the board the weekend before the Tennessee game, and that group ordered Murphy to turn over his job to an interim coach. Elmer Gilb, a sophomore member of that team, recalled that the board got "some town person" to coach the team. "We just sulked around and wouldn't play under this other guy," he said. "We went on strike and made them bring 'Murph' back." After the board reversed its decision, Murphy agreed to accompany the team to Knoxville, but he let it be known that he was through as UK coach and would not accept a new contract if it was offered to him. He would be succeeded the following year by Harry Gamage of Illinois.

Curtis M. Sanders

If ever there was a football trainer's nightmare, he was Curtis M. Sanders, probably the best fullback ever to play for the University of Kentucky. A virtual iron man, the six foot, 185-pound farm boy from Nicholasville averaged almost 60 minutes a game for four years, playing in constant pain from midway through his sophomore year until his final game in 1924.

He played five games with a broken right hand in a cast, had his nose broken four times, played with both shoulders separated, had bones chipped in both ankles, and kept right on tackling despite damaged cartilage and vertebrae in his neck.

It was enough to cause Wildcat trainer Frank Mann to throw up his hands in despair and exclaim, "Sandy, if you had any brains, you'd quit!"

"I told him I couldn't let my buddies down," the 72-year-old Sanders said as he sat in his farmhouse at Berry, Kentucky, on the afternoon of Superbowl IX in January, 1975. "You know, I can't recall a game in my senior year when I wasn't knocked out. They made me a special helmet with heavy canvas straps across the top on the inside so my head wouldn't touch the helmet, but you know leather gives and helmets sometimes go sideways.

"There were no fancy training rooms or equipment in those days. I remember the trainer did a lot of massaging of bruises, and he had an infrared machine. I 'cooked' those shoulders in the shower, and that was our 'whirlpool.' Our ankles were taped regularly before every game. We never thought about playing without tape.

"There were no scholarships, and I didn't get any help, if

Curtis M. Sanders.

you know what I mean. There wasn't too much support for the players. We even paid our own tuition. I worked in tobacco, as a lifeguard, plumber's helper, millwright's assistant, night clerk in a hotel, waiter, elevator operator, fraternity house manager, and bill collector.

"I pushed a concrete buggy, parked cars in an all-night garage, drove a bus, sold dry cleaning tickets, worked on a railroad repair gang, drove T-Model Fords from Cincinnati for $5 each trip, and helped build Dix Dam.

"During my sophomore year, my eyes went bad, and I dropped out in March and worked in my uncle's lumberyard in

West Helena, Arkansas. I meant to stay out there, but I came back to tell everyone good-bye and I saw them out there scrimmaging and I went in and got me a uniform and joined them."

He came to UK as an 18-year-old freshman in 1920 and played only class ball that year. He then played four years of varsity ball under a rule that was changed a short while later.

The victory over mighty Alabama in 1922 ranks as the most notable UK triumph during Sanders' varsity career. Sanders caught a 20-yard pass and gained nine crucial yards in three carries to help set up a seven yard scoring run by Bruce Fuller, and he had 29 of UK's 53 carries and 93 of its 125 yards.

The *Courier-Journal* reported, "The outstanding star of the fray was Curt Sanders. 'Sandy' gained yard after yard through the enemy line and was responsible for putting the Cats in position to score. He was the main cog in the Cat defense, making a large part of the tackles, even in the line of scrimmage and blocking Alabama passes in the first moments of the game."

"When players get a little shoulder separation now, they're out," Sanders said. "I couldn't raise my arms above my eyes without pain. That was in my sophomore year, and I had my right shoulder knocked down first. They made me a special shoulder pad, one that was heavy and had no 'give.' Then I got the other shoulder knocked down, and they made another one of those heavy, stiff pads and laced the two of them together. I could hardly move my arms, but I played almost 60 minutes of every game.

"In my senior year, I bought me a rubber nose guard that you held in your mouth, but Coach Murphy laughed and said, 'You'll lose all your teeth.' I didn't wear it, and I got my nose broken again. I broke it a fifth time when I was coaching at Paducah, and the doctor said, 'Curt, it's pulverized. I can make you any kind of nose you want.' Did a good job, didn't he?"

Sanders was captain of the 1924 Wildcats and had the honor of scoring the first 16 points on the new Stoll Field. Louisville was the opponent for that dedication at the beginning of the season. Before 5,000 fans in the finished half of the stadium, Sanders started the scoring by plunging through center from one yard out and kicking the extra point. In that same first quarter, he threw a key pass to Charles "Turkey" Hughes and kicked a 25-yard field goal. He scored his final six points on a 25-yard run in the second quarter. The Wildcats scored 13 more points in the second half to win, 29-0.

Against Georgetown the following weekend, Sanders scored a touchdown and hit five of five extra point attempts in a 42-0 rout. Despite that good start, the Wildcats finished with a 4-5 record, losing to W&L, Centre, Alabama, VMI, and West Virginia. They managed a 7-0 win over Sewanee on a touchdown and an extra point by Sanders, and he scored two touchdowns and kicked three extra points in a 27-6 victory over Tennessee at Knoxville. Against the Vols, Murphy made only one substitution, sending Ted Creech in for Charles Sauer just before the end of the game. Sanders, Rice, and King were injured in that game but continued to play after a time out was called in each instance.

"You could only be substituted once, and you played both ways," Sanders said. "If you came out, you could only go back once."

Sanders scored 51 points that year and was the Wildcats' best defensive back. For years all UK fullbacks would be compared to him and found lacking, both in overall ability and total dedication. At UK he was a member of Lamp & Cross, Omega Delta Kappa, and Delta Chi. He attended summer schools on coaching at Notre Dame, Northwestern, Wisconsin, and four years at UK.

He coached football, basketball, and baseball six years at Paducah Tilghman High School; basketball two years at Paducah Junior College; and returned to Lexington as basketball coach and teacher of mathematics at the old Picadome High School. He coached basketball and baseball 14 years at Berry High and was vo-ag instructor at the consolidated Harrison County High before retiring to the 355-acre farm on which he has tobacco, hay, and a herd of Hereford cattle. And lots of memories.

Roll Out The Barrel

Although Centre was still considered the University of Kentucky's big football rival in the early 1920s, Wildcat fans were beginning to savor the trips to Knoxville every other year. The Tennessee game was gaining in importance. Graydon Bower of the *Herald* captured the flavor in the following account of the 1924 game in Knoxville:

> When a heavily laden outfit of huskies with head gear strapped to their suitcases detrained at Knoxville at 7 o'clock Wednesday morning, went to the hotel and worked through a snappy practice session at Tennessee's field Wednesday afternoon, Knoxville was aware that company was coming for Thanksgiving.
>
> That was Wednesday. Knoxville awoke Thursday morning to find that the University of Kentucky as represented by the famous University band in its khaki, a husky-voiced crew of Wildcat fans that detrained from a special Pullman in the Southern parade at 7 o'clock and a vari-clad contingent of blind baggage travelers and others whose muscles were cramped from a long rest in the narrow confines beneath a lower berth. Nearly 100 fans detrained with the band and hiked the seven blocks to the Farragut Hotel, where the bell boys and clerks retreated into the corners and gave Kentucky full sway.
>
> The streets were lined with yellow and white, with occasional appearances of blue and at 10:30 o'clock Tennessee's student body and band paraded downtown and halted in front of the hotel for a contest. Everybody yelled and hats came off when the Vol band swung into 'My Old

Kentucky Home' and many a khaki-clad University cadet stood a trifle straighter as the familiar air was played.

At 1 o'clock, Ed Gans unlimbered his baton and the Kentucky band led the way to the heights on which Tennessee's buildings stand. The University musicians were cheered all along their line of march, and rewarded the crowd with a real exhibition of marching technique.

It was after the game, which the Volunteers had lost after a gallant battle, that Tennessee won the hearts of the Kentucky crowd. The team, band and fans were invited to one of the fraternity houses for a tea and dance, with Tennessee students looking out for them from the time they left the hotel until they got back at 6:30 o'clock in time for a break-training turkey dinner, with smokes allowed for one night by Coach Murphy.

Joy was unconfined in the temporary Kentucky camp set up in the hotel lobby. At 7 o'clock the band gave an hour's concert, including a variety of selections, which was applauded at length by the crowd of Knoxville people and Tennessee students who thronged the lobby. The Kentucky delegation separated in all directions, to be reunited beneath the arc lights of the Southern station at 12 o'clock.

It was the following year that UK alumni Guy Huguelet and Rollie M. Guthrie conceived a plan to stimulate the Wildcat-Volunteer rivalry to greater heights by something material to denote supremacy between the two. Here's how Guthrie, a retired insurance man living in St. Petersburg, Florida, in May, 1975, recalled the incident:

"We were having Cokes in Casey Jones' Lexington Drug Store, the hangout for Wildcat fans, and talking about Purdue having the Old Oaken Bucket and Michigan the Little Brown Jug when we decided to come up with something symbolic of both states, and we immediately thought of moonshine whisky and started to hunt a whisky barrel. When the Women's Christian Temperance Union got wind of what we were going to do, their protests were vigorous, so we settled for a beer keg, which we obtained from John G. Galvin, a Lexington distributor."

It also became necessary to rechristen the barrel, since the Anti-Saloon League, WCTU, and similar organizations evidenced horror at the thought of even a beer barrel symbolizing the rivalry. They seemed to interpret such a proclamation as approval of the return to light wine and beer. So, the keg was carried onto Stoll Field on Thanksgiving Day of 1925, incognito, with "Ice Water" painted on it.

"I remember we went down to J. D. Purcell's and got some blue and some orange cheese cloth and pinned them on the pants of two members of SuKy and two members of Tennessee's pep group," Guthrie said. "We made a stand for carrying the barrel and also made some 'battleaxes' from tin, with plaster lathes as handles and had two other boys from each side carrying them."

That first ceremony was described as nothing less than spectacular. Kentucky's blue-and-white-clad band marched from one end of the gridiron and the Tennesseans, in orange and white, came from the opposite goal. Six representatives from each school, their trousers decorated accordingly with either the blue of UK or the orange of UT and both wearing white waists, preceded the bands. They met at the 50-yard line, where the keg rested royally. A representative from each side drank from the barrel, filled with water, and toasted the honored foe. Then, to the tune of "How Dry I Am," the traditional ceremony was completed.

The alumni's decision to officially label the keg as an "ice water barrel" was described in an editorial carried in the *Lexington Leader* November 29, 1925. The editorial said, in part:

> There was a good deal of agitation in some quarters when it became known that at the Kentucky-Tennessee football game a beer keg would be dedicated and used as a trophy. The feeling was quite general that this was an unfortunate choice, and quietly protests were made and immediately those who had charge of the matter saw the reasonableness of the objection raised and named the trophy the "Ice Water Barrel."
>
> It was obvious that no offense was intended in the beginning. Certain angles of the matter were overlooked, and as soon as complaints were made action was taken by the University authorities and the alumni to meet them.
>
> This is a happy solution. There were very good reasons why a beer keg—a relic and typical of the saloon system in America, now forever banished—was not suitable as a trophy and a symbol. There has been too much of a disposition to treat prohibition lightly and to joke about it. It is a tremendous social experiment, fraught with con-

sequences, in its success or failure, which will be far-reaching and profound, and has been written indelibly upon the Constitution of the United States.

...everything is quiet along the Potomac, and the University management and the alumni are to be congratulated on their prompt action and broad treatment of the situation. May the "Ice Water Barrel" stay here, and never run dry.

Len Tracy, who would later teach English at the university, scored three touchdowns, two of them on passes from Ab Kirwan, and Gayle Mohney kicked a field goal for a 23-20 UK victory and first possession of the trophy. The *Kernel* described the enthusiasm in Lexington following that first game for the keg:

"A wildly singing, whooping rah-rah crowd of University

Kentucky cheerleaders reclaim the Beer Barrel after the Wildcats defeat Tennessee, 20-6, in Lexington in 1957.

of Kentucky boys, tearing madly down Limestone Street Thursday afternoon, following Kentucky's victory over the gold and white clad Tennessee eleven, staged a celebration that nearly eliminated Lexington.

"And so far did they go in their celebration as to (shall we say) borrow the flag poles from in front of the various public buildings and stores in the business section of downtown. Not even was the seat of county justice, the Fayette County Courthouse, an exception...."

In future years the rotating trophy would stimulate the grid rivalry between the two schools and would be involved in many shenanigans on the part of rival student bodies. Following a UK victory in 1953, disgruntled Tennessee students would raid the UK campus and "kegnap" the barrel—holding it until persuaded to return it by threats of reprisal against their coon dog mascot, Smoky. In 1955 UK students would visit the Tennessee campus hiding place of Smoky and "dognap" him. UT students would promptly retaliate by painting up the UK campus in a surprise raid and carting away "Colonel," UK's stuffed Wildcat mascot. A trade would be engineered at the game that year.

The stunts would erupt again in 1958, with Vol students catching a guard "napping" and sneaking away with the stuffed Wildcat. Despite promises to return it at half time of a nationally televised basketball game, the mascot would not be given back until four months later.

In a peculiar turn of events the beer barrel would be "kegnapped" from its hiding place in Lexington in March, 1961, by Vanderbilt students seeking support of Vol fans for the Commodore basketball team which was meeting the Wildcats in Knoxville in a playoff for an NCAA Tournament booth. Embarrassed Vandy students did not return the trophy until several months later.

Another chapter was added to the keg's history that year when two UK freshmen players forgot to bring the barrel to the game, and the Vols left town without claiming it. Kentucky sent the keg on to Knoxville later.

When the keg first turned up missing in 1953, Guthrie noted, "We should hope they bury it. It carries mostly memories of headaches for Kentucky. Virtually nothing but Tennessee wins. Now would be a good time to start a new one for a long string of Kentucky wins coming up.

"This time, we should get a barrel which has seen more rugged service than as a container for beer. We should have a barrel with more dynamite behind it. One that has carried white mule, say, from the hills of Kentucky and Tennessee. If somebody will find such a barrel, I'll do the paint job as I did on the first one 28 years ago."

His suggestion has gone unheeded. The same barrel was en route from Knoxville to Lexington when the Vols traveled to meet the Wildcats in 1975.

"Gloomy" Harry

They called him "Gloomy" during his seven years (1927-33) as head football coach at the University of Kentucky, and anyone who knew Harry Gamage will tell you that he lived up to the nickname in every respect. The situation at UK was enough to concern any coach, but it seems that Gamage was one of those natural worriers who always entered a season or a game as if a little black cloud hung over his head. The *Atlanta Journal's* "Old Timer" wrote what must be one of the best descriptions ever given of Gamage in the fall of 1932:

Kentucky is coached by the debonair Harry Gamage, who is a movie hero in manly pulchritude and who was a hard-boiled center of Zuppke's at University of Illinois in the not-so-distant past. Harry is a very serious-minded young man over whose head Mr. Timer's antic wit flies without making the slightest impression. Mr. Timer, upon arriving in the beautiful village of Lexington, will say, for instance, "Well, Harry, I assume, without having heard a word, that you are beset with injuries, poor material, hookworm and malaria among your squad; your quarterbacks are morons in intellect, your halfbacks suffer from palsy and athlete's foot, your linemen are victims of malnutrition, and the depression has just reached your fair city." And Harry without so much as a smile, will say, "Mr. Timer, your imagination is inadequate and fails utterly to portray the actual dire situation." Then he will proceed to give facts and figures to support the theory that he should have never gone into the business of coaching because fate and the forces of nature are permanently arrayed against him.

But invariably, his teams beat everybody they play except Alabama and then they top their brilliant season by tying Tennessee, who in the meantime has beaten everybody in the conference.

Mr. Gamage is assisted in his coaching by a small but select staff consisting of Bernie Shively, one of the best guards that ever functioned in the Big Ten; Monk Campbell, whom I believe to be the best back Wallace Wade ever had at Alabama, despite the praise heaped on Johnny Mack Brown, Flash Suther, Tony Holm, et. al.; and a young alumnus named Miller. It is a compact body, and I should venture the guess, it is highly efficient.

Mr. Gamage has one idiosyncrasy. He flits from this system to that, as blithely as does a butterfly from Sweet William to hollyhock. He is wedded to none, and he has the brave idea that systems should be adapted to fit the men, and not one set up as a sort of Procrustean bed in which the sleepers must fit the dimensions of the piece of furniture.

The players who played for Gamage and the coaches who served under him are unanimous in the opinion that he was a fine coach, especially on defense, and all are sympathetic with his courageous attempt to bring big time football to the university.

A native of Macomb, Illinois, he attended Western Illinois Teachers College and the University of Illinois. He did such a good job coaching high school teams at Fairmont and Parkersburg in West Virginia that Robert Zuppke called him to Illinois in the fall of 1924 to direct the freshman football team. Gamage turned out a fine team his first season as frosh coach and was retained for two additional seasons.

When the athletic council at UK asked Zuppke to recommend a coach for the Wildcat football team, the veteran Illinois coach promptly named Gamage, who was put under a two-year contract by the university, beginning what proved to be a constant and frustrating struggle to make UK one of the leading teams in the South. Barring injuries and other bad luck, he might have produced that championship team he so desired.

During the first 90 years of football at the university, only Paul Bryant (1946-53) and Blanton Collier (1954-61) would serve longer as head coaches than did Gamage. Charlie Bradshaw

Harry Gamage (1927-33).

(1962-68) would equal the seven-year tenure. And only Bryant (60-23-5) would have a better record than Gamage (32-25-5).

The situation was anything but bright when Gamage arrived on campus in the fall of 1927. The 1926 team had opened with a victory over weak Maryville and registered only an 18-13 decision over Florida and a 13-13 tie with Virginia Tech. They had lost six games. Gamage did not fare much better his first year, tying Maryville in the opener and defeating Kentucky Wesleyan, VMI, and Centre. He lost to such teams as Indiana, Florida, Washington & Lee, Vanderbilt, Alabama, and Tennessee.

However, the victory over Centre was UK's first over the Colonels since 1916. In winning nine consecutive games over UK, Centre had scored a total of 230 points and had limited the Wildcats to a lone field goal. Kentucky made up for some of that in 1927 by blasting the Colonels, 53-0. Gamage's teams defeated them two more times, 8-0 the following year and 33-0 in 1929. That was the end of the series as UK dropped the longtime rival in favor of the University of Virginia.

In October, 1931, Bruce Dudley, *Courier-Journal* sportswriter and Centre graduate, raised the first howl for Gamage's scalp. He charged that Gamage was instrumental in Kentucky's dropping Centre. From that time on, the Louisville newspaper would continually insist that UK play other schools in the state in both basketball and football.

Delmar Adams, in the April 6, 1933, *Kernel,* noted that each year the UK teams were better, and each year the opposition was tougher. "Had Gamage been content to rest on his laurels and played the teams within the state of Kentucky, all would have been well, and the 'Cats would have had several undefeated seasons," he said. "But the ambitious coach sought strong foes and was able to topple some of them. In 1928, the strong Northwestern Purples were held to a 7-0 win and three times Gamage's teams kept the Tennessee Vols from Southern Conference championships by administering ties in 1928, '29, and '31."

At that time there were no athletic scholarships, per se, at UK, and very little aid of any kind was officially received by football players. Joe Rupert, an end and team captain in 1934, said that in his freshman year (1931) he was given a scholarship consisting of tuition. "In addition, we were given jobs by business firms in downtown Lexington to pay our room and board.

We worked two to three hours in the evenings to earn $7 per week, which was ample in those days to pay for three large meals per day and a clean bed to sleep in. This I am sure is quite different from what the athlete receives today.

"Because it was so hard to get cash, an event that sticks out in my mind is a 50-yard dash between Frank Seale and myself at spring track meets. The fans would raise a pot of $10 to $12 to be given the winner. Frank was fast for his size but received a 10-yard handicap for his great weight. I ran the 50 and he ran the 40. I have forgotten who won, which was not important, but I do remember who got the money because, without the knowledge of anyone else, we agreed to split it equally. Five or six dollars was a lot of money in those days."

Gamage recruited Frank Seale when he stopped to visit at Seale's home in Big Stone Gap, Virginia, while on a business trip to Middlesboro, Kentucky.

On the day of Gamage's visit, Seale was hunting game in the hills surrounding his home and did not get in until late afternoon. "Gamage waited around all that Saturday, barking up a post," Seale recalled 46 years later. "As I came out of the hills and walked toward my home, people in every house along the way would stick their head out and say the coach wanted to see me. I just mosied on up to the house in my old pair of overalls and logging boots. My mother introduced me to Gamage, and he said 'Son, I don't wait all day for a guy and then hear he's going to the University of Virginia. You're going to Kentucky.'

"He gave my coach a $20 bill, told him to buy me a round trip ticket and see that I was in Lexington the next weekend. When I arrived at UK, somebody picked me up and showed me around. Gamage had written notes telling me everything I was to do, where to report, etc.

"Gamage was very tough. He ruled with fear, a whole lot like 'Bear' Bryant. We never got close to him. He was standoffish. He was a great believer in scrimmages for getting you in shape. Even during the season we scrimmaged on Tuesday and Wednesday."

Elmer "Baldy" Gilb played his junior and senior years under Gamage in 1927-28 and later was an assistant coach. Gilb said, "We just didn't have any recruiting. I thought Gamage got as much out of the material as any coach. He was an excellent defensive coach. Nobody ever scored much on us.

"I played in the last Centre game, when we beat them 55-0

in 1927. Gamage introduced a special system for that game. He moved me to guard, where I was to either block the end, if the play went to the left, or the halfback, if it went to the right. Our fullback would turn and back into the line with the ball, and one of the wings would get the ball or he would keep it. On one play he backed into the line for 10 yards. Gayle Mohney and Paul Jenkins were the wings, Len Miller was the quarterback, and Al Portwood the fullback.

"There was more interference in front of a player then. We never ran a play without somebody in front of the ballcarrier leading interference. Now they try to fool people more. Our defense also was more standardized. I backed up the line my junior and senior year. I was having a picnic in the Alabama game at Montgomery because I knew what they were going to run. They didn't huddle up, and their play calls were the same as ours. If they called an end run, I was waiting; if they came through the middle, I was waiting; if they threw a pass, I was waiting. I was in on every tackle.

"With the score tied 0-0 right after the first half, they called a 'No. 50,' and I tried to get Max Colker in position for it, but he wouldn't pay any attention. 'I know it's going to be a pass,' I said, and the Alabama guys heard me. They went into a huddle, came out, and scored on the first play. They beat us, 14-0."

The Wildcats' best season under Gamage was 1929, when they won six games, lost only to Alabama, and tied Tennessee. The following year they were 4-0 when powerful Alabama came to town for what was UK's No. 1 homecoming of that era. Both teams were undefeated, and both were rumored as possible Rose Bowl candidates. Some believers favored the Wildcats on the basis of their 37-0 victory over Sewanee (Alabama had beat Sewanee 25-0), their season record of 174 points in four games (Bama had 162 in five games), and the presence of "Shipwreck" Kelly in the UK backfield. Scouts of Grantland Rice were in the stadium to report Kelly's All-American possibilities. With so much at stake, football spirits were high.

A UK custom in those days, originating back when football teams played without shoulder pads and headgear, directed that the grid squad go without shaving for at least one game each season. The Wildcats chose the Alabama game as their shaveless one that year. A SuKy contest offered a valuable favor and the honor of shaving before a Pathe cameraman between

Members of the 1930 UK coaching staff. Left to right: Len Miller, Adolph Rupp, Birkett Pribble, Elmer Gilb, Harry Gamage, Bernie Shively, and Pete Drury.

halves to the student with the longest beard, and the nonshave habit swept the campus. Almost every one of the 2,000 male students appeared with chin foliage within a few days.

On Friday night before the game the finals of the SuKy contest were held at a mammoth pep rally, with approximately 25 men presenting their chins for inspection. Harold S. Ray of Independence, Kentucky, was named winner, and a special barber and barber chair were obtained for the shaving ceremony. Also featured at half time was Major Duke Redd, an 84-year-old Confederate veteran, who rode up and down the sidelines on a prancing horse, waving his saber.

Years later "Daddy" Boles, business manager for athletics, recalled that 19,500 fans attended that game—a record until the stadium was enlarged years later. "The reserve seats in the concrete stadium and the field boxes were sold in advance," he said. "Bleacher seats were sold as long as there were fans to buy them. We always had a reserved section for colored fans. Well, on the occasion of that game the advance sale of these tickets was very light. But on the day of the game the colored fans swept down on the ticket sellers in droves. So rapidly were the tickets sold, the man in the booth had neither time nor space to place his money in the money drawer. He dropped each bill on the floor. Finally, I received an SOS from this seller. He was in difficulty. I rushed to his booth, and when I opened the door, I saw a sight I had never seen before. That ticket seller, on my word of honor, was standing in dollar bills up to his knees. We had 2,000 standees that day."

The Wildcats lost that game, 19-0, and then lost to Duke at Durham, beat VMI at home, and lost to Tennessee, 8-0, for a 5-3 record. They were 5-2-2 in 1931, 4-5 in 1932, and 5-5 in 1933, losing to Alabama, Duke, Tulane, and Tennessee each of those last two years.

Gamage switched from the Zuppke system of double wingbacks and a balanced line to the Notre Dame shift and various adaptations of his own ideas. However, his teams never seemed to have the ability to push across the winning score at a strategic moment against top competition. During the 1932-33 seasons, they lost several games because they lacked the punch, and it seemed that several of those games should have been theirs since they out-gained and out-fought the foe.

After the 1932 season the school newspaper decided to run a series of editorials on the athletic situation, but the first of these stirred up so much strife on the campus that the editor decided against writing any more. Presently, a student petition was presented, asking for the removal of Gamage. Printed but unsigned handbills were scattered across the campus, accusing him of exerting undue influence on the selection of football captains over a period of three years. The *Kernel* threatened to conduct an investigation, but Gamage was cleared of any wrongdoing and his contract was renewed for three more years. Alumni interest soon turned to other things, such as UK's membership in the newly formed Southeastern Conference which also consisted of Georgia, Georgia Tech, Alabama, Alabama Polytech (now Auburn), Mississippi, Mississippi State, Tulane, LSU, Tennessee, Sewanee, Vanderbilt, and Florida.

In 1933 the Wildcats got off to a fine start once again—defeating Maryville, Sewanee, Georgia Tech, and Cincinnati.

Their joy was short lived as they lost to Washington & Lee, Duke, and Alabama; defeated VMI; then lost to Tulane and Tennessee. Tulane scored four times in the first quarter and once in the second en route to a 34-0 victory in New Orleans. Tennessee scored twice in the first quarter on a 56-yard run by Beattie Feathers and a pass from Vaughn to Ponders. At no time did the 'Cats make a serious scoring threat against the Vols.

Wildcat fans considered 1933 the most disastrous season in UK football history. The 5-5 record was not that bad, but fans had their sights set on a high finish in the newly formed Southeastern Conference and were not satisfied with ninth place. Gamage called it quits and moved to the more peaceful climes of Vermillion, South Dakota, where he had a long and relaxing career as head football coach at the state university there.

Time Out: Shipwreck Kelly

To many Kentucky football fans, John Simms "Shipwreck" Kelly was Horatio Alger, Huck Finn, Jack Armstrong, and a host of other All-American heroes rolled into a six-foot, 190-pound package of blazing speed, rare cunning, and indisputable courage.

He came out of the little farming community of Springfield, Kentucky, bowled over would-be tacklers like tenpins at the University of Kentucky, was an idolized professional player in Brooklyn, married the debutante daughter of a New York millionaire, became a successful businessman, and was part owner and president of the old football Dodgers.

He conjured up his gridiron magic at UK during the varsity years of 1929-31, when the Wildcats compiled a composite record of 16-6-3. Their best season was 6-1-1 in 1929, when they lost only to Alabama at Montgomery. And Shipwreck Kelly did not make that trip because his grandmother was ill in Springfield.

His attachment to the grandmother had brought him to UK in the first place. His mother had died when he was three days old, and his grandmother raised him. His grandfather, John S. Simms, was a graduate of Notre Dame and naturally would have been pleased if the young Kelly had chosen to wear the football green of the Irish. There were other pressures along that line, especially from Walter Clemons, a friend of Knute Rockne. Clemons kept insisting that Kelly attend Notre Dame.

"I wanted to go to Kentucky to be close enough to visit my grandmother," Kelly recalled by telephone from his Manhasset, Long Island, home in April, 1975. "I was a kid then, and

I had those feelings. I lived about 50 miles from Lexington. They had raised money to bring players to Lexington, but the feeling then was that if you lived that close, you couldn't play football."

Although Springfield was a little off the beaten football path, he had attracted much attention because, as he so aptly put it, "I used to run through a lot of teams. Like I had always been *the team*. I knew I could play. The Lord did that. He gave me a good body, speed, and quickness. When you've got it, you've got it. When you break through that line, what's going to stop you?"

He enrolled at UK without benefit of scholarship, which really did not worry him too much since he received money from home—"My grandfather had two big farms and we did all right"—and he encountered no trouble whatsoever in quickly lining up a sponsor among the "horsey" set.

"Let's face it, Ed Madden (owner of Hamburg Place) was good to me," he said. "He was a great track man, and he got a big kick out of coming out to track meets. 'Daddy' Boles was too cheap to send the track team on long trips, and I sometimes went as the team. Mr. Madden sent me to Chapel Hill, and I won the 100, 220, 440, and broad jump. I would run for the New York Athletic Club in the summer, and I was beaten out of the 1932 Olympics."

A flamboyant person with a flair for the spectacular, he acquired his nickname at a time when another man known as "Shipwreck" Kelly had achieved fame of a sort by living on top of a flagpole for a month. John Simms Kelly announced that he would imitate the flagpole sitter. He climbed to the top of a flagpole on the Lafayette Hotel in downtown Lexington where he remained for a few hours. Asked why he came down, he replied, "I had to go to the bathroom."

By the time he left the university, it was said that he would visit the local Greyhound bus station in a chauffeur-driven Cadillac and send the chauffeur in to pick up wages for which he never toiled.

"It really wasn't a Cadillac," he said in 1975. "It was a LaSalle. I had the Cadillac earlier. A convertible. Babe Wright (a star tackle) would drive. If we won a game, it was wonderful to let the top down, drive all over town, and have people say, 'Look at that Shipwreck Kelly.' I was living."

And if there ever was a "Big Man on Campus," it was

Shipwreck Kelly.

Kelly. One year the *Kentuckian* devoted a full page to him, depicting him decked out in football togs and in dress clothes beside a large fish hung in the usual Florida tourist pose. It also ran a full facial shot and labeled the page, "Lady's Man."

The bride he took June 30, 1941, was oil-rich Brenda Diana Duff Frazier, society's No. 1 glamour girl since her $58,000 debut in 1938. He was 31, she was 20 at the time. A few months later she received $3,500,000 from a trust fund.

In his first year at UK, Kelly was relegated to the second-team freshman squad, which meant that he competed against high schools. When he started running over the opposition, frosh coach Birkett Pribble elevated him to the first team for the final game with Centre. With the Kittens trailing, 14-0, Kelly was inserted in the final quarter and scored three touchdowns.

"Gamage made it tough for me," Kelly recalled. "He tried to break me down. In my sophomore year he used to keep me with the first team; then I'd go with the second team and sometimes with the scrub team until everybody would go in. I'd then go up and ask him if he'd mind if I took a couple of laps. I'm built that way. When you're gaited a certain way, you can't help it."

Kelly burst onto the collegiate football scene in his first varsity game, against Maryville on October 29, 1929, the first night game held in Kentucky and perhaps the first in the South. He scored on runs of 40, 20, and 70 yards for the Wildcats' first three touchdowns and then caught a 20-yard touchdown pass from George Yates. Frank Hoover of the *Herald* called the 70-yard run "a sparkling exhibition, he shaking off six tacklers before he really got started." UK won the game, 40-0.

"I remember the first four times I got my hands on the ball, I scored," Kelly said. "We didn't pass much; in fact, every team I played against knew we weren't going to pass. They knew I was going to get the ball and run."

In the second game of the season Washington & Lee had the Wildcats backed up to their three yard line when Covington called a punt formation, threw his headgear aside, went back as if to punt, and caught the General secondary asleep. Tom Phipps took the ball on a crisscross and carried to the 26. On the next play Kelly raced to the right, then to the left, shook off four tacklers, finally reversed his field, picked up his interference, and scored the final touchdown in a 20-6 victory.

Kelly had a 44-yard run in a 58-0 rout of Carson-Newman and scored a touchdown in a 30-0 blanking of Centre. He gained national prominence at the expense of undefeated Clemson, which had whipped five Southern Conference teams in September and October before visiting Lexington. After kicking off to the Tigers, the Wildcats held for downs, forcing a Tiger punt. Kelly returned 15 yards to the Clemson 47. Then on the first play from scrimmage he ran to the right sideline, cut back, and raced for a score. Clemson coach Josh Cody called it a "perfect play." Later in the game Kelly again scored from the Clemson 47 yard line on the same play.

"I told the reporters it wasn't a perfect play the second time because one of their guys got hold of my jersey," Kelly said. "He held onto it for a moment and the shirt gave way and boom!—I was gone. I think we ought to thank the guy who made that shirt."

In the famed "Battle of the Snow" against Tennessee on Stoll Field in 1929, more than 20,000 fans were on hand to watch Kelly and Volunteer All-American Gene McEver. The Wildcats made 14 first downs to two for the Vols and outplayed the visitors in every phase of the game except punting (Bobby Dodd repeatedly punted out of danger for Tennessee). The famous McEver made only 16 yards from scrimmage. However, the game ended up a tie.

Kelly scored 48 points that year, mostly on long runs. The following year he scored 46 points, and he added 30 points in his senior season. Kelly opened the 1930 season with two touchdowns and runs of 15, 26, 40, and 46 yards against Sewanee. Next came his best individual total, in a 57-0 rout of Maryville. Kelly carried the ball 15 times for 280 yards and scored four touchdowns, with his longest gain covering 69 yards.

In a 33-14 win over Washington & Lee in 1930, he gained more than 180 yards, including a 59-yard touchdown and runs of 16 and 22 yards. He had a 44-yard punt return and totaled nearly 300 yards in runs and returns.

His flair for the spectacular and his appeal to the fans were pointed up in an easy Wildcat victory over the University of Virginia (47-0) in 1930. When the Cavalier coach started a second-string team, with only his regular center and fullback in the lineup, Gamage came back with his second-string backfield and a substitute for tackle Babe Wright. The Wildcats dominated the

"Shipwreck" Kelly again sidesteps the famous Alabama line, but UK loses, 19-0, in the 1930 game in Lexington.

game, but there were no real thrills until the final quarter when the crowd began to yell, "We want Kelly!" Kelly entered the game and on the first play from scrimmage went 65 yards for a touchdown.

Carey Spicer, an All-American basketball player who earned football letters in 1928-29-30, visited Lexington in the fall of 1975 and shed some light on the lack of more points in Kelly's book of records.

"We'd use the double wing formation, with Kelly carrying most of the time, until we got inside the 20," he said, "and then we'd go to the single wing, and I would carry. Kelly would make all the yardage, and I would score the touchdowns. I scored a school record 75 points in 1930 that stood until Rodger Bird broke it 35 years later. It was embarrassing because I was the quarterback. I talked to Coach Gamage about it, but that didn't change anything. Kelly didn't complain. He knew the circumstances, but I don't think the public understood.

"Kelly was a tremendous person, a friendly fellow who never seemed to get upset. He was a great believer in himself. He believed he could do anything, and he could. He was cocky, but he could back up what he said he would do."

Utilizing existing records, John McGill of the *Herald* figured Kelly gained 2,101 yards from scrimmage, a career total which stood until Sonny Collins broke it in 1974. However,

only Kelly's long gains are listed for several games in which he undoubtedly had more yardage. In his senior year alone, he gained 1,074 yards on 171 carries.

The team that gave Shipwreck Kelly the most trouble was Alabama in 1930. Kelly caught a 16-yard pass and returned a punt 35 yards. But that was about the extent of his contribution as the big Tide line smothered him several times behind the line of scrimmage. He finished the afternoon with a total of 25 yards in 11 carries. Alabama won, 19-0. Here's what Kelly remembered most:

"Will Stewart, who owned a big garage in Lexington, went to Vanderbilt with Grantland Rice, and he [Stewart] kept writing 'Granny' about me. We hadn't lost a game and Granny was picking All-Americans, so he came to see me play. I was sure we were going to knock Alabama off, but they were tough. I remember carrying the ball so many times and that Granny wrote that we had a five-man backfield and the fifth man was Alabama tackle Fred Sington. After that game I locked myself in my room and didn't come out for two days. Then I was back in the saddle."

Teammate Frank Seale recalls that on the eve of the Alabama-UK game in Birmingham the following year, Kelly asked reporters to be in his hotel room at a certain time for an important announcement.

"I was just as curious as anybody," Seale recalled, "and I went in there at the appointed time, and there was Kelly in bed in a pair of shorts. He said, 'Gentlemen, tomorrow I will make a touchdown against Alabama. Put it in the papers. I want everybody to know it, and it will be more than 50 yards long.'" He scored on a 57-yard reverse, but the Wildcats lost, 9-7.

Will Ed Covington recalled that before the game Gamage had all the small players, including Covington, walk around the hotel lobby in Tuscaloosa to give the impression that Kentucky was a small team.

"Alabama was always the big, rough club one would expect," he said. "On our kickoff to them, the receiver got the ball and picked up three huge linemen and came sweeping up the field. I was the only one between them and our goal. I was able to run fast enough that they couldn't block me out, but I couldn't get to the ballcarrier behind them. I realized that I had to do something or they would cross our goal in that manner. I wheeled and darted in and made a diving, flying block on all three at their knees, with my arms stretched out to try and knock all of them off their feet. I did block the three linemen, and they fell on me. The ballcarrier jumped the entire pile, stumbled, and was caught on our six yard line. We held on downs twice. They fumbled and we recovered, ran two plays, and kicked out of danger."

Tennessee and Tulane were hoping for a Rose Bowl invitation that season, and Tennessee was expected to make short work of the Wildcats as they marched toward Pasadena. The day before Thanksgiving Kelly sent the following telegram to the captain of the Tulane team: "Make your plans to go to the Rose Bowl for we will take care of Tennessee for you tomorrow." The Cats and Vols tied, 6-6. Kelly gained 117 yards in that game.

"I later received a letter from Coach (Bernie) Bierman, thanking me for taking care of Tennessee," Kelly said.

Seale, who centered the ball to Kelly two years, said a lot of people who met Kelly and did not know him had a tendency to dislike him. "I guess he was an arrogant person," Seale said, "but he was one who could deliver. He was a playboy type, but he never dominated the huddle or berated a player. I was devoted to him because of this. He was a pretty good blocker, an extremely good runner, and he could break open a ball game in a hurry.

"I only saw him do one foolish thing. I gave him a long lead, and he got by everybody and was in the clear against Florida at Jacksonville. He turned and waved at the Florida players, hit some sand, stumbled, and failed to score. But we won, 7-2.

"He wouldn't warm up for less than twelve or thirteen thousand people. He'd pretend he had sand in his shoes, take them off, and stall until he felt there were enough people in the stands."

"Sure, I would look around and ask about the size of the crowd," Kelly said. "It helped to relax the team."

Seale also recalled that Kelly would come to his room at night and want to talk. "He'd say, 'Frank, am I as good as the sportswriters say I am?' I would tell him to go to bed."

Ralph Kercheval, who played with Kelly at the university and in Brooklyn, called him a crowd-pleaser, a person who loved to do spectacular things. "I've seen him catch punts many times without thinking of a fair catch, with guys all over him," Kercheval said. "He was extremely fast, game as the devil, and he had high leg action that made him hard to bring down. He enjoyed playing as much as anybody I've ever known. He was kind of a playboy but not a carouser. He was fun off the field, but he took the game seriously."

Kelly's heroics did not end on the gridiron. In the early morning hours of June 21, 1959, he was credited with hustling dozens of people to safety during a fire at the Ambasciatori Hotel in Rome, where he was vacationing. When the fire broke out on the top floor of the five-story building, he dashed from his room wearing a Kelly green bathrobe and slippers to match. The Associated Press reported that "again and again he rushed up the stairs to the smoke-filled upper floors to find guests...to everyone he was the 'man in the green bathrobe'—the man who did the most to get the guests out of their rooms."

While playing "catch" football with a grandson of the movie's Howard Hawks before World War II, he ran into a metal stake and broke a leg. The injury did not heal properly and kept him out of the armed services. However, he worked undercover for J. Edgar Hoover's FBI and, 30 years after the war had ended, was still concerned because some people might think of him "as the draft-dodging football hero who married the heiress."

Ralph Kercheval

Everyone who saw Ralph Kercheval kick a football for the University of Kentucky in the early 1930s will probably tell you that he was the greatest punter they had ever seen.

His old high school coach John Heber said it. Bernie Shively, former All-American guard at Illinois and a coach and athletic director at UK said it. Jim Park, former major league pitcher and all-sports star at UK said it. "Shipwreck" Kelly of the old Brooklyn Dodgers, a pretty good punter in his own right, said it. Tulane fans in New Orleans said it.

The list goes on and on, yet never was there a player more worthy of the accolades but more modest in accepting them.

Standing in front of a picture window in the winter of 1974 and watching some young thoroughbred horses run around a bluegrass pasture on the 3,500-acre Mereworth Farm, which he manages, the 63-year-old Kercheval admitted that perhaps he was finally ready to talk about some of his feats.

"I wouldn't have said anything about them 35 years ago," he said, running fingers through his thick thatch of gray hair. "Perhaps I'm getting softer."

Kercheval was anything but a softie in his football-playing days at Henry Clay High School, the University of Kentucky, and with the Brooklyn Dodgers. "I never got hurt much at all, either in college or pro ball," he said, "but I did have a broken ankle in high school and didn't know nothing about it for three days. I was hopping around, and they finally decided to have an X-ray.

"In my freshman year at UK, I played in all games and had a pretty good year, but I got a concussion in one game and came over and sat on the bench. I was extremely fuzzy. The coach finally said I might as well go to the showers. The gate was locked, and I obviously climbed over the fence and four strands of barbed wire. I took a shower with my clothes on, got in the car, and drove home—all without knowing what I was doing. They didn't pay nearly as much attention to players then."

Kercheval had what might be considered a peculiar style to most punters. He seemed to throw the ball downward as part of his punting technique. In 1974 he explained that he really did not throw the ball down but held it with one hand on top and a little to the side. This allowed the left arm to swing as if one were in stride, which gave excellent balance.

Frank Seale centered the ball to Kercheval for two years. ("He was near perfect," Kercheval said.) Seale recalled that Kercheval wanted the ball centered toward the tip of his right shoulder and directly into his upheld hand. "He would raise the ball slightly as he stepped forward, then push it downward," Seale said. "We went through a 15-minute punting drill daily. He would kick from the 45 and then the 50. When he reached the other 40, he would start aiming the ball out of bounds inside the five or try to bounce it dead at that point.

"He would stand about 11 yards behind the line of scrimmage. His kicks were high and accurate. The center and the ends would try to get down field fast, and his kicks were so high, we usually prevented a return. We had some exceptional wing men in John Frye, Joe Rupert, and Dutch Kreuter."

Kercheval took a secondary role his freshman year; the Kittens overran six straight opponents and his punts were not needed. But he place-kicked the extra points. He had come to the university after a fine career at Henry Clay.

"Even as a kid, I could kick the ball 55 or 60 yards," he said. "When I was about 12 or 13, we used to go over to where the Kentucky players were punting. We'd get behind the goal, in case they missed, and shag balls. Sometimes they'd let us punt. I used to kick it over their heads. They'd get a bang out of that. I remember seeing Red Roberts—he wore a handkerchief over his head—Herb 'Flash' Covington, and his brother Ed.

"We used to climb over the fence, hide, and get lost in the crowd during games. That's when they put up the barbed wire over the cyclone fence. The players had to walk through a garden area from the dressing room to the playing field, and we'd often walk with them, hiding under their blankets. When we got inside, they would turn us loose. I remember seeing UK beat Alabama, 6-0, in 1922. Bruce Fuller went off tackle from about the five.

"My biggest thrill came in the first game I played in. It was my sophomore year. We had two good fullbacks in Tom and Jack Phipps, and I hadn't played in the opener against Maryville. Just before the half was up, we had the ball on our own 35 against Washington & Lee, and we got a 15-yard penalty. Coach Gamage yelled, 'Kercheval, go in there and kick it.' I caught the ball real well, and I kicked it 75 yards in the air. I remember, as a kid would, everybody rose in their seats on both sides of the field, and I couldn't help but see and hear them. When we went back to the dressing room, Gamage sat beside me and said, 'I'm going to start you this half, and we're going to kick every time on first down.' I started every game after that."

John McGill of the *Herald* said Kercheval could be called "the Babe Ruth of Kentucky football. His long punts linger so vividly in fans' memories that his all-around ability is often overlooked."

Kercheval's record for the most punts in one game is 17 against Alabama in 1931, a game that the Tide won, 9-7. On a free kick, he booted the ball 65 yards to the Bama 15. He averaged 40 yards, although one kick was blocked. He rushed for 161 yards in a 7-0 loss to Duke. Against Tennessee he tried his first quick-kick, which was good for 58 yards, and punted one 62 yards out of bounds on the Vol four. He also kicked one 79 yards, which would be a record except for the fact that UK was offside. In his final game as a sophomore, he ran nine yards for a TD to beat Florida, 7-2. His nine punts averaged 48 yards, one traveling 66.

"Shipwreck" likes to tell the story of that victory over Florida in Jacksonville. "We had them beat with fourth down and seven or eight to go about their 20," he recalled. "In the huddle, I told (captain) Babe Wright, 'I want you to do one thing for me. I want to see Kercheval kick one more time.' Ralph took the ball on the 25, kicked it out of the end zone and into the bay. That is the only time I've ever seen a ball kicked out of a stadium."

Kercheval was hurt during the 1932 season, missing the Duke and Alabama games, but he made his presence felt otherwise. He completed six of 11 passes, intercepted three passes, and kicked a field goal against VMI. He was ready to try for the winning point after a touchdown against Tennessee when there was a sudden change of signals. Kercheval explains:

"I was making my mark for the point attempt when Dick Richards, a marvelous blocker and a quarterback with a great voice for calling 'Ready, Hep, Tup, Three, Four,' said in the huddle, 'I think we ought to let Babe Wright kick it because he is captain of the team.' Why he did it, I don't know, but Babe kicked and missed, and the game ended in a 6-6 tie. That goes back to football like it was played then."

Wright, a six-foot, 210-pound tackle, was chosen the outstanding tackle of the year by a committee of 10 sports editors from the South. Ed Danforth called him one of the fastest linemen in the conference. His play in the Tennessee game was one of the greatest all-around exhibitions by any tackle that season.

"Tennessee had been invited to a bowl game, and they had a fine club," Kercheval said. "Bobby Dodd was gone, but Gene McEver and Beattie Feathers were still around. We were kicking from Rose Street up toward Limestone Street, and I got off a good punt, about 65 yards in the air. We were offside, and they took the penalty. I kicked the ball back to the same spot and again they didn't return it and again we were offside. They took the penalty and I kicked it back to the same spot and again there was no return."

It was end Joe Rupert's job to cover Kercheval's punts. He recalled returning to the huddle after that second penalty and asking, "Who the hell was offside?"

"No. 50," said the referee. That was Rupert's number.

"I remember Kercheval was the talk of the Southeast," Rupert said in March, 1975. "In the VMI game in 1933, we had a rather large lead and possession on third down with the ball about the 35. In the huddle Kercheval said he was going to kick the ball over the stadium and give the crowd a thrill. Well, the ball just lacked a little making it, but I'm sure the crowd was thrilled just the same.

"In the summer of that year, Gamage invited several players to his home to review plans for the oncoming season. During the review, he explained a new end-around play that would end up in a pass to the opposite end deep down the field. His comments were that he had a dream in which the play came to him. He said the ball would be on our 40-yard line, second down.

"He said, 'Rupert will take the ball on an end-around, drop

back, and throw a long pass to Johnny Frye—and this will take place against Georgia Tech in the third game of the season and will beat them.' The play was practiced daily but not shown in the first two games. At the exact spot on the field in the Tech

Ralph Kercheval.

game the play was called, and Frye did catch the ball on the goal line, which did beat Georgia Tech, 7-6. When I threw the ball, the only thing I saw was about six charging yellow shirts, and I had to throw—just to get rid of it or else."

In that game Kercheval had a 77-yard punt, longest in the school's history. Later in the game he kicked a 73-yarder, going against the wind, and averaged 45 yards on 16 kicks. He kicked the winning point and made two key defensive plays.

"It was a rule of thumb then that inside the 10, you kicked on first down; inside the 20, on second down; inside the 30, on third down; and inside the 40, on fourth down," Kercheval said. "There was so little field goal kicking, even in the pros, but I used to practice field goals all the time. It's like playing golf—you love to hit the tee shots. I remember kicking one against Tulane here in 1932."

In that game he averaged 42.1 yards on 15 punts, one sailing 65 yards out of bounds on the six. Another covered 63 yards. Kentucky was leading, 3-0, when Kercheval told the team he would send the kickoff into the left corner, away from Tulane's great Don Zimmerman. However, Zimmerman grabbed the ball in the corner at the three yard line and returned it 62 yards, setting up the winning score in a 6-3 game.

In New Orleans the following year, Kercheval had fans buzzing. It was his custom during warm up to first stand on the 40 yard line and kick the ball four or five times through the goal posts. He would then repeat the routine from the 50 and then the 40. At the end of the exhibition he kicked the ball to the goal line from 75 yards out, then to the out-of-bounds line, and finally through the goalpost and into the crowd.

"Everybody stood up and applauded," Kercheval said. "That stands out in my memory as being very self-satisfying."

Tulane won the game, 34-0, and Tennessee blanked them, 27-0, in Lexington. The Vols blocked two of his punts, but he recovered one and then punted it 51 yards. The team had lost five games in a row after winning the first four by outscoring their opponents, 106-20. They were outscored, 57-10, in those five losses.

Kentucky and Cincinnati were both undefeated when they met the night of October 14, 1933, before 16,000 fans in Nippert Stadium (a record at the time for that facility). The Bearcats' fleet halfback Bill Schwarberg described Kercheval's kicking in that game for Bob Rankin of the *Cincinnati Enquirer* in January, 1972:

"We drove to Kentucky's goal line time after time and Kercheval would simply stand back and kick the ball all the way back. In those early days the UC lighting system was not too good and his kicks were so high, we lost them in the lights."

In that game Kercheval had punts of 47, 46, 47, 73, 66, and 45 yards. He had five other kicks of lesser dimensions and finished the game with a 47.0 yard average. With three minutes to play and no score for either team, Kentucky's J. N. McMillan returned a punt 36 yards to the UC 19. Kercheval split the uprights for a 25-yard field goal, winning the game, 3-0.

That year he had 101 punts in 10 games for 4,394 yards, a national record which still was standing in 1975. This propelled him into the pros, along with his former teammate "Shipwreck" Kelly. They went on to set records for seven years with the Brooklyn Dodgers.

"I remember my first year with the Dodgers," Kercheval said. "We were playing in ankle-deep mud with the ball fourth down on the other team's 40. Chris Cagle, the quarterback, called for a kick. Kelly said, 'Hell, you can't kick a field goal in all this mud.' Then he turned to me and asked, 'Can you?' I said yes and I kicked it and we beat them, 10-7. My longest field goal in the pros was 51 yards; my longest punt, 91 yards in the air against the Bears."

"The Chetter"

When Chet Wynne was signed to a three-year contract as athletic director and football coach at the University of Kentucky at an annual salary of $7,500 in 1934, Brownie Leach of the *Leader* said the Wildcats not only were entering a new coaching regime but were about to become potent factors in southern football.

"Oh, I know that sort of thing has been said every time a new man takes over the Wildcat job," he wrote. "If Kentucky doesn't go to the top with Wynne in the pilot house, the Wildcats and their followers might as well give up."

The first Notre Damer to coach a Wildcat athletic team, the 35-year-old Wynne had a fine record as a player and coach. With George Gipp, Frank Thomas, and Johnny Marhardt, he helped form one of the most famous backfields ever produced by Knute Rockne. He coached two football champions at Missouri College and won two more at Creighton. Wynne was also admitted to the state bar and served two years in the Nebraska State legislature. In 1932 he coached the Auburn Tigers to an undefeated season and a conference co-championship.

Ed Danforth, UK alumnus writing for the *Georgian*, said:
> In Kentucky, they look to Wynne as the man to bring peace to the Dark and Bloody Ground that is strewn with the bones of football coaches. . . .Again, it must be realized that football has been a minor sport at Kentucky. Basketball is tops! This creates an unsavory situation. Even on campus they are talking basketball during the football season. . . .Into this unsettled realm, Chet Wynne is going. . . .He is one of the few coaches who can make a go of it. He

is a diplomat from here to yonder. . . .Kentucky needs a diplomat more than they do a football coach. Chet can give them the well-coached football team and bring order out of chaos.

The assignment was the toughest any coach had faced. Spirit on campus was at a low ebb, and the schedule was tough. Wynne's first move was to weed out players who were only participating in football for the exercise and those who showed flashes of temperament. By the time he finished that process, the squad numbered 30 players.

Russell "Duke" Ellington, who lettered in 1934-35-36 as an end, remembered Wynne as a highly educated person, one who loved to entertain and be entertained. This eventually was interpreted as a weakness by the citizenry.

"He kept himself kinda aloof from us," Ellington said. "My dealing was mostly with Porter Grant, the end coach. We started the season by going to Greentree Farm for twice-a-day workouts. We'd ride two buses that weren't air-conditioned, and it would get awful hot and sticky with those uniforms on. Those practices, beginning on Labor Day and lasting until a week before the first game, really showed us who was and who wasn't in shape."

Gene Myers, a sophomore destined to become one of the best centers in the South, said Wynne was somewhat different from the "distant" Gamage in that "he would at least speak to you once in a while." However, Myers admitted that he had little contact with Gamage because the freshmen dealt mostly with their own coach, Birkett Pribble.

Myers said, "On our first day of spring practice under Wynne, he watched us a while, then lined us up, and said, 'I'm going to teach you to run.' It was my fifth year in football, and nobody had bothered to teach me to run. In the fall, some weren't invited back."

In addition to Myers and Ellington, Wynne inherited some fine football players from Gamage—but not enough to survive a hard season unscathed. The list included: Joe Rupert, Jim Long, Norris McMillan, and Stanley Nevers.

Captain Joe Rupert was a 188-pound, pass-catching, punt-covering, deadly tackling end who came to UK to play basketball. He had never played football in high school, but he went out for the freshman football team and was such a sensation that he gave up basketball.

Jim Long, captain in 1935, attended Kentucky Military Institute and never had a football in his hand before attending UK.

Norris "00" McMillan was a diminutive quarterback who got his nickname in 1933 when he returned a punt 65 yards for a score against Maryville. The local newspapers did not say how he got his nickname, but apparently it was a spin-off from the famed "Bo" McMillin of Centre fame.

Stanley Nevers was a 220-pound tackle whose family name was Neverdoski. In 1917 he was a child in Gracow, Poland, when the Poles won their independence from Russia. The campaign was one of hunger, pillage, and hardship. Nevers learned English in a New Britain, Connecticut, kindergarten, worked his way through high school there, and attended UK on an athletic scholarship. He and Myers were co-captains of the team in 1936.

One of the greatest collegiate punting duels of all time took place in Lexington on September 29, 1934, in Chet Wynne's first season as coach. Bert Johnson of the University of Kentucky and Bill Ellis of Washington & Lee, two former Ashland High School teammates, kicked the ball twice as many times as their teams ran plays from scrimmage.

Neville Dunn of the *Herald* said the two native Kentuckians "stood back there in the mud and kicked at each other all afternoon. . . .Seventy times—probably a record—seventy times that grimy, slippery football sailed into the air. Kentucky punted 36 times and Washington & Lee 34.

"Ellis attempted all Washington & Lee punts but one and averaged 40 yards. Johnson kicked all of Kentucky's except about half a dozen for an average of 38½ yards. It was a magnificent performance for both, considering the muddy field, the slippery ball and the uncertain footing. Ellis might have been expected to do that well by the Washington & Lee supporters, but Johnson's kicking was a pleasant surprise to Kentuckians."

Chet Wynne had declared that the punt was football's most important and efficient weapon, and he had searched long and hard in preseason drills for a kicker to replace the great Ralph Kercheval. He finally decided on Johnson, a triple-threat star whose road to that wild punting afternoon had been sprinkled with stardust and paved by the solicitations of a UK alumni.

"When I was playing football in high school, an attorney

from Ashland who went to UK took me to his cabin on Cold Water Lake in Michigan every summer and once took me to the World's Fair in Chicago from there," Johnson explained in February of 1975. "When we got home that summer after my senior year, he let me out of the car at my house and said, 'I'll see you Friday.'

"'Where are we going?' I asked.

"When he said 'Lexington,' I had a pretty good idea of what was going on since I had met the UK freshman coach Birkett Pribble one time in the park where I was playing baseball. I got room, board, and tuition.

"When I arrived in Lexington, they threw me right into a scrimmage against the varsity—'Babe' Wright and all those guys—and I ran through the whole bunch of them, the length of the field, three times. Coach Gamage told me to get out and go to the showers. He didn't say it in an unkind way, and Pribble laughed about it."

Johnson lived on the south side of Ashland while Ellis lived closer to downtown. They played together on the high school team, where Johnson twice was named Prep All-America. While Johnson was loving football as an eight-year-old and playing organized ball about three years later, Ellis owned the only football in the near-downtown area and did not like to play with it. In fact, the *Courier-Journal* said, he would hide on the other side of town when the team was practicing, with more than a little fatherly persuasion needed to point him on the trail to that wet September afternoon of 1934 on Stoll Field.

"The mud was knee deep that day," Johnson said, "and all we did all afternoon was kick. They kept throwing the same ball back in. They would wipe it off with a towel, and it was like kicking a brick, almost. Neither team wanted to keep the ball because they couldn't do anything with it. Bill Ellis could really boom that thing, but he had one or two bad kicks that sluffed off the side of his foot. Each team fumbled seven times. I'm surprised we didn't fumble more."

The game's only score came in the fourth quarter when, as Dunn described it, "an indistinguishable wall of slime-covered football players swept down on Johnson" and blocked a punt on the 37. Billy Dyer picked up the ball for Washington & Lee and advanced it to the 14. Jack Bailey, a native of Maysville, Kentucky, scored two plays later. Johnson said Dick Gumm, another Ashland matriculate at Washington & Lee, told him

Chet Wynne.

later that he blocked the kick.

The Wildcats did not run a play from scrimmage in the third quarter and were credited with 19 carries to 24 for Washington & Lee for the entire game. The *Courier-Journal* credited the Wildcats with three passes thrown, one falling incomplete, the other two resulting in interceptions. The final theft occurred on a desperate UK pass which Jones of Washington & Lee picked off and returned to the UK 16 as the final gun sounded.

It is significant that Gerald Griffin, the new part-time athletic publicity director at UK (Neil Plummer became the first in 1932) had solicited the services of Stoll Field's first football statistician that season. Griffin instructed him to record first downs, passes completed, yards gained, number and distances of punts, and other pertinent data. The local newspapers applauded the move and even published some of the stats.

"I really don't remember much about the statistician or statistics," Griffin said as he sat in his Lexington home in late January, 1975, and looked back at a career which spanned more than 50 years of UK athletic history. "I was writing for the *Courier-Journal* when Chet Wynne came to UK, and I took the publicity job on a part-time basis. I kept records in a little black book which I guess, was lost with all the other records and stuff when Alumni Gym was flooded sometime before World War II."

Although the records are lost, it is a well-documented fact that the teams did punt a total of 70 times. It is unfortunate that Ellis is not officially credited with a total of 33 punts, which would break the current NCAA record of 24 held by three players. By the same token, UK's total of 36 must be some kind of record, as would its total kicking yardage if it were obtained by some measure other than just taking the figure "38½ per kick" reported by the newspapers.

Griffin remembers the old wooden bleachers at Stoll Field and the fact that numbering of players was haphazard. The bleachers "were as dangerous as they could be," he said. "The boards would break and you had to be careful. They also didn't pay much attention to numbering players and at times you didn't know who you were writing about. Sometimes, I would have to go to the coach and say, 'Hey, who scored that touchdown?' It's easy to see how hard it was to tell the players apart in the mud."

Of Bert Johnson, Griffin said, "Bert Johnson had all the tools, but I believe he needed a little more discipline. I felt he and the team could have done better."

Johnson agrees that the Wildcats perhaps should have won more games in that era. "As I look back, I could have put more into it," he said, "and I believe I would have gotten more out of it, but we didn't work as hard then as they do now.

"And about that so-called kicking duel. It must have been a dull game."

Chet Wynne's first season ended with a 5-5 record. The team won four of its first six games but lost three of its last four.

The Thoroughbred Connection

In the land where the horse is king, it is a high honor to be nicknamed after a famous thoroughbred. Chet Wynne was doubly blessed in the seasons of 1935-36, having in his gridiron stable Bert "Man O' War" Johnson and Bob "Twenty Grand" Davis. They were one of the better backfield combinations of their day.

Besides being a punter, Johnson was the tailback in Wynne's Notre Dame box formation. He apparently obtained his nickname after the Wildcats defeated Auburn, 9-0, during the 1934 season. Neville Dunn of the *Herald* called him "the human Man O' War of the Blue Grass" after that game.

Bob "Twenty Grand" Davis made his varsity debut in 1935 when he scored four touchdowns, three on runs of 63, 58, and 47 yards and another on a 38-yard pass from Johnson, in a 60-0 romp over Maryville. Johnson also scored two touchdowns in that game.

A 21-7 victory over Xavier in 1935 was unusual because all scores came on plays of 45 yards or better. Not one was made from scrimmage. Center Gene Myers scored first for UK on a 65-yard return of an intercepted pass, Davis returned a punt 60 yards, and Johnson returned an interception 55 yards. Xavier quarterback Leo Sack returned a UK punt 46 yards for the Musketeers' score.

One of the biggest games played by a UK team in that era was against Ohio State, before 56,696 patrons at Columbus in 1935. "We had never been in a stadium that big before," Myers said. "When the Ohio State squad came out, I thought I'd never seen so many people or so many big people. We traveled with

33 players, played about 19 in a game, and had about 15 good ones in the bunch. We could give anybody a good game for three quarters. When they sent in a third complete team in the last quarter, we had had it."

Johnson also remembered that game well. "We were all about half scared to death when we went out on the field," he said. "They had players sitting on benches the length of the field. They wore us right down into the sod. Every time we looked up, it seemed there was a new man coming onto the field.

"We had worked hard on a razzle-dazzle play where I later-aled the ball, but we hadn't tried it. I broke loose for about 25 or 30 yards, and I heard somebody holler for the ball. It was Gene Myers behind me. I had only one man in front of me, and I think I could have got by him, but I tossed the ball back to Gene. They caught him from behind."

However, that run set up the Wildcats' only touchdown, scored from the five by Davis. The Buckeyes passed for one touchdown, scored the second on a fumble, and scored a third through the line, for a 19-6 victory. When Johnson left the game, the Buckeye fans gave him a tremendous ovation. He had gained 108 yards, punted brilliantly, and prevented two Buckeye markers singlehandedly. He had stopped one runner on the four yard line, and he had knocked down a touchdown pass. The Ohio State players later named him the outstanding opponent they met that season.

When Johnson was hospitalized and missed a game with Georgia Tech, Davis took up the slack, gaining 169 yards and scoring touchdowns on runs of nine and 75 yards and on a 33-yard pass reception. Auburn spoiled UK's hopes for a share of the SEC grid spoils, walloping the 'Cats, 23-0, in Montgomery. Alabama followed with a 13-0 blanking in Birmingham. The 'Cats were never able to get past midfield against the Tide. They defeated Florida, 15-6; lost to Tulane, 20-13; and eked out a winning season (5-4) by defeating Tennessee, 27-0.

The Tennessee game was an important one in that it was the first time UK had scored on Tennessee since 1931. UK outrushed the Volunteers, outpassed them 80-64 yards, and intercepted six passes (a school record which has been equalled but not surpassed). On their first TD drive the 'Cats marched 62 yards to the two and then employed what was described as a "trick play." Coming out of the huddle, only quarterback

Bert Johnson.

McMillan got in position, while the other three backs were apparently arguing with each other. McMillan received the ball from Myers and scooted through center for the score.

Sherman Hinkebein, writing from his home in Evansville, Indiana, in January, 1975, clarified that situation: "While we were in the huddle, our quarterback, '00' McMillan, called for a play we had never practiced—a quarterback sneak. Just before breaking huddle, he said, 'If you linemen don't get me over, we'll all be killed by the coach.' Result—a touchdown. The same situation happened in the second half, and we won the game.

"After the game, in the locker room McMillan said that he was the greatest quarterback Kentucky ever had. Every time he carried the ball he made a touchdown—which was twice. In our offense the quarterback blocked and never carried the ball."

Kentucky scored its second touchdown that afternoon on a 39-yard pass from Johnson which bounced off the hands of a Tennessee defender and into the arms of "Duke" Ellington. It was the first UK victory over UT in 10 years. "God must have been smiling," the *Kentuckian* later opined.

However, the game was marred by tragedy. Herbert Tade, a 21-year-old Tennessee center from Paducah, Kentucky, suffered a skull fracture when UK fullback Elmore Simpson drove four yards to within the UT goal line late in the game. Tade was taken to the Good Samaritan Hospital, where UK players paid him several visits before he eventually was transferred to Knoxville. He remained paralyzed until his death some years later.

The 1936 season opened with a 54-3 victory over Maryville. Davis carried the ball nine times for 167 yards in that game and scored five touchdowns in the following manner: 83-yard run from scrimmage, 68-yard run from scrimmage, 45-yard run after pass of 10 yards from Johnson, and 14 and six-yard runs from scrimmage. Then, in a 21-0 win over Xavier, Davis also made key plays. He caught a touchdown pass from Johnson and also scored on an 80-yard run.

The Wildcats lost to Georgia Tech and defeated W&L before losing to Alabama, 14-0. They stopped the Tide eight times in the first half, but Joe Riley took charge in the second half and scored from the 27 after Alabama drove from their own 26 after the kickoff. Joe Riley scored again from the 16 yard line to culminate a 69-yard march in the final quarter. He had gained 175 yards from scrimmage. At one point in the game Johnson gained 53 yards on four successive tries, passed to

Davis for a first down on the eight, and then was stopped short of the goal line on a fourth and two situation.

Gene Myers intercepted two passes in the game and earned high praise from Tide coach Frank Thomas, who told reporters, "My players told me after the game that they would have scored at least one touchdown in the first half had it not been for Myers, who was a marvelous line backer-up.

"Coming down on the bus, my boys couldn't talk about anything but Myers and how tough he was. I'd sure love to have him on my team."

A native of Harlan, Myers was a big, rugged performer who utilized speed and size well as a linebacker. It was also said that in three years of centering the ball, he never made a bad snap.

The Tennessee game in Knoxville that year was disappointing. Kentucky was trailing Tennessee, 7-6, with fourth down and inches to go for a score. Johnson hit the line and apparently scored; however, the official ruled he had not crossed the line. "You couldn't see the chalk lines," Johnson recalled later, "but our center's waist line was over the goal line, and my head was right over his head." There was no more scoring that day, so Tennessee won.

"Bert ran right up my back on that play," Myers said. "I was laying across the goal line. When I got to the dressing room and pulled off my jersey, there were cleat marks on my back. I was told that was the game where General Neyland got the tear-off jersey idea. Larry Garland caught one of his guys on the 10 by the jersey and pulled him down on the one. A friend of mine with a sporting goods manufacturer told me years later that Neyland had his firm make some tear-away jerseys for the Vols after that game.

"I remember how Tennessee liked to throw that little pass they call the 'look-in' these days. Three backs would get down in the three-point stance, while the quarterback would raise up, catch the center snap just over his right shoulder, and quickly pop it to an end cutting across. On their scoring play, we thought we had stopped them on fourth down after they had banged the line three times from the one. Joe Huddleston and I thought we hit the guy behind the line and stopped him cold, but when I looked up, the official was signalling a touchdown. When I started to argue, he said, 'If you don't shut up, I'll throw you out,' and I shut up."

The 1936 season ended with a 6-4 record, with three of

the losses coming in the last four games. And Coach Wynne was in trouble. When his initial contract expired after the 1936 season, the Men's Student Council endeavored to get him fired. The *Kernel* ran a front page editorial citing three objections to Wynne: "(1) He is not a good judge of material, (2) His assistants on the coaching field are not the highly capable men they were originally thought to be, and (3) Mr. Wynne's personal conduct off the field is not entirely conducive to the setting up of high training standards for the team." However, the newspaper recommended renewal of the contract, and he was signed to a new three-year pact.

However, the pressure on Coach Wynne became unbearable the following season when the Wildcats failed to score against Vanderbilt, Georgia Tech, Alabama, Boston College, Tennessee, and Florida en route to a 4-6 season. The problem was simply a lack of depth and a tough schedule. The Wildcats also deviated from their usual routine of opening with a "patsy" at home and instead visited powerful Vanderbilt. (In previous years Kentucky had not lost an opening game since Vanderbilt defeated them, 28-0, at Lexington in 1906.)

After dropping their 1937 opener to Vanderbilt, 12-0, on a waterlogged field in Nashville, the Wildcats posted victories over Xavier, W&L, Manhattan, and South Carolina. In the W&L game

Gene Myers intercepts a pass against Alabama in 1936 on Stoll Field. Alabama won, 14-0.

Davis scored five touchdowns for the second time in his career, registering on scoring runs of 80, 50, 22, and 60 yards and a 100-yard pass interception return. He gained 267 yards rushing in that game, for a record still on the books in 1975. The team lost to Georgia Tech and Alabama before playing Boston College in Fenway Park, which seated 45,000 but only drew 2,000 for the football game.

"Never has a crowd looked so small and lonesome," said George Keller of the *Kernel.* Sherman Hinkebein, who played on that team, discussed the game in a letter written from his home in Evansville, Indiana, in January, 1975:

"We arrived Friday evening during a terrific thunderstorm. It was the first time in my football career that we were not able to practice because of the weather. The next day when we took the field for the game, the field was 20 percent full of water. During the game it was raining so hard that, being center, I could not see our punter, Bob Davis, to throw the ball to him. I looked around to locate him, and when I turned back to center the ball, it had disappeared. It had blown away on the water surface."

Duke Ellington said the Wildcats had played Manhattan in a sea of mud the preceding year in New York, but Boston was worse. "After we had played five minutes, you couldn't see a number. It was a daytime game, but it was so overcast that it was almost like playing at night with no lights. It was like going out in a vacant lot and playing, and the rain never stopped during the game."

A bad punt late in the first quarter set up the first Boston score. The Wildcats had the ball on first down on the Boston eight yard line twice in the half but could not punch it over. Boston scored once more for a 13-0 decision.

Against Tennessee that year a seven-yard UK punt in the second quarter set up the first Vol score, and Babe Woods scored another in the third quarter. The 'Cats failed to score once from the three. They lost, 6-0, to Florida as substitute halfback Ed Manning ran 58 yards to set up the Gator touchdown. The nearest UK came to scoring was a 40-yard pass juggled on the goal line and dropped.

"The depth just wasn't there that year," Ellington said. "We could stay with anybody, up to a point."

After the 1937 season, assistant coaches Porter Grant and Tom Gorman resigned, causing 70 players to register a protest with the UK administration. Then Wynne yielded to the internal pressure and submitted his resignation. The words of Ed Danforth never rang more true:

"When Chet Wynne left the peaceful precincts of Auburn to take over the job that in a few years had Harry Gamage cutting out paper dolls, your reporter, feeling he was familiar with the problems at Lexington, was prone to admire Chet's courage, but doubt his wisdom."

In his four years at the helm, Wynne had barely broken .500, winning 20 of 39 games. The pattern of victories and losses was similar to the preceding years under Gamage, when the Wildcats compiled fine early season records and then slipped as the competition got tougher and injuries and other factors took their toll.

Wynne's first UK team won four out of its first six games and lost three of its last four. His second edition won three of the first four and lost three of the last five. His third edition won five of the first six and lost three of the last four, while his final UK squad won four of its first seven and then lost its final three games.

During his four years at Kentucky there were four first-time foes: Boston College, Manhattan College, South Carolina, and Southwestern of Memphis. But Wynne lost four times to Alabama, three times to Tennessee, and two times to Tulane, Florida, Clemson, and Georgia Tech. He beat Tennessee, Tech, and Clemson once each; split with Auburn and Manhattan; and lost to Boston College.

A. D. Kirwan

"I know I shouldn't say it," a nationally known football coach said in the winter of 1974, "but he was too brilliant to be a football coach. He could have been a Supreme Court Justice, or just about anything for that matter."

The subject of conversation was Albert Dennis Kirwan, a big Irishman with the features of a scholarly prize fighter, the morals of an apostle, and the nerve to accept the position of football coach at the University of Kentucky after Chet Wynne threw in the towel.

A native of Louisville, Kirwan attended Male High and starred at UK for three seasons, playing halfback most of the time but also seeing duty at end before his graduation in 1926. That fall he remained in Lexington as an assistant to Coach Fred J. Murphy, but the next year he returned to Louisville to coach at Male High.

He was so straightforward in his dealings that he was hired as head coach by Male's bitter rival, Manual. In six seasons at Manual, his teams had a 47-11 record, with four of the defeats coming in his first year. His 1933 team lost only to Ashland High. In addition to his coaching success, he was considered a fine English and history teacher.

At UK, he held the rank of professor, as did Bernie Shively, who was named athletic director that year. Frank Moseley, who was retained as an assistant coach along with Gene Myers and Joe Rupert, was an assistant professor. Neville Dunn of the *Herald* said such a combination had "sounded the death knell for swollen salaries for coaches, contracts for coaches and fierce emphasis on winning or else."

The big question is not Kirwan's ability as a coach, but why he bothered to coach football at all. The answer is probably that he loved the game and played and coached it as he did everything else in which he endeavored—with intelligence and enthusiasm. An example of that enthusiasm occurred when Kirwan played football and was cited by a teammate who remembered the 1924 game with Centre, one of the best teams in the South.

"We got off a nice, high punt, and Ab set sail down the field," the teammate said. "By the time the ball came down, Ab was charging like a ferocious bull at 'Flash' Covington, who was playing safety for Centre. Ab tore into Flash for all he was worth and nailed him in his tracks. The only trouble was that Ab hadn't noticed that Flash had made a fair-catch signal. The 15 yards we were penalized started them on their way to the game's only score."

Kirwan would later remember most vividly the Centre and Tennessee games of his playing days. In his sophomore season, he played left halfback as the Wildcats lost 10-0 in a game that dedicated Centre's new stadium, Cheek Field, before what the *Herald* described as "a crowd of 10,000 of the wettest fans who ever witnessed a football game." His biographer, Dr. Frank Furlong Mathias, relates that Kirwan so seldom got past the line of scrimmage that he finished the game with an average yardage of minus two. Years later, Kirwan finally heard the story behind his dismal showing: "I ran into Minos Gordy...who played offensive fullback and defensive end for them. I asked (him)...what happened to me that day; it worried me....'Well,' he said, 'after the first few plays when the color of our uniforms was completely obliterated by the mud...our two guards would line up with your team and...simply turn around and tackle you!'....I'm inclined to believe that he might have been telling the truth."

Kirwan would later refer to that Centre team as maybe the best squad the Danville institution ever produced. It won the southern championship, beating such teams as Georgia and Alabama. Although Bo McMillin and Red Roberts were gone, the team had fine backs in Covington and Gordy. A *Herald* reporter noted, "Covington and Gordy did more to the Kentucky line than a laundry can do to a silk shirt."

Mathias said that what might well have been the turning point in Kirwan's life came as a result of the 1923 Tennessee game. The Volunteers had defeated Georgetown College by only one touchdown the preceding Saturday, but it was a different story when they played the favored Wildcats. Quarterback Turner Gregg called on Kirwan three times in one series of plays to carry the ball over from the two yard line, and Kirwan failed. He later fumbled into a Volunteer's arms for a score. Tennessee scored again after blocking a Wildcat goal-line punt and falling on it in the end zone. The final score in an 18-0 UT win came on a runback of an intercepted UK pass.

On the following day, signs appeared on the UK campus reading, "Tennessee 18, Sigma Nu 0," an obvious illusion to the fact that Gregg and Kirwan were fraternity brothers. Kirwan wrote to his old Male High teammate Edliff "Butch" Slaughter, who was on his way to becoming an All-American at Michigan, and asked him about the possibility of transferring to the East Lansing institution. The response by Slaughter was favorable, but Doc Rodes, Kirwan's backfield coach and friend, talked him into staying.

The Wildcat-Centre game in 1925 would be more satisfying for Captain Kirwan. In the early stages of the game on muddy Cheek Field, the UK quarterback made a long run to the Centre two yard line and then gave the ball to Kirwan, who plunged into the line from his right halfback position and was buried under the pileup on the goal line. Here's how Dr. Mathias described the scene:

> The officials were going to have to unravel the mass of gold and blue uniforms before 12,000 frantic fans would know if the Centre jinx had been ended. Down on the bottom, with his left arm pinned and his right arm around the ball, Ab knew the ball was clearly over the goal line. But suddenly the hand of a Centre lineman slithered across Ab's face and started oozing the muddy ball out of his right arm. Ab was desperate: "I reached over and bit him on the arm!" The bellowing lineman cleared several players away as he leaped to his feet, giving the official ample room to see that Ab had possession and to rule a touchdown. Meanwhile, the lineman showed the referee Ab's toothmarks on his arm. Ab admitted it, explaining the circumstances. The referee then said, "Let's play ball," whereupon the Wildcats put a 16-0 bite on Centre for the first time in a decade.

Kirwan decided at the end of his football career that he wanted to be a lawyer. He changed his academic major from engineering to English, with the thought of entering the Kentucky Law School in his mind. While attending summer school to complete 15 required credits in English, he decided against going to law school. He remained as an assistant in Dean C. R. Melcher's office and helped his former coach, Fred J. Murphy, with the football team. Murphy hired him as backfield coach in 1926, giving him firsthand experience with disgruntled alumni and the heartbreaks of a losing season.

Kirwan left UK that year and went to work for the Midcontinental Petroleum Co., promoting Diamond brand oil and gasoline throughout the "Little Egypt" area of southern Illinois. He returned to Louisville in 1927 and accepted an offer to teach English and serve as assistant to football coach Tom Johnson at Male High. He and Johnson produced winning teams from 1927 through 1931. In his spare time he attended law classes, won his law degree, and then coached at Male one more year after being admitted to the bar. His short-lived career as an attorney ended in 1932, when he was offered the position of head coach of the Manual football team. He was hired mainly to defeat Male, something the Crimson had accomplished once since 1918. During his six years at Manual, his teams would beat Male three times and compile an overall record of 42-11-2.

While he was capping a fine 1937 season with a 19-12 victory over Male, the University of Kentucky was planning to replace Chet Wynne. Wynne apparently had lost control of his team, and rumors of scandal had circulated after the Wildcats failed to score in their final six games. The situation had reached a point where a reorganization was effected in early 1938 to bring athletics more fully under control of the university.

In essence, the setup placed the athletic department in the College of Arts and Sciences, where coaches would be faculty members laboring under the same privileges and restrictions as other professors. It gave the president power to appoint an advisory council on athletics from among the faculty and students, increased the powers of the athletic director, and put all sports finances in the hands of the business office. The object obviously was not to win at all costs.

Kirwan was a logical and popular choice as UK coach in 1938. He was respected both on the athletic and academic

"Ab" Kirwan.

scene, was friends with President McVey, and was known and liked by other members of the faculty and administration. An equally popular appointment among all segments of the athletic situation was that of Shively as athletic director. Even the school newspaper applauded the move:

"The old order has changed. We have something now to anticipate. The era of gloomy Saturdays in the fall may be at an end, despite the hardships that our athletes will encounter during the first months. . . . One thing is certain. We have not only a new slate to cheer for, but a clean and virtuous one."

Kirwan wisely refused to predict a championship team, pointing out that the competition in the South was the toughest anywhere. He only promised to work hard, and he set about immediately to organize booster clubs throughout the state. The annual $10 dues charged each member went to pay football players and other athletes for jobs performed, all in accordance with conference rules and with the UK business office handling the funds. He also sent his assistants on the recruiting circuit and stepped up efforts to entice Kentucky boys to the state university.

Described by his players as brilliant and ingenious, Kirwan was always trying new things on the football field. He operated from the single wing, running what amounted to a split-T option. The tailback would start on a sweep and either give the ball to the fullback off tackle or keep it himself and key on the end and linebacker before either cutting in or going wide. He also utilized a short punt formation, with the punter seven or eight yards deep where he could still run the regular offense, either going off tackle on power plays, running around end, passing, or executing the buck lateral play.

He also instituted a two-platoon system, playing entirely different units in alternating quarters.

"I played only in the first and third quarters," said Carl "Hoot" Combs, a running back in 1938-39-40. "I never was in a game in the second and fourth quarters. We'd go down to the one-inch line, the quarter would change, and the other team would come in. We had so many football players we didn't know what to do with them. Kirwan tried to be an inspirational type coach. He would take fits in the locker room. He would scream and holler, and once he threw a chair through a window. His favorite saying was, 'You don't have to get beat!' He said it once when we were three touchdowns ahead at halftime and had no intention of getting beat."

Dr. William McCubbin, head of the Physical Education Department at Virginia Tech, remembers his old high school and college coach in a different vein. "I could go to him for advice, and he would give me some real answers—his judgment was almost like being part of the family," he told Dr. Mathias. "He would walk and think and always click his heels. All of a sudden, he would say, 'We're starting today with . . .,' and he'd name the players for (each position). Then he'd remind us of things we'd prepared for that week. . .warning us not to be afraid if they do something unusual."

Speaking from his office in Blacksburg in May, 1975, McCubbin recalled that Kirwan would raise his voice when he needed to get the attention of the overall squad. "He would change the inflection of his voice to change the tempo."

The 1938 team opened with impressive victories over Maryville and Oglethorpe but lost its seven remaining games. At the annual football banquet Kirwan dismissed the season by saying, "The quicker it is forgotten, the better it will be." The UK president, Dr. Frank L. McVey, said the Wildcats did the best they could under existing circumstances and that he had "never heard of a team losing seven straight games without some coaches losing their heads."

McVey compared the championship goal of the Wildcat football team to Joshua's when he marched seven times around the city of Jericho. "We have marched around the wall once," he said. "We will march around it again next year, and the next, and perhaps seven times in all before we take the city." He turned out to be quite a prophet, since the university would field six more football teams before hiring youthful Paul Bryant as its football coach in 1946.

Junie Jones, who lettered as a back in 1939-40-41, thought Kirwan's two-platoon system was great. "The first team was made up mostly of seniors, and the second team was mostly sophomores," he said. "The seniors would start the game and play the first quarter, and the second team would come in and play the second quarter. The seniors would play the third quarter, and we would finish the fourth quarter. This was very good because both teams were even in ability. In fact, it became a challenge as to which team could score more points. I am glad to say the second team, or sophomores, outscored the first team."

Led by Combs, Jones, and Ermal Allen, the 1939 Wildcats defeated Vanderbilt for the first time in 43 years, vanquished two other foes, and tied Alabama before playing Georgia Tech in Atlanta. Prior to the Tech game, Joe Creason of the *Kernel* called UK's perfect record the "most unexpected thing to hit football since the flu epidemic of 1918," and the football spotlight of the nation focused on Grant Field, where a bowl bid apparently awaited the winner.

On the night before the game, Kirwan and 33 players boarded a special sleeper which would take them to Atlanta. The other cars were filled with UK boosters, as was a special train across town which hauled 500 more fans and the Wildcat band. Somewhere in Tennessee, the team train hit a passenger car. Nobody was killed, but an air line setting the brakes on the train was damaged, causing a delay in reaching Atlanta. Upon arrival, the players went directly to the field.

On the second play of the game, Tech's Billy Gibson got off a quick kick which was downed on the UK one yard line by

Bob Ison. Joe Shepherd kicked back to almost midfield, and Johnny Bosch returned to the UK 34. Bosch completed a pass to the 26, setting up a play which was described by Larry Shropshire of the *Herald-Leader* as "dastardly deception." Hoot Combs, the person it was to affect the most, explained the play as follows:

"It was a belly series, and Georgia Tech ran it better than anybody. We'd never seen it before. Luke Lindon tackled the fullback in the line, but the tailback had faked the ball to the fullback, taken it from his belly, and given it on an end-around reverse to Ison, who had paused for two or three counts. I was pointing to Luke Lindon saying, 'Great tackle,' or something like that, and that's when the newspaper took a picture of Ison scoring, with me looking the other way."

The Tech lead of 6-0 held up until early in the final period when Tech drove 82 yards, completing three long passes in the process, one coming on an 18-yard completion off a fake kick. The Wildcats got a touchdown in the closing minutes on a pass from Allen to Jim Hardin. After the final whistle sounded, a fight erupted among the players. Joe Creason told his *Kernel* readers, "Here in the land of 'Gone with the Wind,' Kentucky's bid for football empire collapsed like a house of cards."

"The Atlanta newspaper ran a picture of that touchdown play the next day," Combs said, "and it didn't show that there was another defender behind me, out of the picture. A national magazine ran the picture and called it the best executed play of 1939. When we got home from Atlanta, my ceiling was plastered with those pictures, and they were stuck up all over the campus. That was the first time I realized how cruel people could be. It was a helluva disappointment and all that, and even today people keep reminding me of it."

The Wildcats defeated West Virginia and then turned their thoughts to Tennessee, with a possible invitation to the Rose Bowl resting on the outcome of the game. They fumbled eight times and bowed, 19-0, to the Vols. Their 6-2-1 record, which would be Kirwan's best season during a six-year reign, resulted in much optimism among UK fans, an optimism that he did not share because he realized full well that the conference teams would be ready for him the following year. And they were. He tied Vanderbilt and Georgia, beat Georgia Tech, and lost to Alabama and Tennessee. He particularly relished the tie with Georgia (which was coached by his old Louisville high school coaching rival Wally Butts) and the fact that the Wildcats held the heralded Frankie Sinkwich in check. He had recruited Sinkwich the year before, but lost him to Butts' Bulldogs.

After that 5-3-2 season, Joe Creason wrote, "It's not nearly as simple as simon, and good strong men have been driven to padded cells by much simpler jobs than coaching a Kentucky football team.

"Yet Ab Kirwan. . .is planning no perpetual motion machine, doesn't think he is Napoleon and, to tell the truth, appears entirely sane. He has not allowed the Kentucky set-up to loosen even one bolt of his mental structure.

"For years prior to the appointment of the Kirwan posse, Kentucky had been notorious in football circles as the club with more outside interests than a Follies dancer. For instance, the alumni were supposedly responsible for many of the coaching decisions, while dirty stories concerning the influence that local betting commissioners, the boys who make a living by outsmarting the suckers, had on the teams were thicker than ants at a picnic.

"Everything had been tried in an attempt to give Kentucky a football shot in the arm except allowing the coach to run the team.

"Kirwan let it be known he was running the team, took off closed practice signs, constructed bleachers for fans and drafted for his squad members a strict code of rules."

Kirwan's 1941 team won five of nine games while his wartime 1942 team defeated only Xavier, Washington & Lee, and George Washington; tied VPI; and lost to Georgia, Vanderbilt, Alabama, Georgia Tech, West Virginia, and Tennessee. The main criticism was that his teams would play good ball in one half and then play poorly in the other. That year he produced Kentucky's first All-American, Clyde "Big Train" Johnson, a tackle from Ashland.

Donovan reportedly met with the athletic council after that season, and there was some suggestion that Kirwan be retired, "or something." Donovan pounded on his table. "What we need is manpower," he said. "We have the coaching power. I have absolute confidence in all my coaches. . . .I believe Kirwan is the equal of any coach in the Southeastern Conference. I'll stand by him through thick and thin. We can't meet Tennessee, Alabama, and Georgia Tech on equal footing because they have

Clyde Johnson, first UK All-American.

more manpower than we possess. We can't cut them down to our size, so that leaves one alternative—we must build the University of Kentucky up to their size."

When Kirwan accepted the UK job, the Wildcat athletic program was definitely low key in comparison to the huge athletic funds and emphasis on winning that would be prevalent during the years following World War II. All athletic expenses during his era had to come from football and basketball gate receipts, and he felt that all of the expenses of intercollegiate athletics had to be earned. In a statement before the executive committee of the Southeastern Conference in 1952, he would touch lightly on his coaching experience at UK:

". . . .I make no pretensions that I was a good coach, but for one reason or another, perhaps because of my inferior ability, but I choose to think there were other causes, I was not a successful coach at Kentucky.

"We broke no rules while I was coaching at Kentucky. We had only sixty scholarships in football at that time, forty varsity and twenty freshmen. We not only broke no rules in awarding grants-in-aid, we did not even grant the full scholarship permitted. We gave only board, room, books and institutional fees at Kentucky at that time. We gave not a cent to any athlete for laundry or for any other purpose. And yet I had many opportunities to do so. Frequently sports fans came to me with offers of money to make illegitimate inducements to promising athletes to enroll at Kentucky, but I spurned all such overtures. I claim no particular credit for having done so. I am one of those unfortunate people with a tender conscience—I even observe speed limit signs along the highway. I am unable to enjoy any peace or happiness whenever I think I have done anything illegal."

Kirwan was confronted at UK with the same major problem that had faced coaches before him and would dismay most of his predecessors—that of recruiting good players for his teams. The number of high schools fielding football teams in the commonwealth was limited, but, more importantly, he despised trying to lure high school heroes to UK. He said he once took a trip outside the state to talk to high school boys and did not like it.

Kentucky canceled football in 1943, and Kirwan began teaching five sections of freshman history to the large influx of student soldiers on the UK campus. He started work on his master's degree in the spring of 1944, commuting to Louisville for classes and talks with his advisor. He would get that degree in February, 1945.

The Wildcats returned to football in 1944 and won only two of eight games, losing 2-0, to Michigan State early in the season and dropping two games to Tennessee. Surmising that he was not the kind of coach who could compete in the SEC with the limited support (financial and otherwise) that he was getting, and not liking the rivalry that had existed for years between football coaches and Adolph Rupp, Kirwan submitted his resignation to Donovan. Donovan assured him he need not resign, but Kirwan finally convinced him that he never intended to coach another football team. As Dr. Mathias relates: "Donovan pushed himself back in his chair, saying 'All right, now I would like to know how in the world a man like you ever coached football in the first place?' Ab had no answer for that one except to divulge his great love of teaching and his hopes to reenter the field. Donovan was impressed."

While Kirwan pursued an academic career which would lead him to fame as a historian, an author, a dean of students, and eventually to the UK presidency, Shively would fill in as interim football coach until Dr. Donovan could launch the university on an ambitious postwar football program.

Time Out: Ermal Allen

"We had this fence around our practice field, and one day Ab Kirwan looked up and saw this little fellow, dressed in a Morristown High School uniform, climbing over it," Hoot Combs said. "Ab went over to run him off, and the kid said, 'I came here on your invitation and I'm going to play.' It was Ermal Allen."

Allen, now assistant head coach of the Dallas Cowboys, said during a visit to Lexington in February, 1975, "I was so small that when they asked me to get on the scales, I put one of those five-pound weights—the type you add to weigh different-sized people—in my jock strap."

At five-foot-ten and 145 pounds, Allen did not present an imposing figure to assistant football coach Gene Myers, who had accompanied Adolph Rupp on a recruiting tour of the Morristown, Tennessee, area in early 1938.

Allen said, "My coach told Gene there was a big old tackle at our school he might be interested in, and then he pointed to me and said, 'but here comes our best athlete.'

"I ate with them at the drugstore, and Coach Rupp said, 'Coach Petey Siler tells me you're a good football player.'

"'I play basketball, too,' I told him, but he didn't seem impressed. When he left, I could tell that I hadn't sold him that I was a basketball player. The trip was not to see Ermal Allen. It was just an accident. But they invited me up to Lexington.

"I met Dana Bible, the Texas football coach, through one of his family members who lived at Jefferson City, near Morristown, while he was playing golf, and he talked to me about coming to Texas on a golf and basketball scholarship. When he said I was too little for football, I more or less forgot about

Texas.

"Myers wrote me a letter and told me when the freshmen would start practice at UK. When I showed up, Frank Moseley looked kinda startled and asked, 'What in the world is he doing here?' When Myers told him I was going to try out, Moseley said, 'Why, he's not big enough to play football.'

"The greatest thrill in my life was when they didn't cut me from the freshman squad, but I didn't play any at all that year. They wanted me to grow a little.

"I was kinda glad Kirwan had the two-platoon system because I got to play the second and fourth quarters of each game. I hadn't been in my first game—against VMI—five minutes when someone made a tackle and the ball squirted up into my arms and I scored a touchdown. That's the type of thing you stay awake at night and dream about."

In the memorable 21-13 victory over Vanderbilt in Nashville in 1939, Allen hit seven of 11 passes and carried for 75 yards. In the closing eight minutes against Georgia in Louisville, he connected on an 80-yard scoring bomb to "Junie" Jones, but Georgia came back with a long pass and three plunges for a score. The 'Cats drove 72 yards, scoring the winning touchdown on a pass from David Zoeller to Hardin.

Kentucky was trailing Alabama, 7-0, well into the fourth quarter as the result of a blocked punt that the Tide turned into a touchdown. Then Allen advanced the Wildcats from their own 35 to the Tide 11. Sophomore Noah Mullins carried to the one in three carries and then plunged over and Hardin kicked to tie the score. This set up the all-important game with Georgia Tech in Atlanta, in which Kentucky scored on a 67-yard pass from Allen to Hardin.

"I remember the train hitting that vehicle in Tennessee," Allen said. "We got in there just before game time. Some of us had eaten on the train. Some still were munching on sandwiches. I felt like the trip hurt us."

Mullins joined Allen in the UK starting backfield in 1940 and became the first person to return a kickoff for a touchdown under Kirwan, rambling 95 yards on a return against Washington & Lee. Mullins also caught two passes from Allen for touchdowns in the first quarter of that game. Two games later Mullins scored on a 90-yard kickoff return against George Washington. In that game Junie Jones kicked a 16-yard field goal, first for a UK team since Ralph Kercheval kicked one in a 6-3 loss to

Ermal Allen.

Tulane in 1932.

When Kentucky played Vanderbilt, assistant coach Paul "Bear" Bryant was in charge of the Commodores. Coach Red Sanders was in the hospital with an appendectomy, though he was "with his team" via a telephone loudspeaker hooked up to his bed. Kentucky tied the Commodores, 7-7.

In the rest of the 1940 season Kentucky defeated George Washington, tied Georgia (7-7), lost to Alabama (25-0), beat Georgia Tech (26-7), and then lost to West Virginia (9-7) and Tennessee (33-0). In the game with Georgia Kentuckians deemed it a minor miracle that the Bulldogs only scored one touchdown and UK escaped with a 7-7 tie. The Tech game was notable because Dave Zoeller went 65 yards for a touchdown on the opening play. And the West Virginia game in Morgantown is remembered for mud and snow. Barely 5,000 persons turned out for that game, and the field was so deep in mud and snow that it was likened to quicksand.

"I guess you could call me the 'hero' of that game," Allen said and chuckled. "I tried to pass, and the ball was so slick it fell from my hand. We recovered, but it scored as a safety for them and they beat us, 9-7."

In 1941 Allen and Mullins were rated among the best backs in the South. However, their interference was often lacking. Time after time Allen was smothered behind the line as he attempted to pass, and Kirwan never found a successful field general to replace Jones, who was switched to blocking back. Sensational touchdown runs by Allen and Mullins, along with Allen's bullet passes, highlighted the campaign, while backs Jones, Claude Hammond, and Bob Herbert gave creditable performances. The best newcomer was Phil Cutchin, a sophomore halfback who could run, pass, and kick with skill. In the line Bill Portwood ignored a broken nose and other injuries to keep on playing and was named to several All-SEC sophomore teams.

The university's big social-athletic event in 1941 was its Golden Jubilee of Football, celebrated during the weekend of the October 11 game with Vanderbilt. In their first two games the Wildcats had defeated Virginia Tech, 37-14, and Washington & Lee, 7-0, so optimism was high.

"Before that Vanderbilt game we seniors got together and

said we were going to have the best year we could possibly have," Junie Jones said. "We passed, ran, kicked around, over, under, and any way we could the first half and were leading, 15-0, with one minute to go in the period. Vandy threw a pass to Jack Jenkins around the goal line and Allen, Mullins, and I went up for the ball and smacked it down as hard as we could, and we knocked it right in the hands of Jenkins, who was flat on his back on the ground. We wore ourselves out so much the first half that Vandy came right back and beat us, 39-15. We were really sick and downhearted after that game."

Jones ended his football career at Kentucky holding two records, which were not to be broken for many years. "I held the UK record for the longest touchdown by pass reception, which was 80 yards in the Georgia game played in Louisville in 1939, until Dicky Lyons broke it in 1968 (92 yards from Dave Bair vs. Georgia in Lexington). Ermal Allen threw the pass. I also kicked 16 straight extra points one year, and Bob Jones broke that with 18 in 1969."

The Wildcats finished the 1941 season with five victories, none over conference foes, and four losses, all within the conference. Allen was awarded his third football letter that year and had a total of nine letters in football, basketball, and golf when he graduated in 1942 and entered army service at Fort Benning, Georgia. Gen. Bob Neyland had him transferred to Yale, where he trained and played football for six weeks under the coach from Tennessee. Playing three games in one eight-day stretch, that team defeated the New York Giants and the Brooklyn Dodgers and lost to the Chicago Bears.

Allen returned to the university after the war and played in two games for Bear Bryant before being declared ineligible. He played one year for the Cleveland Browns and then was an assistant coach for Bryant and Collier at UK before joining the Cowboys.

"I have played or coached under six of the most successful coaches in the business—Bryant, Rupp, Paul Brown, Collier, Neyland, and Tom Landry," he said during that 1975 visit to Lexington, "and they were all different types of people.

"Neyland was very cold-blooded, regular Army before and after he coached, but he was far ahead of his time, especially in the kicking game.

"Rupp's secret was that he could really get more out of you game after game.

"Bryant is a great recruiter and great leader. He had a dominant personality. If he walked in this room and smiled, you would smile.

"Paul Brown was very highly organized, as was Collier. Both had excellent football minds."

And how does football today compare with when Allen played at UK?

"In my days, most guys didn't even smoke," he said. "You'd wait until the end of the season to have a beer. Things have changed. I want to feel like they had more pride in those days. Maybe."

Time Out: Bernie Shively

The setting was a quiet cove and a week-long, two-man, penny-a-point gin rummy game in an isolated cove on Lake Cumberland near Jamestown, Kentucky, in the summer of 1967, and Bernie Shively was in a relaxed and expansive mood.

"I remember when I had a pretty bad arm and shoulder injury once at Illinois," the big UK athletic director recalled, "but I wanted to play very much. I had a score to settle with an opposing lineman on the team we were to meet. He had broken my nose the season before.

"I asked our trainer to shoot something in my arm to kill the pain, but he refused to do it. I went to a physician and had him give me a shot of novocain, which I paid for out of my own pocket. In the locker room before the game, I told Coach Zuppke that I was ready. He looked at me, shook his head, and said, 'You're crazy, you can't even move that arm.' When I moved the arm, he told me to get dressed. I played and really gave that other guy a rough time. In fact, I got him thrown out of the game. I poked him once and knew he'd do the same to me on the next play. I told the official to watch him, because he was slugging me. Sure enough, he slugged me on the next play, and the official was watching and threw him out. After the drug wore off, I really was hurting.

"My job on offense was mostly to block for Red Grange. We both made All-American. I was also heavyweight wrestling champion of the conference, and that came in handy a few years ago when a guy tried to swindle me out of some basketball tickets in New York. I chased him for several blocks in that city traffic, caught him, and held him until police arrived. I'm not sure I could do that now."

Shively was 65 years of age at the time. He would die six months later of a heart attack.

"I played with Harry Gamage at Illinois and came with him to the university as line coach," he said. "That was 40 years ago. We had some good years and some not-so-good years, several fine players, but not enough, which always seemed to be the problem.

"When they hired Chet Wynne in 1933, I transferred to the Department of Physical Education. They named me athletic director after he left in 1938. I consider Ab Kirwan one of the finest men I ever knew. I helped him with the line after we brought him over from Louisville, and I also coached track and baseball. We recruited hard and worked hard, both on and off the football field, but it was always a matter of too little money, not enough good players, and a tough schedule.

"During the first year of the war (1942) we played Georgia, which won the Rose Bowl and the so-called national championship; Alabama, which was in the Orange Bowl; Georgia Tech, which was in the Sun Bowl; and Tennessee, which was in the Sugar Bowl. We were leading Georgia, 6-0, in Louisville until the final five minutes, when Sinkwich scored a touchdown and their extra point kick was good.

"We drove from our own territory to the Vanderbilt 15, but one of our boys was called for clipping, and they beat us, 7-6. I remember dedicating the new stadium in Roanoke, where we led Virginia Tech by two touchdowns at half time, but they came back to tie the game, 21-21. West Virginia beat us when one of their passes in the last minute bounced off Charlie Kuhn's hands and fell into the arms of Fred Morecraft, who stepped over the goal line. We lost the Alabama game on a fumble and pass interception. I guess Georgia Tech was the only team that beat us bad, along with Tennessee, which we played without Clyde Johnson, who was injured.

"That was the year Clyde was named to the Associated Press All-American team. He was the university's first player so honored. Of course, we've had quite a few since that time, and it's hard to realize just how big it was then. Ab said it should make it easier to persuade prep school boys to come to UK to play football because it showed them that it was just as easy to become a great ball player at Kentucky as at any other school.

"He said a lot of kind words about Clyde and about the

Bernie Shively.

fact that I coached him, but it was just a matter of letting Clyde do what he did best. He came to us from an Ashland team that had won all its games his senior year and had outscored its opponents something like 140 points [134] to two.

"We called him 'Big Stoop,' and he was the biggest player at UK up to that time. He was six-foot-six, weighed about 240 pounds, and had the determination to go when the game was hardest. In fact, he played better against the good teams. He had real long arms that helped him bring down ballcarriers that an ordinary player wouldn't have gotten close to.

"We had him on the 'Z' team when he was a sophomore, which meant we probably would have held him out so he could play five years, but John Eibner got hurt on the opening kickoff against Georgia, and we put Clyde in at tackle. He was a starter after that.

"I remember Clyde was quiet and unassuming. He didn't talk much and always seemed at ease, but he was really very nervous. The night before a game he would read and pace the floor. Once I saw him out walking before breakfast, and I'm sure he hadn't slept at all."

Clyde Johnson, who retired as coach at East Los Angeles Community College in 1961 and still was teaching and operating a sports shop there in April, 1975, recalled that it was more a matter of rising early than staying up late.

"I'd wake up every morning at 5 o'clock," he said, "and I'm still an early riser. And I'll tell you, I woke up sore many of those mornings. Trainer Mann kept me in the ball games. He had an old bathtub, a table, and some heat lamps in a room in the old gym. He'd fill the tub with Epsom salts, and after others had left the Sunday meeting, he would soak me. I'd be so weak, and he would rub me with oil and liniment. He'd put that heat lamp on every sore spot he found. We'd do that three or four days a week.

"In my senior year, I'd be so stiff on Monday I could hardly walk. It was just that I played so much, both offense and defense, and my style was to throw my body around a bit. We played a hard-knock type of football then. It was more running, blocking, and short yardage. All the teams had outstanding runners. Clark Wood was my roommate, and he also played all the way through at the other tackle. Charlie Bill Walker was a linebacker, and no better have I seen—then or now. He would kick me in the butt if I didn't do my job right.

"Kirwan was awful smart. He would read Shakespeare to Daddy Boles on trips. I remember 'Shive' never had a kind word. He worked me harder than any mule. He'd keep me in until the last minute. He'd play you so much you had to improve. We had Alabama tied, 0-0, at half time, and the coaches and everybody got excited. Then we'd play a while, and they'd send in a whole new set of shirts, then another new set. They had depth. We had about a team and a half. When I got clipped and hurt my ankle against Tech, I told the coaches if they would get someone to hold me up after each play, I would stay in the game. That's just what happened. I played the whole game. When I made All-America, it was a shock. 'Shive' took me down to the newspaper to show me the story and a picture of the AP squad. I owe a lot to him."

UK did not have a football team in 1943, but it was one of the first to get a team together the following year. "We had a squad of about 60 men, mostly freshmen, 4-F's and 17-year-olds," Shively recalled. "We taught them the T-formation and got off to a fine start by beating Ole Miss, 27-7. We lost our other five conference games and also lost to Michigan State, 2-0, when they blocked Wilbur Schu's punt behind the goal line for a safety.

"At half time of the Tennessee game, the alumni association presented to me a plaque dedicated to five of our former athletes who were killed in the war. We hung it in Alumni Gym. After that season Ab asked to be transferred to the Department of History, and I took over as football coach until things got settled and we could go about hiring a new coach and reorganizing the department.

"We thought we would have a good team the year I coached, but to be perfectly realistic, it was just a matter of not having enough players with enough experience. They were still drafting boys into the armed services, and our squad consisted almost entirely of inexperienced players.

"Wash Serini, an all-conference tackle the year before, was back, and 'Dutch' Campbell was a good basketball and football player. I recruited George Blanda, who was a big, strong freshman with lots of potential, but he was green as a gourd. Wallace Jones came down from Harlan and joined the team two days before our first game. He practiced on Thursday and Friday, and I substituted him in the fourth quarter against Mississippi. He made all-conference the next year.

"We had signed Ralph Beard to a football scholarship, and he played three games at fullback before injuring both shoulders and switching over completely to basketball where, as most people know, he was an All-American. We also had Bill Chambers, Jim Barnett, Babe Ray, Jesse Tunstill, Rusty Granitz, Dick Hensley, Gene Haas, and Roger Yost. A few of them would be around to play under Paul Bryant.

"I remember Blanda as being somewhat erratic that first

year, as you can expect a freshman to be. He threw some fine passes and also had some intercepted. However, there was no doubt about his kicking. He could really boom it."

Babe Ray, who was recruited out of Louisville by Kirwan, remembered most the competition between Blanda and Granitz. "They were both Pennsylvania boys, both terrific punters, and both battling for the quarterback position," he said. "About the middle of the season 'Shive' had us line up in the 'T' and shift to the box, with both of them playing. Blanda would be the quarterback and Granitz, the left half shifting to tailback.

"Against Cincinnati, we didn't shift every time but sometimes ran from the 'T.' Granitz came running into the game with a play, and instead of telling Blanda, he called the play. It was a punt and they got into an argument over who was going to kick the ball. That was the game in which I let the ball roll dead on the two yard line once, and they recovered it and scored.

"I knew Shive was just filling in until they could find a coach. After I was drafted in December, I wanted to tell him good-bye, and he told me to get on back there because UK was going to have a good coach."

As the marathon gin rummy game ground to a close in 1967, with Shive quitting when he got one penny ahead, he touched slightly on circumstances leading to the hiring of Paul Bryant as UK football coach:

"The war ended in September, and Dr. Donovan immediately set about to upgrade the football program. One of his first moves was to draw up and approve an articles of incorporation of the UK Athletics Association and approve an agreement giving us use of Stoll Field and Alumni Gymnasium. The athletic council was replaced by an 11-man board of directors, and the new association was incorporated in order that we could pay more than the constitutional salary limit, which was $5,000 a year at the time. It also allowed us to cut the red tape involved in laws and regulations pertaining to equipment, travel, and other details. That made us competitive in the market for a new coach.

"All this was happening while we were ending our football season in 1945. The war had ended in September, so you can see we weren't wasting any time. Donovan had lunch with several prominent business and professional men and laid it on the line: we were ready to build a first class athletic program, but they would have to supply the funds. They raised more than $100,000, which was placed on deposit against a rainy day. That money is still in the bank.

"Guy Huguelet, who was head of Southeastern Greyhound Lines and a prominent alumnus, was head of the committee screening applicants for the coaching job. We wanted a coach with a nationally known name but gave up on that after Bo McMillin couldn't get a release from his 10-year contract at Indiana. When we started looking at the younger men available for the job, the name of Paul Bryant kept popping up. We hired him and were on our way."

During his almost four decades as UK athletic director, Shively guided the development of the Wildcats as a nationally respected power in major sports, garnering personal prestige through a fair-minded approach to many problems. He directly supervised major expansions in UK's athletic plant and at one time saw Wildcat athletics rank No. 1 overall among major powers, with the basketball team winning national championships and the football team playing in four consecutive bowl games.

On the national scene he served as chairman of the NCAA Basketball Tournament and NCAA summer baseball committees and was an influential figure in national athletic circles.

The System

When tall, wavy-haired Paul Bryant stepped through the front door of Alumni Gym shortly after noon on January 18, 1946, he was greeted by 3,000 wildly cheering, horn-tooting, placard-bearing University of Kentucky football fans.

Co-eds in the predominantly female crowd, which filled the sidewalk and spilled onto the street, squealed and cheered. The band struck up "On, On, UK," and everybody began to sing the school song. The president of SuKy placed a cardboard good luck "hoss" shoe around Bryant's neck, and the vice-mayor fumbled for the Key to the City.

"Isn't he handsome?" cooed a blonde as Bryant lowered his head for the draping of the shoe.

"Hubba, hubba, hubba," replied her brunette friend.

The vice-mayor explained he could not find the key; instead, he presented an imaginary key and promised that if Bryant could give Kentucky a winning football team next year, he would give him the city.

"This reminds me of what a little girl once said to me in Alabama," Bryant said. "This is so sudden."

Indeed it was.

Three days earlier there was much doubt and apprehension over the selection of a young "unknown" as coach of the Wildcats. That was before Maryland students established picket lines and held a mass meeting protesting the loss of their coach on the morning of January 15. Bryant explained that the choice was made of his own free will and that Kentucky offered a better job and a better future. He then turned the protest into a rousing farewell party.

Paul Bryant gets a wreath and a gala welcome at Alumni Gym upon his arrival at the University of Kentucky in 1946.

The story and a picture of Bryant surrounded by adoring Maryland students kindled a fire under Kentucky students, who were determined to make his welcome to Lexington more arousing than his send-off at Maryland.

Babe Kimbrough of the *Herald* said if Bryant could secure the backing of the student body at Kentucky as he had at Maryland, he would have solved one of the major problems which would confront him. He described Bryant as "one of those fellows who as soon as you have been introduced to him, makes you feel that you have known him for a lifetime."

Following the welcome, during which he promised to serve his employers—the students—faithfully and loyally, Bryant retired to his newly painted office in cramped Alumni Gym and immediately began to change everything.

"If the uniforms were blue on white, he changed them to white on blue," said Carl "Hoot" Combs. Bryant had the ticket manager, team trainer, and equipment manager replaced. Combs was the first of three publicity men to serve under him before

Ken Kuhn began a 20-year tenure at that job in 1948. There were other turnovers—right down to the secretaries. The intense young coach gave two of them a lengthy lecture when he overheard them trying to interpret the meaning of a news release handed them for reproduction.

From Maryland he brought assistants Frank Moseley, Carney Laslie, Lew Bostick, and Ken Whitlow, whom he had known either at Alabama or in the navy, or both. When Whitlow and Bostick accepted positions with other institutions before the 1946 season began, Bryant hired air force combat veteran Bill McCubbin, who had played and coached at UK; navy veteran Mike Balitsaris, a bowl performer for Tennessee; and navy veteran Joe Atkinson, who was captain of the Vanderbilt team when Bryant was an assistant coach there. All were veterans, all under 40, and all loyal to him.

"The first time I saw Bryant at Kentucky was when he was introduced to the student body at old Alumni Gym," Charlie Kuhn told Tev Laudeman of the *Courier-Journal & Times* in a 1975 interview. "I'll never forget, he was standing on the steps in front and we were standing around—at that point he hadn't had a squad meeting—out on Euclid Avenue and over in front of the old girls' dormitory across the street. . . .He was a very impressive person, although he didn't say much."

Bryant's first meeting with the football players came another day. "It was in old Frazee Hall, the old history building near the Student Union," Kuhn said. "Of course, he knew me because he had tried to recruit me when I was at Male High School and he was line coach at Vanderbilt. He had come to Louisville and spent a couple days with me then.

"He remembered me and made a remark about it at the meeting, about me coming to Kentucky after he had tried to get me to go to Vanderbilt. He knew a lot of other players, too, because he had recruited this area for Vanderbilt before the war. There was Jesse Tunstill, Phil Cutchin, and a bunch of us he knew about."

George "Chink" Sengel also remembered Bryant well. "He could look at you with those steel, cold eyes, and they would drill into your mind. When he walked into a room or even cleared his voice, he got complete attention—he was always right to the point. He seemed to have eyes in the back of his head. He had an office in the corner of Alumni Gym, where he could see out toward the Student Union Building, and we

Members of Paul Bryant's first staff at UK. Left to right: Mike Balitsaris, Bill McCubbin, Carney Laslie, Frank Moseley, Joe Atkinson.

players wouldn't walk by, especially if we were with a girl. If he saw you, he might call you in, suit you up, and have you blocking some big tackle."

Sizing up his prospects for the 1946 campaign, Bryant discovered that he had the nucleus of a consistent loser, plus a nondescript group of pre-war players who had returned to the campus from the armed services. The situation was desperate but not hopeless, thanks to relaxed wartime eligibility rules which were still in effect and allowed freshmen to play varsity football. He acquired a helpful handful of talented freshmen in a lightning raid on the small steel towns in western Pennsylvania. One of these—Harry Ulinski, of Ambridge—eventually developed into an All-South center.

Bryant scheduled his first spring practice on February 11, the earliest such practice in the history of UK football. As it turned out, the practice was forced inside Alumni Gym by a two-inch snowfall. Uniforms were issued to 23 holdovers from the 1945 squad, four war veterans who were members of previous squads, and 18 newcomers.

The number of candidates grew to 69 the first week of practice and fluctuated daily as a steady stream of young men tried out for the squad. For the incoming freshmen and service veterans, he scheduled a six-week summer workout, beginning in mid-June. The squad grew to more than 100 by June 27, when the first contact work was held. Two days later the weather was so hot that practice was held at night. The sessions ended July 12.

An estimated 500 players tried out that first year. "He had so many tryouts coming through the house I lived in on Washington Street, that you would see one face at night and a different one the following night," Don Wedge said.

Bryant mailed invitations to 99 candidates that fall, including discharged veterans Bill Moseley, Phil Cutchin, George Sengel, Leo Yarutis, Len Preston, Jay Rhodemyre, Matt Lair, Bill Griffin, and Gene Meeks of the 1942 squad and Doctor Ferrell and Norman Klein of the 1944 squad. The 1945 squad was represented by nonveterans Washington Serini, Gene Haas,

Carney Laslie, Frank Moseley, and Paul Bryant inspect the practice field as Bryant's first spring drills at UK, scheduled to begin February 11, 1946, are postponed because of heavy snow.

George Blanda, Dick Hensley, and basketball star Wallace "Wah Wah" Jones. Jones reported to camp in late August after receiving a flood of telephone calls and telegrams pleading for him to reconsider an earlier decision not to play football. He would become the first player in the SEC to make the all-conference list in both football and basketball.

Before that fall practice Bryant made his only speech of the year to the squad: "Some of you kids have seen a lot of combat. Maybe you'll have a hard time getting excited over a football game. I'm not going to ask you to go out and win for 'dear old Kentucky.' If you win any games this fall, win them for yourself."

"Coach Bryant had a philosophy," Bob Gain told Dick Fenlon of the *Courier-Journal*. "He said if you were going to do anything, you ought to do it like hell. If you played, you played like hell and if you worked you worked like hell and if you partied....well, then, you partied like hell. I did that one night, most of the night, and when he got hold of me the next day, you know what he said?

"'Damn, Bob,' he said, 'you shouldn't a-done that.'

"When you talk about what Coach Bryant was able to do, you've got to remember this: When I was there we had guys just back from the war—one who saw his twin brother shot by a sniper on Guadalcanal, another who had three ships shot out from under him. When you can get guys like that to go down the line for you, you're doing something."

Leonard Preston, a retired Army major who was serving as director of married housing at UK in January, 1975, was one of several married veterans on the squad who attended school on the GI Bill, lived at Cooperstown, and obtained a scholarship under Bryant. He recalled the practice sessions:

"On at least one occasion Coach Bryant, after getting a running start, charged through a group of players who were not paying any attention to plays being run against the 'Z' squad like a bowling ball blasting through bowling pins and said, 'Pay attention, dammit!' On another occasion, he gave 'recognition' to two players who had poorly executed their offensive assignments by grabbing them behind their shoulder pads and running them together with such force that both players dropped to their knees.

"He would openly praise a player for a good performance and ridicule for poor performance. One or two times he 'fired' a man on the spot—told him to turn in his uniform. He would make or break a man who consistently failed to perform well by running him laps, by a combination of running and ridicule, or playing him on the 'Z' squad, etc. Sometimes a practice session for a player would consist of running around the field for two hours or more for days on end. If he stuck with it, he would be allowed to practice with the rest of the team. Sometimes the player would quit.

"He did not encourage familiarity between players and coaches, and the coaches did not try to be 'one of the boys.' On the practice field when a player executed a block, tackle, etc., poorly, he was corrected on the spot and sometimes required to get off to one side for extra work or take laps. Fundamentals were stressed to perfection. Condition was a must—through laps, wind sprints, agility drills, and drills related specifically to player skills, quickness, power, strength, and endurance, each until a player, even some in good condition, would sometimes fall when walking. This type of conditioning took place during spring practice and during the first part of the regular season."

Bryant's philosophy of conditioning was revealed in a statement about the 1946 freshmen: "You don't know how a horse is going to pull until you hook him to a heavy load. We know all these boys show promise, but we have a lot of hard work to do before we can handle the heavy loads which are scheduled to come our way."

In the summer of 1952, he wrote to his players:

> Winning isn't imperative, but coming from behind and getting tougher in the fourth quarter is. I don't want you to think that you have to win, because you don't. On the other hand, if you can go out there ripping and snorting and having fun by knocking people around, I assure you, you will win.
>
> I honestly believe that if you are willing to out-condition the opponent, have confidence in your ability, be more aggressive than your opponent and have that genuine desire for team victory you will be the national champions.
>
> If you have the above, we will acquire confidence and poise and you will have those intangibles that win the close ones.

In 1972 Ben Zaranka said, "I remember when Gain, Wannamaker, and I—the entire left side of the line—were not listed for practice the Monday after a game. We stood around for

Clowning for the photographer are (left to right) Doc Ferrell, Norm Klein, George Blanda, and Wallace Jones (1946).

three days, practically ignored by Bryant and everyone else. On Thursday we were listed with the freshmen. The following day Bryant asked us, 'How do you like being nobodies? How do you like being on the freshman team? That's just where you'll be from now on if you don't improve.'

"When we left the dressing room to go out on the practice field, he would say, 'As soon as you go out that door, you don't have a friend.' I worked in a steel mill in East Chicago, Indiana, my first summer and then spent the next three summers at UK, playing baseball and practicing football. We worked out twice a day as freshmen in the heat. They gave us lemonade that was actually salt water.

"He said that football may be a game to a lot of people, but it could be a good example to us to take this game into life. 'You'll have good days and bad days,' he told us. 'You'll feel like you want to quit, but there's one thing I'm going to teach you. You may be down to your last breath, but you'll give it all you've got.'

"I would avoid him. Anytime he ran across you, he would stop you and talk football, no matter what the season. Every man on the football team at one time had to block him or be blocked by him. He would put you in back of the center like a quarterback and have seven men pound you. Saturday was the best day for us because scrimmaging or playing a game was fun after what you went through on the practice field all week. I remember one time when Pat James and Bill Wannamaker got in a fight, and he just made a circle and let them fight."

During eight years at the university, Bryant never let up on practice sessions. In August of 1949 he invited his varsity squad to a fishing expedition on the Kentucky River for one week prior to the formal opening of fall practice. Inasmuch as fishing on the river is at its best at dawn and dusk, he thoughtfully took along athletic equipment to help condition his charges and to provide them with wholesome recreation during the daylight hours. He and his staff would meet at 5:00 a.m., plan the day's activities, and then take everyone fishing at 6:30 a.m. Breakfast was served at 8:00 a.m., and a morning workout was held at 9:30 a.m. The team would eat lunch at 11:30, work out in the afternoon, and then eat dinner before returning to their fishing spots.

Pat James arrived for practice late and was made to remain after the drills and cover up manure in the cow pasture where drills were held. When Bryant was late the following day, allegedly because the trainer had neglected to awaken him, James informed him that the players had held another "kangaroo court" and that his punishment was to dig up all the manure, load it up, and cart it off, which Bryant did that night. Since the trainer was not fired, one might assume that Bryant, always an early riser, played a major part in setting up the incident.

Two years later Bryant was unable to obtain a suitable place on a river or lake, so he held the first week of fall practice at Millersburg Military Institute, located 29 miles north of Lexington in a community of 825 persons. The practice field was in a ravine where there was no wind circulation and no water—called "Hell's Hollow" and "Death Valley" by the players who trained there.

"It was the worst place anybody could imagine," "Hooker" Phillips said. "Players dropped like flies. We wore shorts and thongs except at practice and church. We had a choice of practice or church on Sunday, and naturally all the players preferred church. We loaded onto the bus and went to Paris. We went to a movie once. The weather was so hot and muggy at times in the ravine that Bryant would caution us to catch a breath every now and then, 'but when you go, go hard.'"

"I remember that first day at Death Valley," Frank Sadler said. "Was it rough? There used to be a dinky little train that went by there, and they'd stop to watch what was happening. We lost 21 of them that first day, and one of them was a quarterback from Pennsylvania. I asked Bryant if he wanted me to stop him, and he said, 'Aw, let him go.' I asked him again that night if he wanted me to go and bring him back.

"'Yeh,' he said, 'Yeh, you do that. I want to have the privilege of runnin' him off myself.'"

At all practice sessions Bryant used the "challenge" system, whereby a second or third team player could challenge a regular in head-on-head confrontation.

There was a clear-cut caste system among the players. The top performers stayed in No. 147, the best of three "football" houses on Washington Street, and received the most favors. The other two houses—Nos. 121 and 123—had more modest accommodations. A player started living in 121 and worked his way up.

The players ate at a training table in the Student Union cafeteria. Their diet was carefully observed, and records were kept of their weight. For a mild infraction a player would have his plate broken, which meant that his name was deleted from the cafeteria list. When some of the players were caught gambling, a "Downtown Poker Club" was formed, with meetings held after each practice session. Wind sprints were the order of business.

Spurning psychological buildups and crying-towel tantrums, Bryant concentrated on toughening the players physically. He taught them elementary, hard-blocking plays run off the Notre Dame box offense, and he worked them incessantly to minimize the three major errors that lose football games—intercepted passes, blocked kicks, and fumbles. In eight years at UK his teams would compile a 60-23-5 record, win the school's only SEC championship, and participate in three major bowl games.

The Salesman

"I wish all requests that I receive were as easy to comply with as yours regarding Coach Bryant," Virginia Tech athletic director Frank Moseley wrote in January, 1973, and he went on to explain:

The man who is head football coach at Alabama today is essentially the same man who accepted the head football job at Kentucky in 1946. His coaching philosophy, working hours and recruiting methods are just about the same today as they were 26 years ago and, incidentally, no different from any number of successful coaches today.

The big difference is the man himself. He is and always has been the most dedicated of all men associated with college football. His greatest asset probably is willingness to work, but dedication to work in itself isn't enough. Many coaches are willing and dedicated to devoting endless hours, but Coach Bryant's approach has been more directed and effective.

Over the years he has commanded utmost respect and admiration because he always has been willing to sacrifice himself and not the people around him. He is just as loyal, or even more so, to his assistant coaches and players as he expects them to be to him.

He is a demanding man, but he also has a "super salesman" quality that promotes and elicits both the personal and team discipline necessary to winning.

A successful coach has to be an excellent recruiter, and in this regard Coach Bryant has no peers. He has blended honesty, sincerity, hard work and an unusual knack for evaluating talent.

His straightforwardness as well as appreciation and consideration of their efforts has maintained for himself and his associates good rapport with the media.

In my estimation, Paul Bryant would have been highly successful in most any field of endeavor for which he had been trained.

College athletics and in particular college football are extremely fortunate that Coach Bryant chose what he did for his life's work.

If there was one phase of football in which the young Paul Bryant stood head and shoulders above the crowd, it was recruiting, and he involved everyone around him in the task of enticing outstanding players to Lexington. A chronic user of the telephone, he would call anyone—from the local grocer to the governor—at two or three o'clock in the morning and ask him to help recruit a player, and he organized meetings with key persons throughout the state, usually remaining in their towns for dinner sessions and enough time to get acquainted.

"He was in my home town of Pikeville, speaking at a gathering, when he told the parents of Bill Wheeler and Clark Ratcliffe that their sons were doing well," Robert "Hooker" Phillips said in 1973. "Then he turned to my parents and said, 'I don't know about that son of yours. I think he's sold his books.' The people of Pikeville told me in no uncertain terms to shape up.

"When Bryant bragged on me a little bit one time, it was in my home town newspaper, and the people there said it was about time I did something.

"One day my father visited me at practice and called to me as I went after a kicked ball near the sideline. When I replied 'Yeah,' Bryant shook me and said, 'You don't ever say "yeah," especially to your father. You say "yes, sir" and "no, sir."' My father said it was about time I learned some good manners.

"I was recruited heavy for Bryant by the people around Pikeville, and several of the assistant coaches visited me. I had met Bryant and was awed. I came down to the Bluegrass the summer after my junior season; stayed with the family of my

Kentucky coach Paul Bryant, 1946-53.

coach, Clayton Powers, at Frankfort; worked out there with Powers and in Lexington with Babe Parilli and about 35 others who were participating 'on their own.' Actually, there was always a coach watching, and the sessions were organized. We started something like 5:30 a.m., working out on the practice field next to Stoll Field and on a large field in another part of town. A lot of guys would come and go."

When Emery Clark's father made three trips to Lexington from Carlisle in an attempt to sell his undersize son as a football candidate, Bryant told him, "Mr. Clark, I really think I am doing you a favor. I think your boy is just too small to make the grade here, and my advice is that you send him to another college where he can get a chance to play." However, Emery Clark enrolled at his own expense and later would be selected second to Vito Parilli as the most valuable player in the 1952 Cotton Bowl.

Jim Proffitt, who played end for Bryant in the early 1950s, said, "I was first recruited to Kentucky when I was a junior at Manual High in Louisville. I received a letter from Coach Bryant. Thereafter, I was contacted periodically by Ermal Allen, who was in charge of the Louisville area.

"When Kentucky played in the Orange Bowl, they flew Bunky Gruner, 'Deep Wing,' and myself down to Miami in an Air National Guard plane. Later when I was a senior, I signed to go to Indiana University. This was in 1950. In August of that year Coach Bryant and Ermal Allen came to my house and convinced me that I should attend the University of Kentucky. Coach Bryant took me to Lexington two weeks before practice began and got me a job so that the people from Indiana could not find me. My parents said they came to the house several times looking for me."

In 1950 a Notre Dame coach said the Irish would have had a fine team if they had not lost so many players to Bryant. The list included Ralph Paolone, a 1948 Pennsylvania All-State performer who transferred to the University of Kentucky after attending Notre Dame one year, and Gene Donaldson, a three-year All-State player and undefeated wrestling champion at Roosevelt High in East Chicago, who was regarded so fondly by Leahy that Midwest talent scouts did not waste their time soliciting his services.

During a friendly call on the Donaldsons, Bryant pointed out that, in addition to Kentucky's obvious curricular merits, ample religious facilities were available for young Gene, within two minutes walking distance of the campus. Leahy accused Bryant of dressing manager Jim Murphy in a priest's outfit to recruit Donaldson and of hiding the player out in Yellowstone National Park. Bryant replied that he would have said Murphy was Pope Pius if he thought he could get Donaldson that way.

Bryant set up such an efficient recruiting organization in Pennsylvania that other conference coaches began screaming that he had gone into the Keystone State (considered a private preserve by Wally Butts of Georgia, Bob Neyland of Tennessee, and whoever was coaching at Maryland) and signed 100 or more prospects—far more than he could possibly take care of in Lexington.

The university provided only the aid prescribed by regulations. But local business and professional men (known as "sponsors") took some of the players, especially the better ones, under their wing and saw to it that they got little extra favors, a system still in vogue in some institutions.

As an incentive UK players received what Dom Fucci called "gratuities," usually in the form of extra tickets. As a matter of routine, the starters got more tickets than the second team players, the second team got more tickets than the third. The value of the tickets was determined by the boosters who purchased the tickets from a person who sold them for the players.

There was also a system for rewarding individuals for big plays, Fucci said. "For a pass interception, you would probably get two tickets—and five tickets if you scored on it—two tickets for a blocked punt, and one ticket for a tackle behind the line. There were also rewards for recovering a fumble, scoring a touchdown, etc. If you played an exceptional game, Bryant would tell you to go down and get a hat or suit. His great bet was a hat."

Some of that money came from the STAC ("Cats" spelled backward) Club, which the by-laws stated was organized to help needy students attain an education. The club was managed first by an assistant coach and then by Frank Sadler, a diminutive former high school quarterback from Alabama who was Bryant's water boy at Great Lakes and had organized a student protest when Bryant left Maryland. Sadler came to Lexington after receiving the following letter from Bryant in early 1946:

This is strictly on the Q.T. and I don't want you to

mention it to anyone now or later here. Anyway I am sure you know how much we think of you but in addition to that I think you have a lot on the ball and should accomplish something in the future.

In short I would like for you to come to school down here at Ky. We have a new quarter starting March 25 and you could enter then. I will help you all I can but will guarantee to give you your meals during regular football season, give you a room year round and $10 per mo. spending money. Maybe more but the above for sure.

I wouldn't mind taking you away from there since you are not a player but if you do come don't say anything about my helping you—nor mention to anyone here.

We have 3 mgrs. but they are. . .poor and I am going to run them off.

Say hello to everyone and let me know immediately.

Sincerely,

Coach Bryant

Sadler was denied admission to UK immediately, so he attended summer school at Transylvania College and worked in a service station—all the while managing the Wildcat football team. He enrolled in UK that fall.

"He always called me 'MGR,' not 'manager,'" Sadler recalled in 1973. "'MGR do this,' he'd say, or 'MGR handle this.' I remember one day he told me to get the lights turned on. I told him I couldn't because they had been disconnected at the top. 'MGR,' he said. 'I want light.' I don't know if he can walk on water, but he sure caused me to climb four high telephone poles, and he got his lights.

"After I graduated from UK, I was working in an auto dealership in Middlesboro when he asked me to take over the STAC Club. The membership fee was $15, carrying with it the privilege of purchasing two football tickets at face value. We were allotted approximately 3,000 tickets in sections C & D, from the 50 to the 10 yard lines. I turned the collected dues and donations over to Tom DeZonia, who was vice president of Mr. Huguelet's Southeastern Greyhound company. Mr. DeZonia distributed the money."

Although some of the alumni were assisting players, most of the better performers attended the university because of the lure of a free education, a monthly stipend for laundry, all the food they could eat, and an opportunity to participate immediately in an exciting new program.

Ben Zaranka, of East Chicago, Indiana, a two-time All-State player sought by all the Big Ten schools, Notre Dame, Tulane, Washington, and various institutions, and by three major league baseball teams, showed no interest when two of Bryant's assistants visited his home in 1947.

"I was a collector of all types of sports information, and I couldn't find anything good about Kentucky in my books," Zaranka said. "I told them I had seen the school's pathetic football record of the past, and I wasn't interested. They visited me a second time, and I told them I wanted to go where the goal was to win. Bryant then visited me. I remember him as a great politician. He pointed out that the UK record was bad, but that he and his coaches were trying to get the best players in the country. There was a new discipline and hard work at Kentucky, he said, and no one had a position secured. In other words, I could make the team as a freshman if I proved myself qualified.

"I visited Lexington for the weekend, got off the train, and thought I had never seen grass so green, the sun shine so bright, and the air so clean. I was taken to dinner at a cafeteria where I saw tackle Wash Serini seated all alone at a table with an enormous amount of food. I never saw so much food in my life. When they told me that all that food was for Serini and that any UK player could eat all he wanted, I was convinced."

Fucci, a high school star from New Village, New Jersey, visited UK during Easter vacation. "I got to Lexington on Friday night and started to leave on Sunday," he said. "Coach Laslie said, 'You can't go home. We want you to finish spring practice.' I told him I wasn't out of high school. I went back home, and on the night of my graduation I got on a train and came back to Lexington. I got here on Friday. We had a helluva scrimmage on Saturday." Fucci's punting would be a vital factor in Kentucky's 1951 Sugar Bowl game with Oklahoma.

Among Bryant's first crop of recruits were such players as Harry Ulinski, Al Bruno, Ralph and Carl Genito, and Bill Boller. He recruited Bob Gain in 1947 and signed Vito Parilli, along with a host of other fine players, in 1948. The NCAA's so-called "Sanity Code," which became effective in 1949, curtailed mass recruiting activities and tryouts. But by then, Bryant had recruited enough skilled players to form the nucleus of a fine football program.

Bryant pictured with some of his 1947 freshmen. Front row, left to right: Richard Horton, Harold Woodell, Robert Jones, Lawrence Howard, Russell E. Knoerl, Trento Serini, Ben Zaranka. Middle row: Ogden Thomas, Bob Gallner, John Dorman, Clayton Webb, Jim Swenck, Sherwin Gandee, Bob Pope, Bob Wodtke, Don Frampton. Back row: Norbert Moranz, Walt Painter, Joe Davis, Bobby Brooks, Bill Leskovar, Al Bruno, Bill Conde, Bill Robertson, Bob Koontz, Bob Gain, Larry Flamm, and Jim Pickens. Eleven of the 28 would earn a K-letter.

The Blanda Years

The Kentucky football team had just completed a practice session on a hot Wednesday afternoon in July, 1945, and tackles Wash Serini and Hugh Shannon were having a friendly discussion over the talents of a 195-pound freshman from Pennsylvania named George Blanda.

"Why, George can pass the ball over those goalposts," Shannon said.

"I'll bet he can't," Serini replied.

Some of the players went to the dressing room, got Blanda out of the shower, brought him back to the field, gave him a ball, and told him to throw it.

The *Leader* reported that Ken Campbell waited on the goal line to receive the pass and only had to take a few steps forward to catch the ball. Serini reportedly put his arm around Blanda's shoulders and said, "That's all right, George. The wind was against you."

"I think it went about 78 yards," Blanda said in February, 1975, as he thought past a long pro career back to that scene at UK 30 years earlier. "I've never seen anybody throw 100 yards."

Blanda's recollections of playing football at UK were dimmed by "all that has happened since that time" and perhaps because his accomplishments as a Wildcat were not all that outstanding during his early undergraduate career.

Blanda was eligible for varsity competition in 1945 under a wartime ruling. He started that career in a rather modest manner, completing only three of 10 passes against Mississippi and having one errant toss returned for a touchdown as the Wildcats lost, 21-7. He did not enter the next game until late in the third quarter. And then he fumbled on the 27 yard line while trying to pass, to set up Cincinnati's lone marker in a 13-7 Wildcat victory.

"As marksmen, the UK pass-flingers would have made good sewing-machine salesmen," the *Herald* said.

Blanda did have his good moments that season. In a game against Georgia he connected on five of six passes. One was a 15-yard scoring strike to Hal Phillips with less than two minutes remaining in the game. Blanda then tossed the ball 66 yards in the air to Bill Chambers, who juggled it but held on for a spectacular reception as the game ended. Blanda also scored against Cincinnati, passed well against Alabama, and completed a 40-

George Blanda.

yard pass to Chambers before carrying the ball over against Marquette. But, alas! The Wildcats lost all those games.

Then the veterans came home. First, Ermal Allen, fresh off a boat from the Philippines, walked into Bryant's office and said, "I hear you need a tailback?"

"That's right."

"You're looking at him," Allen said.

Just before the opening game against Mississippi, Allen was declared eligible under a wartime ruling. The Wildcats won that game and then defeated Cincinnati before Allen was held out of a romp over Xavier and declared ineligible. Phil Cutchin, another prewar letterman, was inserted into the all-important spot of field general in Bryant's Notre Dame box.

During all the preseason tryouts, shuffling for positions, and insertion of returning servicemen into the lineup, Blanda was a somewhat frustrated young man. Bryant first relegated him to the role of quarterback, which was actually blocking back. Then, when Blanda sulked, Bryant demoted him to linebacker on the "B" team, a move Bryant later admitted might have been one of his "dumbest." "If I had gone to the T-formation that year and had been more experienced, Blanda might have made All-America," he said in his book.

"George was bigger in stature than most of the guys," a teammate said, "and when he was moved to blocking back, he got mad; but he was really fuming when he was moved to linebacker. He tackled like a wild man. Bryant said he had to take him out to keep him from hurting someone or hurting himself. The experience apparently came in handy because Blanda later played linebacker some when he went with the Chicago Bears."

In Bryant's first starting backfield at UK were Allen, Don Phelps, Bill Moseley, and Bill Chambers. On defense, Harry Ulinski and Blanda played in place of Moseley and Chambers.

That first season under Bryant began with a fumble-plagued victory over Ole Miss and ended with a loss to Tennessee and a 7-3 record. This was the first time since 1912 that a UK team had won as many as seven games. Along the way they became the first UK team to travel by air and were involved in all kinds of unusual plays and formations as Bryant sought to make the best of the widely assorted talent at his disposal.

"I remember we lost the ball four times on five fumbles against Ole Miss, with three of the fumbles coming inside the Rebel 20 yard line," George Sengel said. "I committed one of the fumbles on an end-around and missed two touchdown passes. Bryant was wild on the sidelines, but after the game he came to see me in the locker room and said, 'Chink, forget about this game. Hell, I dropped them in the Rose Bowl.' I caught a touchdown pass in the next game, and we beat Cincinnati."

Bryant's first loss as UK coach was to Georgia, 28-13, in Athens, where the 'Cats again had trouble holding onto the ball. In a letter to the writer in 1973, substitute back Ralph Genito recalled being summoned by Bryant to warm up just as Kentucky ran for two first downs and appeared to be launching a scoring drive, when Cutchin committed another fumble.

"I was taking snaps from the reserve center on the sideline," Genito said, "and when the Georgia fans roared, I looked up to see what had happened. At that minute, the center snapped the ball and it bounced off my hands and onto the field.

"'Okay, Genito,' Coach Bryant said, 'go in for Cutchin. You're ready.'"

George Sengel particularly remembered the plane ride to Montgomery to play Alabama. "I'll never forget that first plane ride because I was a bombardier in the air force," Sengel said. "They took two of those old C-47 army transport double-prop jobs and converted them. There were bucket seats on the side. We strapped our gear in big piles in the middle of the aisle. We were about three hours getting off at Blue Grass Field because of the weather."

On the return trip one of the planes developed engine trouble and was grounded at Montgomery. The other plane took one load to Lexington and then returned for the remaining members of the party.

After the Wildcats lost the Alabama game and lost to Mississippi a year later after traveling by plane to Oxford, Bryant vowed never again to transport a team by air. However, he relented in 1949, when his schedule included games at Baton Rouge, Oxford, Dallas, Tampa, and Miami. Perhaps he was superstitious. He also devised a new jersey numbering system in 1953 and quit using it after his team lost two games wearing those numbers.

Superstition aside, he considered himself a "field" coach, as opposed to a tactician. He believed that techniques and tactics were overrated, that a field coach who could get boys to play to the best of their abilities could beat the tactician. However, his game plans were highly organized and efficient, and he was prone to gamble and try new and often spectacular tricks.

Two weeks before playing Alabama in Montgomery, Bryant had decided that the only way to beat his old coach, Frank Thomas, was to gamble. His offense included a pass on his own goal line, but his daring went for naught. The Tide took advantage of his strategy of having the safety play up close, to prevent Harry Gilmer's deadly short passes; they capitalized on three quick-kicks over the safety's head to set up touchdowns for a 21-7 finish.

"I remember those short passes because Bryant was upset about them later," Sengel said. "As we were playing the latter part of that game, they completed a couple of passes leading to scores. There was some question as to whether the passes were legal because they could be construed as 'pick' passes—where a defender is picked off by one of the intended receivers before the pass is thrown. During the heat of the contest we didn't realize what was happening, but Coach Bryant did, and he was

Dopey Phelps takes a lateral from George Blanda as the Wildcats lost to Alabama, 13-0, November 2, 1947, on Stoll Field.

fuming on the sidelines. We lost, and we stayed in Montgomery that night. . . . I was on the same [plane] trip with Bryant, and he was dejected because Thomas had used those passes to beat him.

"The next week, we had a similar pass in our repertoire. We called it '28 Special, with blocking,' but we didn't plan to use it unless in dire need. When Michigan State came into Lexington highly rated and was leading us at half time, we decided to use the play against them. We lined up in the 'T,' shifted to the box, and slipped Phelps in there as the blocking back. The play was designed where the tight end runs a curl pattern and annihilates the linebacker, while the wingback goes on a deep curl and blocks the halfback. It starts out like a power sweep to the right, and the tailback gives a soft, easy pass over the line to the blocking back drifting out into the short flat zone. All he had to do was catch the ball and use his afterburner, which Dopey did. It happened so fast that Michigan State didn't realize what was going on. Dopey had a field day. Check the record."

That game had hardly gotten under way before the speedy freshman, Dopey Phelps, took a five-yard pass from Babb and dashed the additional 40 yards for the first marker. Then after the Spartans had knotted the count only a minute later, he put UK back on top when he took a pass from Boller and ran 61 yards to the one yard stripe, then plunged over on the next play. With UK trailing 14-13 in the second half, he took the ball on his own 15 yard line and galloped 85 yards to score. Phelps scored his fourth touchdown of the day on an 11-yard heave from Cutchin.

"We fooled heavily favored Cincinnati with a beautifully executed variety of the old Statue of Liberty play," Sengel said. "Cutchin took the ball from center, faked a hand-off, and nonchalantly placed the ball on his right side until Jack Farris came by, grabbed the ball, and scored.

"Vanderbilt was looking for that play when we met them two weeks later. Cutchin took the ball from center and placed it on his right side. When Dopey went by, the whole Vandy team went with him. Cutchin still had the ball. He threw it to Wah Jones, who was all alone in the end zone. That was the first touchdown scored on Vanderbilt that season, and it was also their first loss."

Blanda carried the ball two times that season, losing five

yards against West Virginia and failing to gain against Marquette. He threw two passes and attempted no field goals. However, he did share the punting chores with Cutchin and kicked 28 times for 1,106 yards, a 39.3 average. He intercepted a pass to set up a touchdown against Mississippi and caught a two-yard pass against Vanderbilt. That was the extent of his offensive endeavors.

In the opening game of 1947, a 14-7 loss to Ole Miss, Blanda carried the ball two times for minus 13 yards rushing; completed two of seven passes for a net gain of four yards, including a two-yard scoring toss to Wah Wah Jones; and had two passes intercepted. Fans blamed him for the loss, although the Rebels were one of the better teams in the nation.

Bryant said the turning point in Blanda's career came the following week when he assured him that the students and fans would soon be cheering for him. Noticing the old clothing Blanda was wearing, Bryant told Blanda to go down to a local men's store and purchase a new outfit, head to foot, and charge it to his account.

In his first game after the loss to Ole Miss, Blanda set up a touchdown with a 35-yard pass to Phelps and kicked two extra points in a 20-0 victory over Cincinnati. Improving with each game, he guided them to consecutive victories over Xavier, Georgia, previously undefeated Vanderbilt, and Michigan State.

"There was a big change between 1946 and 1947, when Bryant installed the T-formation," George Sengel said. "Otto Graham, Don Hutson, and Bobby Dodd helped us with it.

"I remember the time we were dressed for scrimmage one Saturday afternoon, and Bryant had us all sitting around near the goalpost. He called out the starting offense, starting defense, and the game officials. The coaches kept standing around. All at once they opened the gates and a big bus drove in. There was a football team on it. They go to the other end of the field, get out, and do calisthenics. We lined up and played a regulation football game, beating them, as I recall, 7-0, on a punt return by Don Phelps. We had six or seven first downs, and they had 20.

"When that team got back on the bus, we stayed and scrimmaged some more. We found out later the coach was Sid Gilman, and team was Miami of Ohio. They had Dietzel, Parseghian, Pont, and all those guys.

"That year we were the first team to use any type of spread formation. We dabbled very little with it, but we really went into it later. Against Alabama, we utilized a formation which spread three men in a triangle formed by an end, a tackle, and Phelps, with the three placed to the left or right of the rest of the team. Phelps, the rear man, would take a long lateral pass from Blanda before starting to run. I remember he made a 20-yard gain against Alabama, but we lost, 13-0."

Their most unusual play was known in the huddle as "Abba Kadabba, who's got the ball?" Guard Len Preston recalled that opportunity knocked on his door against West Virginia. Rules at that time permitted linemen to carry the ball under certain circumstances, and that was just what he did. The team lined up in a tight "T," Blanda took the ball from center, pivoted 180 degrees, and seemingly was operating a power sweep. But during the pivot, he slipped the ball to Preston, who was crouched with his inside arm open and his outside arm shielding the ball as Blanda continued the faking action.

"All the backs were crouching like they were blocking for a sweep to the right," Preston said, "and I took a low count to about five and pivoted away from the play, put the ball on my outside arm, and tried to get to the left sideline. Dick Hensley, our left end, had forgotten the play, and I stumbled over him and fell down."

"On that trip to Morgantown we sent our equipment ahead in a truck," Sengel said. "Those shoulder pads, helmets, and other items of gear would fly out as the truck whipped around those mountainous curves. State police all along the way were salvaging the gear. When we got to Morgantown, Bryant was furious because the field was wet and it hadn't rained a bit. Everybody who made the trip, except the players, was pressed into service changing the regular cleats to those big three-inch mud cleats. It was really something to see Shively, McCubbin, and those guys back there working like beavers. I remember one big play, a blocked punt by Jay Rhodemyre. We beat them.

"After the game Bryant told Frank Sadler to open a trunk in the locker room and give us cigars, cigarettes, and $5 each. He then sent us back to Fairmont, where we had spent the previous night, and he and his assistants went to Washington for a professional game. We relaxed and drank beer at an air force club before boarding the train for Lexington shortly after midnight. He gave us Monday off and then worked us hard the rest of the week. I guess it was significant that we were scheduled to

George Blanda, senior and quarterback on the 1948 team, is congratulated by Coach Paul "Bear" Bryant upon receipt of the Jerome Lederer trophy presented annually to the outstanding senior on the team, as selected by teammates. Blanda was also elected honorary captain of the team.

play Evansville, which wasn't so good, that next Saturday."

The Wildcats closed that season with their annual loss to Tennessee on a cold, rainy, snowy day. Then they defeated Villanova in the first and only Great Lakes Bowl in Cleveland Stadium. Insignificant as it was, that game was UK's first venture into bowl competition. The team finished with an 8-3 record. Not since 1909 had UK won more than seven games. Blanda had a fairly good year, completing 53 of 114 passes for 484 yards, averaging 39.4 yards per punt, and making 17 of 24 kicks for extra points. In the only field goal attempt of his UK career, he kicked the ball from the 26 yard line against Villanova. It not only went through the goalposts but cleared the skinned infield and went into the baseball dugout.

Blanda got his senior season off on a spectacular note by

lateralling to Phelps; Phelps passed into the end zone, where Jones made a circus catch in the 48-7 romp over Xavier. However, Blanda completed only one of nine passes for eight yards against Mississippi and fumbled to set up a Rebel score. He ended the frustrating afternoon by throwing to an official rather than to the intended receiver. The Wildcats lost, 20-7.

The Wildcats had lost three of four games when Phelps, Bill Boller, and Jim Howe were left home, and the 'Cats beat Marquette, 25-0, in Milwaukee. Blanda hit Jamerson with a beautiful 46-yard pass in that game. He also averaged 49.8 yards on four kicks, with two punts traveling more than 60 yards each. The 'Cats defeated Cincinnati; tied Villanova on a 69-yard broken field run by Howe after a pass from Blanda in the final 45 seconds of play; won their first conference game as Blanda completed 11 of 13 passes, three for touchdowns, against Florida; fought Tennessee to a scoreless tie; and defeated Miami, 25-5. Thus the season ended with a 5-3-2 record.

During the three years Blanda played for Bryant, UK teams compiled a 20-8-2 record, the best three-year total since before World War I. Blanda began his professional career with the Chicago Bears and played as quarterback for Houston when the American Football League was formed. In 1975 he was the "Grand Old Man" of the game, still active as a place-kicker with the Oakland Raiders.

It is ironic that he only kicked one field goal for the Wildcats. But he punted during his four years on the team. In the pros he became an all-time great place-kicker but never assumed any punting chores. "When I went to the Bears, it was just a matter of need," he said. "They had a punter; they needed a kicker."

Time Out: "Cholly Mac"

A postluncheon session with Charles McClendon at the DeSoto Hilton in Savannah, where the Southeastern Conference was holding its annual meeting in March, 1975, failed to materialize.

"But we'll get together later this afternoon," the highly successful LSU football coach said, and, sure enough, there he was, among the first persons to arrive at a predinner social hour held in the foyer outside the main ballroom.

"Let's get back away from everybody," he said as he chose a small corner table with two chairs. "Now, let's talk Kentucky football."

A native of Lewisville, Arkansas, McClendon attended Magnolia Junior College before serving three years in the U. S. Navy. He then spent three years at UK.

"I remember very well my first visit to Kentucky," he said. "I went there with Joe Joe Dean, who tried out for the basketball team. Carney Laslie had recruited me through friends of Coach Bryant in Arkansas. They were holding a football clinic at UK, and Otto Graham was there. My job was to catch the balls thrown by Otto. I can't even remember whether I caught one or not.

"I had a great respect, or perhaps fear is a better word, for 'Wah Wah' Jones. I had read a lot about him. He was a real fine football and basketball player, maybe the last to be that good in both sports. I'll never forget that Pat James entertained me. I still accuse him of keeping that $10 they gave him. I think we got in that picture show free.

"It didn't take very much to get me to sign because I was

awful anxious to play and get an education. I went back home, and they were checking me real close to see if I really wanted to come. I may not have impressed them. There was no reason to think I could play. Looking back, I never played a down of high school football. I was lower than this floor. I went to junior college on a basketball scholarship and ended up playing on the football team.

"My wife had never been away from home. I thought I had made a mistake. She knew I had. I remember she had a hard time getting adjusted. We first lived in a little one-room apartment, and when I walked in after my first day of practice, she was crying. She had tried to fix her first dinner with a hot-plate oven, and nothing had panned out. What she didn't know was that I wasn't hungry. We had worked so hard that I was too tired to eat.

"Charlie and Martha Bradshaw kinda took us under their wing. Pat James was married and still is one of my best friends. So are Gene Donaldson, now at Shreveport; Harold Woodell, now at Houston; and others. It's amazing how my teammates are spread out, and we're still friends.

"One of my LSU teams played Kentucky one time in Lexington when Charlie was coaching, and I had my game plan on a little clipboard. We were throwing a pass to one of our men in the open, and a UK man almost intercepted it. In the excitement I had hit my leg with my game plan, and the board flew up into the crowd. I turned toward the stands, and this voice said sweetly, 'Here, Charlie Mac.' It was Martha Bradshaw handing me my game plan.

"When we all lived at Cooperstown (married veterans' housing project) and I didn't have any transportation, William 'Moon' Conde and I would pedal each other on his bicycle as far as we could and then push it the rest of the way home after we got too tired to pedal.

"The work was demanding, but when you deal with numbers, you've got to find out who wants to play. I really didn't think about it as a player. If you're going to win, you've got to give yourself completely. Being older, I understood it. I felt I was so far behind, anyway. There were about 25 of us who stayed out several times and worked after the lights were out.

Charlie McClendon.

They wanted to find out if we really wanted to play football. Most of us were veterans and knew how to take orders. There were also fewer problems because you couldn't move around much.

"Buckshot Underwood was supposed to have been tough, but he had a heart of gold, and you kinda knew he was pulling for you. Ermal Allen was one of the sharpest coaches I've ever seen. He expected the players to be just as good as he was.

"The thing I remember most about Coach Bryant is when I started work for him (as an assistant in 1951), and I would drive him to banquets. We've shed tears together, and you'd think you were close to the man as a man could be until you met him the next day in the hallway and he didn't know you. I understand now. He had something on his mind and decisions to make to keep him ahead of the game.

"I remember taking him one day to catch a plane, and the assistant's job came open at Vanderbilt. I wanted to stay at UK, and I told him if he'd pay me more money, I wouldn't have to go. 'If I wanted to pay you any more, I would,' he said. I know now that he was instrumental in getting me on at Vanderbilt and later at LSU.

"Remembering some of the players then, we thought Bob Gain was a giant, but he would be just another player size wise today. I don't know any player who got involved in it any more than Gain when the whistle blew to begin a game. He was a super player, and he'd still be class today.

"Babe Parilli was something else. He not only had the ability to do his job, but he could get other people with him to do their job.

"But let's give credit to the *Leader* (Bryant). He had everything to do with it.

"I remember best when we beat Ole Miss, 47-0, and Jim Mackenzie scored a touchdown in that game. The largest crowd that ever met us was at the airport. They were all the way out on the highway. That was really something.

"The Tennessee games were always very much of a frustration for me. In my years there, we did not beat them. I remember the closeness of the games and playing in the snow in 1950 at Knoxville. I coughed all the way home because of the cold in my lungs. It seemed like they were going to come out.

"We had snow on the field before a game with Florida in Lexington, and they burned it off, with gasoline I think. Anyway, it made a heckuva odor when you hit the ground. I also remember running sprints after a game...for conditioning. That would seem a little strange now."

McClendon earned varsity letters in 1949 and 1950 as a defensive end. One of his better games was the 1951 Sugar Bowl, when UK snapped a 31-game Oklahoma winning streak. In his book, Bryant said:

"Early in the game Charley McClendon came off the field with the side of his face torn off. When I turned to call the trainer and looked around he was already going back on the field with the defense. His tackling caused three fumbles that day."

"Billy Vessels was running (with the ball) and I thought I had him," McClendon recalled, "but he had more speed than I thought. He got by me, and his feet hit me in the eye; however, I managed to knock him out of bounds after he got a pretty good gainer. Thank goodness there was a penalty on the play.

"They put cotton on the wound and froze it with whatever they used in those days. I remember so vividly praying, 'Don't let that thing fall down on my eye.'

"Now that I look back on it, Kentucky didn't run all those players off when Coach Bryant first went there. They sorta disqualified themselves. I don't know how it happened that I made it. Maybe I played in fear of not excelling, which is the way I coach...with a fear of losing. I realized if I didn't make it, I'd probably be digging the longest ditch in Arkansas."

A Minority Opinion

A lone dissenter among all those former players who praised Paul Bryant for the job he did at the University of Kentucky is Don "Dopey" Phelps who, in January, 1975, felt that 27 years was too long to hold a grudge.

"It's about time he got off my back," said Phelps, who was probably the best running back to play under Bryant at UK. "There are some things he said about me in his book that just aren't true."

Phelps particularly resented Bryant saying that he had a "problem" remembering plays and that Dan Chandler told his father, A. B. "Happy" Chandler, that after having a class with Phelps, he could understand why people called him Dopey.

"Dan Chandler was six or seven years behind me," Phelps said. "He graduated from UK in 1955 or 1956. I was in Owensboro, Kentucky, at the time. Bryant also said the only problem I had on the field was remembering the plays. Any player is subject to missing an assignment."

At the time of the interview Phelps was in the Margaret I. King Library on the UK campus, checking microfilms of local newspapers to determine whether or not he set national records in punt and kickoff returns in 1946.

"I got my nickname when I was in the ninth grade, and the 'Snow White and the Seven Dwarfs' movie was out," he said. "I was always kinda shy and tagging along behind. When I came out of the dressing room one day, wearing that old football gear and that old leather helmet with the ear flaps out, one of the guys saw me tagging along and said, 'C'mon, Little Dopey.'

"I always had speed, but I didn't know how to use it. Danville was a rough, tough town, and I was rough with it. Fear didn't enter into it. With my speed, I was a hard-running back. Schools all over the country were after me.

"Kentucky was down. Not that they didn't have the material. They just had a lot of conflicts. I wanted to play with a team that was winning. I really chose Tennessee for the simple reason that they played the single wing, which I played in high school. General Neyland was a good friend. Before entering the service, I visited Tennessee and practiced with them in the summer.

"When I got out of service, my father was ill with a stroke. He was a great football fan of mine, and he wanted me to go where he could watch me practice and play. I didn't know Bear Bryant. When I went to see him, he told me he would get my father a box at the games, and he could watch me practice.

"The first day we met Bryant on the playing field, we had a two-hour scrimmage, and he ran off 48 players. He made a list and called out mostly all the vets and lined them up against all the 18-year-olds. We made up the plays in the huddle. The old vets didn't want to hurt the kids.

"'That's what's wrong with you s.o.b.'s,' he said. 'You can't beat your way out of a paper bag. I want you to start hitting people.' He ran a lot of kids off. He was just a rough, tough, mean individual.

"Most of us vets had played semipro ball, so to speak, in the service and were used to being kicked around and could take more than the younger players. I thought we had a pretty good team that year. With Ermal Allen, we would have had a better record. We had the material, but I guess it took Bear Bryant to get it out of us.

"We had a better record in 1947. The best game I ever played was against Georgia that year. They were a top contender in the country. I mean they had Johnny Rausch and some other fine players. They were loaded. We kicked off and held them to three downs. I caught their first punt and returned it 60 yards for a touchdown. I ended up making a couple touchdowns, intercepting a pass, and setting up a few other guys. That, in my opinion, was the start of UK in the Southeastern Conference. It was the first time we had beaten any of the 'Big Three'—Alabama, Georgia, Tennessee—and from that time on UK had found its place in the conference."

Dopey Phelps led the team in rushing (80 carries for 416 yards), kickoff returns (nine for 163), punt returns (20 for 224), and scoring (30). He completed four passes in four attempts, caught five passes for 89 yards, and averaged 44.1 yards on seven punts. He put together a 15-yard run, a 15-yard pass, and a one-yard plunge for a UK touchdown in a 7-6 victory over Michigan State.

Prior to the 1948 season Bryant told Larry Boeck of the *Courier-Journal,* "Halfback Don Phelps is our biggest 'if.' He undoubtedly could contribute more to the cause than anyone else—unless it were Blanda. If Don reaches top physical condition, learns the offense adequately, learns to block, to play defense and to fake, and takes more pride in carrying out assignments when he isn't running the ball, he could become as fine a back as the South has ever seen. I have been remembering Phelps in my prayers for the last two and one-half years and this is the year we could use the bounty from heaven."

Phelps got off to a spectacular start that season, taking a lateral from Blanda and passing to Jones in the end zone as UK beat Xavier, 48-7. He also intercepted a pass and returned it 29 yards. He gained 65 yards in 14 carries in a loss to Ole Miss, gained 54 yards in seven carries in a 35-12 loss to Georgia, and slipped to only 20 yards in 10 carries in a 26-7 loss to Vanderbilt.

"That is the year in question with me and Bryant," Phelps said. "Before the fifth game, with Marquette in Milwaukee, he called me into his office and said I wasn't playing the type of game I was capable of playing and that he guessed I had too many outside interests. I admitted I wasn't in shape, but my family came first. My two-year-old baby was ill at the time and keeping me up nights. He said he would leave me home to practice with the freshman squad, and the way he put it didn't hit me right. I didn't practice with the freshmen, and he dismissed me from the squad after returning from Wisconsin. I continued to go to school because Blanton Collier of the Browns wanted me to.

"I rejoined the team in 1949, after Bear had considered me as a student not on scholarship. He said I would have to earn the right, and it would be tough because I would be under a lot of pressure. He put me on both offense and defense in intra-

Don "Dopey" Phelps.

Bear Bryant bats as Dopey Phelps catches during summer outing in 1949.

squad games and called me up to the 'B' squad just before the first game and said the stats showed I was ready to play on the first team."

Wildcat statistics for that year credit Phelps with 118 carries for 443 yards. He completed his only pass attempt for a 15-yard touchdown, caught seven passes for 105 yards and two touchdowns. He also punted 14 times for 580 yards. He led the team in kickoff returns with seven for 231 yards, and punt returns, with 24 for 201 yards, and in scoring (43 points).

"In some respects, I felt I did not get to show my abilities," he said. "I was an outside man so to speak, but I ran 24 times around end in 1949, about 15 times off tackle, and 80 times in the middle of the line. The rest of the time I was used as a decoy."

Phelps played three years with the Browns and then returned to Kentucky, where he pursued a career in private business before entering employment with the state government.

"Sweet Kentucky Babe"

There never was a Kentucky football team like the 1950 one, and there never was a UK football player quite like Babe Parilli.

The team represented four years of hard and dedicated labor by Bryant and his staff, the realization of the five-year goal he set for himself when he accepted the UK job in 1946.

Parilli was the "accident" that made it all possible.

Parilli was the son of Italian immigrant parents. The six-foot-two, 190-pound football player came to Lexington in the spring of 1948, unsolicited and unknown, and hung around while Skip Doyle, his Rochester, Pennsylvania, high school backfield teammate, tried out for Bryant.

Doyle already had made up his mind to attend Ohio State, but he agreed to look the UK situation over if he could bring Parilli with him.

"The other guy was a big shot," quarterback-coach Ermal Allen recalled. "While Bryant watched him, he told me, 'You go watch John Doe.' A short while later I returned and told him, 'That John Doe can really pass and punt.'"

"Where did you see him punt?"

"Over there."

"Why, that's Babe Parilli," Bryant said. "He just came along for the ride."

"On that first visit, I didn't even get to talk to 'The Bear,'" Parilli would recall in the spring of 1975. "They talked to Skippy, and when they got through, we went back to Pennsylvania. A couple of months later Coach Bryant came up and said he wanted me to come down and visit the campus. I told him I had already been down there. He said, 'Well, why don't you come down again?' So I did, and they worked me out with some of the varsity people. When I got through, they decided that I could probably play quarterback for them.

"After I played in an all-star game in Pennsylvania, several colleges were after me, but I really wanted to go to Kentucky all along. Other fellows from around the valley had gone there, boys three or four years ahead of me in high school. They were my heroes; they liked it there. And when you go to a new school and new surroundings, it's nice to know there's somebody from home."

Parilli's transition from single-wing fullback to T-quarterback began the moment he arrived back in Lexington. "We worked him all summer long," Allen said. "There was a strategy session in the morning and a workout on the field every afternoon. In addition, he practiced each night before a mirror, handling the ball in the up-back position, and he did it so much that he became a superb ball handler and was able to do a lot of faking. He also had that fine ability to spot a receiver and get the ball to him."

Zipp Newman of the *Birmingham News* said, "Parilli could take an elephant out on the field and, told that it was a football, hide it." Walter Stewart of the *Memphis Commercial-Appeal* said, "He handled the leather with the baffling skill of a trans-Atlantic card shark, and can dot a receiver's eye (right or left as the occasion demands) at 80 yards."

In his book, Bryant called Parilli the best fake-and-throw passer he had ever seen, one so quick and strong with his hands that he could pump three times before he threw. "We adjusted to Babe, not him to us," he said. "We built around him." He visited Parilli's room every night and had him in his office every day to play a game where they were quarterbacks and another quarterback would referee and tell them how much they gained or lost on a given play against a given defense.

Bob Hardy, an understudy to Parilli, said, "Those daily sessions in Bryant's office placed us under so much pressure to call the right plays for downs and distance, to know the ability of their backs, and—from the scouting reports—to know what defense the opposing team would be in, that it was a pleasure to be in a game and not in a 9 x 12 room with Bryant."

Allen said that when Parilli stepped onto the playing field as a sophomore, he was ready. "I'm glad he felt that way," Parilli said in 1975. "I think one thing Bryant teaches you is the fact that you really don't ever think you're good enough or ready for a game. I don't think he'd ever let you get overconfident."

He had a fine supporting cast that first year (1949). The offense included ends Zaranka, Bruno, and Odlivak, and backs Phelps, Boller, Clark, Hamilton, Brooks, Howe, Jamerson, Martin, Lawson, Leskovar, Genito, and Webb. The best man on defense was Bob Gain, a six-foot-three, 230-pound tackle from Weirton, West Virginia, who was described by Allen as a person who would "hit his mother" if she were on the other side of the line. His supporting cast included such familiar names as Claiborne, Pope, Mackenzie, Moseley, Wannamaker, Donaldson, James, Ignarski, McDermott, Yowarsky, Fuller, Bradshaw, McClendon, Fucci, and Bentley.

While the defense tackled and intercepted its way to a No. 1 ranking nationally, Parilli had a banner year. In the opening game, against Mississippi Southern, he completed 12 of 16 passes for 166 yards and two touchdowns. Kentucky won, 71-7. Against LSU he threw a 33-yard scoring pass to Phelps the first time he got the ball, and he started a 47-0 romp over favored Ole Miss with a 29-yard strike to Howe. Parilli went on to throw a four-yard strike to Fucci in a 25-0 victory over Georgia; score two touchdowns in the first quarter of a 44-0 victory over The Citadel; throw a 26-yard completion to Fucci for the only UK score in a 20-7 loss to SMU; and spark two third quarter touchdown drives to beat tough Cincinnati, 14-7.

Tennessee intercepted four of his passes and beat UK, 6-0, in Lexington. However, the Wildcats rebounded with a 21-6 victory over a strong Miami team and accepted an invitation to the Orange Bowl, their first major postseason classic. In the game Parilli hit Emery Clark with a 52-yard touchdown pass, but UK lost, 21-13, to Santa Clara. They finished the 1949 season with a 9-3 record.

The defense that year earned its top ranking by allowing 153.9 yards per game and only 53 points in 11 games (averaging 4.8 per game). It set national records in yards returned on intercepted passes for a season and for a game. Jerry Claiborne set a school record of nine interceptions. Gain and Ulinski were accorded All-Conference honors.

Babe Parilli.

The best lineman in the nation in 1950 was the big, agile Gain. He was one of the few persons who played both offense and defense and was equally adept at both. He had lettered in 1947, drawn praise from many sources in 1948, and was mentioned on every all-star team selected in 1949. Elected co-captain with Jamerson in 1950, he was a one-man wrecking crew. He blocked a North Texas punt in the opening game, picked up the ball on the 30, and returned to the 19, to set up a touchdown plunge by Parilli. Six games later he pulled a similar feat—blocking an attempted quick-kick by Georgia Tech and recovering the ball on the Tech 13 to set up a score.

While the defense was superb, Parilli was nothing short of sensational. Against North Texas State he completed four of 11 passes for 40 yards and scored from the one. Some of his lateral flings sped off the mark, but others were real bull's-eyes which had too much oomph for the receivers. After that game, a 25-0 victory for UK, Gain and Jamerson led the squad in wind sprints as amazed fans filed out of the stadium.

Bob Fry, a UK tackle in that game, was on a scouting mission for a pro team 23 years later when he met a former North Texas State player who also was in the game. "He said what really irked them was the fact that we started running 100-yard dashes and sprints before they left the field," Fry said. "We ran 11 of those. Looking back, they had a pretty good team. About five of those guys played pro football."

Parilli received a groin injury in the North Texas State game and spent the early part of the week in the infirmary. "Bryant came to me with the whole offense against LSU," he recalled in 1975. "He threw them out on the bed and said, 'Learn them.' I couldn't walk, I couldn't move, but that Saturday night I was out there playing. This guy was something else. He believed you could do anything you wanted to. He was a great motivator. He got you up for a game better than anyone I know.

"Going into that game, he told me, 'Get in there and start throwing, and throw until I tell you to quit.' The first nine plays were passes, and 16 of the first 18 plays were passes. I threw 16 times in the first quarter alone. Before the game Pat James had told the offensive linemen he would personally kill them if they let anyone lay a hand on me, and nobody did."

Parilli completed seven of 20 passes for 48 yards and threw one interception in that game. Late in the first half, linebacker

Harold Woodell intercepted an LSU pass. Leskovar carried a delayed handoff from Parilli to the one foot line and then scored on the next play. In the second half the Tigers were stopped on the one foot line. Parilli scored the second and final touchdown on a one-yard sneak. The final score was 14-0.

With the groin injury healed, he marched the Wildcats 84 yards for a score on the opening kickoff and then sneaked over from the one after completing two long passes to Bruno in a 27-0 blanking of Ole Miss. He threw four touchdown passes and scored on a 38-yard run against Dayton before sitting out the entire second half. The Flyers were a 40-0 victim, marking the fourth consecutive shutout for the Wildcats.

Cincinnati scored a touchdown and an extra point but was swamped, 41-7, as Parilli threw five touchdown passes to tie a conference record set earlier that year by Billy Wade of Vanderbilt. He hit 18 of 29 passes for an SEC record 338 yards in that game. Bruno caught three of the scoring tosses.

In a 34-7 victory over Villanova, Parilli hit nine of 19 for 161 yards and a touchdown, but the visitors ended his string of completions without an interception at 50. He completed 12 of 18 for 102 yards and two touchdowns in a 28-14 win over Georgia Tech; hit eight of 14 for 119 yards and two touchdowns against Florida in a snowstorm in Lexington; and connected on 13 of 21 for 232 yards and three touchdowns in a 48-21 win against a Mississippi State defense ranked No. 1 nationally.

Dave Bloom said, "Kentucky's incomparable Babe Parilli gave Mississippi State a three minute, 35 second football lesson...that the Maroons and 28,000 gasping spectators will never forget...For those scant 215 seconds, this master quarterback legerdemain conducted the Bowl-bound UK to three touchdowns and the momentum carried them to another."

In an 83-0 romp over North Dakota, Parilli left the game after three minutes had expired in the second half, having to his credit 15 completions in 20 attempts, for 198 yards and five touchdowns. He hit 14 of 31 passes for 150 yards against Tennessee but could not punch the ball over, and hopes for a national championship were shattered on that frigid afternoon in Knoxville.

Parilli ended that 1950 season with a fine performance in the Sugar Bowl, completing nine of 12 passes for 105 yards and a touchdown in a monumental 13-7 upset of national champion

Oklahoma. The Wildcats finished with an 11-1 record and their first and, up to 1975, only SEC championship. Parilli set or tied the following regular season marks:

A new all-time national collegiate record for most touchdown passes in one season (23), to eclipse by one the mark set by Nevada's Stan Heath in 1948.

A new SEC record for yards gained by passing in one game (338 against Cincinnati) and in one season (1,627).

A new SEC record for touchdown accountability in one season (28)—23 passing and five rushing.

Twice tied the SEC record for most touchdown passes in single game (5), against Cincinnati and North Dakota.

During the regular season he completed 114 of 203 passes for a percentage of 56.1, just one percentage point off the national record set by Mississippi's Charley Conerly in 1947. Including the Sugar Bowl, he completed 123 of 215 tosses for a net gain of 1,732 yards and 24 touchdowns. He was intercepted 12 times.

Champion passer of the SEC for the second straight season, he ranked as the nation's fourth leading passer and was sixth in the country in total individual offensive gain. He was named by an Associated Press poll as the conference's best passer and most valuable player, an honor he also received from the *Nashville Banner* and the Birmingham and Atlanta Touchdown clubs.

"He is the finest back I've ever coached or seen," Bryant said at the end of that season.

While Parilli was setting records and garnering All-American honors, his teammates also were sharing in the glory. Gain was presented the Outland Trophy as the nation's outstanding lineman, Yowarsky was named the most valuable player in the Sugar Bowl, and Bruno shared the SEC record of 10 touchdown receptions with Al Lary of Alabama. Gain's 10 extra points against North Dakota tied a conference record set in 1946, while UK's 11 total extra points from placement set a new one-game record. The Wildcats also set conference records in scoring passes, first downs, and yardage allowed in punt runbacks. They tied a record of 27 first downs in a single game set by Tulane in 1937.

Without Parilli, Kentucky would have been a mediocre team in 1951. The line was good but far from great on offense;

Bear Bryant is flanked by All-Americans Babe Parilli (left) and Bob Gain.

there were no outstanding running backs (Leskovar was plagued by injuries) to vary the attack and divide enemy attention with the Wildcat pass patterns. Everybody knew that Kentucky had to pass to win, and the Wildcats passed. In the opening game, a 72-13 win over Tennessee Tech, Parilli threw and completed passes on the first three plays from scrimmage for a 65-yard touchdown jaunt. He completed a total of 11 of 16 before retiring early in the first half with three touchdowns to his credit.

Against Texas at Austin, Parilli almost won the game in the final hectic two minutes. He tossed the ball from a short punt formation to Jim Proffitt, who had the ball in his arms in the end zone but coughed it up when hit by a Texan.

The Longhorns got a touchdown earlier in the game, when Parilli faded back, raised his arm to pass, but was hit from behind and fumbled on the 28. The Wildcats scored in the third quarter but lost, 7-6, as holder Herbie Hunt could not get the ball on the kicking tee for the extra point.

The Wildcats scored first against Mississippi on a field goal by Harry Jones but lost, 21-17, on two Ole Miss touchdowns set up by UK fumbles. After undefeated Georgia Tech won, 13-7, in Lexington, state police formed a cordon to protect the officials. They had penalized UK 138½ yards while calling only one offside and three delay-of-game penalties on Tech. The outcome of the game had hinged on a fourth down gamble on the UK 33 early in the final quarter. The Wildcats had gone almost nine yards in three tries but missed the crucial first down as Harry Jones was nabbed behind the line. Tech then drove for a score. Bryant said he would do the same thing over again if the opportunity presented itself.

A game with Mississippi State was 10 minutes old when Bob Fry blocked a punt, scooped up the ball and ran to the State three, setting up the first of three UK touchdowns in a 27-0 victory. The defense of undefeated Villanova, conqueror of Army, Penn, and Alabama, made the mistake of boasting how it was going to stop Parilli; he passed for three touchdowns, two of them to Meilinger, for a 35-13 victory. He threw two touchdown passes in a 14-6 victory over Florida and three each in shut-out victories over Miami and Tulane.

Once in the third quarter against Miami he faked to three men before throwing, and he performed so smoothly on each fake that the Hurricane defense was completely baffled. He missed only two tosses against Tulane, throwing one over the end zone and completing the other out of bounds. Most incompletions that he threw were dropped or jarred out of the receivers' hands. In a 47-13 conquest of George Washington, he threw touchdown passes to Meilinger, Fillion, and Max Mason.

He hit 15 of 25 passes against Tennessee for 179 yards. However, the No. 1-ranked Vols won, 28-0, to hand Bryant his worst defeat. Thus, the 1951 season ended with a 7-4 record. Kentucky went on to the Cotton Bowl, where Parilli bowed out with two touchdown passes in a 20-7 victory over Texas Christian University. He was named the game's most valuable player.

"We had played hard football in losing to Tech—and to Ole Miss and Texas—but costly errors here and there hurt us," he told Larry Boeck of the *Courier-Journal*. "We were a bunch of glum guys in the dressing room after we had lost to Tech. Coach Bryant came in and we had a good bawling-out coming to us.

"'Don't feel too badly about it,' Bryant said. 'You played a good, hard game against a helluva fine team. You're going to have your backs against the wall many times in the years ahead, so you might as well get used to it.'

"We were criticized some by fans and others after that third whipping in a row. But Bryant, on his television show the next day, said: 'It's my team now. Before, when we were winning, it was everybody else's team. Well, now it's my team, and I'm proud to have it.'

"That bucked us up, and we went on to get a Cotton Bowl invitation and beat Texas Christian in that game. I don't think we had a great team, but I think it was one that was loaded with courage, the desire to play the game as well as it could, and competitiveness.

"All this, I've been told, is part of good character, and Bryant certainly did a lot to instill that in us."

In 1952 Parilli played for the Green Bay Packers. He later played for the Browns, Patriots, and Jets.

Time Out : Steve Meilinger

The best player on the Kentucky football team after Babe Parilli completed his eligibility in 1952 was Steve "Horse" Meilinger of Bethlehem, Pennsylvania. He was the younger brother in a family of modest means, and he helped out in the fields at an early age and had little time for sports.

Meilinger was big for his age and allegedly was spotted accidently one day by Bethlehem High School coach John Butler. Butler passed a field in which the youngster was plowing and inquired as to the whereabouts of another boy. As the legend goes, Meilinger lifted the plow to point the direction, causing Butler to forget all about the other boy.

"That was the story Coach Butler always told the press," Meilinger, now a deputy U. S. Marshal in Lexington, said with a smile in the winter of 1974, "and I'm not one to spoil a good story. But it really was just a little cultivator, not a big plow."

As far back as Meilinger can remember, he started playing organized football, but he gave up his prep career temporarily when he quit junior high school, got a job, and started playing in a sandlot league.

"Our high school coaches used to referee those semipro games, and I was playing when one of Butler's assistants spotted me," Meilinger said. "The guys I was playing with and against represented a multitude of ages—right up to 40 years—and I was 14 or 15, over six-feet, and weighed about 197 pounds.

"I was working at a landscaping nursery, and Butler came by to see me one day when I was taking care of a mule. He began to rib me about it. My mother and daddy had come over here from Europe, and they believed him when he said the school board would fine them if I didn't go back to school. My mother made me go back."

Meilinger was captain of the 1948 All-Pennsylvania team. In later years Butler would often remind him, "You'd probably still be back there in that nursery leaning up against that old jackass if I hadn't come and got you."

"I enrolled my senior year at Fork Union Military Academy in Virginia and was named to the All-Virginia team," Meilinger said. "Coach Carney Laslie came up to see me and brought along the Orange Bowl film. My lifetime dream was to be an All-American and go to a bowl game. I wanted to go to the University of Pennsylvania, but it was only 50 miles away, and the thought kept running through my mind that I would be home every other weekend and not get much done.

"Laslie persuaded me to come to Kentucky by pointing out that most of the UK ends would be seniors my freshman year, and I would get to start as a sophomore. What impressed me most was that I had read a lot about Babe Parilli. There was no doubt in my mind that I would be good enough to make the starting team, which meant that I would get to play one year with Parilli, and that would help me learn a lot about pass catching and help me when I hit the pros. I had my eye on the pros even then.

"When I visited UK spring practice in 1950, I met Bryant and Ermal Allen for the first time. Bob Gain and Allen Hamilton took me around and introduced me to people. I was impressed with the coaches, the system, and the townspeople, who were very friendly. That enticed me to come to UK."

As a six-foot-two sophomore end in 1951, Meilinger played exclusively on offense, ranking third in the conference with 38 pass receptions for 515 yards (not counting three receptions for 61 yards in the Cotton Bowl). His eight touchdown receptions surpassed other conference receivers, ranking him 12th among the nation's receivers. He was named to the All-Conference team and received much preseason publicity as an All-American candidate.

"I really didn't find myself until the Villanova game that year," he said. "We had won our opening game against Tennessee Tech, 72-13, but I only caught three passes. We then lost to Texas, Mississippi, and Georgia Tech, before beating Mississippi State. Villanova came to Lexington with a perfect record, and we beat them, 35-13. I caught four passes for 108 yards and

Steve Meilinger.

scored touchdowns on catches of 50, 24, and 18 yards.

"I caught two touchdown passes in the Miami and Tulane games and one against George Washington. We were 7-3 when we played Tennessee that year in Lexington, and I remember the game real well because Coach Bryant put in a new type offense where I would come into the backfield, more or less on every play, as a man in motion and was used mostly as a blocking back. After I'd go back, Babe would pitch the ball to someone, and I would be the leading blocker. I caught one pass for 16 yards. We lost, 28-0.

"The Cotton Bowl was the realization of my childhood dreams. I didn't score a touchdown, but I set up two scores for us, being tackled once on the one and once on the four after catching passes. We beat TCU, 20-7."

Jimmy Breslin wrote in *Sport Magazine* that Meilinger "has the knack of throwing his hands up at the last possible moment to pull in a pass. And instead of trying to grab the ball while on the run, Meilinger will stop dead and leap into the air, trying to grab the pigskin at the highest possible point. You don't make many interceptions when a boy as big as Meilinger begins scrapping for the ball."

Meilinger explained, "I didn't wait for the ball to come to me—I got up and got it. And I guess I could do that pretty good because I was bigger than most of the defensive men covering me. In that 1951 game against Villanova I scored two touchdowns, not because I outran the guy, but because I outjumped him."

With Parilli gone, Bryant changed to the split-T formation in 1952, visiting the University of Oklahoma that spring to study the offense and filming five spring games in Lexington in order to study the moves of each player over and over in an attempt to get the best out of rather limited talent. Sharing the quarterback position early in the season were Harold Gruner, a halfback on the 1951 team, and Harry Jones. Dick Shatto started the fourth game after Gruner was dismissed from the squad.

In the opening game against Villanova, Meilinger played left end on offense, but the absence of a passer of Parilli's caliber to throw to him soon became obvious. Meilinger carried the ball one time, picking up a bad center snap on a punt attempt and running 13 yards through the big Villanova forward wall. The Kentuckians threw only two weak passes the first 30 minutes and had a meager seven attempts, with one completion for eight yards. They scored on a 73-yard run by Harry Jones but ended up losing, 25-6. It was the first loss of an opening game in Lexington since 1896.

"I guess my major contribution in that game was in the punting department," Meilinger said. "After Babe left, it seemed everybody was on an even keel. We had no superstars, and we didn't have a punter. I used to go out and fool around with the kickers in my sophomore year. Bryant said he didn't like my style but that I could probably kick the ball with my knee and get 35 yards out of it. I kicked off that year, too, but I don't think I did too good. I don't remember ever getting it inside the 20."

Meilinger gave a fine two-way performance against Ole Miss, playing end, defensive halfback, and safety. In addition, he occasionally was assigned to run with the ball on an end-around or to fade back and pass after faking a run. He climaxed his efforts with a catch of a perfect 24-yard pass from Larry Jones in the final period and ran 40 more yards for a touchdown. Herbie Hunt picked up a bad snap from center and placed it perfectly as Jones kicked the point to tie the score, 13-13.

In a 10-7 victory over Texas A&M at College Station, Meilinger kept the Wildcats out of trouble repeatedly with booming punts into enemy territory. He played a good game at safety and caught passes in the clutch for valuable yardage.

He caught nine-yard passes for Kentucky's only scores in two games: a 34-7 loss to Louisiana State and a 27-14 loss to Mississippi State. He performed with equal brilliance at defensive safety and offensive end for almost 60 minutes in a bitterly fought, 14-6 victory over Cincinnati. He strengthened Kentucky's pass defense, backing up the line nobly when the Wildcats twice stopped the Bearcats within the shadow of the goal line. In one of the finer plays of the season he made a desperate, leaping bid for a long, high pass from the UK 26, caught the ball, hipped off one defender, and outraced two pursuing defenders on a 77-yard touchdown run.

"That was the year we didn't have a quarterback," Meilinger said. "In order to run the split-T, you have to have a quarterback who can run the ball. Coach Bryant said his quarterbacks were not big enough or fast enough.

"On Monday after the Cincinnati game he and I ran

around the field twice, before practice, with him teaching me to flip the ball with my wrist after faking to an imaginary halfback.

"'This is your start for the week,' he said, and that was how I got the word that I was moved to quarterback. It was quite an adjustment but not near as bad as it sounds. If you played end or halfback for Bryant, you had to know the assignment of everybody in the backfield.

"I practiced the position four days, and when we got to Miami, we worked out in a public park where there were a lot of spectators. Bryant didn't want the word to leak out, so I ran at end. Joe Koch said some of the defensive players didn't know about the switch. And when we ran the first play after the kick-off, Miami immediately called time out."

Awkwardly effective, Meilinger caved in Miami's ninth-ranked defense, shattering the Hurricanes on quarterback-keep plays, smashing like a fullback from the up close position, and going back to his regular end slot to catch a nine-yard pass for a touchdown. He was "Player of the Week" in the South. "Quarterbacking was tough," he recalled. "I never really did learn how to play that position. I wasn't fancy enough. That ball handling killed me. I didn't carry out a fake. I just handed the guy the ball and said to myself, 'good luck.' I was like a cow on ice, as Bryant used to say, but I got the job done."

Luther Evans of the *Miami Herald* reported, "To say that Meilinger was anything but great in his debut as a field general would be slander. He directed the team with unbelievable skill, despite only two days of practice at the position, scored two touchdowns, rushed for 82 yards, and set up a touchdown with a 49-yard pass to the one-yard line."

For the second week in a row he set the pace for an upset victory as the Wildcats humbled Tulane, 27-6. He had a hand in three Wildcat touchdowns, passing for one, running for the

Steve Meilinger, versatile workhorse in the University of Kentucky football stable, posed with his animal-world namesake, "Meilinger," at Keeneland race track in Lexington. A high tribute in this horse-conscious Bluegrass, the highly regarded, two-year-old thoroughbred colt was named after the Kentucky football star by owner-breeder S. S. Gano of Georgetown, Kentucky.

other two, and putting on one of the greatest one-man shows ever seen on Stoll Field. "That was the game I ran a quarterback sneak for 41 yards and a touchdown," he said. At the end of the season the Tulane team voted him the honor of outstanding opponent, an accolade usually reserved for an entire team. In that game he accounted for 183 of UK's 481 yards, averaging 10.5 yards per try on 10 rushing attempts and adding 78 yards and a touchdown by passing.

He sat on the sidelines with an ankle injury as the Wildcats defeated Clemson, 27-14. This was the only game he missed in his football career, and he wept openly before the game. Against Tennessee he rallied the Wildcats to two touchdowns in the final minutes of play for a 14-14 tie. In addition to expert generalship, he shifted to an end on several occasions and was a superb decoy. He also ran with devastating power and caught a pass to set the stage for one of the UK touchdowns.

"That was a thrill," he said. "We had gone three years without scoring on Tennessee. We scored 14 points in the last five minutes, with the second one coming on a pass from Hunt to Proffitt with 20 seconds on the clock after we had recovered an onside kick."

Alternating freely between quarterback and halfback against Florida, he gained 110 yards in 17 carries, but his heroics were in vain. The Wildcats lost, 27-0, to end the season with a record of 5-4-2.

"At the time, Bryant let the players decide whether they wanted to go to a bowl," Meilinger said. "We had an offer to play in the Gator Bowl that year, and he called a meeting and said he was going to leave the room and let us vote. We voted not to go. Everybody thought he was just trying to get in another spring practice. Besides, we didn't think the Gator Bowl was much. When he returned and heard the verdict, I've never seen him so mad. He almost tore the door down. As he left, he turned and said, 'All right, boys. Just remember, we've got spring practice coming up, and I'll remember this.' But everything was soon forgotten.

"The next season I couldn't understand why we didn't get a bowl bid. We lost our first two games, beat Florida, tied LSU, and won the rest.

"I remember most the 6-6 tie with LSU. There were just a few seconds left, and we had tied the score. We tried to get Bryant to go for a field goal, but for some reason we didn't kick. He put me in at quarterback for three plays. We tried to run the quarterback sneak from the one and failed the first two times. We called time out and asked him again to try for a field goal. 'No, run the quarterback sneak again,' he said. I fumbled the ball, and they recovered on the two or three yard line. I'll never understand why he did that."

In a newsletter distributed midway of that season, Bryant said he felt he lost the game by not playing the percentages. "The percentage play was, of course, to attempt a field goal, on fourth down on the one-yard line," he said. "I considered it but remembering that we had only kicked two out of seven points, I had more confidence in our ability to run it over than our kicking. This proved to be a mistake.

"You probably saw by the press where I did not know the final score. This is true as I thought we had lost, 7-6; however, the press report saying that I had chewed the boys out and later apologized was ridiculous. I learned at the Orange Bowl to never say anything to a team immediately following the game if we lost. I did go up to where the kids were eating and told them and we had a good laugh over that."

Kentucky closed out the season with a 27-21 win over Tennessee. Meilinger said, "It was a controversial game where they said Bob Hardy's knee hit the ground before he pitched out to Ralph Paolone for a 22-yard touchdown. Had we received a bowl bid that year, I think we would have gone."

Meilinger realized his two childhood ambitions at UK, making All-America in 1952 and 1953 and playing in the Cotton Bowl. He then played professionally with the Washington Redskins and Green Bay Packers. In 1974 he joined the Wildcat Football Network as "color" announcer.

Bear Goes Bowl-ing

The University of Kentucky's first appearance on the major bowl scene was in 1950, when the Wildcats lost to Santa Clara, 21-13, in the Orange Bowl. They upset national champion Oklahoma, 13-7, in the 1951 Sugar Bowl and defeated Texas Christian University, 20-7, in the 1952 Cotton Bowl.

They defeated Villanova, 24-14, in the first and only Great Lakes Bowl in 1947, but that was a box office disaster which attracted only 15,000 fans to Cleveland Stadium and could hardly be classified as a major event.

Dr. Emery Clark of Carlisle, Kentucky, who participated in the three major bowl games, reminisced about those times during a brief stopover in Lexington in February, 1975, while en route to Louisville with his son's high school basketball team.

"I was always hard-nosed," the former farm boy said. "I didn't think you could work too hard, but I'm convinced that's what beat us in the Orange Bowl.

"It was sleeting and snowing when we left Lexington for Cocoa Beach, where we were to train for the game. We walked off the plane dressed in overcoats and heavy clothing, and it was hot as it could be. I remember Bryant saying to the team manager, 'We're going straight to the practice field.' We practiced on a field where a baseball team had its spring practice. Everybody put on shoes and jocks and waited for him to come in the dugout before putting on shorts. But when he came in and said, 'We'll be on the field boys in two minutes,' we knew he meant pads.

"We practiced more than two hours, and about 13 guys at one time had passed out from the heat. He [Bryant] asked

Smokey Harper, the trainer, 'Can't you keep them off the field?' We had moved all around that big field to avoid the bodies, and there was no place to practice where somebody wasn't laying down.

"We'd leave the hotel at 9:30 a.m., ride the bus to the field, and practice until noon. On the way back we'd stop at an orange stand, and we'd drink as much pure orange juice as we could while lying in the shade of the building. We'd get back to the motel and try to get a little rest, but by the time you laid down, it was time to get up and eat. We'd have 'skull' practice at 1:30, spend about one hour in the room, and practice from 2:30 p.m. to 5:00 p.m. as hard as we could. We went in full pads morning and afternoon. We'd go back to the motel at 5:30 p.m., eat, and then have another skull practice at 7:30 p.m. or 8:00 p.m. After that you were free, but there was nothing to do—which, of course, was the way they wanted it. I don't remember anything about Cocoa except walking out on one of those fishing piers. Smokey warned them we were exhausted, but it didn't do any good."

While the Wildcats toiled in the sun and sand, Coach Len Casanova and his Broncos had a leisurely trip from California, stopping overnight two or three times along the way to rest and admire the scenery. Casanova also heeded the advice of the father of his backfield coach. Jack Roche's father was a greyhound dog trainer who said you could not work greyhounds hard in Miami and expect a good showing out of them, and that human beings were very much the same way.

Kentucky was leading, 7-0, with possession on the Santa Clara two yard line near the end of the first half, when Parilli called two rush plays. But time ran out with the Wildcats still a yard short of the goal. "I should have sent in a pass play," Bryant said in his book. "If it failed, the clock was killed. Then we could have tried a field goal. Instead, I did nothing. I think it cost us the ball game."

Santa Clara scored twice in the third quarter and again in the final period. The tired Kentuckians finally managed a score on a 52-yard Parilli-to-Clark pass. "I remember going deep and throwing a body block at the halfback," Clark said. "He jumped over me, and I rolled over and came up running. I was wide open, and Babe just lofted the ball to me. At half time was the first time I heard Bryant's expression that his backs ran like they had pianos on their backs. He usually ranted and raved when we lost, but after that game he wasn't mad. He said, 'Boys, hold your heads up. It's my fault. I just worked you too hard.'"

En route to the Sugar Bowl the following year, Bryant put his squad through a week of workouts in Mobile, gave them a short layoff, and then another week of drills in Baton Rouge. "We practiced only an hour and a half in shorts each morning and not near so long in pads in the afternoon," Clark said. "Bryant told us he had learned something at Cocoa."

Carney Laslie said he had never seen a game unveil so much the way a coach planned it. To counteract Oklahoma's split-T, Bryant employed four tackles on defense in one pattern, and he succeeded in upsetting the precision of the Sooner assaults centered around quarterback Claude Arnold.

The key Wildcat player in that defense was Walt Yowarsky, a native of Cleveland, Ohio, who reputedly was dressed in a gray, pegged-leg, "zoot" suit when he arrived at the UK football camp in 1947 and brazenly asked, "Where's 'The Bear'?" He then walked up to Bryant and said, "Paul, my name's Walt Yowarsky."

Bryant assigned Bill McCubbin to the job of running him off. Each day Bryant, who could not pronounce Yowarsky's name, would ask, "Is that guy 'Smitty' still around?"

Before the Alabama game Yowarsky was given a red jersey with All-American Harry Gilmer's number on it and was made to carry the ball all afternoon. During those trying days, he kept telling McCubbin, "Coach, you might withdraw my scholarship, but you can't run me off."

Yowarsky was in Lexington to scout a UK football game in 1974 for the group of professional teams he represents. He would neither deny nor confirm the "legend." "I remember the running, but I wasn't alone," he said. "They were trying to get me in shape and find a position for me. I thought I was a player, but I *wasn't* by their standards. They tried to make me a defensive back. Then I was a linebacker and center. They put you where they needed to in scrimmage, and there was no necessity to find a position for you until they thought you were ready."

In essence, Yowarsky was playing as an end in the 1951 Sugar Bowl game and was in good position to nail the Sooners' outside runners. On the way to being named the game's most valuable player, he set up the first Wildcat score—a pass from Parilli to Jamerson—by forcing and recovering a fumble by

Bryant instructs Charlie McClendon on sidelines during Sugar Bowl game.

Arnold on the Sooner 22 less than three minutes after the kickoff.

Jamerson scored again in that half, plunging over from the one foot line after a 40-yard pass from Parilli to Bruno. "Bryant told us at half time that we were two up on them, but two big plays would kill us, and they were perfectly capable of doing that," Clark said. "We didn't throw, and we didn't run any wide stuff in that half. I would dive behind Donaldson for those precious few yards on my side, and then Jamerson would dive on his side."

The loss snapped the Sooners' 31-game string of wins. Coach Bud Wilkinson said, "I had the feeling that if we had managed to score again, Parilli could have come right back and pitched Kentucky to another touchdown."

In the Cotton Bowl in 1952, TCU had first downs three times within the UK eight yard line in the first half. The Horned Frogs reached the four, the five, and the one yard lines, but on

The Wildcats whoop it up after their 20-7 victory over Texas Christian in the 1952 Cotton Bowl.

each occasion they lacked the wallop to put the ball across. Their passes failed, and the UK line rose fearlessly to stifle ground threats.

Kentucky scored on its second possession, covering 53 yards in eight plays, including a 31-yard pass from Parilli to Meilinger and a five-yard touchdown pass from Parilli to Clark. Jones kicked the point. The Frogs came right back, marching 50 yards in 11 plays, but Clark intercepted a Mal Fowler pass on the 17 and returned it to the UK 43. The 'Cats then marched to a score, with Clark leaping high in the end zone to catch a 12-yard toss from Parilli. Jones missed the point, so UK led, 13-0, with five minutes remaining in the half.

The Frogs once again made a valiant effort. They were in scoring position after a pass by TCU's McKown was deflected by Fry and fell into the hands of Ted Vaught on the UK 30. Clark caught him on the three for Kentucky, but Vaught crawled over the goal line; however, an official ruled Vaught's knee touched on the one. TCU's Bill Doty got six inches on the next play. A substitute came into the game, and TCU was penalized for excessive times out. Doug Moseley stopped McKown on the three, and Atkins stopped the next play on the two. An incomplete pass halted the drive.

Gil Bartosh took the Frogs 80 yards in four plays, with Bobby Jack Floyd scoring on a 43-yard dash around left end in the third quarter. That was their only cause for celebration; Kentucky wrapped up the game with a three-yard plunge by Ed Hamilton and was on TCU's six yard line when the final whistle blew.

Parilli was named Most Valuable Back; and TCU linebacker Keith Flowers, Most Valuable Lineman. But the player who attracted widespread attention on defense was Ray Correll, a strapping, thin-thatched blond farm boy described by Bryant as the most unorthodox football player he had ever seen. His stellar play in stopping TCU backs for sizable losses when UK was nursing a one-touchdown lead earned him a unique honor for a sophomore—selection to the All-Time Cotton Bowl team—and caused wonderment as to how a guard could carry out his blocking and defensive assignments and still be in the enemy territory so often.

One of Correll's trademarks from that time forward was an uncanny ability to be the first man down field on punts. His vicious tackles of safety men in 1953 alone caused no less than eight fumbles. And his senior year he was named an All-American.

"The best techniques that Ray uses on offense are his own and not what we've taught him," Bryant said in 1953. "He'll line up crooked, use some unorthodox feints, and even follow the play sometimes in a bewildering way. But the amazing thing is that it all works. So we don't fool with that boy's style of play. We're just delighted the way it works."

Ermal Allen later said, "We turned Correll loose then much the same way as we later did Bob Lilly of the Cowboys."

Correll and Tommy Atkins were co-captains in 1953, when Bryant walked into the training room where the players were eating and told them the university had received a bid to the Gator Bowl.

Assuming that his captains would be the first ones to vote in favor of accepting the bid, he asked, "How many centers want to go?"

When no hand was raised, he asked, "How many guards want to go?"

Again, no hands.

"Hell, we can't play without centers and guards," he said and stomped out.

Twenty-three years later Kentucky still has not appeared in another bowl game.

Seeing Orange

An inability to beat Gen. Robert E. Neyland's Tennessee teams was the most frustrating experience of Bryant's tenure at Kentucky. Neyland tormented him as he had every other UK coach since 1926. In fact, no Wildcat team ever whipped one of Neyland's teams. UK's last pre-Bryant victory over the Vols was in 1935, when Neyland was on active duty in the Philippines.

The first meeting (1946) between Neyland and a Bryant-coached UK team was a brilliant defensive duel for three quarters before Tennessee's Walt Slater tucked a George Blanda punt under his arm and returned 54 yards for a touchdown. Charlie Mitchell kicked the extra point. Thus, some 6,000 UK rooters, in a crowd of 40,000 at Knoxville, went home to brood another year over a 7-0 defeat. The Vols went to the Orange Bowl.

On a muddy field before 24,000 homecoming fans in Lexington in 1947, one of Neyland's worst teams (a five-time loser) defeated the Wildcats, 13-6, after recovering two of four UK fumbles in the first half. The 'Cats scored on a spread formation pass from Blanda to Bill Farris to tie the score, 6-6, at half time, but Hal Littleford went off tackle for a 20-yard score with four minutes remaining to win the game.

The Wildcats narrowly missed victory in 1948 when Gain's field goal attempt from the 27 was wide of the mark. They never got beyond the 48 in the first half of that game and had three attacks fizzle in the second half. Their big opportunity came after Blanda kicked 68 yards and the exchange gave UK the ball on the UT 39. That set up Gain's field goal attempt. The game ended in a 0-0 tie.

In preparation for the 1949 game in Lexington, Bryant

draped the goalposts in Tennessee orange and dressed his scrubs in orange jerseys. He took the varsity to the Circle M Farm, while Tennessee checked into a downtown hotel amidst blaring bands, parades, raucous alumni, and milling thousands. The Wildcats needed a victory to keep conference and bowl hopes alive, so they practiced in snow flurries on Thursday. The Vols did not scrimmage all week.

Tennessee harassed Parilli as he had never been harassed before—or since. The Vols intercepted his first pass and marched 35 yards in five plays, including a 15-yard roughing penalty, for the game's only score. They intercepted four of his passes and yielded only four first downs. The disheartened Wildcats were in tears when they left the field after the 6-0 defeat. Bryant took the blame, figuring Parilli was unnerved by the tension.

Tons of snow had to be swept from heavy tarpaulins protecting Shields-Watkins Field in Knoxville before the 1950 game. The gridiron was frozen, and the game was played in 16-degree weather. Parilli was smeared on the unyielding turf time after time. Throwing with near-frozen fingers, he completed 14 passes for 150 of the 1,734 yards he gained through the air that year. Whenever the ball changed hands and Tennessee took to the offense, hand warmers were applied to his fingers so he could handle the ball normally for a couple of plays when UK got the ball. The bitter cold numbed his fingers, and he did not dare attempt many of the multiple fakes he ordinarily performed mechanically.

"The ground was like concrete," Emery Clark said. "I would go in on punts, and I couldn't tell if my feet were touching the ground. I knew I was walking, but that was all."

As the university was trying for its first perfect season since 1898, the battle was hard and bruising. Smashing blocks and tackles, as well as chilled fingers, caused numerous fumbles. A Wildcat fumble midway into the second period led to a UT score. After Hank Lauricella's kick from the 35 hit the ground on the UK 40, the ball took a crazy bounce and hit Pat James on the leg. The Vols recovered. On fourth and 14, Lauricella passed to Rechichar, who stepped over after catching the ball on the one. Shires kicked the point. And Tennessee won, 7-0.

"I remember Rechichar caught that pass right in a snowdrift," Clark said. "One of our backs turned to the other and said, 'Where were you?' The other answered, 'That was your

Coach Paul Bryant, 1946-53.

man.' Pat James stole the ball from Rechichar later on a reverse, but he was tackled about the 30. Then we lost it again on a fumble."

"To this day, I would tell Tennessee coach General Neyland or anybody in the state of Tennessee that the officials took that one," Bryant said in his book. "I'm trying to be more humble and all now, but they took it from us. We had a tackle eligible play, a favorite of mine until the rules committee outlawed it in the late sixties, and I had alerted the officials beforehand. We ran it three times and made a mile, and instead of giving it to us they brought it back and penalized us every time."

Walt Yowarsky remembered those passes well. He caught two of them. "I made 47 or 48 yards on them, but they were called back," he said. "It was an old Cleveland Browns' play. Coach (Paul) Brown threw a tackle-eligible pass to Lou Groza. Consequently, coach Bryant put it in for our Tennessee game that year."

In 1951 Tennessee defeated the Wildcats, 28-0—the worst defeat suffered by a Bryant team up to that time. It was also the first time a Bryant-coached team had lost four games in one season. The powerful Vol running backs—Lauricella, Rechichar, and Andy Kosar—methodically advanced behind perfect blocking, converting each UK mistake into a Tennessee break.

The Wildcats got a small measure of revenge in 1952, playing the role of "spoiler." They tied Tennessee 14-14 and dashed UT's hopes for a share of the 1953 SEC title. The UK facts book described the game as a "snow bowl" fight in Knoxville, with the Wildcats pulling from behind in the final five minutes to score twice with chilling swiftness on a one-yard plunge by Hunt and a 17-yard Hunt-to-Proffitt pass. Tennessee did not throw a pass in the wet, 18-degree weather. UK completed only two of nine.

With Neyland retired in 1953, Bryant finally defeated the Vols. The Wildcats moved the ball to the UT 15 after the kickoff but lost it on a fumble. Tennessee—out of character—fumbled right back. Kentucky recovered on the 17, with Meilinger scoring on three carries. Hardy kicked the point. The Vols stopped UK drives to the 29 and 22, but then the Wildcats moved 68 yards on 10 ground plays, with Bradley Mills scoring from the five. Hardy's kick was blocked.

Tennessee scored its first touchdown after recovering a UK fumble on the 25 and then scored again after another Wildcat fumble to lead, 14-13. The Wildcats marched 63 yards in 11 plays for a score, but Tennessee took the lead again, 21-20. Kentucky's big break came when Harry Kirk crashed through on a Tennessee punt play and hit the ball, with Atkins recovering for Kentucky. Three plays later Hardy, who was knocked down by the crashing Vol line, pitched out to Paolone. He raced wide and went 22 yards to score. Hardy kicked the point, and the Wildcats defeated the Volunteers, 27-21, for the first time since 1935. After the game Bryant and Gov. Lawrence Wetherby posed with the beer barrel, symbol of victory. That was the last game Bryant would coach at Kentucky.

Bear Says Goodbye

Within one hour after the Kentucky football team returned to the campus from its 1952 triumph over Texas Christian in the Cotton Bowl, Paul Bryant startled the grid world with a new recruiting policy which he described as a unique plan to "cease all recruiting of football players outside the state of Kentucky."

The plan in essence said that UK would not conduct or condone recruiting outside the state's borders, and immediate emphasis would be placed on encouraging the best Kentuckians to attend their state university. Out-of-state students would be accepted under highly selective limitations.

Bryant directed that there would be a limit of "no more than five football scholarships in any one year to non-Kentuckians." In all instances, he pointed out, out-of-state students "must seek us out and apply for scholarships. We will make absolutely no effort to recruit them."

He explained that the allowance of five non-Kentucky scholarships was designed, in most part, to accommodate sons and brothers of alumni and to keep the out-of-state ratio on the football team in line with the ratio of non-Kentuckians in the total student population. At the time, Bryant's staff had signed 40 out-of-state players and planned to honor its commitments.

Despite the fact that only 108 Kentucky high schools fielded football teams in 1951, Bryant declared, "We have confidence in the ability of Kentucky boys to stand toe-to-toe with those of neighboring states and hold their own in football."

The plan was out of character for him since many of his stars—Parilli, Gain, Meilinger, to name a few—had been from out of state. Persons in the know immediately surmised that the plan was not of his own choosing. The university was on the verge of backing off from its attitude of "win at any cost," and the recruiting plan was just one of many steps to place athletics in a more "proper" perspective.

The beginning of UK's athletic decline and Bryant's dissatisfaction with the situation came in October of 1951 when three members of Adolph Rupp's national championship basketball teams of 1948 and 1949 confessed to manipulating the point spread on games. Their contact man in the gambling-bribe conspiracy was Nick Englisis, who had left the football squad shortly after Bryant became coach in 1946. As more Wildcat basketball players became implicated in the nationwide investigation, the three confessed former players testified to various violations of rules by the university. Their testimony included accusations that football player Gene Donaldson had been employed at one dollar an hour by a local architect, Chet Lukawski was given $100 to purchase clothing, and both football and basketball players violated rules by accepting gift certificates and bonuses from local merchants.

Hoping to set its house in order, the university adopted a program designed to slant its athletics toward campus and made suggestions that the SEC help cut down on the "big-time" cost of athletics. Despite UK's obvious good intentions, the executive committee of the SEC unanimously voted in August, 1952, to require UK to suspend all intercollegiate basketball in the conference for the period of one year. The NCAA followed suit. The conference also suspended Donaldson and Lukawski from football competition and fined Kentucky $500 for each. After that the crackdown on athletics at UK was so tight that Donaldson remarked in April, 1953, that "an athlete strolling across the campus can't even ask somebody for the time of day."

Bryant was extremely unhappy about the basketball scandals, which were keeping many athletes from attending UK, and he felt that the university was governed by basketball at the expense of football. He said in his book that a major factor in his dissatisfaction was a clash of objectives with Rupp: "We were too much alike, and he wanted basketball No. 1 and I wanted football No. 1. In an environment like that one or the other has to go."

However, it also should be noted that promised changes in the athletics' policy had not been made and that he was bitterly

Bryant is pictured behind successful UK basketball coach Adolph Rupp, which was often the case during the Bear's eight years at Kentucky.

disappointed because Paul Hornung of Louisville, the best football player in the state, had cast his lot with Notre Dame.

Bryant had what was probably his second best team returning in 1954, but the outlook was bleak beyond that point. The Kentucky-only recruiting policy would begin to be felt. Because of the unsettled athletic situation, Bryant also lost many players he had been banking on to fill the holes left by a sizable departure of seniors from the previous season's team. And he had a difficult time coaching a team disturbed by the continuation of the scandal.

Back during the first season under the new recruiting rule, only four out-of-state players were accepted. Bryant claimed to be pleased with the job his boys did in 1952, but it is hard to picture him accepting a 5-4-2 record with good humor. He also must have begun to wonder if he could get all the high school players in the state he wanted and if the fans who purchased the tickets and filled the stadium would be satisfied with a team that would win some and lose some. He had submitted his resignation shortly after the 1952 season ended, planning to accept the head coaching job at the University of Arkansas, but he had relented after Huguelet and Donovan assured him some changes would be made.

At the time he had a contract for an unprecedented 12 years, extending from January 1, 1951, through December 31, 1962—believed to be the longest to which a coach of a major school had been signed with the exception of Rube McCray's lifetime contract at William & Mary.

After receiving the Kentucky Press Association's outstanding citizen award in January, 1951, he had said, "Every day, I thank God that I wanted to be a Kentuckian and that you wanted me to be one."

Then at a luncheon held in his honor on December 28, 1952, in Frankfort, he received a new automobile and was proclaimed a citizen of Kentucky "now and henceforth forever." A group of 25 intimate friends, including the governor, chipped in and purchased the car, and the governor made him a lifetime Kentuckian by proclamation "so that neither Alabama nor Arkansas nor anybody else can claim him."

In January, 1954, Bryant refused an offer from LSU. He stated on January 8, 1954, "As for myself, I hope my services rendered to the University of Kentucky shall always be of the caliber that is desired. I also hope I am fortunate enough for Kentucky to be my home forever."

Less than one month later he resigned to become head coach and athletic director at Texas A&M. UK first threatened to refuse his resignation but relented and released him as head coach on February 7, 1954. Significantly, its announcement did not carry the customary expression of thanks for a job well done or good wishes for the future.

Any remorse UK fans had over Bryant's resignation was dispelled four days later, when UK announced it had hired Blanton Collier as its new football coach. The 47-year-old backfield coach of the Cleveland Browns had twice refused the offer, but he finally succumbed to pressure from the "home" folks and accepted a three-year contract at $12,000 annually, plus a $2,000 expense account.

Collier was described by his boss, Paul Brown, as a determined but quietly patient person who was solid in football fundamentals and meticulous in technique. He was considered the perfect choice as a goodwill ambassador who could charm away the differences between football and basketball at UK. First and foremost, he had strong ties with the basketball family. Harry Lancaster was his aide at Paris High School, and Rupp had acknowledged Collier's basketball know-how by employing him as a scout. In addition, Collier's prowess as a coach for 16 years at Paris was as great in basketball as in football. His 1932 team was regarded as one of the best teams ever to perform in the state tournament. In four trips to the big tournament, he advanced twice to the semifinals.

Collier was born in Millersburg but moved to Paris at a preschool age. He lettered in football and basketball at Paris High and Georgetown College. Upon graduation from college in 1937, he was named coach of all athletics at Paris and held that position until entering the navy in 1943. He also did postgraduate work at Kentucky, earning a master's degree in educational administration.

During an official welcoming celebration for Collier, Rupp started off his part of the ceremonies by offering the new coach a bottle of aspirin—"the first thing you'll need in this business"—and numerous other pill bottles and boxes. Rupp prescribed one medication after another for the various troubles that Collier and his companion coaches would experience.

Dr. Donovan briefly reviewed the history of UK's athletic plant before presenting the keys to McLean Stadium, and to the football houses, to Collier. He then gave the coach a giant-sized copy of the team's schedule, which he termed "murderous," and a Japanese samurai sword, with the admonition, "Mow 'em down."

"I'm beginning to wonder if this is a welcome or a scare session," Collier said. He went on to say, "When criticisms come, I hope you're not as vehement in your condemnation as you are gracious in your welcome. . .that would be a much more difficult thing to face than losing to one of the teams on that schedule would be."

Both Rupp's pills and Collier's fears would prove prophetic in the eight years ahead.

Blanton Collier

By his own admission, Blanton Collier was a compulsive teacher, but that was no secret to anyone who knew him.

"He just likes to teach anything," said Billy Grimes, who was a student in a general science class taught by Collier at Paris High School. "You know, he was quite a swimmer. Used to swim all the time at Paris Country Club. But he'd notice somebody not doing something right, and he'd start instructing them. He picked me out one day because I couldn't swim a lick. That didn't bother me—matter of fact, I didn't want to know how to swim. But it bothered Collier. He made a swimmer out of me."

Ermal Allen said Collier analyzed everything to get out all the fine points. "He can coach any position," Allen said. "He tries to know the strict, minute details of each. That's the way he approaches it. Any coach who ever coached with Blanton Collier, no matter how long he had coached, would learn something."

Among the coaches who served as assistants to Collier during his eight-year term at UK were: Bill Arnsparger, named coach of the New York Giants in 1974; Charlie Bradshaw, who would succeed Collier as UK coach; John North, coach of the New Orleans Saints in 1974-75; Don Shula, highly successful coach of the Baltimore Colts and the Miami Dolphins, winning Super Bowl championships; Howard Schnellenberger, who had a brief term as coach of the Baltimore Colts in 1975; and Chuck Knox, coach of the Los Angeles Rams.

"Fundamentals, fundamentals, fundamentals," was the way Harry Lancaster, who retired as UK athletic director in

Blanton Collier.

July, 1975, remembered Collier. "Blanton insisted there was only one way to do a thing, whether it's solving a math problem or executing a shot—the right way. When I was at Paris High, even your ears had to be right or he'd crop them. To be brief, he is a perfectionist to an infinitesimal degree."

Buckshot Underwood, a Collier assistant in 1954-55, recalled that in Collier's home was a coaches' room equipped with big, school-type chairs, movie projector, screen, blackboard, paper, pencils, coffee maker, water fountain—and no telephone. During the season Collier and his staff would meet for hours on end.

"I remember sitting in that basement four hours with him and trying to decide whether to cover an opponent's split end with a linebacker or an end," Underwood said. "When I fell asleep, he woke me up and said, 'Buckshot, you're not very interested, are you?' I said, 'Coach, I made up my mind two hours ago.'

"That's the way he coached. He had to make less mistakes than his opponents. He believed that if a team didn't make any mistakes, it would win. If I had to know the truth about something, about what to do technique-wise, I would go to Collier. He studied films all year. Where other people played golf and what have you, Collier got his thrills from football. He studied it harder than anybody."

Former All-American Lou Michaels recalls one day when he was a freshman at UK. "I was trying to block a guy and I couldn't move him," Michaels said. "Collier came running from the other side of the field. He must have run 50 yards. He called me to the side and said, 'Hey, you know what you're doing wrong?' I told him I knew I was bigger than the other guy and I was hitting him with everything I had, and I asked, 'What's wrong?'

"He said, 'Hey, fellow: one, two, three, four—move your feet—one, two, three, four.' And you know what? I blocked this guy, and I knocked him back 20 yards."

During a visit to Lexington in April, 1975, Collier said he had not planned to coach when he came out of college. "In fact, I didn't intend to teach," he said. "I took no courses in education on purpose. My reason for that was that my mother's two brothers and a sister were college professors. I had heard that all my life, and I was obsessed with the idea that I wasn't going to teach or coach. I came out and started selling bonds for

Kentucky Utilities Company. I probably happened to come out of the house one day at the wrong time. I was going to work and ran into a high school friend in late November, 1927, and he told me that the basketball coach at Paris High had resigned, and he had seen the superintendent and suggested that he get me. The next day the superintendent called me, and I wound up coaching the basketball team. I had to teach in order to coach, and the superintendent got a provisional certificate for me. I coached all sports the next year and taught five classes. I did that until I went in the navy in December, 1943."

After graduating from Great Lakes Naval Training Base, Collier went to Bainbridge, Maryland, where he taught survival swimming. He developed ear trouble and was transferred to the naval hospital in Philadelphia.

"I felt great except that I couldn't hear," he said. "I would do extra duty in order to get off weekends, when I scouted the Eagles, the Redskins, and every college game I could find. At Bainbridge they had that great football team. To me, it was a great opportunity, and I took notes and scouted and had an enjoyable time learning a lot about football."

Due to the ear ailment, he was shipped back to Great Lakes, where his barracks was beside the field where Paul Brown was conducting summer practice.

"I was working in the Green Bay area," Collier said. "I would catch the late bus and get over to watch practice every afternoon. I would take notes on what he was doing, his organization, and everything.

"One day I missed the bus, and Green Bay commander Alden W. Thompson picked me up and drove me in his car. I just facetiously said, 'You're a life saver. I was about to miss football practice.'

"He looked at me and said, 'You're not playing football?'

"'That's right,' I said, 'but I watch them practice,' so he and I watched it together.

"He asked me a group of questions, found out how interested I was, and I thought no more about it. He came by the next afternoon, and I was watching practice again. The next morning he called me into his office and said, 'How would you like to be on Paul Brown's staff?' I said I wasn't paid to do that. He was able to work it out, and I became an assistant on Brown's staff.

"When I got out of the Navy, I came to UK and worked on

my master's degree. I had intended to go on to a doctor's degree and probably wind up on the faculty of the College of Education. Meantime, I had talked with Bear Bryant, who was coaching at UK at the time. He and I had agreed that I would work with him in an assistant's capacity. Along in June or July, while I was in summer school, a call came from Paul Brown, who wanted me to come to the Browns. I told him I would love to, but I couldn't. I had already accepted a job with Bear. Brown called up the next day and asked if I would mind going to Bear and talking to him. 'I will,' I said, 'but I promise you, if there's any reluctance on Bear's part at all, I won't be there.' Bear was wonderful about it; he seemed to understand. He told me he thought I had to go ahead. I went with Paul Brown in July, 1946, and worked with him eight years until I came to the university."

Collier was Brown's right-hand man as Cleveland won four conference championships and then went into the NFL to win more championships. When asked why he left the Browns for less money at UK, Collier said, "From my boyhood I had always wanted to coach at the University of Kentucky. I'm a guy that likes to coach football, and Kentucky was my school.

"You know, Paul and I were talking about the Kentucky job one night, and the very next morning there was a story about Paul Bryant signing a new contract. Well, it didn't look like I would ever go to Kentucky. A month later Paul Bryant quit to go to Texas A&M, and I was offered the job.

"Paul Brown and I were close friends. Knowing how I had always felt about wanting to coach at Kentucky, he helped me to finally make a decision.

"One of the first things Dr. Donovan asked me was, if I planned to restrict recruiting to the state of Kentucky. I told him, 'I don't think you can. I have not been in Kentucky for a long time, but I don't think there are enough football players to win with, even if you get them all. You have got to go out of state to recruit.' He agreed with me 100 percent. There were some players who had been recruited from other states but not very many.

"The big problem, as I saw it at that time, was that the program had lost contact—was out of touch—with those out-of-state people who had been helping Kentucky in their recruiting, and they had transferred their allegiance to other schools. Besides, it was late in the recruiting season. I don't want to discuss it in a negative way, but you have to have football players to win. We had some pretty good football players when I first went to Kentucky, and we had a pretty good team that first year. A lot of people don't know it, but the players turned down a bid to the Gator Bowl that year."

Billy Mitchell, a halfback who returned to UK as an assistant in 1973, remembered that all the players were looking forward to the transition from Bryant to Collier. "This man had been at the top level, in the pros," he said, "and it just took us a while to get started, to know his system. It was completely different on both offense and defense. He threw the ball a lot more and operated the belly option system out of the old split-T.

"Practices were no easier than they were under Bryant. In fact, I think he worked the first and second units a lot harder, but I guess that was due to a new staff coming in and getting their feet on the ground."

Bill Wheeler, a tackle that season and later team physician for the Wildcats, said, "Everybody stayed on the field, and all left at the same time. Under Bryant, some got to go in early as sort of a reward. Some of the players resented having to stay out that first spring, but that all passed on.

"We always felt that Collier had the ability to take someone with talent and teach him the fine points. Bryant could take somebody without talent and teach him to play. If some of those people who left UK under Bryant had stayed, I probably wouldn't have played five minutes."

In Collier's debut at UK, a 20-0 loss to Maryland, the Wildcats were in scoring position five times but threw five interceptions and lost two fumbles. In a 28-9 loss to Ole Miss at Memphis, the 'Cats and the Rebels set a conference record, being penalized a total of 305 yards (UK: 16 for 123 yds.; Ole Miss: 15 for 182 yds.). The first UK score under Collier was a 14-yard field goal by Delmar Hughes in that game.

Collier's first win at UK was a 7-6 conquest of LSU, with the winning touchdown being scored by Dick Mitchell on a four-yard run culminating a last-minute drive. The Wildcats defeated Auburn, 21-14, but lost to Florida, 21-7. However, they then went on to defeat Georgia Tech, Villanova, Vanderbilt, Memphis State, and Tennessee. The Tennessee win was the first in 30 years in Knoxville.

For that 7-3 season, Collier was an almost unanimous

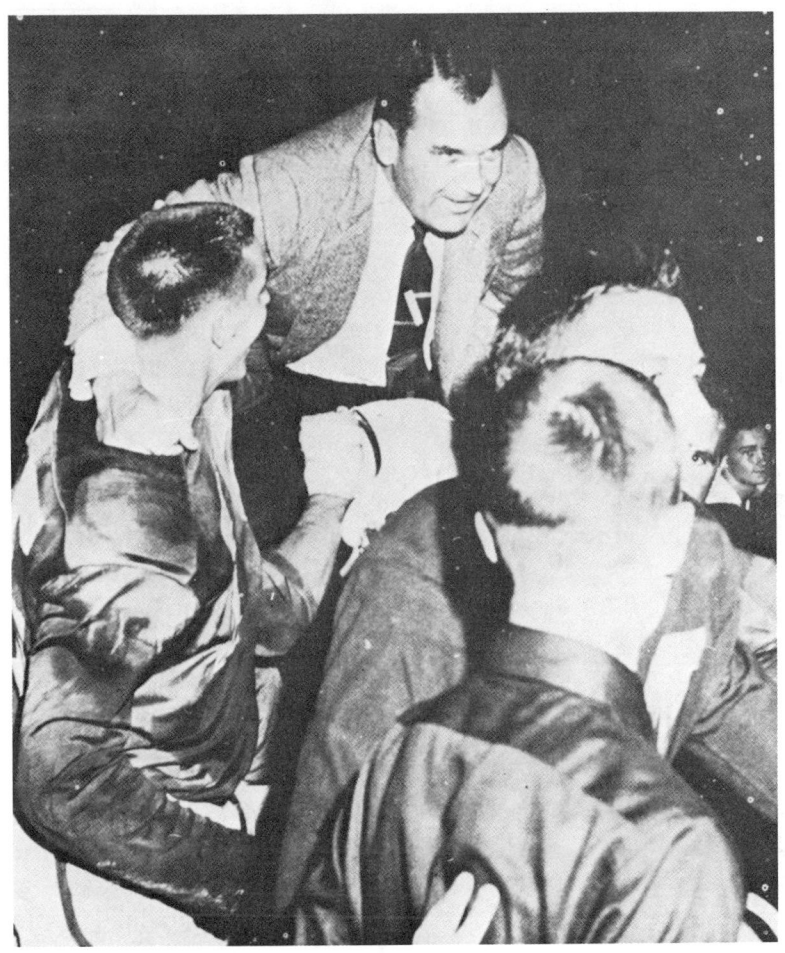

Blanton Collier gets victory ride after UK defeats Tennessee, 14-13, in his first season as head coach.

choice as SEC Coach of the Year, becoming the first coach in the 19-year history of the poll to be so recognized in his initial season in the collegiate ranks. He was also the first UK coach ever voted the award, and he finished high in the poll for National Coach of the Year.

Hardy, who would repeat as All-SEC, and Schnellenberger, who would make All-American, were both seniors the following year and formed one of the best passing combinations in the South.

The most promising new player was tackle Lou Michaels.

Bob Dougherty, a power runner, was back after two years in the marines and a season of inactivity necessitated by his transfer from the University of Cincinnati. The Wildcats lost to Mississippi State and Vanderbilt and tied Auburn, but their 6-3-1 record in 1955 included a 23-0 victory over Tennessee in Lexington.

Without a strong aerial attack in 1956, the Wildcats finished with a 6-4 record. They appeared for the first time on national television in their opening game in Lexington, but they lost the game, 14-6, to Georgia Tech. Collier suffered his only loss to Tennessee that year (20-7) as the Wildcats outplayed the visitors on paper but fell to the undefeated Vols and the heroics of John Majors.

The honeymoon was over in 1957. Collier had one of the best players in the nation in Lou Michaels, but the supporting cast was not up to the schedule. The Wildcats lost in succession to Georgia Tech (13-0), seventh-ranked Ole Miss (15-0), 17th-ranked Florida (14-7), No. 1 ranked Auburn (6-0), LSU (21-0), and Georgia (33-14). Next Kentucky whipped Memphis State (53-7), lost to Vanderbilt (12-7), beat Xavier (27-0), and defeated Tennessee (20-6). It was the worst record (3-7) since the 1945 Wildcats were 2-8. And it was the first time a UK team had lost six games in a row.

The Wildcats were 5-4-1 in 1958, 4-6 in 1959, 5-4-1 in 1960, and 5-5 in 1961. That was the period during which the administration adopted a policy requiring that all students make a minimum standing of 2.0, equivalent to a C grade. The old rule had required freshmen to average 1.4, sophomores 1.6, and juniors 1.8. The new policy also required that out-of-state students be in the upper 50 percent of their graduating class to enter UK. In February, 1959, 37 percent of the freshman football players at UK would be declared ineligible.

Dr. Frank Dickey, who succeeded Donovan as president, openly opposed the practice of "redshirting" (holding a player out of competition one year), and the school newspaper was a constant critic of Collier and his players. The students at one time hung him in effigy, along with Premier Kruschev of Russia, on the John Hunt Morgan horse in the courthouse square in downtown Lexington.

Although Collier received a five-year extension of his contract after the 1958 season, he still lacked what he considered proper support for his program. The situation came to a head after he committed the unpardonable sin of losing to Tennessee in 1961. The athletics association held a special meeting January 2, 1962, and voted to buy up the remaining three years of his contract for a total of $51,000.

For the next three years UK was paying out $36,000 yearly for head football coaching—paying one to coach and the other, not to coach.

Collier returned to the Cleveland Browns as offensive backfield coach and later won some championships as head coach of that team. Many Kentuckians would remain bitter for years to come over what they considered rather shabby treatment of a fine gentleman and an excellent student of the game. And there was little consolation in the fact that his two immediate successors would fall short of his record (.531) at the university.

Time Out: Bob Hardy

In a letter to the author, former All-SEC quarterback Bob Hardy described how he "decided" on Kentucky and recalled his years under Bear Bryant and Blanton Collier.

"Dear Russell:

"In the spring of 1951, after visiting Notre Dame and Coach Frank Leahy, I decided I would attend the University of Notre Dame. There were not many people in Paducah who were in favor of that decision.

"Early one morning in the first week of June, I received a phone call from Coach Bryant. He said he would be in Paducah the following evening and would like to have dinner with myself and two fellows that played end with me in high school. I had never talked with Coach Bryant; the recruiting from Kentucky had been done by Coach Ermal Allen and Charlie McClendon.

"The following night we had dinner and then went to a Kitty League baseball game. At the baseball game Coach Bryant said to me, 'I saw Leahy in Washington this past week and he told me you were going to Notre Dame. I told him that was a mistake, that you were going to Kentucky.' He had never lacked for confidence. I left the ball game that night still going to Notre Dame and very impressed with Coach Bryant.

"The next morning at 7 o'clock the phone rang at my home. There was a phone beside my bed and I was the first to answer it. It was Coach Bryant. He said, 'Bob, I have a private plane at the airport and I will be by in 30 minutes to pick you up to take you to Lexington. You spend a couple of days with us and see how you like it,' and hung up. I did not have a chance to make one comment. In the meantime, my folks had picked up the phone and heard the conversation. We had 10 minutes of looking at one another and then, coming to the conclusion that there wasn't much to do in the next couple of days, decided I might as well make the trip.

"Lexington was great fun. The first day I was there I played golf with Coach Allen, Coach Laslie and a young fellow by the name of John Y. Brown, Jr. I virtually moved into the Brown house. I saw Coach Bryant only twice in the 10 days I was in Lexington (it started out to be two days). I played golf with him one day at the Idle Hour Country Club. The other time I saw him was with Governor Wetherby, who told me in no uncertain terms that a Kentuckian who was going to live in Kentucky should go to the University of Kentucky. The Governor was very influential.

"The Browns were fantastic. I stayed with John and was entertained by the whole family. I played golf every day and had a gorgeous dinner at their house every night with five delightful young ladies—the Brown sisters and Mrs. Brown—and, of course, the always entertaining John Y., Sr. They were as responsible as anybody for my going to Kentucky. The Browns are my friends today and I probably have no better friend than John Y., Jr.

"Ten days after my first day in Lexington, I was called to Coach Bryant's office and without any hesitation he said, 'I think you should go to summer school. Here are the keys to a car. Go to Paducah and get your clothes and be back for summer school.' I did just that and to this day I am delighted that I chose to make that decision, although I am not sure whether I chose or he chose.

"I had great fun in summer school—there were a lot of us there. Freshmen were eligible in 1951. Fall practice was indeed a time of growing up. We went to Millersburg. I will never forget the first day in Lexington when they said, 'backs circle up for calisthenics.' There was not room for the linemen! There must have been at least 50 backs. I could not believe that there were that many football players in the world.

"In three days, some of us went to Millersburg and there I got to see the great Babe Parilli and the Bear Bryant that I had never met before. We were in the football business; two practices a day, two meetings a day and a lot of guys leaving. You had to walk from Millersburg to Paris to catch the bus and people leaving probably created the biggest traffic jam that road has ever seen.

"My biggest competition was a quarterback from Pennsylvania by the name of Rudy Matteoli. He decided about 11 o'clock one night to leave and I loaned him the money to catch the bus. Why I stayed I will never know, because I wanted to leave every day. As a matter of fact, I felt like it would have been easier to stay than to go back and face Paducah.

"The first half of the freshman year was a great one for me. I got to play in some varsity games and made some trips. However, against the Georgia Tech freshmen about mid-season, I played the worst football game of any quarterback in the history of Kentucky, I think. The rest of that year was not much fun.

"The spring practice of 1952 was not a good spring. We were changing to the split-T and I lost confidence in myself and the coaching staff lost confidence in me at the same time. It was decided in the fall of 1952 that I would be a redshirt. We went back to Millersburg that fall. It was the same old Millersburg; hot, 24-hour-a-day football. Kentucky had a fair season in 1952. Coach Bryant used Meilinger, Hunt and Shatto at quarterback. For me, it was a miserable three months. I was the opposing team's quarterback every week. Some days I played guard, linebacker, or whatever position needed to be filled with a body. As it turned out, I learned a lot of football. I learned to take care of myself. Off the football field I was a miserable student. I almost flunked out of school, almost changed schools, almost did a lot of things; however, in the final analysis, I stayed.

"The spring of 1953 was not much better because I had not shown enough improvement to create an interest from the coaching staff. During the spring sometime, I decided I was the best split-T quarterback that we had and in the last few days of spring practice I began to show some improvement.

"I worked hard the entire spring and summer at being a split-T quarterback and at throwing the ball. My biggest drawback was I had no speed. Coach Bryant called me 'paddle foot.' I had quickness, but no speed. I knew the game as well as anybody. Split-T football to me was much like fast-break basketball, except you didn't have to dribble and I was the guy in high school who ran a fast-break basketball team.

"With all the many, many quarterback meetings I had

attended with Coach Bryant—and that is great training—and all the positions that I had played while being redshirted, I knew the game of football. I understood defenses, could recognize them, knew what could succeed against them, understood sequences of plays, and Coach Bryant's whole program of downs and distance.

"We came back in September of 1953 and I assumed my same position, fourth string and running the opposing team's plays. Things did not look very good. Two guys who were running in my backfield at the time were Joe Platt and Ralph Paolone (they later started with me). The first two games we lost. We had no offense and everybody was pretty disgusted. On Thursday before the second game I was so frustrated that I got into a fight with one of the tackles. On Monday after that second game, Coach Bryant called me into his office and said to me, 'You have not done much since you have been here. I am going to start you Saturday and if we don't win, I think you ought to pack your bags and go on back to Paducah.'

[It was simply by the 'grace of God' that Bryant happened to hit on Hardy as a quarterback for that game. 'Frankly, during that long ride from Oxford back to Memphis, I had decided on another quarterback, but it was not Hardy,' he said in an October, 1953, newsletter. 'However, during practice on Tuesday and Wednesday he moved the football better than the rest and sort of in a desperation move, I decided to give him his chance. Needless to say, he came through beautifully.' Hardy completed seven of 10 passes for 131 yards and two touchdowns against a Gator team that was leading the nation in pass defense, having allowed only four completions in two games. For engineering the 26-13 upset, he was named SEC 'Back of the Week.']

"We ended up having a great season. We tied at LSU; Coach Bryant thought we got beat. We were playing both ways and a great many new substitution rules were in effect, and with about two minutes to go in the game I threw Joe Platt a pass and he got knocked out of bounds on about LSU's three yard line. At this time Coach Bryant thinks we are behind 7-6. He wanted two specific plays called and he sent Herbie Hunt in to call those plays and brought me to the sidelines to get ready for the third and fourth plays if we needed them.

"Coach Bryant had forgotten that I could not go back into the ball game with the new rule change. The first two plays didn't work. He had his hand on my shoulder pad and he told

me to go in the game and score. I said, 'I can't, I'm dead.' He threw me right over the telephone table and did not even know he had done so. Needless to say, the last minute was total confusion and we did not score. Enough has been written about that ball game.

"As I said, 1953 was a good season. We beat Jackie Parker and his crowd at Mississippi State. We beat a good Rice team at Houston. I think Rice won the Southwestern Conference that year, because we thought we were going back to the Cotton Bowl and the Cotton Bowl did not want us to play Rice again. Some of the nicest things that were ever said about me as a football player were said by Jess Neely, the Rice coach. Of course you know that we beat Tennessee. I went to the infirmary after the Tennessee game to get my nose sewed up. I did not realize how high my emotions were and I sat there in the infirmary and cried for two hours. When that was over I was the best-feeling human being that had ever walked on that campus.

"Just before the semester break in January, I had a great visit with Coach Bryant on plans and preparations for spring practice. I went to Florida with a group of kids between semesters and the third day in Florida I picked up the morning paper, which said that Coach Bryant had left Kentucky to go to Texas A&M. I was flabbergasted. I called Lexington and they told me this was true. I couldn't believe that he left without telling us. (I found out later that things happened so fast that he did not have time.) I felt bad because I was just beginning to understand him, to have complete and total confidence in him and in myself. I was scared to death of him, but I was firmly convinced he was totally responsible for my success and I felt sure he was developing the same confidence in me.

"Playing football for Blanton Collier has no relationship to playing football for Coach Bryant. They look different, they act different, they teach different; they are like daylight and dark.

"When you compare Coach Bryant and Coach Collier and you say that Blanton is the teacher and Bryant is the motivator, you leave the impression that Coach Bryant is not a teacher which is, of course, completely false. I think teaching and motivating are approaches rather than assuming the one teaches and does not motivate or that one motivates and does not teach.

"We had a good football team in 1954 and Coach Collier

Bob Hardy.

was easy to get along with. I think on many occasions too easy. I feel today as I did then, that 19 and 20-year-old boys are boys and occasionally they need a bump on the backend to get their mind on what they are doing. This was not Coach Collier's method.

"Coach Collier inserted a new passing attack and a new concept in defense. Other than that, we ran the same offense and defense that we had in the previous year. As I said, we had a good football team, mostly because we had some outstanding guys on that squad—Howard Schnellenberger, Dr. Bill Wheeler, Joe Koch, Dave Kuhn, and a host of other guys who really provided a great deal of leadership.

"Collier's practices were long and tedious. We went over techniques time after time; such as the timing and steps of a guard pulling, or a post block by a tackle. Coach Collier felt that these points were vital. I did not want to disagree with him because the guards and tackles were my best friends, but there were times when 21 guys stood for 10 minutes while he demonstrated to a guard or tackle. He was totally thorough and if you executed his teaching, you would be the best.

"A split-T scared Coach Collier to death. When I graduated, he put in specific steps that a quarterback would take. Throwing the football around behind the line of scrimmage was not his idea of a well-designed play.

"He really knew the passing game and the moves for the ends to make to get into the open. He could watch me warm up and make an adjustment that would solve any problem I had. The feet are so important in throwing and he knew all the tricks and techniques to help you get your feet into the right position.

"Blanton Collier was an honest man even when he was going into a football game. An example is Georgia Tech in 1954: we had just gotten the daylights beaten out of us the previous week in Florida and our co-captains were hurt, so Schnellenberger and I acted as co-captains and just before we went out on the field to flip the coin Coach Collier said to the squad, 'I want you to play hard today. Georgia Tech has a great football team. If they have an off day and we are at our best, the game could be close.' He was not trying to pump anyone up. He was being plain honest with his observation of the two teams. As Howard and I walked out to the coin tossing, we really could not believe that he did say that to the squad and much to Coach Collier's surprise—and maybe a great many other people—when the game was over, it was Kentucky 13, Georgia Tech 6.

"We beat Tennessee at Knoxville in the rain. A last-minute pass to Schnellenberger put us out in front to stay. I hope no one ever forgets that Bradley Mills punted the ball out of his own end zone—in the rain—30 yards in the air, left-footed. He was a right-footed kicker! Somebody smiled at us that day. I could name 20 other instances.

"1955 was the finale for me and a dozen other guys. During spring practice we spent a lot of time on technique. Coach Collier was enjoyable to play for. He had a great family—the older girls were in school with us and, of course, Mrs. Collier was, is now and will always be one of the most delightful ladies I have ever known.

"We had a lot of fun in 1955. We won some and lost some but we beat Ole Miss, we beat Rice and Tennessee. That made it three for three for the seniors against Tennessee.

[With a little more than six minutes left and Rice ahead, 16-13, Hardy guided the 'Cats 66 yards in nine plays, scoring the winning touchdown himself on a 12-yard run, then kicking the extra point. He carried the ball six times in the final push, including an 18-yard pass completion on a fourth and 10 situation that mended the drive just as it seemed to crack. The pass put the ball on the Rice 24 and after two plays, carried to the 12. Hardy scored through left tackle on a keeper. He completed 10 of 17 passes for 125 yards, rushed 11 times for 35 yards, and scored 14 points for a tremendous one-man show that earned him national 'Back of the Week' honors. He was virtually a unanimous All-SEC choice his junior and senior years. Over a four-year span he had a passing percentage of better than 52 percent, including 18 touchdown passes and 2,367 yards. After guiding the 'Cats to a victory over Tennessee in his final collegiate game, he received a standing ovation from the crowd as he trotted toward the UK bench, where he danced a happy jig with Collier.]

"I do not mean to rush through 1955, because it was a good year for Kentucky football and for those of us who were graduating, but it was the beginning of the downfall of Coach Collier at Kentucky and Kentucky football as Kentuckians had known it the past eight years.

"Coach Bryant had instituted a new recruiting policy at Kentucky before he left, which allowed only five out-of-state players per year to come to Kentucky. Although we had nine or

10 Kentuckians starting in 1954 and 1955 that policy will not succeed. The State of Kentucky does not produce enough high school football players to allow that policy to succeed. Coach Collier was having assistant coach problems. He had some great assistant coaches and they have proven themselves, but there were constant rumbles and disagreements and the squad knew about them.

"The organization of out-of-state recruiters had deteriorated. The organization that had been headed by the late Mr. Huguelet was sputtering and I think Coach Collier and this group had trouble communicating. I feel it is inappropriate to place blame because the factors mentioned above all contributed to grinding down a solid organization and a very difficult period of time for Blanton Collier. He and his family went through personal hell. We were close then and now and I thought he should have resigned earlier for his own interest. I saw no way to change the tide of events and I saw no reason for he and his family to suffer. You can't lose and recruit and if you can't recruit, you can't win. Therein lies a small piece of the story.

"Regardless of all the problems, there are two things that stand out in my mind. Coach Collier helped to mold the top coaches in professional football and there is no question that many of his ideas have made professional football the great spectator sport it is today.

"Blanton Collier, to me, is a story of success, as a coach and a human being. I am thankful that he was my coach and friend.

"This has been enjoyable for me to go back and recreate my time at UK and two great football coaches. How fortunate can a young man be? To have Paul Bryant make you grow up and realize it and to have Blanton Collier work at polishing the result. I wish my children could be so fortunate, for those were great times.

Bob Hardy"

The Actors

If Oscars were given for acting on a football field, Howard Schnellenberger and Bob Collier of the Kentucky Wildcats would have been sure nominees for the 1954 and 1955 statuettes.

Schnellenberger earned accolades for an act which produced a game-winning touchdown on a slippery gridiron in Knoxville in 1954, and he was also involved in a bit of theatrics which resulted in a field goal that beat Florida, 10-7, the following year.

Ed Harris of the *Knoxville Journal* explained the 1954 incident:

> It was second down and 17 to go for a first down by the Cats on the Tennessee 22. . .Schnellenberger blocked as if providing protection for the passer, quarterback Bob Hardy. . .the six-foot end slipped off a Vol and fell to the ground, got up slowly and started trotting down the opposite side of the field, the Vols in pursuit. . .Hardy finally spotted the end all by himself for an easy toss, a 22-yard touchdown pass and a victory.
>
> . . .To thousands of fans on hand yesterday it was the first time they had ever seen a Kentucky team defeat Tennessee in Knoxville. . .The last time that happened was in 1924. . . .It was also the first time in modern football history that Kentucky has ever won two straight over the Vols.

Schnellenberger also had a hand in a bit of fakery involving guard Bob Collier in that 1955 game with Florida. With only 23 seconds remaining and the score deadlocked, reserve quarterback Delmar Hughes, suffering a broken nose and other facial injuries from earlier action, came in to boot a successful 20-yard field goal. Gator coach Bob Woodruff later unofficially protested that Hughes' entry into the game was made possible by sideline signaling and a faked injury. Blanton Collier was visibly upset by the implied reflection on his personal integrity and declared he had never signaled for a fake injury and had never coached any of his players to resort to such tactics.

Twenty years later Dr. William Wheeler, who was a UK tackle in that game, shed some light on the incident. "Bob Hardy, Schnellenberger, and I grabbed hold of a sophomore (Bob Collier) and told him on the next play he was hurt," he said. "Blanton Collier didn't know a thing about it. After the game (Bob) Collier walked around on crutches three days, but he wasn't hurt."

Delmar Hughes, a career air force officer serving in Thailand in 1975, recalled that his real injuries were "annoying" him quite a bit and that it was hard to keep his eyes from watering. "I could see Hardy and the ball, but I couldn't see the goalposts," he said. "I knew they were up there some place, so I just kicked and hoped."

Wheeler, one of the only group of UK seniors who never lost to Tennessee, fondly recalled beating them, 23-0, in 1955. "All we did was double-team the tackle on both sides of the line and give the ball to Bob Dougherty," he said. "Bob outgained the entire Tennessee team that day."

Wheeler also recalls the game with LSU: "I remember we went down to Baton Rouge for the opening game that year, and we thought we were in good shape. But in that heat and humidity we found out that we weren't, and we lost, 19-7, in what was considered one of the big upsets."

LSU took a 6-0 lead early in the first quarter and held on determinedly, but the Wildcats doggedly fought back. They had just narrowed the LSU lead to 13-7 when LSU's Joe May returned a kickoff 96 yards for a touchdown.

Blanton Collier also remembered that game vividly. "I had never been to Baton Rouge," he said, "and I didn't realize how hot and how humid it was going to be. I had made up my mind that it was important that we rest the first team. We had a good team but were not strong in reserves. I played the first team half of the first quarter and then took them out, and that's where I made my mistake. Due to the excitement, the heat, and the

Howard Schnellenberger is all alone for a touchdown reception in UK's 14-13 victory over Tennessee in the mud at Knoxville in 1954.

humidity, they were completely worn out after 7½ minutes of action. . . .I've never seen a group of boys so completely deflated physically. They were drained. By contrast, a short time later we played Miami in the Orange Bowl Stadium, and I took the first team out at the end of three minutes and beat them."

Bill Wheeler recalled a 20-14 loss to Mississippi State that year. "Hardy had scored from inside the 10 to put us ahead with less than a minute to go. We kicked off and had them inside the 20 when Collier took out a whole bunch of guys because he thought they had been playing so much that they must be tired. We let them complete an 83-yard pass for a touchdown. I was on the ground, and I remember seeing the ball going over the head of our defensive man and into the arms of Bill Morgan on about the 50."

"We had an injury in that game that shook us up a little," Coach Collier said. "Dick Moloney, who was one of the most aggressive, hard-nosed football players I've ever been privileged to coach, was playing a great game with us, and he had a head-on collision that knocked him out completely. Darrell Royal was coaching Mississippi State at the time, and I remember that long pass too well."

That play cost the Wildcats the national leadership in pass defense. Without that 83-yard gain against them, the per-game average allowed opponents via the airwaves would have been 39.6 yards, which would have bettered the top mark posted by Florida (42.0). As it was, UK finished sixth in the nation with a 47.9 average.

Collier had his third best season (6-4) in 1956. After opening with losses to Georgia Tech and Mississippi, the 'Cats defeated Florida and then lost to Auburn, 13-0, as Tommy Lorino got off a 68-yard touchdown run. They beat LSU, 14-0. Then they edged Georgia, 14-7, with a 43-yard pass from Ken Robertson to John Cornelius in the closing minutes. Billy Mitchell had a 78-yard punt return for a touchdown in a 14-0 blanking of Maryland, and Hughes threw a 21-yard scoring pass to Doug Shively and then kicked the extra point for a 7-6 victory over Vanderbilt.

"One of the most unusual plays of the season happened in that game," Mitchell recalled. "Vanderbilt had the ball fourth and 10 on about their 33, and a substitute quarterback was back to kick. I was back to catch the punt. The Vandy guy took a step forward, saw that none of our linemen were rushing him, and he started running. Everybody was running down the field and looking up besides me and that quarterback, who was running behind the 20 other players. We stopped him on the 22. The guy later threw the ball, had it slapped back into his hands, and threw it again.

"Against Tennessee that year, we were ahead 7-0 and had them backed up on the five, when Majors quick-kicked and I caught it on the 40. Instead of going straight ahead, I started running in a circle trying to get open and ended up losing 20 yards. In addition, we were penalized for clipping on the play and for unnecessary roughness after the ball was dead. We were back to the 10 by this time. We lost, 20-7."

That was Blanton Collier's first of only two losses to Tennessee. The difference was Majors, who battered the Wildcat line for two touchdowns in the late going, with his second score coming after consecutive runs of 23 and 31 yards. When he fumbled once on the 10, the ball sailed forward into the arms of tackle Gordy for a touchdown.

Graduating from UK after the 1956 football season were such fine players as Mitchell, Pack, Butler, Frankenberger, Bennett, Curnutte, Kuhn, Hughes, Netoskie, and Dougherty. They would be sorely missed.

Time Out: Lou Michaels

A nationwide television audience and 30,000 local fans got their first look at an All-American when the 1956 football season got underway on Stoll Field. With Georgia Tech poised on UK's one foot line, a six-foot-three, 230-pound Wildcat applied a bone-jarring tackle to a Tech runner, stopping the drive cold. Then on the ensuing play, that same Wildcat exploded a spiraling 61-yard punt from his own end zone, setting the activity back on Tech's 39 yard stripe.

That was Lou Michaels, described by those who knew him in Lexington as the best football player they had ever seen.

"He was probably the greatest athlete I ever played with here," said Billy Mitchell, now an assistant coach at UK. "When he stepped on the campus, he was ready. You can go through the games he played in four years here, and you couldn't come up with a bad one.

"He was also the only guy I ever knew who loved to practice. He would wake up in the morning just dreaming about playing on the practice field. He took discipline as well as anyone—in fact, better than most. He loved to work, and as a result, he got better and better."

Buckshot Underwood, who was UK line coach during Michaels' sophomore year, said, "He was the greatest football player I've ever seen at UK. On the day we played Tennessee that year, he was the greatest player in America. He was football indoctrinated. Everything he did was based on football. If we were traveling through a town, he might say, 'This town is no good. They don't have a football team.' That was the way he judged them.

"And was he rough? He would fight a circle saw. He was one of the meanest football players I've ever seen. He would tear your head off if you didn't get out of the way."

The possibility of Michaels attending UK was so uncertain at one time that Collier must have awakened in the middle of many nights, shuddering at the very thought of losing him. The association between the player and coach began in 1954 when Collier was backfield coach of the Browns and Walt Michaels, Cleveland's stellar lineman, was preparing to send his younger brother (Lou)—a fine football prospect—to college. Since Walt was a prominent Washington & Lee graduate, he was expected to use his influence to send Lou to that institution. However, almost simultaneously with the announcement that UK had hired Collier, Washington & Lee revealed that its athletic program was to be de-emphasized.

"I thought of Washington & Lee indirectly," Lou said by telephone from his Lou Michaels Inn in Swoyerville, Pennsylvania, in April, 1975, "but I never really intended to go there. Everybody planned it for me, but I was interested in a larger school."

He checked in on the Kentucky campus and immediately issued advance notices of his varsity prowess. His brutish assault

Lou Michaels and Blanton Collier.

on the rival yearling squads verified it, and he earned the respect of the Wildcats, both frosh and varsity. Perhaps the best appraisal came from UK's Larry Hennessey, a veteran who earned four letters and in 1975 was a longtime assistant to Paul Bryant at Alabama.

"I've been in a lot of two-on-one drills," Hennessey said in 1954, "but that freshman out there is the toughest three-on-one yet."

"I had it so easy at Kentucky, blocking the material they had there," Michaels said. "Anybody that ever got in front of me, I was able to block. I was very fortunate. I never had any trouble one-on-one, two-on-one, but Buckshot Underwood got so he never used me in those drills. . . .

"He told me one time to hit a guy in the face. 'You mean, you want me to hit this guy right in the face?' I asked. 'This is the only way you're going to be an athlete—and win,' he said. 'If you don't hit them right in the choppers, you're not going to win.' There's the man who taught me the rules."

Such crowd-pleasing feats as those pulled before the nationwide NBC-TV audience in the 1956 game with Tech were a steady diet for Michaels during his three varsity seasons at UK. While the press ran out of adjectives to describe his prowess, rival coaches were just as lavish in their praise.

"Not since Bob Gain have I ever seen a player dominate the action like that Michaels fellow," enthused Tech's Bobby Dodd. "His 61-yard, on-the-fly kick from Kentucky's own end zone was one of the greatest pressure punts I've ever seen. We won the game (14-6), but Michaels definitely was the game's best player."

Michaels indeed was magnificent that sunny September afternoon, making 14 tackles—eight of them unassisted—and his performance against Maryland a week later was almost a replica of the opener. Throughout the season the nation became well acquainted with his exploits. Of the 21 organizations announcing All-American teams, 14 listed him as a first-teamer. The other seven had him on the second unit. He earned spots on eight of the 10 All-American checklists compiled weekly by news services for distinguished performances.

Statistically speaking, Michaels probably meant the difference between success and failure for UK's 1956 campaign. In

Lou Michaels.

his 57 punting assignments, he posted a 38.3 average and registered a 3.7 out of a perfect 5 on the coaches' system of grading game movies. "Against Tennessee, he graded 96 percent," Underwood said. In 10 games he saw 556 minutes of combat. It was a case, as one assistant coach put it, of being just too valuable to rest. Besides his reckless thrusts at the enemy, his power made him a long-range field goal threat. His 30-yard boot against Florida in the rain put the Kentuckians ahead to stay.

Collier, reminiscing in 1975, said Michaels did not use a tee on the slick grass and kicked the ball so close to the ground that the Florida people thought he almost punted.

"The next thing that happened was we had the ball on the goal line," he said. "It was pouring down rain, and we needed a touchdown badly. On fourth down I sent in the same pass—No. 66—the same one that beat Tennessee the year before. But this time we had changed it a little, with Kenny Robertson, our quarterback, throwing to Jim Urbaniak instead of Schnellenberger.

"When Urbaniak was a freshman, he had caught the ball so poorly that we almost put him in another position. But we did a little therapy on him and tried to help him, and through dedication on his part, he became a good receiver. In that Florida game we faked the running play and threw to Urbaniak for the winning touchdown. Shortly after that we were backed up on our own goal line, and ahead, 17-6. Rather than let them block the kick in that rain, I elected to give them a safety, and I will never forget that Michaels was fit to be tied. He didn't want to give them anything."

"Football was my game," Michaels said. "I loved it. I wanted to eat, sleep, and live it. Everything I wanted to do in life was win. This is the thing that stands out."

It was hard to pinpoint the things he did best. He was most spectacular on defense, being blessed with a great "nose" for football, an ability that let him "luck out" with sensational tackles more often than not when he relied on guesswork to figure out where to be to stop an opposition ballcarrier. It was not unusual for him to make a tackle well behind the line of scrimmage at a spot far removed from his normal area of responsibility. His bone-jarring tackles caused a half-dozen or more fumbles by the enemy in 1956, with three of those proving the springboard for crucial touchdowns.

While he admittedly was a defensive giant, Michaels was

also tremendous in offensive performances. The coaches made much use of his quickness, speed, and downfield blocking ability by having him pull out to lead interference or smash through to knock down key secondary men.

"Lou Michaels does everything well," Collier said. "He does all that's asked of him and then some. He's superb on defense, equally good offensively, and extremely effective as a kicker. I haven't seen a better man on the field in a long time."

Although the Wildcats were 3-7 in 1957, Michaels repeated as a consensus All-America and was again almost a one-man show in a stunning 20-6 upset over Tennessee before 36,500 fans at Stoll Field. Cited for his bruising play, his superlative punting, and his all-around alertness, he got the Wildcats off to a good start by recovering a UT fumble in the end zone in the first quarter for his first and only collegiate touchdown. He made it 7-0 with his 11th consecutive conversion of the season.

Seventy seconds later he sent a booming kick to the Vols' Bobby Gordon in the end zone, then tackled Gordon so hard that the Vol back coughed up the ball. Jim Urbaniak recovered on the 39, setting up a four-yard touchdown three plays later by Bob Cravens. Again Michaels kicked the goal. His first miss of the season came after Cravens scored the final touchdown for UK.

The key to the defense was moving Michaels to middle linebacker for the first time. The Wildcats were strong at left tackle but weak at the other tackle, and teams would run away from Michaels. Collier decided to put him at a position where the opposing team could not run away from him. The Wildcats had two weeks to prepare for the Vols, and Michaels worked the entire time at linebacker, with instructions to forget about the pass and go where the ball was.

"We had felt that Tennessee would not throw passes on early downs or in the early part of the ball game," Collier said, "and we hoped to win the toss and kick the ball in order to gain field position. We wanted Michaels to kick the ball into the end zone, forcing Tennessee to begin play on the 20. We had set up the defense to stop the run three straight times, force the Vols to punt, and get possession about midfield.

"We had not shown Lou at linebacker in any other game up to that time, and we told him he had no pass responsibilities. All I said was, 'Where the football is, you go get it.' He played a fantastic defensive game."

"That is one game that happened the right way for me," Michaels said while in Louisville for the 1975 Kentucky Derby. "The fact that it happened on my last day on Stoll Field was a tremendous thing. I knew what Blanton Collier was going through. The man was under pressure. I felt so sorry that I wanted to do everything I could. I wish I could have made all the tackles that day."

And Michaels added, "I just want to say that Collier was the greatest football coach that I ever had. Put that in big quotation marks. He really knew the game."

All In The Family

Family acts are certainly no rarity in collegiate football, and the University of Kentucky has had its share of fine brother combinations. There were the Rodes brothers—J. W. and Pete—in the pre-World War I era; the Phipps brothers—Frank, Jack, and Tom—from 1926 to 1930; and Bob and Dameron Davis just before the outbreak of World War II.

Bryant got a lot of mileage out of Allen and Ed Hamilton, from 1946 to 1951, and the Jones twins (Harry and Larry), from 1950 to 1952. The twins occupy a unique niche in UK football history, having been better known for the numbers they wore—1A and 1B—than for their exploits on the field. Bryant dreamed up that numbering system in the fall of 1950.

It is an interesting coincidence that the brothers Rodes, Phipps, Davis, Hamilton, and Jones were all backfield aces and that Blanton Collier's famous brother combination—Delmar and Lowell Hughes—would both play quarterback and defensive back in that era of one-platoon football.

Collier would also have the fine halfback Calvin Bird in 1958-59-60 but would miss by a couple of years the equally talented halfback Rodger Bird, who would make All-America in 1965. Billy Bird would earn a backfield letter for UK in 1961, and another brother, Jerry, was a fine forward on Adolph Rupp's basketball teams of 1954-55-56.

In their time, the Hughes brothers were two of the most highly touted players ever to come out of the eastern Kentucky hill country. Delmar was the first to matriculate at Prestonsburg High, where he completed 271 aerials in 397 attempts for 3,401 yards over a three-year span, passed for 51 touchdowns, scored

25 himself, and added 67 extra points. Lowell rewrote those records, passing 347 times for 225 completions and 3,482 yards. Outside of his freshman season, in which he scored 30 points in five games, he tallied 46 touchdowns himself and kicked 46 extra points.

During his first freshman-eligible season under Bryant and his first two subsequent seasons under Collier, Delmar played in the shadow of Bob Hardy. He completed 50 percent of his passes and kicked a UK school record of 17 consecutive extra points over a two-year span. He was starting quarterback the first two games of 1956 and then shared the assignments with Kenny Robertson.

Lowell was a levelheaded, versatile performer as a sophomore starter and field general during the ill-fated (3-7) 1957 season. He was the fourth best passer in the SEC and one of the team's outstanding defensive men. His best defensive game was against Mississippi, when he intercepted two passes, and his best offensive game was against Memphis State, when he had a 64-yard touchdown run and threw two touchdown passes to end Jim Urbaniak.

Lowell Hughes scores in a 14-7 loss to Florida in 1957.

In 1958 Lowell had a knee problem against Auburn, had the flu and played only 3½ minutes against LSU, and sprained an ankle the week of the Mississippi State game. However, he still managed to play 302:11 minutes in nine games. The Wildcats had defeated Hawaii and Georgia Tech and lost to Ole Miss before the Auburn game. Lowell left in the second quarter against Auburn. The Tigers scored on a long pass in the final quarter and then added a safety when they trapped Calvin Bird in his own end zone as he attempted to return a punt.

"Hughes got his knee hurt playing basketball for Coach Rupp," Collier said. "It had to be operated on. He took himself out of that game. He came to the sideline and told me, 'My knee is not bothering me, but I can't concentrate on what I'm doing. I think you had better put somebody else in.' That was one of the finest displays of moral courage I have ever seen."

Collier said the loss of Hughes was the single cause of UK's poor showing as they lost to LSU. The Wildcats also lost to Georgia before beating Mississippi State, 33-12, in Lexington. Rain, mud, fumbles, and intercepted passes cost them a frustrating scoreless tie with Vanderbilt. Pascal Benson kicked the wet ball off the mark as a 30-yard field goal attempt failed on the last play of the game.

In the Mississippi State game Collier was calling plays from the sideline, which was strictly against the rules. "At the first of the game we had the ball backed up near our own goal line on third down," he recalled. "I had a play I wanted to run, but the official was watching me. I had a special play—a pass from punt formation—to use when we were in trouble, and the signal was a salute. But that wasn't the play I wanted to use. I was trying to get this other play in, and the official sees me, and I wave like I'm throwing a spitball. It never dawned on me that Eisaman mistook it as a signal for the special pass play until he went in punt formation, threw that pass, and completed it out to about the 50. We took it in and scored."

In one of the oddest plays of the year, Jerry Eisaman literally stole the ball from Tennessee fullback Carl Smith in open field to set the stage for UK's lone touchdown in a 6-2 win over the Vols. The unusual action came on the Vols' first play from scrimmage following a safety after Bird was trapped in his own end zone.

Bird, who had the dubious distinction in 1958 of scoring for three teams, was the Wildcats' chief offensive threat in the

1959 season. He started only four games but was named SEC "Sophomore of the Year." He led the conference in pass receiving with 21 catches for 373 yards and four touchdowns. He also scored five touchdowns and five extra points to rank second in conference scoring.

His best game in the 4-6, 1959 season was against Tennessee, when he personally scored 19 of UK's points in a 20-0 decision over the Vols and was named to the UPI's "National Backfield of the Week" and SEC "Player of the Week." Although he received a slight shoulder separation in a midseason clash with LSU, he started every game and turned in consistently good performances. He made his best showing in kickoff returns (third nationally) and punt returns (11th nationally), ranked third in the SEC in receiving after leading that department in 1958, and was third leading scorer with 55 points.

Another game of significance in 1959 was played at Miami, where the Wildcats were penalized 148 yards but defeated the powerful Hurricanes, 22-3. Miami filled the air with footballs, utilizing the dangerous passing arm of Fran Curci, but the Hurricanes registered their only score on a first period field goal by Al Dangel. Bird had a 55-yard punt return early in the game and added a final touchdown with a 30-yard jaunt in the fourth

Jerry Eisaman steals the ball from Tennessee's Carl Smith in UK's 6-2 win over Tennessee in 1958.

quarter.

Collier confused his players with his signals in the game with Georgia Tech that season, and he recalls the game.

"For some reason we played Georgia Tech in Lexington again that year," Collier said, "and Bobby Dodd was still kidding me—and to this day kids me—about the year before, when we beat him in the pouring rain on what he claimed was a 'fair-weather' play. We had a boy named Bob Cravens from Owensboro, and we had a special forward pass play for him. We said if we ever got to a certain point on the field—the 30 yard line—the play was to be called. We called it, and Cravens scored standing up.

"For that 1959 game I had a signal system mostly centered around how I did my program. Sometimes I had a pocket-type pass, and I would put my hands in my pocket. I told Lowell Hughes if I walked away from him, he was on his own. We had the ball back about our 20 on fourth and seven or eight. I turned and walked away from him, but I put my hands in my pocket; and he forgot about that walking away bit and called a pass play—and completed it. They had us, 14-12, in the latter part of the game, and we got down to the goal line and couldn't get it across. We missed a field goal."

Quarterback Jerry Woolum and end Tom Hutchinson were a promising sophomore passing combination the following year (1960). But the Wildcats got off to a terrible start, losing to Tech, 23-13, in Atlanta, to eventual national champion Mississippi, 21-6; and to Auburn, 10-7. However, they ended a four-year scoring drought against the Plainsmen when Bird scored late in the second quarter, after Auburn had tallied on a 47-yard run by fullback John McGeaver. With the game deadlocked, 7-7, UK quarterback Tom Rodgers gambled on a pass from deep in his own territory. Auburn halfback Jimmy Burson intercepted the ball, and injured Auburn fullback Ed Dyas came in and kicked a 28-yard, game-winning field goal after the drive faltered.

One of the oddest plays of the season set up the UK score in the LSU game. A 28-yard field goal by Clarkie Mayfield was to win the game for the Wildcats, and it occurred after a strange play on a fourth and one situation on the LSU 25. Woolum elected to gamble on a sneak for the key first down. He plunged into the Tiger line and seemingly was stopped, but before the official blew the ball dead, the UK quarterback tossed an improvised pitchout down the line of scrimmage to sophomore halfback Gary Steward. Steward gathered it in and moved forward to the 19 for the first down that led to the field goal.

Mayfield, head coach at Jacksonville (Alabama) State University, recalled that game in a letter to the writer in February, 1975:

"John North, now coach of the New Orleans Saints, told me before I tried it, 'Mountain Boy, if you miss it, just keep on running because you won't eat another meal here.' Also in my sophomore year, I kicked a field goal in the last few minutes of the game to tie 10-10 against Tennessee."

Both Hutchinson and Woolum had fine sophomore seasons. Hutchinson, who kept bees for a hobby at the family farm at Tell City, Indiana, hauled in two passes from Eisaman and three from Woolum in his debut against Georgia Tech, and he sparked a comeback that almost derailed the highly regarded Engineers. Although never starting a game that season, he caught 30 passes for 455 yards and four touchdowns to place second in the SEC and be named All-Conference. On a deep and winding pattern against Tennessee, he completely outwitted safety Billy Majors, then stopped and reversed field to make a sensational catch of an underthrown Eisaman pass. This set up Mayfield's field goal. A similar catch against Auburn in 1961 would score the second UK touchdown in a 14-12 victory over the Tigers.

Among the 16 lettermen lost via graduation in 1961 were backs Bird, Sturgeon, Poynter, Eisaman, and Rodgers; end Dick Mueller; and lineman Lloyd Hodge. However, there was much optimism as Collier entered his final season at UK. In addition to Woolum and Hutchinson, he had halfbacks Bill Ransdell, Gary Steward, and sophomore Darrell Cox; ends Dave Gash and Tommy Simpson; tackles Junior Hawthorne and Herschel Turner; and center Irv Goode, who would be named All-American.

The 1961 schedule seemed a little lighter, with Miami (Florida) returning as opening foe in place of powerful Georgia Tech. However, quarterback George Mira and end Bill Miller teamed to lead the Hurricanes to a 14-7 victory in Lexington. It was Miami's first win ever in 14 games against Wildcat teams.

Mayfield kicked two field goals against Mississippi, and UK trailed only 7-6 in the first half. But the Rebels came to life in the second half, returning an intercepted pass 69 yards and driving for another third quarter score. Ole Miss won, 20-6. Mayfield's extra points beat Auburn, 14-12, however, and the Cats also beat Kansas State. Then came a 24-14 loss to LSU, when a UK upset failed to materialize, and a 16-15 loss to Georgia, when the Wildcats lost six fumbles. Georgia got its final touchdown by recovering a Woolum bobble in the end zone. They defeated Florida State, 20-0, but lost the services of Woolum, who broke a leg.

At the time of his injury in the Florida State game, Woolum was third leading passer in the nation with 70 completions in 125 attempts for 892 yards. Without him, the Wildcats had trouble subduing weak Vanderbilt and troublesome Xavier. Tennessee took its first win in the series since 1956, and first in Lexington since 1951, as sophomore Mallon Faircloth ran and passed the Vols to a 26-16 decision. The Vols scored once in the first and second quarters and twice in the third before UK gained two quick markers through the air. Hutchinson scored the final touchdown on a play covering 73 yards. He caught 32 passes for 543 yards that season, a UK record at the time. Four catches were touchdowns. At the end of the season Hutchinson was named All-SEC for the third consecutive year, and he made second team All-American.

Charlie Bradshaw

Shortly after Charlie Bradshaw was named head football coach at the University of Kentucky in January of 1962, he walked into the Wildcat squad room and received a standing ovation from the 88 players he inherited from Blanton Collier.

"I remember it like it was yesterday," said Dave Gash, who played end for both Collier and Bradshaw. "At that time, all the players 19 and 20 years of age felt like we needed a change. We thought Bradshaw, with his experience under Bryant, was going to turn the program around and win. We were tired of finishing 5-5 and not winning the big games. That ovation was out of respect for him, but I imagine any other coach coming in then would have been treated the same way.

"Charlie talked that day of inner toughness, sacrifice. He said we were in for a tremendous experience, but the price of victory would come high. He promised us the hardest work we'd ever known and said that we must be dedicated and, most of all, must have discipline."

The 37-year-old Bradshaw, a former marine corps drill instructor, meant exactly what he said. Before the Wildcats played their first game that year, more than 50 of their original number would desert the ranks.

He brought back to UK the system of recruiting tough, aggressive players, impressing upon them that the only thing that matters is victory. He trained them to an absolute peak of condition and taught them to hit until the opponent inevitably falters and then capitalize on his mistakes. It had worked for Bryant at UK in 1946, at Texas A&M in 1954, and again at Alabama in 1958. Described by Auburn coach Ralph Jordan as "the new hell-for-leather, helmet-busting, gang-tackling game they're playing here in the Southeastern Conference," it suddenly seemed the only game that could win.

"Charlie expected no less from his players than he had given himself," Athletic Director Bernie Shively said. "Everything he ever did was done the hard way and by being tough inside. His father died when he was 14 months old, leaving his mother with three children. And the only way for him to get a college education was to earn it, and he did it through athletics.

"I remember when he [as a player] had an emergency appendectomy after the first day of fall practice in 1946. He had a McBurney incision, which parted the muscles instead of cutting them, and he participated in a scrimmage 10 days later. He played in the opening game less than three weeks after the operation. To me, his coaching of football reflected along the same lines."

Bryant, asked in 1963 where he first met Bradshaw, replied, "It was in 1940, at Montgomery, where I was trying to recruit his older brother for Vanderbilt. This little brother was only 15, but I never forgot his face, his manners, his eagerness."

"The depression was rough," Bradshaw once recalled. "Then, in the middle of the 1930s, I worked as a newsboy, bellboy, carpenter, with a bottling company, and lots of other jobs. But I got time to play football at Sidney Lanier High School (in Montgomery, Alabama). When I was 15, I started in football. The little sacrifices I've made are coming back to me. . . .I love football because I know what it has meant to me. Without it, I wouldn't have gotten an education and wouldn't have been in position to render service, not just to football players, but to other young people."

Upon graduation from Sidney Lanier, he attended UK one semester before entering the marines. He returned to UK to play on Bryant's first three Wildcat teams, earned his first of four letters as a center in 1946, and picked up his three subsequent letters as a 165-pound end. As a graduate student he was ruled ineligible for further competition after participating in three games in 1949. He remained on the coaching staff as a student assistant and returned to Montgomery the following year as coach and coordinator of the junior high program at Sidney Lanier.

Chosen an aide in 1954 on Blanton Collier's first staff at UK, he remained in Lexington five years as end coach and later offensive backfield coach before moving to Alabama. He gained much recognition as line coach and then as offensive coach for the national champion Tide in 1961.

"When Charlie got to Alabama, they already had their off-season program," said Chink Sengel, a holdover assistant coach from the Collier regime. "He was trying to change the image of the whole thing at UK—study habits, attending classes regularly, keeping up with assignments, dress code. Really nothing different from today, except that coaches today have better rapport. Charlie tried to make one big change instead of going into things gradually. It came as a big shock."

"You would never believe it possible what we had to do in an hour," Dave Gash said. "We would wrestle 15 minutes, lift weights 15 minutes, hit dummies 15 minutes, and run and have agility drills 15 minutes. Pretty soon people started dropping out, and I felt this was good. We definitely had some dead weight on the team. . .people getting free rides and not doing the things necessary to win. They needed to make up their mind whether they were willing to pay the price. It got to the point where I felt we had lost the dead weight, but then spring practice started, and we started losing people who could take the physical punishment but not the mental harassment."

"Not all the players quit, and not all who quit were bitter," Tom Hutchinson told *Sports Illustrated*. "The practices were tough physically, but we all took the same knocks. I don't believe anyone was unequal to the butting and the banging. It was the mental stress and the day-after-day demands that wore a lot of the guys down. I suspect that this thing just snowballed and got out of hand—sort of like mass hysteria."

The better players among those who quit were Dale Lindsey, a sophomore fullback who would become a Little All-American at Western Kentucky and a starting linebacker for the Cleveland Browns; center John Mutchler, a two-year letterman whose father was a principal at Paducah Tilghman High School; Dan Riviero, a junior end who transferred to Tampa; Phil Branson, a sophomore fullback who quit during the season and later played for South Carolina; and Darrell Cox, star sophomore halfback.

Darrell Cox had led the SEC and ranked fourth nationally in punt returning with 21 returns for 281 yards in 1961. Despite a broken hand received in the Auburn game, he had seen 331:38 minutes of action in nine games, including three

Bradshaw with quarterback Jerry Woolum and end Tom Hutchinson.

starts at halfback. And he posted UK's longest scoring play of the season—an 86-yard punt return versus Florida State. He was a fine defensive back (four interceptions), caught 10 passes, and averaged 34.9 yards on 50 punts.

"To make a long story short, 19 of us quit after a hard scrimmage," Cox later told Earl Cox of the *Courier-Journal*. "It was the silliest thing I've ever done, but my friends were leaving and I did too.

"Mr. Bob Hardy, who used to play at Kentucky, and Mrs. Helen Fishback, our housemother, talked to me when I quit and convinced me what a mistake I had made. I wanted to go back, but Bradshaw said no.

"I signed a release from my scholarship and moved out of the football house. I got a little basement room out in town where I stayed two weeks, confused as any boy ever was. I wanted to stay in school, but I wasn't financially able without a scholarship.

"Tommy Simpson, one of the seniors on the team, came

to see me. He said he had talked with Coach Bradshaw about me. Tommy convinced me that I should talk with Coach Bradshaw. I did and Coach agreed to let me come back—but only if every member of the team wanted me back. And he told me that if I came back, no one else would ever be allowed to quit and come back. And no one but me was allowed to come back, although several tried to.

"Because I had missed practice two weeks, I had a hard time keeping up. And then came a crisis that only a few people know about. I let my grades fall down. The first thing I knew I had to enroll for nine hours (six is considered a normal load) during summer school to get eligible to play. And not only that, I had to make A's in all three courses.

"I didn't do a thing but study all summer. I studied harder than I've ever studied in my life and I came up with three A's."

"We were glad to get Cox back," Gash said. "We needed all the help we could get. I knew Mutchler and Lindsey wouldn't be back. Mutchler said he was going to stay in the spring to show them he could take it. That first spring was awful. You'd get so fatigued mentally and physically that you didn't give a damn, but I'll tell you what—when we came back that fall, we were in shape."

Clarkie Mayfield kicks field goal to defeat LSU, 3-0, in 1960.

Clarkie Mayfield remembers how much weight he lost under Bradshaw. "In the spring before my senior year, when Coach Collier left and Coach Bradshaw came, I weighed 204 pounds, and for my last game the next year against Tennessee, I weighed 162 pounds," he said. "I remember how hard we thought it was, but looking back, I think it was because we had never had indoor workouts before. Consequently, several quit... an awful lot quit. I even thought about it myself.

"We ended up with 26 players that year, and we would play 17 or 18 players a game while the other teams would play 40 or 45. We had a joke that the other teams would change complete teams while Tommy Simpson would go in for the center and I would go in for the quarterback. The other nine members of our team would stay in."

Bradshaw said the lack of numbers was not a concern of a single coach on his staff. "That we are strong in the quality of each of our members is all that matters," he said. "If we are better and are tougher mentally and are willing to give whatever it takes to win, then we will win. All our kids are lean, skinny, and feel their responsibility as we muster our forces."

The Thin Thirty

Midway into fall football practice at UK in 1962, some of the team leaders were so concerned with the diminishing numbers that they called a squad meeting and told the other players: "You're either with us or you can leave. We're depending on every man, and we don't want anybody holding down a position and then leaving at the last minute so that somebody else will have to learn it all over again. If you want to leave, we'll help you pack. There are no hard feelings behind this. Get out now, or stay and work."

Those who remained will be known forever in UK football annals as "The Thin Thirty." Lining up as starters for the opening game against Florida State that year were:

Ends—Proven pass catchers Hutchinson and Gash, who would be cast in different roles in the run-oriented offense Bradshaw brought from the Capstone. However, Hutchinson would manage to equal his 1961 total of 32 catches and finish with a career total of 94 catches for 1,483 yards and nine touchdowns. He would be named All-SEC for the third straight year and would make some second and third team All-American squads.

Tackles—Herschel Turner, a steel worker's son from Alexandria, Kentucky, who was the "iron man" of the squad, playing 52 minutes a game, and Pearl "Junior" Hawthorne, who had spent his early years in a children's home, appeared in juvenile court, and finally gave up a job with a carnival to play football in high school. Both would make All-SEC that year. Turner would be an All-America in 1963.

Guards—Jim Hill, a former high school backfield star from

Neon, Kentucky, and Vince Semary of Cleveland, Ohio, a converted fullback who pursued sculpture as a hobby.

Center—Simpson, son-in-law of Frank Chelf (congressman from Lebanon, Kentucky) and a favorite of Bradshaw.

Quarterback—Woolum, a slow-of-foot but fine "pocket" passer who would be less effective under Bradshaw than he probably would have been had Collier remained at UK.

Fullback—Perky Bryant, a tough five-foot-nine, 190-pound mountain boy from Evarts, Kentucky, who would lead Wildcat scorers with 24 points that year.

Halfbacks—Gary Steward of Henshaw, Kentucky, who would average 3.6 yards a carry, catch 10 passes, and return two interceptions 11 yards; and Cox, who would lead the Wildcats in rushing (81 for 402), punt returns (13 for 131), kickoff returns (14 for 296), interceptions (three), and finish second to Hutchinson in receptions (32 for 485). Ken Bocard would start the final four games in Steward's place.

Also listed on the roster were Giles Smith and Terry Clark, who were medical casualties before the season began. Smith, a sophomore end from Lexington, was hospitalized in April after a routine game scrimmage. Emergency cranial surgery was performed to correct dangerous bleeding from lacerations of the brain stem. What caused the sudden hemorrhage was never determined by doctors. A review of game films offered no clues. After a second operation Smith lapsed into a coma for a long length of time, underwent three months of intensive hospital care, returned to his classwork, and served as a manager of Wildcat teams until his graduation. Clark was held out because of a back ailment, but he later lettered for UK and was a successful high school coach in 1975.

Against Florida State's "Chief," "Renegade," and "Warrior" platoons, Bradshaw played a total of 25 people, and the Wildcats emerged with a scoreless tie against a fine team. Their best chance to score came after they had driven from their own 39 to the Seminole 11, but Mayfield's 24-yard field goal attempt fell short.

Against seventh-ranked Ole Miss in racially troubled Jackson, they gained a first down inside the 20 but failed to score and lost, 14-0. Johnny Vaught called them "the best conditioned and hardest hitting Kentucky team we've ever faced." Auburn beat them, 16-6, on three field goals and a closing-minutes touchdown.

The "Thin 30" Center: The coaching staff headed by Charlie Bradshaw (kneeling) and including (from the left) Homer Rice, Dave Hart, Bill Jasper, Chuck Knox, George Sengel, Bob Ford, Bud Moore, George Boone, Leeman Bennett, Ralph Hawkins, and Matt Lair. Top Row: The players (left to right), Jim Foley, Terry Clark, Dennis Schrecker, Ray Heffington, Jim Hill, Jerry

Finally the Thin Thirty gave Bradshaw his first victory, a 27-8 verdict over Detroit. Perky Bryant scored three touchdowns against the Titans.

They held off fourth-ranked LSU's three platoons of talent until the final 10 minutes before losing, 7-0, in Lexington, and received a standing ovation from a near-capacity crowd on Stoll Field.

"I shall never forget that game and the great Jerry Stovall," Simpson said. "Coach Bradshaw told me that Jerry was my man and for me to handle him. I did it with the help of other teammates (especially Turner and Hawthorne) because he had fewer yards in that game (74 in 17 carries) than the five-yards per carry he was averaging."

Woolum, Elmer Jackson, Ken Bocard, Frank Sakal, Perky Bryant. Third row: Jesse Grant, Junior Hawthorne, Bob Kosid, Joe Parrott. Second row: Jim Komara, Howard Dunnebacke, Giles Smith, Phil Pickett, Tom Hutchinson, Bob Brown. Bottom row: Dave Gash, Bill Jenkins, Tommy Simpson, Clyde Richardson, Vince Semary, Denny Cardwell, Gary Steward, Darrell Cox, Herschel Turner, and Clarkie Mayfield.

The Wildcats led Georgia on a 10-yard scoring pass from Woolum to Bocard midway into the second quarter but settled for a tie when Bingham Woodward intercepted a Woolum pass on the UK 31 and returned it for a touchdown. They also led Miami for three quarters before wilting on a humid night in the Orange Bowl and losing, 25-17. Miami scored three touchdowns in the final 18 minutes. Woolum had his best night, connecting on 18 of 31 passes for 274 yards, while George Mira hit nine of 17 for 91 yards.

Capitalizing on only one of nine scoring opportunities, they defeated Vanderbilt, 7-0, for their first win of the season on Stoll Field and in SEC competition. In the third quarter Commodore quarterback Hank Lesesne dropped back to pass and had the ball taken away by Turner. This set up a UK touchdown from the 16.

The low point of the season came one week later when they lost, 14-9, to Xavier. Xavier had been scheduled as a pre-Tennessee game breather. The victory was only the second in 20 games with UK for the Musketeers.

"We didn't practice one day for them," Gash said. "It was the most horrible game of my life, like a nightmare. Everything we did was wrong. . .offside, missing passes, fumbling. We fumbled a pitchout from Woolum to Steward on the one foot line, and by the time Steward had kicked it and Woolum had kicked it, Xavier recovered on the 29."

Playing a total of 22 men against Tennessee, the Wildcats surprised the Vols with a shotgun offense built around the versatile Cox, who among other things gained three more yards (111 in 19 tries) than the entire UT team, caught a 58-yard touchdown pass, threw a six-yard pass, recovered two punts, averaged 41 yards on four punts, broke up four UT passes, and got the necessary yardage in four of five critical third down situations.

The Vols scored first on a field goal in the opening quarter, but UK tied it with a 36-yard boot by Mayfield. Tennessee jumped into another lead early in the fourth quarter after a 73-yard interception return to the UK one yard line set up an easy score. But UK retaliated on a 58-yard pass from Woolum to Cox. A two-point PAT gamble failed, and things looked dark for the 'Cats until Mayfield kicked another field goal (19 yards) in the final 16 seconds for the winning margin, 12-10.

After the game Cox told the following to the *Courier-Journal:*

> When practice started this fall, I wanted to make good so that I could show Charlie Bradshaw that I had quit because I was confused and not because I couldn't take it. I started out on the second team. But worked hard and made the first unit the second week of practice.
>
> Charlie Bradshaw doesn't give many compliments, so I felt like a million dollars when he told me before today's game, "Well, you made it; you've become a man." I was "up" for this game more than any except the Miami game (I'm from Miami).
>
> I was still thinking of what Coach Bradshaw said when I carried the ball on the first play of the game. That

Tennessee end came right at me. I could go either right or left. But I ran right into him and fumbled.

But I didn't let it shake me. I played the best game I've ever played, thanks to the guys up front who blocked so well. I wouldn't trade those guys for anyone.

Bowden Wyatt, UT coach, said, "Cox alone did enough to win for Kentucky. The boy was simply great."

Bradshaw said, "Cox's performance equals anything I've ever seen in a college football game. He'll be one of the best college backs in the country next year."

It is ironic that Cox would not be on the starting offensive team as Bradshaw's sophomore-dominated squad lined up for the opening of the 1963 season.

Bringing home the barrel after defeating Tennessee, 12-10, in 1962 are (clockwise) Clarkie Mayfield, Darrell Cox, Ray Heffington, Frank Sakal, Jim Hill, Jim Komara, Herschel Turner, and Jerry Woolum.

The Die Is Cast

The scene was Mississippi Memorial Stadium in Jackson where UK had just upset No. 1 ranked Ole Miss, 27-21. On that sunny September afternoon in 1964 the Wildcats had come up with their biggest victory since the 1951 triumph over Oklahoma in the Sugar Bowl.

The Wildcats carried Bradshaw off the field, let out a jubilant yell as they entered their dressing room, and then suddenly quieted down as they recognized a stranger in their midst.

"I've never seen a bunch of boys deserve to win as much as you," said Rebel coach Johnny Vaught. "You should have beat us 40 points. I'm proud of you. You're a good bunch. If anybody had to beat me, I'm glad it's you."

On the first play of that game Rodger Bird started to run an end sweep and suddenly improvised and threw a 79-yard scoring pass to Tom Becherer. The play was called back because a UK lineman was illegally downfield. Bird tried the same play early in the second half, and Rick Kestner hauled it in for a 32-yard touchdown. Kestner caught two other touchdown passes, both from Rick Norton, and was accorded national "Lineman of the Week" honors.

The juniors on that squad represented one of the finest groups ever recruited at UK. The class roll included Kentuckians Norton, Bird, and Sam Ball, each destined for All-American honors the following year; All-SEC end Kestner; and such fine out-of-state players as John Andrighetti, Doug Davis, Tony Manzonelli, and Becherer.

Their road to that victory over Ole Miss in Jackson had been paved with blood, sweat, tears, hard work, and long practice sessions, plus a 3-6-1 record in 1963.

"The discipline put on the players was similar to a military school," said Bird, a successful businessman in Henderson, Kentucky, in March, 1975. "There were strenuous workouts, a lot of dissatisfaction and turmoil, and racial problems were just beginning to come on the scene. There was a lot of bad publicity both locally and nationally toward the system Bradshaw was trying to implement. However, I felt that 1963 was the beginning and not the end for UK football."

Norton, a highly sought prep star who had preferred Georgia Tech but succumbed to recruiting pressures from the home state alumni, said he really was not aware that the players had undergone such strenuous training that first spring under Bradshaw. "I didn't realize so many had left," he said. "When I got there and began to talk to the ball players, I was shocked. I don't think people knew what was going on.

"Of the guys who reported for that first practice, 10 or 15 quit, a lot of them from Louisville. In the pros I talked to guys who played under Bryant, and they said Bryant never saw the day he worked a team like Bradshaw.

"We used to have what they called a 'gut-check'—it wasn't a big accomplishment under Bradshaw, but they tell me that 'Bear' would hug you and all that. Charlie made football negative; at the same time, that type of atmosphere made players closer to each other—they stuck together for self-survival.

"As the years went by, it got easier. I don't know if I would have stayed that first spring. Bradshaw talked a lot about the value of self-discipline and made you understand you could overcome a lot of problems if you developed a will. I always felt deep inside he thought what he was doing was right—whether he really understood it or not. But I don't think he understood what one assistant coach was doing to the players.

"My freshman year the varsity had some of the finest passing personnel in Woolum, Hutchinson, Gash, and Cox. They had capabilities to throw on anyone. Woolum was a helluva passer, but he was a slower runner than I was. They used him on a sprint-out, option type. That shocked me as much as anything. They did have a good defense.

"As a starter the next year, I set conference records—for the most interceptions and most consecutive throws without an interception. We ran the sprint-out, which was not my forte. Other teams would blitz me and force me to run. We had a good football team that year."

Rodger Bird got that sophomore season off to a good start by returning the opening kickoff 92 yards for a touchdown in a 33-14 victory over Virginia Tech, which was coached by former Wildcat Jerry Claiborne. Only Noah Mullins had returned a kickoff farther (95 yards vs. Washington & Lee in 1940) for a UK team. "It happened so quickly," Bird said. "I had good blocking from the line and a final block from Kosid." He also gained 157 yards rushing in that game. Norton was less impressive, having two of his six passes intercepted.

The Wildcats lost to defending SEC champion Ole Miss, 31-7, and to Auburn, 14-13. After trailing the Plainsmen, 14-0, for 29 minutes, Norton hit Bird with a 61-yard scoring pass and then cut it to 14-13 on a pass to Kestner. He tried to hit Kestner for a two-point play, but Auburn broke up the pass.

The 'Cats beat Detroit, 35-18; lost to LSU, 28-7; and fell to Georgia, 17-14. In the Georgia game a 17-yard pass from Norton to Kosid in the closing minutes was just shy of a first down on the Bulldog three.

"I feel we lost some we shouldn't have lost," Norton said. "Auburn, with Sidle and Frederickson, had us 14-7 at the half. I still think we could have beat them. In the second quarter I had Kestner on a post for a first down, and an Auburn guy knocked him down, chopped his legs from under him, but there was no flag. We kinda jelled as a team after that.

"We had LSU, 7-0, and were on their five with fourth down near the end of the half. The crowd was so loud that we'd get down and then go back, get down and then go back. I told the official, and he said he was going to give me a delay of game penalty. They went crazy with their running game in the second half. At Georgia I had one of my better games. That's when we started getting a reputation as a hitting club. Georgia had Rakestraw, and, if I'm not mistaken, we put two or three of his receivers out of the game.

"Our scouting report said Miami always ran a draw to the strong side and screen to the weak side, away from the wide side. Two of their big plays came just opposite that. That was the game where they threw a pass back to Mira (28 yards), and it put them in scoring position. They won, 20-14."

Darrell Cox, a starter on defense but relegated to a substitute role on offense, had a 53-yard touchdown run and gained 130 of UK's 145 rushing yards against the Hurricanes. George

Mira hit 21 of 36 passes for 223 yards.

The Wildcats' worst game that season was a 0-0 tie with winless Vanderbilt. They were in Commodore territory only twice, both times as the result of interception runbacks. Prior to that game Norton had thrown an SEC record of 68 passes without an interception.

Talbott Todd, a successful insurance executive in Lexington in March, 1975, remembered the game well:

"We were on our way home [after the game], and Bradshaw walked back through the plane and said, 'We'll be dressed and in our seats at the Sports Center tomorrow morning at five o'clock. Lights will be out tonight at 9:30.' The plane got to Lexington at 9:15.

"Giles Smith woke us up at 4:30 Sunday morning. When we got to the Sports Center, all the lights were out. Our equipment manager, Buster Brown, hadn't got there to turn them on. The bags containing all the equipment we had used in the game were lying around on the floor. We used cigarette lighters and matches to find our stuff, got dressed, and were in our seats, in the dark, before five o'clock.

"About 4:55 'Big Dad'—that's what we called Herschel Turner—said, 'I'm hungrier than a bastard rat.' We all burst out laughing, and just as the laughter died down, Bradshaw flipped on the lights. He gave us five minutes to warm up, and he sent all the assistants up on the tower. Giles had the game chart, and we began with the opening kickoff and played the game over, running the same plays we ran in the game. If a play had gained five yards and we made 10 in the replay, the ball would be brought back five yards.

"When the final whistle blew, it was about seven o'clock. The birds were chirping. Bradshaw called us together and said, 'We're going to have one hour of going in offense and one hour of going in defense.' He called us together again after that was over and said, 'We're going to cover punts for one hour for laughing in the meeting room.' During that drill Seiple was just kicking it out of sight. He couldn't kick it short to save his life. It about killed us covering those punts.

"Two of the guys got in a fight, and Bradshaw told them to pull off their headgear and go to it. We were all pulling for them to fight because it would give us a rest. The fight was going on when the team doctors came onto the field. They broke it up and fussed at Bradshaw.

Herschel Turner.

"After the punts Bradshaw sent the backs and receivers in and kept the line out. They worked another hour on blocking. On Monday we all figured he was going to kill us again, but when we got to the Sports Center, there was this big sign, 'First team offense and defense in sweats.' We liked to fainted. We went out the whole week in shorts, and we beat Baylor in Waco."

"That Sunday practice led to the eventual quitting of a bunch of guys who made up their minds they weren't going to around much longer," Norton said. "It was after that Vanderbilt game when we really started taking a look at what was going on. When we practiced, it wasn't with the idea of improving—it was going out there and trying to kill somebody. You just don't do it that way.

"Baylor was one of the better games we played. Kestner had a helluva game. Trull was their quarterback, and we played the best pass defense we played during the four years I was there. Mississippi was the best team we had played up to then. They were both in the same class.

In that 19-7 upset of the bowl-bound Bears, the Wildcats had their best showing of the year. Don Trull, the nation's leading passer, operating without injured star receiver Lawrence Elkins, who hurt an ankle after catching an eight-yard pass in the first quarter, completed 17 of 30 passes for 248 yards and a touchdown. However, the Wildcats intercepted three of his tosses, including one which Cox returned 42 yards for a touchdown in the second quarter. Turner was named national "Lineman of the Week" for stalking Trull and keeping him off balance throughout the game. He was responsible for dumping Trull for 44 yards in losses. On one occasion, after the Bears had been penalized to the 14 in the third quarter, Cox spilled Kelly Roberts for a five-yard loss. This forced the Bears to go to the air. On the next play Bird intercepted a Trull pass on the five to pull the 'Cats out of danger.

Pres. John F. Kennedy was assassinated the following week, and many sporting events were canceled; however, the UK administration elected to play the Tennessee game on Stoll Field. A chilled, saddened, near-capacity crowd saw the 'Cats drop a 19-0 decision to a fired-up UT team which was bent on gaining a measure of revenge for a 70-0 shellacking of its yearlings by the Kittens that year. Short UK punts held back by the chilling wind set up the Vols' first and third markers. Behind the passing artistry of tailback Mallon Faircloth, UT got all its scores via the aerial route. UK managed only to pick up 85 yards on the ground, with Bird personally contributing 55 yards.

Joining the varsity in 1964 were such fine sophomores as Machel, Spanish, Withrow, and Antonini. Maurice Moorman, a big tackle from Louisville who had opened gaping holes in opposing freshmen lines the preceding year, quit the squad that fall. He eventually became an All-America at Texas A&M and was a fine professional player. His dissatisfaction began when he reported back a few pounds overweight and was made to run a mile after each practice session until he got down to the desired weight.

"Personally, I also quit between my freshman and sophomore year," confessed Seiple, who in 1975 was a veteran punter with the Miami Dolphins. "I was going home, but I talked to guys like Bird and Norton who were starters on the team, and I stayed. The attitude of the team toward Bradshaw was one of the things that hurt.

"I can recall how hard the work was and how you couldn't please some of the assistant coaches, no matter how hard you tried. They were looking for the bad part. It was a completely different ball game from what I experienced in high school and in the pros. Everybody on the field was afraid.

"When they played that Vandy game over, I was a freshman. Believe me, I was scared because I just knew they were going to call us also at five o'clock, but they didn't. However, we played many of those games over."

The 1964 season started off with an unimpressive 13-6 victory over Detroit, Bird scoring both UK touchdowns. After the upset of Ole Miss, the Wildcats defeated fifth-ranked Auburn, 20-0, in Lexington. Bird again scored two touchdowns, one on a 95-yard return of a wayward pass tossed by Jimmy Sidle. He gained 112 yards rushing and prevented two sure Tiger scores with timely tackling from his safety position. Norton and Kestner contributed the final touchdown after a 40-yard run by Bird.

The Wildcats were ranked No. 7 nationally when they journeyed to Tallahassee to meet undefeated, untied, unscored-on Florida State. The Seminoles had a potent offense led by six-foot-five quarterback Steve Tensi and flanker Fred Biletnikoff, along with a defensive line which lived up to its nickname, "The Seven Magnificents."

The Seminoles put points on the board in every quarter, including three in the opening frame. They ate up ground consistently behind the passing of Tensi to Biletnikoff while harassing Wildcat passers and runners effectively. The UK offense never could get rolling until Antonini scored in the final 29 seconds. Florida State won, 48-6. The Seminoles finished the season 9-1-1 and made a decisive conquest of Oklahoma in the Gator Bowl.

"We gave them three easy touchdowns on weird plays," Norton said. "The first was a Statue of Liberty play on third and 15. The receiver came around the end and went to the one. The next was the punt they claimed hit Bird's leg, which set up a touchdown, and the third time was when Biletnikoff caught a 69-yard scoring pass with nobody on him. In the second half they started running a sweep that our coaches didn't pick up until they saw the game films the next day. They got three of the quickests touchdowns you ever saw off it."

"I've thought about that game time and again," Seiple said. "We had bad practices all week. Bradshaw was a firm believer that if you put out in practice, you would put out in a game. We had a slow, sluggish practice on Friday, and he told us at the Saturday pregame meal if we went out and got beat, we were going to have a helluva workout when we got back, and we'd wish we were somewhere else—or something to that effect."

"They brought us back to Lexington and had us running on Sunday," Norton said. "I have never run so much in my life. Guys were throwing up all over the place. We got so tired, we could hardly walk. He took a good football team that had beat two of the best teams in the nation and lost a game, and he actually tried to kill us. It just didn't make any sense."

Unable to rise from the ashes of that defeat, the Wildcats fell to LSU (27-7), Georgia (21-7), and West Virginia (26-21) before edging Vanderbilt (22-21) at Homecoming in Lexington.

"I scored on the first play from scrimmage in the LSU game," Bird said, "but they were too deep for us. A lot of people don't realize that we were going both ways that year. I played safety and halfback and returned punts and kickoffs. But I didn't mind that as much as the practices."

After losing to Baylor, 17-15, the Wildcats salvaged a

break-even season by whipping Tennessee, 12-7, in Knoxville. They were trailing the Vols, 7-6, midway into the final quarter when Norton threw a 68-yard pass to Kestner just inside the back line of the end zone for the winning marker.

Although he was not mentioned on any All-SEC team, Norton was the conference's total offense and passing leader with 1,319 yards total and 1,514 yards in the air. He set school records for most plays (272 on 70 runs, 202 passes) and most passes he had intercepted (18).

Kestner broke the school record for catches (42) and yards gained by a receiver (639), erasing marks set by Steve Meilinger and Tom Hutchinson. His 185 yards against Mississippi was a school record. Rodger Bird led team scoring with 60 points.

Thanks to the victory over Tennessee and to the fact that several fine players were returning, UK fans looked forward eagerly to the 1965 season. They would settle for no less than a winning season and bowl appearance. Bradshaw's moment of truth had arrived.

Run For The Roses

Just before the 1965 football season began at the University of Kentucky, Bradshaw told Earl Ruby of the *Courier-Journal*: "This is the 'Derby' year—you might say—my first crop of seniors. If we are going to establish a winning momentum here at Kentucky, this is the best year to do it.

"You know what my problems have been. We first went with emotion alone. We didn't win many. Then we moved up last year to where we had emotion and ability. This year we have emotion, ability and depth—and we are going all out. This is our 'Run for the Roses.'"

His squad totaled 70 players, including 27 lettermen, and he was able for the first time to establish complete offensive and defensive platoons. He moved Mike McGraw and Becherer to defense and left Antonini and Seiple on offense to complement Bird and Norton, establishing a fine balance between passing and running. Wingback Bob Windsor was a highly touted transferee from Montgomery Junior College.

They opened with a 7-0 victory over powerful Missouri on a hot (88 degrees), humid day in Columbia. The score came on a fourth and seven situation on the UK 36 with 50 seconds remaining in the half. Choosing to gamble, Norton passed to Seiple, who caught the ball on the 12 and scored. Some powerful running by Johnny Roland and bulldozing plunges by Barry Lischner gave the Tigers a first down on the UK three in the fourth quarter. Three running plays netted less than two yards before Roland tried a final plunge and was met head-on by a host of blue shirts. When the pile was untangled, UK's Mike McGraw held up the ball. The official signaled a safety, then quickly changed the sign and gave UK the ball on the 20. Terry Beadles, playing safety in his first varsity game, intercepted three passes for Kentucky, including one in the end zone. This was to tie a school record. Seiple had punts of 63 and 64 yards.

"That was probably the best club we played the whole time I was in college," Norton said. "I felt like I could have thrown all day on them, but I never could get time to throw it. They didn't have much of a pass defense, but they had a helluva rush. Eight or nine of those guys went to the pros."

Ole Miss was next on the schedule. The Rebel's coach John Vaught had a hard time pronouncing Seiple's name—"I fear that 'See-Pull,'" he said in a telephone hookup to the Lexington Quarterback Club. However, Vaught would long remember the UK punter. Seiple was standing with the ball on a fourth and 41 situation on the UK 30, with the Wildcats leading, 9-7, and 30 seconds on the clock. When no one rushed him, Seiple went 70 yards for a touchdown and a final score of 16-7.

"They formed a wall to our left side," Seiple recalled in 1975, "and nobody came in to block. I wasn't going to run. I started to kick, and nobody was coming. I hesitated and started to kick again, and nobody was coming. You stand there 15 yards behind the center, and you can see everything. I saw an opening and took off. I saw somebody digging their feet in front of me and getting nowhere. It was Windsor, trying to angle for a block. I shoved him into the Ole Miss player. Calvin Withrow, the center, led me into the end zone. We were about the only ones who knew what was going on. We had rehearsed the play on Wednesday, but I was just horsing around in practice. I never wanted to do anything like that. After that run Bradshaw told me in no uncertain terms that there was no way in the world that I would ever do that again while playing for him. I believed him!"

(Seiple pulled a similar feat in the Dolphins' victory over the Pittsburgh Steelers in the 1972 NFC play-off game.)

"In training camp my second year in pro football I met the Ole Miss player who was supposed to contain on that side, and he told me he got more hell the following week than any player in the history of football," Seiple said.

The Wildcat game plan against Auburn was to control the ball by running a lot, Norton said. "But they took the ball and rammed it down our throat. They had picked up a weakness in our defense. They had a guy free all day on pass rush. He must

Larry Seiple takes off on his celebrated impromptu touchdown run off a fake punt in a 16-7 Wildcat victory over Ole Miss in 1965 in Lexington. Other Wildcats are J. D. Smith (86), Rich Tucci (63), Calvin Withrow (54), Sam Ball (73), and Frank Antonini (47).

have hit me 30 times. He laughed and said he never had an easier game. On important downs they used a defensive maneuver which was hard to handle. I learned about it when I got to the pros."

Auburn took a 17-0 lead in the third quarter and withstood a barrage of Norton passes, including touchdowns of 76, 74, and 44 yards, to win, 23-18, as three UK two-point tries failed. Seiple caught touchdown passes of 76 and 44 yards.

Doug Davis caught two tackle-eligible passes in a thrilling, 26-24 victory over Florida State. The first came on a third and four situation on the FSU 15, with UK trailing, 17-14. Kestner moved into the line to the right of end Windsor, while Andrighetti, the other end, backed off the line. That left the six-foot-four, 238-pound Davis as an eligible receiver.

"I was supposed to run a wide pattern, go down about seven yards, and turn in," he said. "I don't know what I ran, I was so excited." He caught the belly-high pass for 10 yards and a first down on the five. Bird scored four plays later.

The next Davis catch came with UK on Florida State's 33, while the Seminoles were leading, 24-20. Norton passed to the tackle on the 18, and Seiple plunged over from the one a few plays later. Bird scored three touchdowns. FSU had a 100-yard kickoff return in that game. Bill Moreman caught the ball on the goal, ran 13 yards up the middle, and leaped high to lateral to T. K. Wetherell. It was the longest kickoff return on record against the Wildcats until Willie Shelby of Alabama matched it in 1973.

The Wildcats fell behind LSU, 17-0, in Baton Rouge and lost, 31-21. The Bengals intercepted six of Norton's passes. Next, in Athens, Georgia chose the strong wind and scored 10 points in the first quarter. When it came UK's turn to go with the breeze, Norton passed for four touchdowns in the second quarter and a 28-10 victory.

"LSU used a three-man line with four linebackers and four backs, and we tried to throw into it," Norton said. "We had a draw, a sweep, a trap, and neither would work; at half time Homer Rice wanted to come out in a power-running game. They dared us to run, but we didn't run. Labruzzo went crazy, and Doug Moreau caught his first collegiate touchdown pass.

"It was real windy when we played Georgia and we went crazy. They had two or three weaknesses on pass defense, which they changed at the half. We had Kestner going on a post, Bird out and deep, and Seiple splitting. They were trying to cover them with two men. It was just a matter of me picking the right guy. We kept Andrighetti back to block on their blitz. Kestner, Bird, and Seiple each scored on the play."

Before bringing his West Virginia team to Lexington, Coach Gene Corum mispronounced Seiple's name ("Sip-Pel") during a telephone interview. Seiple gained 111 yards rushing and caught five passes for 86 yards in a 28-8 UK decision.

Vanderbilt assistant B. N. Crowe, substituting for Jack Green during the next week's hookup, said, "Seiple is one person we don't intend to antagonize. Inform Larry that we pronounced his name correctly." Seiple responded by returning the opening kickoff 60 yards, sending UK on its way to a 34-0 victory. Bradshaw termed that game, "The best overall game since I've been here."

"We had an opportunity to go to the Gator Bowl after we beat Vanderbilt," Seiple said. "Bradshaw came into the dressing room and told us we had the bid, and we could take it or refuse it. He wanted to beat Houston and play Arkansas in the Cotton Bowl. We put it up for a vote. I, Norton, and a couple others voted for the Gator Bowl. The others went with Charlie."

Bradshaw's dream of meeting Arkansas in a major bowl game and ending the Razorbacks' long winning streak, as his old mentor Bryant had done to Oklahoma 14 years earlier, was dashed by Houston on the Astrodome field. The Wildcats led, 21-16, at half time, but Bo Burrus threw three touchdown passes as the Cougars outscored the Wildcats, 22-0, in the second half. Not only did the Wildcats lose the game, 38-21, but they lost the services of Norton, who left with a knee injury in the closing minutes of the game. He had kept Houston in constant danger with his passes, connecting on 19 of 23 attempts for 373 yards and two touchdowns, one a 75-yarder to Seiple. By comparison, the UK running attack netted only 13 yards.

The Astrodome scoreboard flashed the news that Norton had broken Parilli's all-time offensive record, and the injured quarterback received a standing ovation when he left the field. He was just one yard shy of tying Zeke Bratkowski's passing record of 1,824 yards set in 1952, and he had outpassed Parilli 163 yards while playing in seven fewer games.

"Houston was running 'quick-ins,'" Norton said. "They would hit Post on one side and McVey on the other. This is when we started seeing a lot of pro stuff. We got beat watching

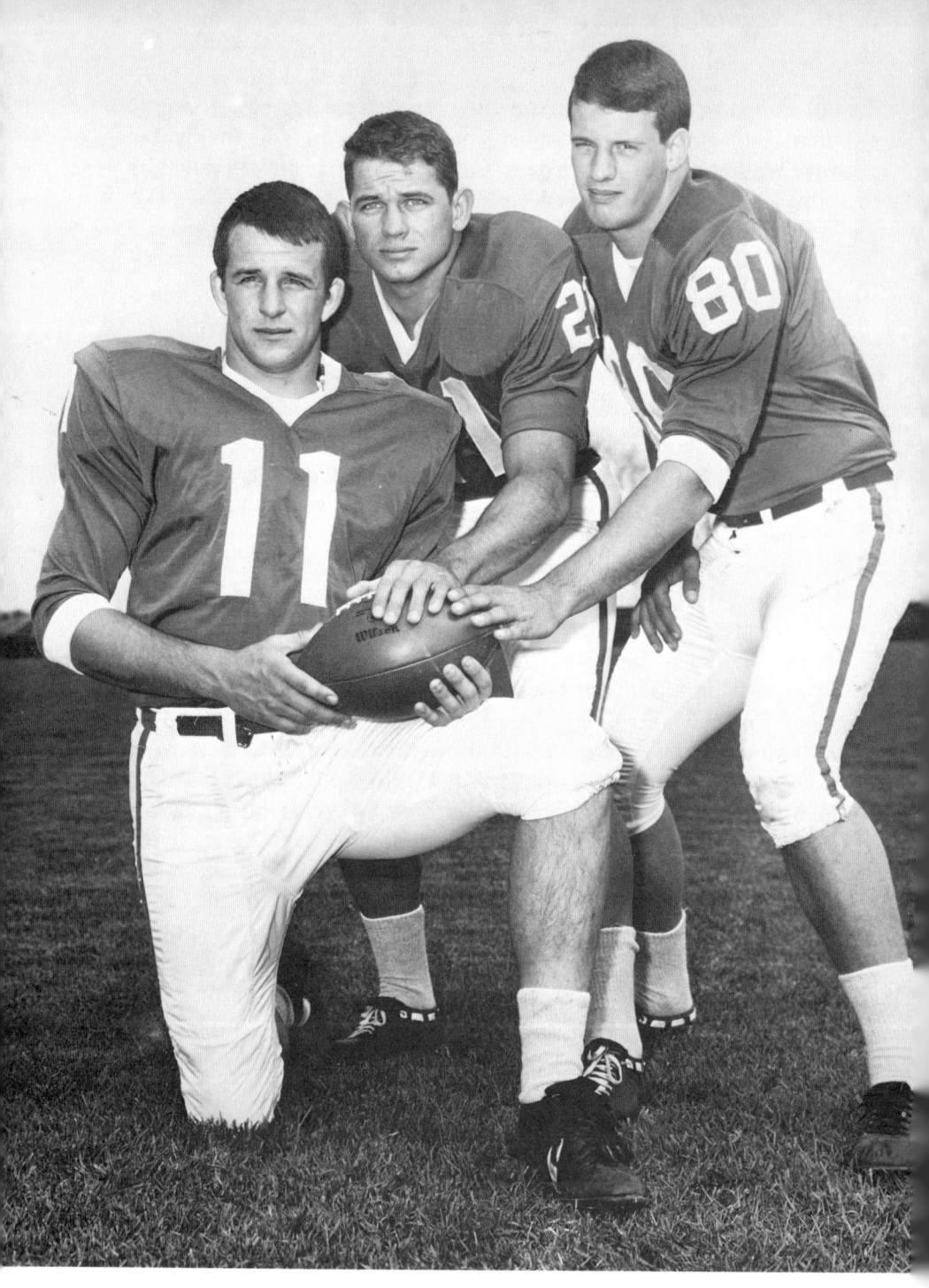

Rick Norton, Rodger Bird, and Rick Kestner.

pro techniques. In the second half they adjusted to shut off Bird's sweep and our passing game to Kestner and Windsor—doubling them with two people each. They took away everything we had done in the first half."

The UK players felt there was no way they could beat Tennessee without Norton. "We basically had two different offenses with Norton and Beadles," Seiple said, "and that hurt us because we didn't have a backup quarterback who could start. I had a chance to break the season record for yards by a receiver in that last game, but Beadles didn't throw to me. He wasn't a passer. I was upset at the time, but it doesn't bother me now."

Walz had opened at quarterback but soon relinquished to Beadles. Together they mustered only 59 yards in the air, compared to UT's 130. It was the first time since 1963 that the Wildcats had been outpassed. Each team got an early field goal, and the score was tied, 3-3, late in the third quarter. Then, in a five-minute span, the Vols, aided by pass interceptions, produced two quick touchdowns and trapped a gambling Beadles in his own end zone for a safety and a 19-3 Tennessee victory. Bradshaw's "Run for the Roses" had died in the stretch.

Time Out: Dicky Lyons

The most controversial and perhaps the best football player at UK during Bradshaw's last three years as head coach was Dicky Lyons, a six-foot, 185-pound all-purpose back from Louisville. Lyons made it a habit of figuring in every statistical department of a game and was known to commit interesting acts of violence.

In the midst of a game in 1967, he decked one of his teammates, a 225-pound offensive tackle, for missing a block. He once dropped another teammate with a forearm for repeatedly failing to execute a block during a preseason scrimmage.

He was such a competitor that when a teammate started past him in the 40-yard dash, he reached out, grabbed the overachiever, threw him aside, and won the race. He even admitted that when his wife was beating him in Monopoly, he picked up what play money he had left and "threw it in her face."

And when Raynard Makin took his time assuming a ready stance, Lyons stepped up and planted a knee to the rump, sending the burly sophomore fullback pitching forward on his face.

"It's just kind of silly when you've got 10 guys doing the right thing and only one guy who is messing up," he said.

Lyons could be equally harsh on himself. He once trapped a pass on one bounce in the Georgia end zone and raged at himself because he felt he would have caught it had he dived for the ball. When the referee returned the ball to the line of scrimmage, Lyons booted it into the stands.

"You gotta get excited to play football," he said. "If a guy can't get mad, he doesn't have any business out there."

Bradshaw said Lyons' competitive spirit made him a

"do-everything" player. "It's pure, simple, unadulterated guts," the coach said admiringly. "Why, he came down here when he was in high school for the state track meet and had never pole vaulted over 11 feet in his life, and he vaulted 12 feet and won it. . .he didn't have any business winning the hurdles either, but he did.

"He is a great runner because he accepts the rudiments of contact that is paramount to the game of football. He likes it and enjoys that part of it."

In his first varsity game in 1966, a 10-0 victory over North Carolina, Lyons set up a touchdown with a 31-yard punt return and then set up a field goal with an interception return. However, what he remembered most was being in on some offensive plays late in the game.

"Bradshaw wanted me to score," he reminisced by telephone from New Orleans, where he was sales manager for Tac Amusement Co. in April, 1975. "I was so tired I could hardly run. When I went to the huddle, I could hardly talk. I told Beadles to just run me to the right. I went to the goal line and fumbled. They recovered. It could have gone either way."

The following week he averted a sure Ole Miss touchdown when he cut in front of a Rebel receiver on the UK two, intercepted a Jodie Graves pass, and returned it 23 yards. However, the 'Cats lost, 17-0.

While Lyons was waxing heroic on defense, Bradshaw was trying to shore up an offensive platoon decimated by the loss of Bird, Norton, Kestner, Davis, and Ball—an offense that had received a grand total of one million dollars in pro bonuses. After a complex system which encompassed 60 possible plays had resulted in only one touchdown in those first two games, Bradshaw said, "We're going to make it simple. We'll do a few things and do them well."

The simplified offense put 17 points on the board while the defense limited Auburn to seven the following week, but it was Lyons who turned the tide by blocking a Jimmy Jones' field goal attempt on the Tiger 24. End Doug Van Meter caught the ball, headed goalward, dropped it on the 12, and then recovered it on the 15.

"I couldn't believe it," Van Meter said. "I don't know what happened. I didn't get tired. I just dropped the ball. I didn't know whether anybody was after me or not. I'm defense. I don't know much about it."

Dicky Lyons.

Lyons could not believe it either. "I was sitting there on the ground and watching Van Meter run down field with nobody within 20 yards of him," he said. "Then I saw the ball go flying. But we scored after he recovered it. I remember in the squad room Bradshaw did a war dance on the table and said we were on our way. I was hurt when we played Virginia Tech the next weekend, and they beat us, 7-0. We got minus yards on the ground."

After LSU held the Wildcats to 33 yards on the ground, and won 30-0, Bradshaw moved Windsor from wingback to tailback, Seiple from tailback to wingback, and Lyons to fullback.

That combination put two touchdowns on the board, but Georgia won, 27-15.

"I played both defense and offense, a total of 57 minutes in that game," Lyons said. "I was so tired that I could hardly walk."

Against West Virginia at Morgantown, Beadles hit Seiple for a 56-yard touchdown. The 'Cats settled for a 14-14 tie after a pass interception in the end zone in the final quarter spoiled the UK victory bid.

"I had started getting the feel of things by then," Lyons said, "and it was in the Vanderbilt game that I threw my first pass. It was called No. 26 Crackback, a checkoff option for the quarterback and pitch man on the short side, and we had run the play all afternoon and saved the option until the last. We had the ball first and 10 on the 23 with less than three minutes to play when Beadles came in with the play. He pitched out to me, and I passed to Dan Spanish, who had faked like he was blocking the cornerback. Spanish carried to the two, and I scored the winning touchdown." (UK won, 14-10.)

Against No. 1 ranked Houston the Wildcats took the opening kickoff and marched 73 yards for a touchdown. Later Lyons returned a punt for a UK record 97-yard touchdown, Beadles completed a 70-yard pass to Seiple, and Windsor had a 43-yard run. However, Homecoming fans on Stoll Field had little else to cheer about as the Cougars gained 649 yards from scrimmage—beating the 629 chalked up against UK by Alabama in 1945—and stomped the 'Cats, 56-18. Lyons had 309 yards in returns to beat Don Phelps' UK record of 289 set against Marquette in 1946.

"That game was a track meet," Lyons recalled. "I thought I was never going to get to the end of the field on that 97-yard run. I must have run 300 yards. Usually you let the ball roll in the end zone, but we were so far behind that I thought, 'What the hell?' A Houston guy finally caught me, but I was in the end zone."

Kentucky scored three touchdowns against Tennessee, something no other team did that season, but Tennessee's Dewey Warren hit a host of talented receivers for 14 completions, 275 yards, and four touchdowns. Beadles hit Seiple for a 78-yard nonscoring pass, and Lyons returned a punt 72 yards as the Wildcats lost, 28-19.

"I was in the best shape of my life when we came back the

following year," Lyons said. "I felt faster and quicker and was ready to be the running back, but Bradshaw switched me to quarterback when Forston got hurt, and I was later switched to tailback and also played fullback."

"I would have confidence playing Lyons anywhere," Bradshaw said at the time. "Even at tackle. The tougher the situation, the tougher he is."

However, Lyons only played half of the 1967 opening game against Indiana when he shared quarterbacking chores with Beadles. "I guess Bradshaw didn't think I had enough experience," he said. "I was at quarterback when Roger Gann scored a 56-yard touchdown on the second play of the game, and we were ahead, 10-0, at half time, but they beat us, 12-10."

Lyons figured in just about every offensive statistic for the 'Cats in 1967. He carried 138 times for 473 yards and eight touchdowns, completed 15 of 41 passes for 195 yards and a touchdown, caught eight passes for 76 yards and a touchdown, punted 46 times for 1,733 yards, returned 24 punts for 390 yards, returned 18 kickoffs for 474 yards, hit a field goal, and kicked four of six extra points. He led the SEC in scoring with 73 points.

He scored both touchdowns in a 26-13 loss to Ole Miss; returned a punt 72 yards against Auburn to give UK a 7-6 lead before the Plainsmen bombed them, 48-7; and scored a UK record-tying, 95-yard, kickoff-return touchdown in a 30-7 loss to LSU. He passed to Phil Thompson for a touchdown in a 31-7 loss to Georgia. Finally the Wildcats' eight-game losing streak (dating back to the Houston game of the preceding year) was broken when Lyons scored all the Wildcat points in a 22-7 victory over West Virginia.

In that West Virginia game Lyons plunged for three touchdowns from short yardage, kicked an extra point, and made good on his first and only collegiate field goal attempt. He next scored on fourth and inches to narrow a Vanderbilt lead to 7-6 and set up a winning touchdown (12-7) with a 51-yard punt return. He caught a 21-yard scoring pass from Dave Bair and scored on a one-yard run in a 28-12 loss to Florida. He ended the season in typical fashion, running 68 yards to the Tennessee three and then plunging over for the lone UK score in a 17-7 loss to the Vols.

"I tore a rib cartilage against Auburn in the first quarter, and I didn't play at all against Virginia Tech," he recalled in

April, 1975. "All I did against LSU was return, but it was my greatest game. I had a total of 160 yards in kickoff returns for an SEC record.

"Georgia was one of my worst games. I think I fumbled four times. After that game I checked into the hospital, dying of the flu. I got out Wednesday, reported for practice on Thursday, pulled a hamstring and could hardly run on Friday, and played against West Virginia on Saturday. The most satisfying thing in my life was when I kicked that field goal. I knew I could kick field goals, but I never had the opportunity. When it went through the goalposts, I was really pleased.

"I remember the Vandy game was in the mud, and we were getting ready to score when the bench called a quarterback sneak, and Vanderbilt must have heard it because they put seven men on the line. I told Bair, 'Don't call it, there's no way,' but he said, 'Shut up, Lyons.' I replied, 'Dammit, Bair, call time out!' When he didn't call time out, I told Kenny Woods, our center, 'Don't snap that ball. There's no way you can block all those guys.' Bair kept calling signals, but Kenny wouldn't snap the ball. Kenny finally turned to Bair and said, 'I'm not going to snap it.' Dave called time out, changed the play, and I scored."

In 1968, Lyon's senior year, the Wildcats were 3-7. However, Lyons felt they had a good ball club and might have won six or seven ball games if they hadn't lost to Ole Miss at Jackson.

"We started off by beating a good Missouri team (12-6)," he said. "They scored on a long pass play (79 yards) from Terry McMillan to Mel Gray in the second quarter. With five minutes left Stan Forston made a smart call. We were second and about eight inside our own 20 when he called a play-action pass. He faked to the halfbacks and then threw to Phil Thompson on a sideline pattern. Phil caught the ball on about the 35 and went to the 26. I scored on the next play with good blocks from Gann, Freibert, and King.

"It was a real hot day (82 degrees), and I think Missouri was fussing about not having ice on their sideline. Dan Devine said his team might have done better if it had worn cool fishnet jerseys like we had, but he said Missouri was on some kind of austerity program and couldn't afford a lot of extra uniforms.

"The turning point was that (30-14) loss to Mississippi. We had all the confidence in the world and we had a 14-10 lead going into the fourth quarter when I dropped a punt and they

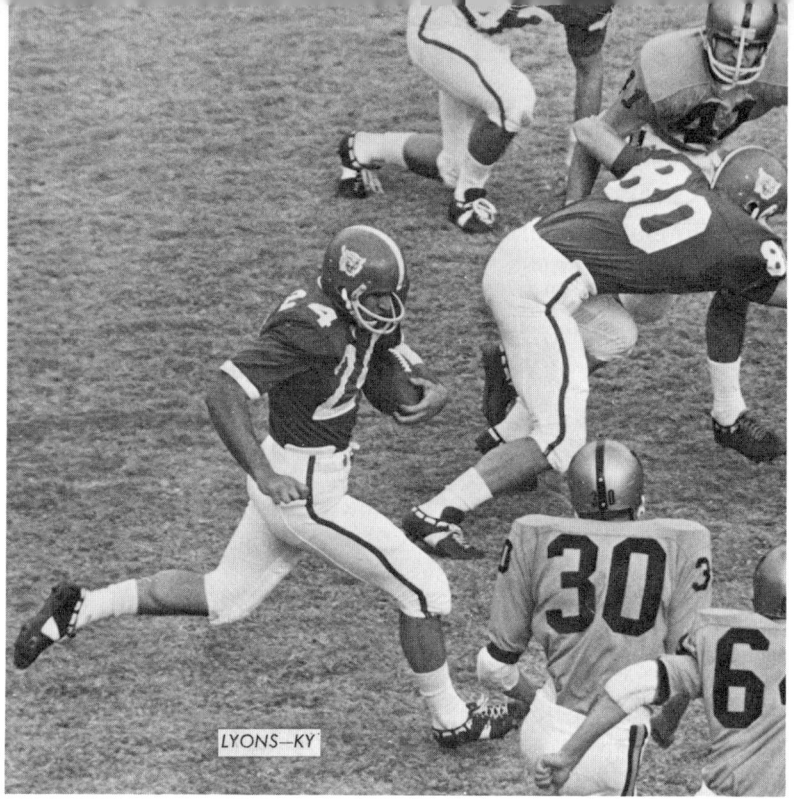

Dicky Lyons sets national records for kickoff returns and punt returns on first play of game with Vanderbilt in Lexington in 1968. Lyons was injured on that kickoff return, and the Wildcats lost, 6-0.

scored.

"The Auburn game was the only game I was ever knocked out in, and I was knocked out twice. . .not completely. It was always one of the toughest teams we played. John Riley set an SEC record by kicking four field goals against us, with one of them going 47 yards. Ron Yarbrough blocked a punt in our end zone and gave Auburn a touchdown. I scored my fourth touchdown in three games, and we lost, 26-7."

Lyons felt one of the best games he ever played in was a 35-34 victory over powerful Oregon State in Lexington. He scored three touchdowns as the Wildcats came from behind three times. The most dramatic moment came midway into the fourth quarter, when OSU pulled to 35-34 and Larry Richart's try for point from placement was wide. Earlier in the game Beaver fullback Bill "Earthquake" Enyart scored four touchdowns and was stopped inches short of scoring a fifth. It was the first one-point win for UK since the 1964 game with Vandy. OSU's 34 points represented the highest total ever made against UK by a losing team. (It erased the 1903 mark of UK over KU, 38-28.)

"As far as the fans were concerned, it was a most exciting game," Lyons said. "They were going crazy."

The Wildcats lost to LSU, 13-3, the following week in Baton Rouge—a game Lyons thought they should have won. "We were all over them, but we couldn't get the ball in the end zone," he said. "We came within inches three times, but they got the break in the end.

"Forston had an emergency appendectomy the following Tuesday, and that was our downfall. He was a cool quarterback, a good leader. I feel we could have broken even or better if he had stayed with us."

Pressed into service against Georgia was Bair, who ironically had been inserted into the UK lineup as a starter against the Bulldogs the previous year. He completed 14 of 35 passes in that 1968 game, including a UK record 92-yard touchdown toss to Lyons. But Georgia intercepted four of his passes, including two returned for touchdowns by Jake Scott, and the Bulldogs won, 35-14.

"I remember Scott's interceptions and Bill Stanfill being in our backfield all night," Bair said. "On that long pass play I faked Lyons into the line and let him go downfield eight or 10 yards because the linebackers were clearing out so fast."

In returning the opening kickoff 34 yards against Vanderbilt, Lyons injured a shoulder, but he set a national career record of 2,199 yards for combined kickoff and punt return yardage. The Commodores won, 6-0, for their first blanking of a Wildcat team in 23 games.

"I feel I could have gone all the way on the outside on that kickoff return," Lyons said, "but I tried to go between two guys and make it on the inside. I fell and hurt my shoulder."

Lyons played only three plays in UK's final two games, losses to Florida and Tennessee, and finished the season with a career record of 2,253 yards in returns.

"I never had any regrets about attending UK," he said in 1975. "People say, 'Dicky, you lost for three years.' Nobody likes to lose, but I had a great time. I had a lot of respect for Bradshaw. He did a lot for me. He was just there at the wrong time."

The Black Cloud

The appointment of Dr. John W. Oswald as the sixth president of the University of Kentucky in June, 1963, had met with the approval of Wildcat football fans who sought in him some semblance of a Messiah who would deliver the embattled program from continuing losses and the embarrassment of an NCAA investigation then in progress.

Honored by *Sports Illustrated* as a member of its Silver Anniversary team, he had played guard in football and was team captain his senior year at DePauw University, where he also threw the discus and tried basketball. Contacted at his home in Berkeley immediately after his acceptance of the UK job, he admitted to an interest in athletics but emphasized that the athletic program should be kept in its proper place in the overall plans of the university. He also agreed with a UK decision to integrate its athletic teams; he let it be known that he expected all coaches to recruit black players and that UK could lose a large amount of its federal funds if its athletic teams were not integrated.

The NCAA investigation had begun in the spring of 1963, when the athletics board invited that body to make sure the proper procedures were being followed in the Wildcat athletic scholarship program. The investigators took an unscheduled look into the off-season training program conducted by Bradshaw and placed the football team on probation one year, beginning April 20, 1964. This meant that Kentucky could not participate in a postseason bowl game that year.

Bradshaw first felt the heavy hand of "The Big O," as Dr. Oswald was called by many in the football camp, when the president demanded an explanation of a closed scrimmage session held on Monday after the Wildcats lost to Georgia, 21-7, at Athens in the middle of the 1964 season. The school and local newspapers had criticized Bradshaw severely after four players received injuries serious enough to necessitate a visit to the clinic after that scrimmage. Shively, Bradshaw, and a team doctor assured Oswald that the injuries were not unusual or unduly intense for such a practice.

Oswald was in the Astrodome when the Wildcats lost to Houston in 1965, but he apparently was more interested in integrating and stabilizing the football program than in participating in a major bowl game. Bradshaw was given a new contract of indeterminate length on Thanksgiving Day of that year, and less than a month later he broke the UK and Southeastern Conference color barrier by signing Nat Northington of Louisville to a UK grant. Soon afterward he signed a second black, Greg Page of Middlesboro, Kentucky.

The 1967 football season began with the usual optimism but was in shambles before the opening game. Page received a paralyzing neck injury in a routine off-speed drill on August 22 and died 38 days later on the eve of a game with Ole Miss in Lexington.

Three weeks after Page's injury, sophomore end Cecil New received a neck injury in a public scrimmage on Stoll Field and was paralyzed from the neck down. In between those two tragic incidents, sophomore quarterback Stan Forston received torn knee ligaments in another routine drill and Northington dislocated a shoulder. The school newspaper editorially attacked the brutality of football and questioned its value on a college campus.

Forston was out for the season, but Northington played briefly in an opening 12-10 loss to Indiana and then saw 3:17 minutes of playing time against Mississippi, becoming the first black ever to play in a football game between two SEC schools. He left the game early after again dislocating the shoulder.

"I wish I could have played the whole game," he said. "I was just happy to be out there." He would appear briefly in four consecutive losing efforts before staying home while the team lost to LSU at Baton Rouge and then would quit the squad after it returned from that trip.

Guy Mendes of *The Kernal* wrote, "The much-spoken-of character, Lady Luck, seems to have dealt a poor hand to the

A 99-yard punt return by Paul Martin against Florida is nullified as Phil Thompson is called for clipping Steve Tannen. The Wildcats lost, 14-12, to the Gators at Lexington in 1968.

Cats." Nobody realized that better than Bradshaw, who said, "It's tough on the team, but they realize brooding isn't going to help."

Dick Palmer was a "walk-on" who played for the 1965 freshman team, was held out of competition his sophomore year, and then started for Bradshaw in 1967. He remembered most the tall, metal tower in the center of the UK practice complex. During that 1967 season Bradshaw repeatedly came running down the tower as first Page and then Forston were injured. He also made frequent descents to correct some situations.

"Bill Cartwright, George McClellan, and I wrote a song

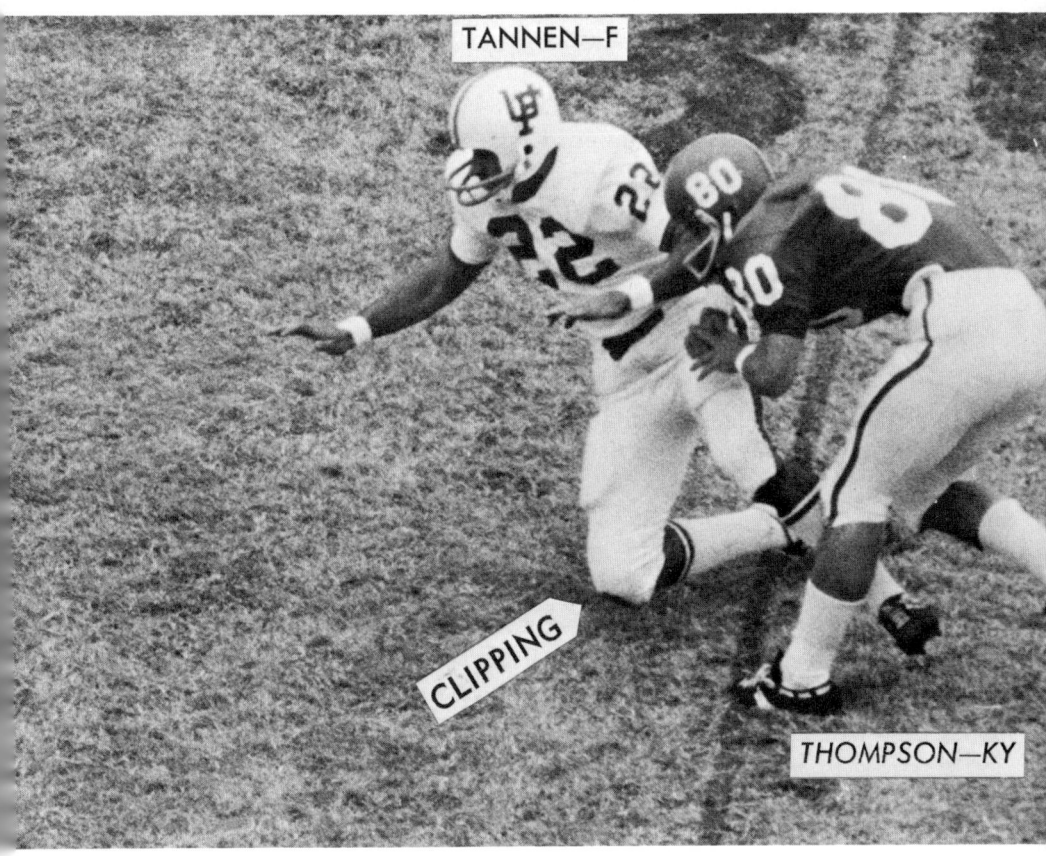

that we called 'The Tower,' Palmer said. "It went like this:

> "Blood and sweat
> Running in my eyes
> Then, I turned around
> Oh, Lord! Charlie's coming down
> From that tower
> That tower
> It haunts me every night
> Oh, Lord!
> Please get it out of my sight."

"Everybody sang it for years," Palmer said. "In summer school, that was our regular Wednesday song. I remember how hard those summer practices were. Although we didn't have a lot of talent, we fought everybody. But there was a long line of games we could have won."

Indiana was one of those games. The Wildcats led, 10-0, at

half time, but the Hoosiers, who would tie for the Big Ten Championship and play in the Rose Bowl, rallied behind sophomores Harry Gonso and John Isenbarger to win, 12-10. Mississippi then beat the 'Cats, 26-13, on the day after Greg Page died, and Auburn humiliated them, 48-7, the following weekend. After those losses Bradshaw said of Forston's preseason injury: "Of all the things that have happened to us, this has been the thing that hurt us most. It necessitated a complete reshuffling of our offensive attack. It affected what we had planned and worked on all spring."

Place-kicker David Weld received a broken leg in a 24-14 loss to VPI, and the 'Cats also fell to LSU and Georgia for their fifth and sixth losses in a row before defeating West Virginia and Vanderbilt. They closed with losses to Florida and Tennessee.

The unfortunate chain of circumstances that had plagued them all season continued. Cancer claimed Claude Sullivan, radio "Voice of the Wildcats," and Bernie Shively died of a heart attack in December. Robert L. Johnson, vice-president in charge of student affairs, assumed the additional duties of acting director of athletics. There was much unrest in the department during the months of his tenure.

Oswald resigned as UK president on April 2, 1968, and returned to the University of California in Berkeley as executive vice-president. Johnson soon followed him there as vice-chancellor for student affairs. Their reign had come during the troubled time of student revolts, and the football situation had not made the burden any easier. Dr. A. D. Kirwan, former UK football coach, was appointed interim president on July 19, 1968, and was instrumental in the appointment of assistant basketball coach Harry C. Lancaster as temporary director of athletics.

Bradshaw's players would remember the final year of his regime as a most frustrating experience. "I thought we could have been 7-3," Bair said. "I look back at some of the stupid games. I remember Phil Thompson catching a pass against Mississippi and an official calling it no good. . .having LSU on the ropes and fumbling. . .talk about bad breaks."

Bob Jones, football coach at Simon-Kenton High School in Covington in 1975, was a place-kicker who came out on his own and made the team. "I also remember the Mississippi game," he said. "We had them, 14-10, in the fourth quarter, and they punted to us. All we had to do was catch it and take it in. We fumbled the punt, and they scored. We started passing in desperation, and Forston threw two interceptions, both resulting in touchdowns.

"In the Florida game Paul Martin ran a kick all the way back—99 yards—for a touchdown, and they called it back on a fairly questionable clipping penalty. That touchdown would have made the difference. At Baton Rouge we had been inside the three yard line three times in the first half and only got three points out of it. We had them 3-0, but we finally got wore down. It seemed to me we were in so many games that were close and could have gone either way."

The Wildcats had lost consecutive games to LSU and Georgia and were 2-4 for the season when Bradshaw met with his players and announced his intention to resign as their coach. "At the time, I really didn't believe it," Dave Bair recalled. "He told us he had promised the people of Kentucky that he would bring them a winner, and he hadn't produced. Everything was silent. There were mixed emotions. Half of us were crying; some were happy. I didn't want to see him leave.

"We decided we were going to win the next game, against West Virginia, for him and the next one for his wife and one each for his kids. We beat West Virginia, but we lost the other three."

Bradshaw closed the books on his UK career with a record of 25-41-4. During the three seasons since his 1965 team won six of 10 games, his squads had defeated only Auburn once and Vanderbilt twice in conference play while losing 17 games to league foes. His overall record against conference teams was 12-30-2. He entered the insurance business briefly in Lexington, was an assistant coach at Texas A&M and Vanderbilt, and then entered private business in Montgomery.

Ray Of Sunshine

Kentucky football's "ray of sunshine" in December, 1968, was John Ray, a perpetual optimist who left the snug position of assistant head coach to Ara Parseghian and Notre Dame's national champion Irish to take over a Wildcat program that had humbled many proud men before him.

Upon being introduced to the press at a conference held to announce his appointment that month, he outlined the following goals:

    1. A conference championship.
    2. Ranking among the Top Ten in the nation.
    3. A bowl game.

And he promised to achieve those lofty goals immediately. Introduced by Harry Lancaster as "the Messiah come to the Holy Land" at a meeting in Maysville a short while later, he told a gathering of 150 UK fans, "We are going to win. And we are not going to wait three years. We are going to win now. I'm convinced and my players are convinced that we will be 10 and zero this season. This may not prove true, but I can guarantee you one thing. We'll never embarrass you."

With only two victories in 10 games, at the end of that first season, he would admit that at least two of those teams embarrassed the Wildcats and that he did not intend to let it happen again.

"Why, he's the guy who wrote that book, *The Power of Positive Thinking*," commented UK's veteran basketball coach Adolph Rupp.

"I'm optimistic by nature," Ray said in 1975. "If I had it to do over again, chances are I'd be a little more realistic. But at that time, they needed it—some positive thinking."

Asked at the very start why he turned down other more seemingly attractive positions in the past and chose to cast his lot with a perennial loser, Ray replied:

"The situation is good at Kentucky and they play in a good league. I don't mean to say the Big 10 or other leagues aren't as good, but look at the bowl situation. Six teams in the SEC are playing in bowl games this year. That is a tremendous incentive."

UK officials had first contacted him prior to Notre Dame's game with Georgia Tech (November 16, 1968), but he told them to clear it with Parseghian and wait until the end of the season. Lancaster and Dr. William Matthews, faculty chairman of athletics, were flying to South Bend in a snow storm to interview Ray when their plane was forced down at Plymouth, Indiana. He drove over to meet them that evening.

"I was very much impressed with him," Lancaster said. "He was very outgoing. I could see where he should be a successful recruiter, and he had been associated with what was considered the best in the business. I interviewed many other applicants, head coaches as well as assistants, and my recommendation was John Ray. He asked all the right questions. . .about schools for his children. . .the town. . .churches. . .industrialization. . .crime. He said he had had opportunities to go other places as a head coach, but he hadn't felt he was ready at that time."

Ray visited Lexington on a Wednesday and was offered the job the following day. He consulted with Parseghian and then accepted the position. Like Chet Wynne, the other Notre Damer who had coached at UK (1934-37), he came to Lexington with fine credentials, both personal and professional. A native of South Bend, he was in the first class to be graduated from John Adams High School in June, 1944, and was a regular center three months later at Notre Dame. He joined the paratroopers, served in the Pacific, and returned to Notre Dame in time for spring practice in 1947. He transferred to Olivet College, where he played three seasons of football and also was afforded an opportunity to be a student assistant on the coaching staff of Frank Ham, who had moved there from John Adams High.

After receiving his bachelor's degree in history at Olivet, Ray coached in Michigan five years, first at Sturgis High and then at Three Rivers, guiding the latter to its first state championship. He became an assistant at the University of Detroit for four years. Then he assumed the position of head coach at John Carroll University in Cleveland, where he masterminded a very successful small college program (29-6) and set several national records in defense. He was at John Carroll in 1964 when Parseghian, who was brought to Notre Dame from Northwestern, persuaded him to become chief defensive assistant of the Irish.

"My family moved to South Bend when I was just three years old," Ray would recall later. "Our home was at 1347 East South Street, right across the street from Jake Klein, Notre Dame's baseball coach. Little did I think that someday the kid across the street would be coaching with Jake at Notre Dame."

At UK he found a situation completely different than what he had experienced at Notre Dame. "We were trying to run a first-class program at Kentucky with a second-class facility," he said by telephone in May, 1975, from his office in Buffalo, where he had been linebacker coach for the Bills since leaving UK. "We had an antique stadium and were competing against teams like LSU and Tennessee which had tremendous facilities. With only 166 high schools playing football in Kentucky, there was also a lack of numbers, forcing us to go outside the state for talent. We competed for players with Notre Dame, Ohio State, Penn State, and teams like that to the north and Tennessee and the other SEC people to the south. Geographically, Kentucky is a tough location for recruiting."

Ray was hired in December, a little late for the recruiting year. He would sign mostly Kentuckians, including running backs Cecil Bowens and Arvel Carroll, safety Darryl Bishop, and linebacker Kenny King, all of Louisville; linemen Tom Clark and Fred Hamberg of Owensboro; and backs Jim Reed of Springfield and Buzz Burnam of Clark County. He would have his best recruiting year in 1970, bringing into the Wildcat fold such outstanding players as quarterback Mike Fanuzzi of Hasbrouck Heights, New Jersey; running back Doug Kotar of Muse, Pennsylvania; tackle James "Bubba" McCollum and tight end Elmore Stephens of Louisville; linebacker Frank LeMaster of Lexington; and receiver Jack Alvarez of Oakland, Maryland. As freshmen, they would win four games and lose only to mighty Ohio State, 10-7, in Columbus.

Ray adhered to the coaching philosophy that when you take over a losing program, you immediately change everything in sight, from the shade of jersey and helmet colors to the paint

John Ray.

on office walls and the carpet on the squad room floors. After he brashly ordered the discharge of an attractive blonde young lady who had been hired previously as a liaison with students, and after he had painted up and carpeted up, he went about the business of letting players know who was boss and of evaluating and distributing their talents into his offensive and defensive plans.

Among those feeling the pressure of the new broom were such veterans as defensive stars Dick Palmer, Cary Shahid, and Dave Roller; quarterbacks Dave Bair and Stan Forston; kicker Bob Jones; and end Vic King. Palmer and Shahid were suspended temporarily for breaking training rules that winter, and Palmer drew a second suspension and would miss the first three games. Bair was transferred to wide receiver and would see no action that year. He refused to enter the Tennessee game as a substitute so that he could preserve a year of eligibility for baseball. Jones would kick a field goal and an extra point in one of Ray's biggest victories but would miss three other field goal tries in that game. Forston would lose his starting position to sophomore Bernie Scruggs and never attain the stardom predicted for him. Roller would have trouble moving from middle guard to defensive end and then to tackle.

Bair said, "The biggest thing I remember about John Ray is when he walked in with that white trench coat on, in the cafeteria where the team was meeting that night, and he talked about Notre Dame. He said that from that point on, he'd never talk about Notre Dame again, but we had the same type uniform, solid helmet and jersey numbering system as Notre Dame."

Jones remembered a pickup truck with a tower on the back that Ray used to observe practice sessions from. "We used to kid each other about taking up a collection to pay the manager who drove the truck to make a quick turn out on the practice field," Jones said. "We were wrong there because you can't win with players acting immature. After each practice that first year, he had a habit of getting up on that pickup truck, with the players gathered in front, and shaking his finger in the air and saying 'We're No. 1,' which went along with his goals. We knew ourselves that we didn't have the football ability to do the things he said. We could look around and see what we were. We knew we weren't going to bowl games or into the Top 10 with what we had.

"This was mixed in with the overall dominating influence

of Notre Dame. I remember he had a sign, 'Home of the Fighting Wildcats,' put up on the entrance of the Sports Center and you could almost picture the word 'Irish' having been written there and marked out and 'Wildcats' written over it."

Roller was an All-SEC sophomore who had been a guard since the sixth grade and was a key man in the new 4-4-3 defense which Ray had instituted at John Carroll and refined at Notre Dame. His transformation was necessary because the defense does not utilize a middle guard. Instead, it has four linemen, four linebackers—two inside and two outside—and three deep backs. Ray expected linebacking to be one of his strong suits. Leading the returnees were Wilbur Hackett, who was coming off a fine sophomore year; Frank Rucks; Cary Shahid; Don Holland; Chuck Blackburn; and promising sophomore Joe Federspiel.

Even without Palmer, the defensive ends shaped up adequately, while Bill Bushong, a sophomore behemoth, was expected to be a major factor at tackle. Dave Hunter was the only experienced hand in the secondary.

Flanker Joe Jacobs would return to the sport under Ray after quitting at the tail end of the 1968 season, while Phil Thompson and King (each of whom snared 29 passes for almost 400 yards in 1968) were considered excellent split ends. Converted fullback Raynard Makin and the rest of the offensive line were question marks.

They opened that season against Indiana before a regional television audience and almost 38,000 spectators on Stoll Field. Coach John Pont brought to Lexington a Hoosier team led by Gonso, Isenbarger, and Butcher. As sophomores two years earlier, they were on the team that defeated the Wildcats in Bloomington and then played in the Rose Bowl as co-champion of the Big 10.

Stan Forston, a hard-luck quarterback under Bradshaw, remembered that game. "I started and I didn't play too well," he said. "I threw a couple of interceptions and (UK's) Bernie Scruggs came in and played pretty good. On that day, I think Indiana was probably the best team in the nation."

The Hoosiers were leading, 24-0, when Scruggs quickly threw a 71-yard scoring bomb to Al Godwin and a scoring strike to Jim Grant on a fourth down fake of a run off tackle. The Wildcats also got a 95-yard scoring kickoff return by Gann, which helped soften the sting of a 58-30 drubbing.

They defeated heavily favored Mississippi, 10-9, in Lexington the following Saturday for what would prove the biggest victory of Ray's career at UK. The Rebels scored first on a 24-yard field goal early in the second quarter and added six more points two minutes later when All-American quarterback Archie Manning ran 64 yards to pay dirt. Hunter blocked the try for point.

Kentucky got on the scoreboard with a 36-yard field goal by Jones in the closing seconds of the first half. Midway of the third quarter, Scruggs put together a 63-yard scoring drive, personally carrying the ball over the goal line from six yards out.

"And then we played Auburn," Forston recalled. "It was a joke. They were on us, 10-0, late in the half. I came in and picked up the team back about the 15. We started moving the football fairly well, completing passes and some nice runs. About their 30, I called a pass play. Both principle receivers were covered, and I saw Houston Hogg standing right at the goal line. I let loose with a pass and he turned around to see where he was just before the ball got there. It hit him on the chest and bounced off. We got a field goal on the next play and with 17 seconds left, we kicked off and this guy returns it for a touchdown. It was all Auburn the rest of the day."

In that 44-3 victory, sophomore quarterback Pat Sullivan passed for 200 yards and three touchdowns, the Tigers chewed up UK's defense for 271 yards on the ground, and John Riley set a conference record with a 56-yard field goal. Kentucky's quarterbacks completed only 11 of 34 passes for 114 yards and had three intercepted, while the UK runners gained only 21 yards on the ground all afternoon.

At the time some writers and publicity men were jokingly referring to Ray as the "Mouth of the South" and were looking forward to his jaunts into Dixie. With about eight minutes left to play, Ralph "Shug" Jordan put his first offensive unit back in the game. Moreover, Sullivan, who had an especially brilliant receiver in sophomore Terry Beasley, was still throwing the bomb. This visibly upset Ray, who confronted Jordan in their postgame meeting at the center of the field.

"Coach Ray was unhappy and took exception to our passing in the latter portions of the game," Jordan told reporters. "I don't remember Hanratty and Seymour easing up on anybody at Notre Dame. This is the first time in my 31 years of coaching that I've run into an upset coach like that. It is not our inten-

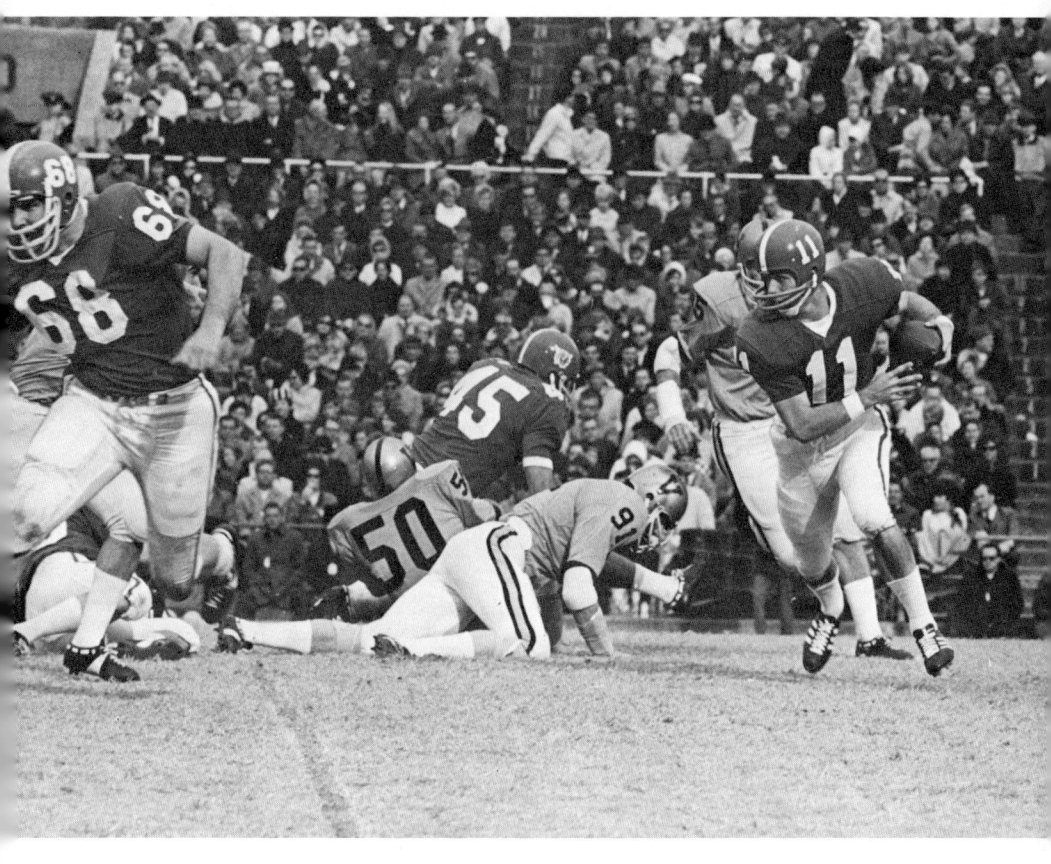

Stan Forston.

tion at Auburn to embarrass anybody. I'm very sorry that Coach Ray is upset. That upsets me."

"I figured that Auburn game was the turning point for Coach Ray," Forston said. "I think for the first time he realized how they play football in the SEC. It's not your typical Big 10 type of football. He was very conservative after that. We went down to Georgia with an offensive philosophy that we were going to establish a running attack with a power backfield consisting of three backs and one wide receiver. They didn't have to play any pass defense. They just killed us. I went in with two minutes to play and we were trailing, 30-0.

"The next week we played West Virginia at our homecoming in the rain. Scruggs played all the way. We had a special play something like a basketball screen with two wide receivers crossing that we put in for a two-point play. Against a man-to-man defense, we would simply run the outside defender into the middle and screen off the inside defender so he couldn't get out and that should leave one of our backs open. We scored and were trailing them, 7-6, with four minutes to go when Bernie called the play. It worked perfectly, but the official called Jack Mathews for interference on the inside defender and we lost.

"Before we went to Nashville to play Vanderbilt the next week, we had a contest to decide who would play quarterback. Ray brought Bair back over from the prep team and he, Bernie, Hugh Bland, Steve Tingle, and I entered the contest. Basically what they did was put four defensive backs and linebackers across the line of scrimmage. We had two receivers and we were supposed to pick out the open one. Whoever completed the most passes was going to start. It turned out to be Bernie. He had a lot of bad luck early in the game. The next half they put Steve Tingle in, and he started completing passes. Steve Parrish caught a UK record (10 receptions to tie Calvin Bird vs. Mississippi, 1958), but we lost, 42-6.

"The next week was the low point in my stay at UK. Ray called me in for a talk before we were to play Florida and said he was thinking about switching me to defensive back so I could cover Carlos Alvarez, who only happened to be the outstanding receiver in the nation that year. I told him I couldn't play defensive back for him. He said, 'You've got another alternative. We're going to put you on the prep team.' I ended up making the trip to Florida, but I wasn't even wearing thigh pads or knee pads. Tingle threw 41 passes in that game, a UK record. Alvarez and John Reeves were every bit as good as they said they were. (Florida won, 31-6.)

"All Tennessee had to do the next weekend was walk in and pick up the remains, but it was a good game. Tingle was doing a good job when he sprained an ankle. Bernie got hurt and I just walked out onto the field and told him to go on in. It was in the last two minutes, we needed 40 yards and we were trailing by two touchdowns. I called a pass that sent two wide receivers deep, with Gann delaying down the sideline. I guessed right. Gann was standing wide open, and I hit him with about a 50-yard pass. The next play was a sprint out for another eight and we were near Tennessee's goal line. This time, they dumped me for a loss. We called time out and Vic King said to me, 'Stan, buddy, this is the last ball game in my career. You've got to look for me, because I guarantee you I'll be open,' so I called

Former UK coaches Blanton Collier (1954-1961) and J. J. Winn (1923) are greeted by John Ray during a practice session in 1969.

the same play as the pass to Gann, but to the other side. Later on, I had to admit to Vic that I didn't look at him first. I looked at Roger first to see if he was open and then I saw Vic across the middle. The minute I let loose of the pass I thought it was going out of the stadium. But Vic made a diving catch in the end zone. We never got the ball back and lost, 31-26."

The season ended with Ray having the dubious distinction of tying Bernie Shively (1945) and Charlie Bradshaw (1967) for the worst record (2-8) in UK football history. He would beat that record the following year when his team would win only two of 11 games.

Close Doesn't Count

On the afternoon of November 21, 1971, John Ray and his UK football players were thinking how nice it would be to go for a two-pointer and beat Tennessee for the first time in seven years. They had the ball on the Vols' nine yard line second down and six, trailing 14-7 with only three minutes remaining, and were moving with authority.

Then the unexpected happened, as was too often the case with the Wildcats. Defensive end Carl Johnson caught a misguided pitchout from Bernie Scruggs on the 15 and had clear sailing ahead as he zipped by a startled Ray. Ray thought Johnson had been thrown out of the game during a first-quarter altercation which resulted in the ejection of UK center Dan Neal.

"An official came over and told me a Tennessee player was ejected too," Ray said later. "They told me from the press box that it was No. 59 (Johnson). Then later in the half, I protested to referee R. P. Williams, and he said actually no Tennessee player was put out because they didn't get his number. I asked, 'If the infraction canceled out, why was my player ejected and none of theirs? Can I put my center back in?' Williams shrugged, but after a conference of officials at half time, it was decided that Kentucky could not put Neal back in the game, even though the officials didn't know the identity of the Tennessee player."

While the big play had salvaged a bowl trip for the Vols, it had also completed an incredible era of struggle and privation for Scruggs. Arriving on campus five years earlier, he had been held out of competition his sophomore year and then had been

Bernie Scruggs.

the No. 1 quarterback during most of the Wildcat games his three varsity years. During that period, Kentucky had played 32 games and lost 25 in almost every conceivable way. Sitting dejectedly in the UK dressing room after the game, he could look back on many frustrations.

There was the Tennessee game of two years earlier when he had taken over for an injured Tingle with the Wildcats trailing, 24-7. He completed 11 straight passes for 168 yards and brought the Wildcats within four points of the Vols, only to lose it all when someone hit him while he was trying to pass and he fumbled into the end zone for the clinching UT touchdown.

And who would forget when he ran 88 yards on a keeper play against Georgia, stumbled into the end zone—but not before his knees touched on the three—and then fumbled to the Bulldogs on the next play?

There were also some good moments. As a sophomore he had engineered the big upset of Ole Miss, and the following year he completed 25 of 39 passes against LSU at Baton Rouge and marched the Cats from their own four yard line to the Bengal 12 before time ran out with UK trailing, 14-7.

Those 25 completions set a UK record, while the 39 tosses were two shy of a record set by Tingle vs. Florida in 1969. Scruggs also tied Rick Norton (vs. LSU 1965) when he had six of his tosses intercepted by West Virginia in 1970.

After closing his career, Scruggs said, "I thought I could make the big plays, but I couldn't. I'd make one good one, then a bad one. Maybe that's what Kentucky needs, just a couple of guys who can make the big plays."

The Wildcats had gotten some big plays that season but not enough. In the opening game at Clemson, Kotar returned the opening kickoff 98 yards for a touchdown. Later Tom Kirk kicked a 27-yard field goal to preserve a 10-7 UK win after a Clemson punt hit a Wildcat safety and rolled into the end zone for a Tiger touchdown. After a fine rookie season with the New York Giants in 1974, Kotar would remember that run:

"About the 50, I started cutting to the sideline and out of the corner of my eye, I could see Coach Ray running right alongside me. I thought if he could keep up with me, the Clemson guys could catch me, but they didn't."

Darryl Bishop, a sophomore safety, gave the Wildcats big plays in their other two wins in 1971. Against Virginia Tech, he got two of four UK interceptions off Don Strock, the nation's leading passer, in the first four minutes of the game in Lexington. The Wildcats went ahead, 20-0, in that first quarter; Tech tied it, 20-20; and UK took a 27-20 lead into the locker room. After UK went ahead, 33-27, in the last quarter, Jeff Woodcock intercepted a 55-yard Strock pass in the UK end zone with less than two minutes to play.

The following weekend Bishop pulled what must rate as one of the most unlikely plays in the UK-Vanderbilt series when he returned an intercepted pass 44 yards for a touchdown after time had run out. On that cold, miserable, rainy day in Nash-

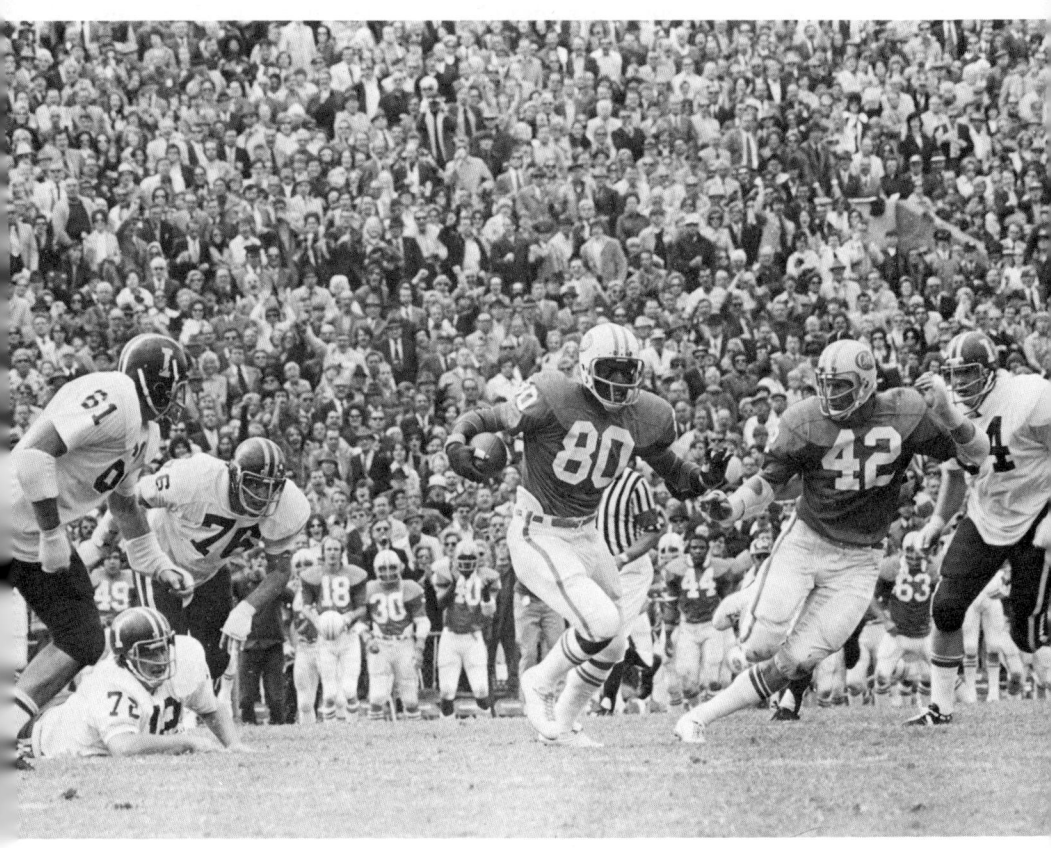
Darryl Bishop returns an intercepted pass vs. Indiana, 1972.

ville, the game seemed destined to end in a 7-7 tie. The Wildcats, faced with a fourth-and-eight on their own 44, elected to punt with slightly less than 50 seconds left.

"We talked about it on the sidelines," Ray explained later. "We thought the fans would make them throw it. We thought that we might get an interception and get a chance for a field goal try, but I didn't think it would end like this."

Walter Overton had made the catch of Gary Knutson's punt on the Vandy 30. On first down, quarterback Steve Burger kept for a four-yard gain. On second and 14, he brought Vandy out of the huddle for the game's final play.

"I thought, 'Oh, my God! He's going to run the play,'" Ray said. "But with scattered boos filtering down from the stands, Vandy elected instead to pass."

The ball was thrown about 10 yards short of the intended

receiver, and Bishop had practically clear sailing for a touchdown return which gave UK two wins in a row for the first time since 1967.

(In Lexington the following year, 1972, Bishop would return an intercepted pass 97 yards for a touchdown in a 17-13 victory over Mississippi State. With UK leading Georgia, 12-7, in Athens in 1973 and the Bulldogs threatening on the Wildcat 29 after six straight pass completions, he would intercept an Andy Johnson pass, return it a few yards, hold the ball up triumphantly and fumble it. Frank LeMaster would recover for UK with 37 seconds left.)

There had been an unusual play in a UK-Vanderbilt game in 1970, with Vanderbilt on the receiving end. The Wildcats had built up a 17-0 lead in the first quarter and held it until after the half. Then a Burger pass was bobbled by one Commodore and two Wildcats before nestling in the arms of Jeff Peeples, who scampered unmolested for a touchdown that sparked Vandy to an 18-17 victory.

The only other Wildcat victories in 1970 were a 16-9 upset of Kansas State and a 27-2 win over North Carolina State, both in Lexington. Roller earned national Lineman-of-the-Week honors for his harassment of State quarterback Lynn Dickey. After that game the Wildcats lost five straight, including a humiliating 35-6 loss to Utah State.

That Utah State game, for all practical purposes, was the swan song of Forston as a front-line quarterback. "We had lost to Ole Miss and Auburn before that 'infamous' game," he said. "They got ahead of us, 14-0, before we had thrown our first pass.

"Once I started passing, I hit Grant with a couple of long passes and we were down on their goal line in just five or six plays. Then came disaster for me as far as the coaching staff was concerned. I just barely overthrew Hunter, and a Utah State guy intercepted it and returned it 95 yards before Hunter caught him on the five. They actually didn't score. We get the ball back on the 20, and I go onto the field, greeted by boos from the crowd.

"I complete a couple more to Grant, moving the ball to their five. We get an illegal motion penalty and then I'm moving down the line of scrimmage, facing the end and trying to option him. He takes my option away and I pitch to Cecil Bowens. Either I pitched too fast or Cecil wasn't really watching for it because the ball bounced away and Utah State recovered it on the five. Again when I came off the field the whole crowd was booing, and I figured I knew who it was for then. Coach Ray said, 'Bernie's going in.' I figured that was the last I was ever going to play at Kentucky and it was, except for holding the ball for our kicker and seeing a little action in the Tennessee game."

Ray's lack of success at UK would continue to be mirrored in the fate of his quarterbacks (and not due to their ineptitude). As a rule they were capable young men who had the misfortune of playing with teams which came up short in talent and depth. However, each lacked one or more of the traits that make a quarterback. Such was the case of Mike Fanuzzi, who had a fine freshman year, was an understudy to Scruggs as a sophomore, but was switched to wide receiver because of an inability to pass the ball. He injured a knee in preseason practice and would miss a year of competition before returning to quarterback and operating the run-oriented veer offense for two years under a new coach.

The burden of guiding the Wildcat offense in 1972 rested on the thin shoulders of James "Dinky" McKay, who had quarterbacked Gulf Coast Junior College, near his hometown of Biloxi, Mississippi, to the national JuCo championship. He would lose and regain the starting position during the season and then be declared ineligible by the NCAA for the following year due to a mixup in transferring of credits from the junior college.

John McGill of the *Herald-Leader* described McKay's debut in a 25-7 victory over Villanova as "near sensational." The slender redhead averaged six yards per carry and hit seven of 12 passes as the Wildcats gained a total of 470 yards, with Gary Knutson scoring three touchdowns. Ernie Lewis entered the game in the fourth quarter and fumbled a snap which was recovered by Villanova. He came back to direct a 41-yard scoring drive, including his own 12-yard run and a 14-yard pass to Ken O'Leary to the one. Also making his debut in that game was highly heralded freshman Sonny Collins, who gained 64 yards in 15 carries for UK.

McKay and the Wildcats met their moment of truth the following Saturday when they traveled to Birmingham for the first UK-Alabama game since 1947 and the first UK game against a Bear Bryant team. The 71,000 fans had hardly settled in their seats before McKay had fumbled the ball to Alabama on the second play of the game and then moments later threw an interception. The game was less that six minutes old, and the Tide was leading, 14-0.

McCollum, LeMaster, Bishop, and the other defenders played a fine first half and held the Tide in check until Bama drove for a first and goal on the UK six early in the second half. After three plays netted only two yards, Bryant sent Bill Davis in to try a field goal. The snap from center was bad, but Terry Davis picked it up, rolled to the left, and hit Steve Bisceglia just over the goal line. UK linebacker Ned Lidvall was screened from the play by an official and missed a chance to tackle Terry Davis. Bama won, 35-0.

Kentucky lost six of its first eight games before Ray benched McKay and inserted Lewis as a starter against Vanderbilt in the last intercollegiate football game to be played on Stoll Field. On the second play against the Commodores, Lewis messed up a pitchout to Knutson; Vandy recovered and turned it into the go-ahead touchdown. Given another chance, Lewis handed off to Knutson on a play good for a first down, but Knutson fumbled the ball away. McKay took over and led the Wildcats to the go-ahead touchdown and a 14-13 victory.

Florida was more responsible than Tennessee for ending Ray's reign at UK, walloping the Wildcats, 40-0, at Gainesville. Ray rallied his forces for a gallant losing effort (17-7) to 12th-ranked Tennessee, but the athletics board met shortly thereafter and voted not to renew his four-year contract.

"I feel it will be a lot easier for my successor than it was when I came—and I certainly mean no reflection on Charlie (Bradshaw)," he said. "It's just that we have a new stadium going up and we've brought in some fine players. That's why I especially hope the new man does a good job, because I feel strongly about all these players. It's been a trying experience and an educational one. If I had it to do over, there's one mistake I wouldn't make. I wouldn't come in at the beginning so enthusiastic. I'm afraid I gave the people the idea I was a miracle worker. They thought I meant right now, but I wasn't really saying that. I was talking about what we could accomplish in time. If I hadn't said those things, I wouldn't be in this situation. Still, I felt I had to get people's interest in our program and look what's happened. A new stadium, season ticket sales are up...I'd say the same things if I was starting again. I'd just clarify them a little better."

James "Dinky" McKay.

The search committee appointed by Dr. Otis A. Singletary, who was named UK president prior to Ray's first season with the Wildcats, recommended youthful Fran Curci of the University of Miami. This coach would make it a point to tell people that he was no miracle worker and that in perhaps five years he could look around and tell them just where the program stood.

With the new stadium, some fine senior players, and some good young recruits, Curci would give the Wildcats a taste of victory for the first time in many years.

Super Sonny

Two days before the University of Kentucky was to play Indiana in a game officially dedicating Commonwealth Stadium in September, 1974, Alfred "Sonny" Collins collided with a teammate and fell writhing to the ground. Coach Fran Curci rushed to his star fullback and moaned, "Oh no, this is all we need!"

The Wildcats were in their second season under Curci and in dire need of a victory to atone for a poor showing against West Virginia at Morgantown. The loss was due in part to a subpar Collins, who had received a leg bruise on Wednesday before that game.

After Collins rebruised the leg, trainer R. D. Wilson loaded him onto a golf cart, hustled him into the training room at Shively Sports Center, and later gloomily reported that the defending Southeastern Conference "Player of the Year" would probably miss the Indiana game.

"I knew I would have to do something desperate," the resourceful Curci said. "I don't know anything about acupuncture. But I knew it was better than nothing. Nobody else was going to wave a magic wand and get the guy ready. So I looked around—Cincinnati, Louisville, everywhere.

"Then my wife Pat told me that her hairdresser had an ear problem cured by acupuncture and that's how I found out there was a guy right here in Lexington."

That acupuncture specialist pierced Collins with three electrically stimulated needles for a period of 12 to 15 minutes on Friday morning and then repeated the treatment with three needles about two hours before the game. Here's how John Husar

Sonny Collins at Florida-UK game in Commonwealth Stadium.

of the *Chicago Tribune* Press Service led off his story the following morning:

> Indiana Coach Lee Corso looked like someone who'd been stabbed with a long, sharp needle after a Hoosier rally fell short Saturday, enabling Kentucky to escape with a 26-22 victory....But it wasn't Corso who'd been stuck... The victim—and, in this case, the beneficiary—turned out to be Sonny Collins, Kentucky's outstanding running back ...Rejuvenated last Thursday, he submitted an ailing leg to acupuncture. By game time, he was fit enough to slice 160 yards thru a puzzled Indiana defense and lead the Wildcats to their first defeat of a Big Ten rival since 1918.

Collins had cut the Hoosiers apart enough to create running room for quarterback Fanuzzi, who ran the veer for another 114 yards, and halfback Campassi, who added 80 yards as the Wildcats racked up 382 yards on the ground. Fanuzzi figured in all four touchdowns—recovering a fumble in the end zone, throwing two short passes, and running three yards—but Collins was the star. He zipped up the middle for a 55-yard run to set up UK's first score and established another threat with a 31-yard dash. His fakes kept Fanuzzi darting through wide-open holes all day.

Not all stories surrounding the injury-prone Collins have such happy endings. Six weeks later he would receive a broken leg bone while scoring a touchdown in a 38-12 Wildcat victory over Peach Bowl-bound Vanderbilt. He would miss a Wildcat win over Sugar Bowl-bound Florida, which would assure UK of its first winning season since 1965, and a loss to Tennessee, which would knock UK out of the Liberty Bowl. Collins ended the season with 970 yards. If he had played in those games, he would have broken his UK record of 1,213 yards rushing set during the 1973 season. That total fell just 99 yards short of the Southeastern Conference record of 1,312 yards set by John Dottley of Ole Miss in 1949.

Collins' best game that season (1973) was against Mississippi State at Jackson, where he gained 229 yards and scored four touchdowns to lead the Wildcats to a 42-14 victory, earning for himself national Back-of-the-Week honors. He led the conference in both rushing and scoring, and at the end of the season became the first sophomore since Harry Gilmer to be named SEC Player of the Year. He lost the SEC battle for most yards gained in 1974 but was the leader in yards per carry.

At the beginning of the 1975 season he held the UK career rushing record of 2,685 yards in 30 games, the single season scoring (80 in 1973) and rushing records, and various and sundry other records. Before beginning the fall practice season, he sat in the writer's office and discussed how he came to be at UK:

"I was in the fifth grade at Pride Avenue School in Madisonville, Kentucky, at the time our president John F. Kennedy was assassinated and Jim Brown was starring for Cleveland. Daddy knew the way I felt about Jim Brown, and he asked me if I wanted to play football. I went ahead because he liked it, and we had a pretty good season.

"I started my freshman year at Madisonville High, and I gained over 1,000 yards and then more than 2,000 yards my sophomore year, but I got a detached retina in the final game and missed the play-offs. My junior year was a great year. We played the play-offs here in Lexington and lost to Fort Thomas Highlands. I gained 1,884 yards that year."

In the second game of his senior year, he injured an ankle and missed the remainder of the season. It would take the entire winter, spring, and summer to heal the wound.

"I had to have an ankle operation, and a lot of people thought I could come back from the operation and play, but the doctor told me just to relax and not worry about trying to come back. Well, I started getting phone calls. Rumors began spreading about, and my daddy worried that I wasn't going to get into college with that kind of stuff going around. I could see myself in the coal mines. I worked one summer there. Both of my grandfathers, or at least one of them, died of black lung. I'd always heard about it, but I didn't know how it actually was until I was old enough to go down. Man, it's spooky. You go about two miles down and then you level off for a while. Then you go through a 36 to 42 inch high hole for maybe a half-mile more. There's no way you can stand straight up. You either bend or crawl.

"Probably the best thing you can find down there are rats. I mean big rats. Bigger than basketball shoes. There's a lot of natural gas around coal, and if you see them you know the air is pretty safe to breathe. But if you see them start running or going in one direction, then you'd better start running behind them because something is going to blow.

"With all that worrying, it wasn't too long before I lost all

Sonny Collins.

my hair. I wear a 'fro' off the field now, and I'm a different person on and off the field."

(After his fine performance against Mississippi State in Jackson, Collins would give that Afro wig to his offensive linemen.)

"When I got a letter from UK, I just set it aside because of the bad reputation. . .a black guy getting killed. . .a predominantly all-white school. I went on what I had heard. I was getting letters from USC, UCLA, Nebraska, Notre Dame, and a lot of others. I was more interested in them. A UK graduate wanted to take me to visit the campus, and when I finally got a chance to go with him, I was just waiting to feel that prejudiced atmosphere when we hit Lexington.

"John Ray made me feel like a super great guy...that I was welcome at UK and that they were interested in me. I met the staff and then everybody at the basketball game that night showed so much interest and enthusiasm that I changed my mind. People came up and talked to me, thanked me, and told me they wanted me to come here.

"I was so anxious to play. I remember during the Villanova game Coach Ray looked over at the bench and motioned me to come beside him. 'Well, you're getting ready to play your first college game,' he said. 'I hope you will do well. We'll be rooting for you.' He sent me in for Gary Knutson. I made about 14 yards the first carry, and the people just went wild. The other guys told me to keep my head up and keep going. Since then, I've calmed down and matured more than I thought I could.

"I was sorry to see Coach Ray leave. He wished me the best of luck and told me the next coach would be a great one and I should work hard and keep my pride. After Curci got here, we were kinda feeling each other out. I got in a little college trouble, and I would have to go over every morning and see him and run. Now, I think he is one helluva great guy.

"During the practice week before that Mississippi State game in 1973, he told me, 'You're going to get over 200 yards. All you have to do is run with your eyes open and run hard.' He gave me the game ball after that game. He also gave me the game ball after I reached the 1,000-yard mark in the Tulane game, and then I got the Vandy game ball after I broke my leg last year.

"I knew I was going to have a good game against Vanderbilt, but I was nervous about the television situation. But it was great.

"I guess during these 11 years of football, I've experienced quite a bit...a lot of injuries...a lot of pain, but it's been worth it."

Time Out: Fran Curci

Fran Curci came to the University of Kentucky from Miami, Florida, where he was head coach of his alma mater two years. He had started his coaching career as freshman coach there in 1962 after making All-America in 1959 and then playing as a five-foot-nine, 152-pound quarterback for the old Dallas Texans of the AFL. In four years his Hurricane frosh teams won 12 of 14 games. He later served as varsity offensive assistant for Hurricane bowl teams.

Tampa University hired Curci in 1968 to rejuvenate its faltering football program. In his first year there he guided the Spartans to a 7-3 season, which included victories over Mississippi State and Tulane and earned for him the Florida Sports Writers Association "Coach of the Year" award. His 1969 season was a brilliant 8-2 affair, and his 10-1 record in 1970, including a triumph over Miami, brought the Tampans the nation's No. 1 College Division ranking. Curci was runnerup for College Division "Coach of the Year" honors. Here's how he says he came to be at Kentucky:

"My first association with Kentucky football was when we played them in Miami. We were supposed to beat them because perennially Kentucky was always the underdog. Instead, Calvin Bird ran a punt back to beat us. If we had won that game, we would have gone to the Orange Bowl, but that's neither here nor there.

"Then I went into coaching and became head coach at Tampa University and Kentucky played Florida in a double header at our stadium. I thought they played Florida a great game, but after they scored with a few seconds to go before the half, I was surprised when they were in a blitzing type defense and Florida hit them with a long pass right up the middle, the post route, and a guy makes an 80-yard touchdown which seemed senseless at the time. The only thing I remembered was that you usually go into a prevent type defense, but they didn't do that.

"When I left Tampa and went to Miami, everything was going pretty good down there, but with the professional situation as it was I could see that Miami would never enjoy the status it had attained in the '50s and '60s. The glamour had gone out of the Hurricane situation. The Kentucky job opened up at that time. They contacted me, I made a preliminary visit—more or less just a look-see type thing by both parties—and they invited me back for a more serious talk. They said if I wanted the job, I had it.

"I married a girl from Kentucky. There always seemed to be something about Kentucky. I thought about this as I went back to Miami to make a decision. Fortunate for me, if there is such a decision to be made, my wife leaves it up to me. We had just bought a brand new house and she was getting the new drapes that day when I came in and said we were going to Kentucky. That was good for her, because she wanted to come back home anyway.

"When I first came to visit, the steel structure of the new stadium was just beginning to pop up. I was fortunate enough to be at Tampa when they opened the stadium there and I've always felt such a facility, with the size to handle a large number of people, has got to help a program. That was what I was looking for and it was with that in mind, and not knowing anything about the players, that I accepted the job.

"When I came up here, I thought the talent wasn't spectacular, but I didn't expect it to be. However, I did find a bunch of really dedicated young men who were tired of losing and were looking for somebody—and I think anybody could have done the same thing I did—to come in and show them how to win. They didn't care whether it was Fran Curci or Joe Schmoe. I'm talking about guys like (Frank) LeMaster, 'Bubba' (McCollum) and a lot of others who just wanted to win. So they went about their work and we all just kinda came in here and the first thing we tried to do was find out the needs.

"One situation stands out in my mind. We went to the 'Towers' (high-rise dormitory) to see where the boys ate. There were four steam tables there and they had given one to the athletes. This meant that the other students had to squeeze into three lines while the athlete could walk right through his line without any wait at all, get double helpings, and walk through the other students. Right away, you could see that was an aggravating situation. We immediately broke that thing up and found a place on the campus where we could feed the boys, give them the amount of food they needed and give the other steam line back to the students who rightfully needed it. I think that was an immediate big plus with the student body and for our football players.

"The next thing we did was try to change the dormitory setup. They had put all the football players in one general area. I think the tendency in such a situation is to point the finger and say, 'There's where all the football players live. They can act silly and do stupid things and get away with it.' The football players in turn ignore them and say 'There's nothing they can do about it.' You end up with a group of young people with not a lot of respect shown on either side.

"So we broke that up and put our football players all over the campus and immediately we had a reaction from our players, who said they didn't think that was such a good idea. They thought there would be too many fights and problems and some of the students immediately came over to see me and said they thought it was an unwise decision. But we went ahead with it, and to this day we haven't had the first problem with our players in the dormitories. Some of the players have told me how they respect the other students, and a couple of the students have told me they like the football players. It's a mutual understanding.

"We must remember that football players also are 18 and 19-year-old kids just like other students. They happen to have bigger, stronger bodies and are maybe a little faster, but overall they're just students like anybody else.

"From the first, we thought Doug Kotar was a pretty good back and we knew Sonny Collins was a premier back. Steve Campassi was a pretty good football player in the early stages, but we decided to go ahead with Kotar, Collins and 'Dinky' McKay. The first big crisis we had to overcome was when McKay was declared ineligible between spring and fall practice because of a junior college rule. After we lost him, we had to make some adjustments. At the same time, we had people like

Curci instructs quarterback Mike Fanuzzi during a crucial game.

Harvey Sword, Dave Margavage and Elmore Stephens in the offensive line. We took Rick Nuzum, a second-string guard, and made him a center. The first time I saw these boys working out in the winter program, I told Coach Mirilovich, 'That's going to be our center,' because he was working so hard and was such a dedicated player, the kind you look for at center. Since that time, he has played almost every snap for us.

"We took Mike Fanuzzi, whom I had heard about and knew a little about, and told him he would start playing quarterback, even though he had been away from it a long time. He was quick and he could do some of the things we were hoping to do, even though he couldn't throw the ball well. At this point, Mike didn't fit into the plans at all, but he was still being looked at at quarterback.

"On defense, we had people like Darryl Bishop, who was a

proven athlete but who I believe has never reached his potential; anyway, he still was a guy who could make things happen for you. LeMaster hadn't played much the year before, but you knew he was a dedicated guy who loved Kentucky. I think McCollum was a premier lineman. He kinda held up the middle for us. Then you had people like Fred Hamberg who had never played ever and he really did the best he could and I think his success was due to sheer determination. That was also true of Marty Marks, a 5-9 or 5-10, 200 lb. kid who really had no right playing against people like LSU and Alabama, but he did his fair share. We also had Jeff Woodcock at corner and all these things started falling in place for a bunch of kids who weren't a great collection of athletes, but as a whole, decided they were going to win.

"In our first game against VPI that season, we go out and just dominate the game and then almost fall apart for a lot of reasons. We were so hyperexcited and everything, and they came back and just about beat us. And then we played a spectacular game against Alabama, but that was strictly an emotional game. We were so high and our kids played way beyond their ability. Alabama's efficiency and raw talent beat us in the end, but it was one of the most exciting moments I ever had in athletics.

"The funny thing was the way we started that game. LeMaster was so excited that he gave the wrong call on the flip of the coin. We had gone over that not more than five minutes before kickoff, but he was so nervous that we ended up kicking off against the wind and Alabama couldn't cash in on it. When the wind reversed, we got two touchdowns on them and the score was 14-0 at half time.

"Then we go to Indiana, which was probably the worst game we played that year. We had a lot of fumbles and made a lot of crazy mistakes. Going into that first campaign, Ernie Lewis worked his way into the No. 1 quarterback position. He had played before and seemed to know more about it than anyone else, and then I had one of the toughest decisions I've had to make since I've been here. After the Indiana game, we decided to go with Fanuzzi against Mississippi State. That game was one of those spectacular explosions. Fanuzzi had a good night and Collins had a real great game, gaining 229 yards, scoring four touchdowns and earning 'National Back of the Week' honors. It was a great game on our part and I think a lot

Fran Curci signals touchdown during game with Indiana.

of it was due to Mike's efficiency in running the veer, which fitted his ability. Ernie was more a straight, drop-back 'I' type quarterback who didn't have the quickness that Mike had, which was why we decided to go with Mike and I think this decision turned out pretty good, but was awful tough on Ernie, who has a lot of pride.

"As the season progressed, we became a much better football team and ended up being one of the better teams in the conference. We had a disappointing loss to Tennessee even though we had 19 first downs to their nine and totally dominated the game. We fumbled seven times. Regardless of that, we proved we could play and we surprised the teams in the South, who suddenly realized Kentucky was back in the football business.

"The next year, we come back and we have to replace 17 starters. You just can't replace that many people, so we're starting all over again. We're very fortunate in coming up with an outstanding freshman class, people like Jerry Blanton, Jim Kovach, Mike Siganos, Art Still, Bob Winkel and Dallas Owens, and others. We had to play them. In the opening game against VPI, three or four freshmen started. We caught them flat and had a pretty good game plan, but we really weren't ready to play with so many young kids and I think West Virginia beat us because they were ready to take advantage of our inexperience, which was smart football for them. It took us a few games to get there, but the guys grooved and we played Miami a pretty decent game and perhaps should have beat them, but they were a pretty good football team, definitely more experienced. As these young boys became veterans, we became a pretty good football team, ending up with five freshmen starting.

"When you have a dramatic loss of talent like we had, it's hard to replace them. With the holdovers coming in this year, we shouldn't have to play as many as last year and then what we hope to create is a program where, like all the other teams around the country, you don't have this tremendous loss of talent at one time. We're catching up in that area. That's the most dramatic thing I notice about Kentucky football. The other thing is that UK, in not winning many football games, did not have an opportunity to recruit a lot of outstanding players. Collins and Campassi were so far above anything they had here at the time that they didn't have two or three guys down the line pushing them to make them even better. Once again, it's a matter of depth. It comes down to lack of talent and lack of depth and you find yourself in a real scrambled position.

"What usually happens in a situation like this is you continue to lose and you can't ever get the type of talent it takes to win, while other teams are maintaining their present level of athletics, and you always become a doormat. We had that one big year and we're able now to at least get them to listen to our story. In trying to compete on an equal basis with the big boys—the Mississippis, Alabamas, Georgias and LSUs—we'll always struggle, but at least, I think we're closing that gap very quickly.

"I also noted that people in the state were kinda used to the fact that Kentucky's football wouldn't be that good, and I think that's where the excitement comes in now. It's been such a pleasant surprise to them.

"I think they are building up pride among themselves and in their new stadium. They are now able to come in and have these tailgating parties in a place where they can really congregate, where you can park 10,000 cars and where everybody can kinda visit before a game. They come into the stadium, fill it up, get excited and actually spur the players to play better than they're capable of playing. You get the electricity passing back and forth. The latest word is that every seat in the stadium is apparently sold, which really means that now the people of Kentucky are really getting behind their state school and being that this is the prime state school, we've got a lot of advantages in that we don't have to compete as do Mississippi State-Mississippi, Auburn-Alabama, Florida-Florida State. We've got Kentucky and it's up to us to build a winning program. If it is built here, people will come out. Kentucky people are very proud people, and I think they love winning. They love to get behind something, and I think now they're behind us."

Rupp: "The Way I Saw It"

There are those persons in the State of Kentucky who for years have blamed the lack of Wildcat football success on the corresponding success of Adolph Rupp's basketball teams. Football coach after football coach came onto the UK scene with much optimism and a determination to elevate Wildcat football to the same status as Rupp basketball. Only Bear Bryant came close, and even that strong-willed individual wrote years later that the Lexington campus was not big enough for both him and Rupp. Bryant's favorite UK joke is that he received a cigarette lighter for giving the Wildcats their first and only SEC championship in football and taking them to three bowl games while Rupp received a Cadillac for winning an "umpteenth" SEC basketball crown.

In interviews tape-recorded in the summers of 1971-72 and 1975, Rupp tells of his relationship with UK football coaches during the 42 years that he served as Wildcat head basketball coach:

> Harry Gamage was football coach when I arrived at the University of Kentucky. He came there three years earlier from Illinois. Gamage was a funny fellow in a lot of ways. I never was able to understand him too well. He was a nice fellow in every respect, but he had two different personalities; he wore one when he talked with people like me, the other when he talked in public.
>
> My relations with Gamage were cordial, but a lot of people thought we didn't get along because football supposedly was declining and basketball was building up.

There was tremendous interest in basketball, but I don't think Harry ever felt that basketball was interfering with his football. He was a victim of a vicious circumstance; he did not have any help at all, as did some coaches in the South whose schools were giving financial aid to some athletes. Harry and I didn't have the benefit of scholarships. In fact, we didn't know what an athletic scholarship was until many years later. I don't recall Harry ever going out and getting in his car and banging the roads for athletes. Of course, he didn't have anything to offer them, and the good athletes were drifting from Kentucky to Alabama and other schools.

Harry used a "Double Wingback" offense and the "Diamond Defense" in football. I helped coach, but I knew very little and had less to say about it. My main concern was working the freshman with Birkett Lee Pribble. Our business was to furnish mincemeat for the varsity scrimmages. I think if there was a weakness in Harry's system of practice, it was that he scrimmaged entirely too much and didn't devote sufficient time to the fundamental details. He didn't have the elaborate "chalk talks" and all those things that they have now at evening sessions. When Harry finished his shower and went home, that ended practice as far as he was concerned.

A lot of people thought Harry was a bad coach because he did not win the conference championship. He tied Tennessee and knocked them out of two Rose Bowl invitations. He always gave Alabama a good game. I thought he did a magnificent job with inferior material. His record in seven years here was 32 wins, 25 losses, and five ties for a percentage of .556. His teams were never crushed.

Gamage coached in a different era than now. A big name then was Zuppke of Illinois. Harry played for him. They had great teams. He helped two years at Illinois as an assistant coach. He was well qualified. Other big names were Stagg of Chicago, Rockne of Notre Dame, Fielding Yost of Michigan, Sutherland of Pittsburgh, Jones of California, Wade of Alabama, Neyland of Tennessee, and names like that. They had tremendous alumni backing. Gamage did not have that support here at Kentucky. If he

would have had that support or the benefit of support that they have now, I am sure that he would have been a tremendous coach. He was a student of the game. His record, I thought, was excellent.

And then, to solve everything, the university hired Chet Wynne, of Notre Dame, as football coach. At that time, anyone who attended Notre Dame and knew football, clear on down to the boy who was on crutches studying algebra and managed to get out and see a game, could get a coaching job. It seemed everybody from Notre Dame was coaching football. Knute Rockne had hundreds of coaches out coaching all over the country.

The story is born in mystery as to how we got Wynne, who was coaching at Auburn, but I'll not go into that because I do not have the facts of the case. Some of the men downtown had more to do with bringing pressure on Dr. McVey than the members of the board on the campus. Those downtowners wanted to win regardless, so they brought in Wynne. The Notre Dame system was entirely different than the double wingback. The downtowners felt that by putting in this system of play it would solve all problems. It was known as the Notre Dame shift. When he was not able to get the job done at the end of three years, everyone thought he would get the axe. Imagine the big surprise when the Board voted to give him a new three-year contract. They finally paid him off at the end of the first year of the new contract. After being here four years, he won 20 and lost 19 for .513 percent, not nearly as good as Gamage.

My relationship with Chet was never too pleasant. He told me in no uncertain terms that he thought basketball interfered with football and as long as we had the high interest on the campus in basketball we could not have a good football team. We were really burning things up in basketball about that time. We were going to New York to play games. We were getting more publicity than Chet was in football. He told me one day, "Now, coach, there isn't any room here on the campus for both football and basketball. There isn't room for both you and me. One of us has got to go." I said, "Well, in that case, when you go

Adolph Rupp.

home tonight, you ought to tell your wife to start packing because I don't plan to leave."

I was very frank with Chet. He was the athletic director, but I don't think he could have fired me if he had wanted to. During his last year at Kentucky, we just did not get along at all. I was glad when the Board finally dismissed him. That was in 1937, when I was in the Norton Infirmary in Louisville for a spinal operation that hospitalized me for more than a month. After I returned home, they asked me to coach football and be athletic director. I told them it sounded like a nice arrangement, but I couldn't coach because chances were I'd be in a wheelchair for a while. They pointed out that Rockne coached in a wheelchair. They said they'd get me all the assistants I wanted.

I told them that I was not a Rockne and that the arrangement that they suggested would not work. The Notre Dame system seemed to prevail and everyone tried to imitate Rockne. I remember reading in the paper one Sunday in a game, as I recall, played against Carnegie Tech in Soldier Field, that Rockne spent practically the entire afternoon on his knee along the sideline studying the game as it progressed. It was amusing to me because the next Sunday a columnist in writing said that practically every coach that had played at Notre Dame got out in front of the stands on their knees trying to imitate everything that had happened the previous Saturday. Such was the great influence of this man, although I'll also say this in fairness: Their schedules were not too difficult.

The next day, they were back again, insisting that I coach and take on the directorship. I told them the fastest way I knew to get fired was to be the basketball coach and the athletic director combined. I planned to go on winning basketball games. I didn't know if they could win football games. If the football team didn't win, they would say Rupp was putting all of his emphasis on basketball and the thing to do was get rid of him. I turned them down.

When asked to recommend a person for the job of athletic director, I suggested Bernie Shively, who was coaching physical education over at the University Training School. I felt Shive, whose football coaching contract had not been renewed when Wynne came, would be neutral in every respect. In the meantime, I saw Shive and told him I was pretty sure they were going to offer him the job and he should take it. I told him we always would get along and that I would do anything that I could to help him. I had Shive stop by my office and told him of my conversation with three members of the board that morning. I would not take the job under any condition and suggested that he go and see two of these men that evening.

In those days, the Board did not fool around the way they do now for months and months hunting an athletic director. They announced Shive's appointment in less than 24 hours. Then they decided to get a football coach from within the state high school ranks. They hired A. D. (Ab) Kirwan of Louisville Manual, a very fine student who eventually wound up as president of the university. I do not know how many books he wrote, but he had a whole shelf full of them. He later was considered one of the brightest professors on the campus.

I am sure Ab knew as much football as any other coach. The university's problems in football have not stemmed from stupid coaches. The problem has been not getting the right boys. It was my privilege to ride with Ab on recruiting trips in Kentucky, Ohio, Virginia, and West Virginia. We visited some fine high school and military academy players. I thought Ab did a nice job in presenting the university to those young men, but I never felt at any time after we talked to them that he had a chance to get them. We did get commitments for some of the boys to visit the university, but I do not believe many of them attended.

Ab worked hard at being a football coach. He won 24 and lost 28. Then World War II came along and we did not field a team one year. They had a team the next year, but Ab told them he was not interested in coaching anymore. He wanted to get in the academic side of things. He was a very brilliant young man, far too brilliant to be a football coach.

When I came back from Europe, where I conducted clinics for the Army, I stopped to see Shive, who had decided to coach the football team. They were going to play Alabama the following day in Louisville. He wanted me to go with him. "Shive, I can't," I said. "I want to see my farms." He said, "No, they will be there Sunday or Monday or Tuesday. You can see them then. I want you to go with me because you've never seen us beat Alabama. I want you to be there when this happens." I asked if he was sure. He said, "Just as sure as you're standing here, we're going to beat Alabama."

I sat on our bench. They kicked off to us. We lost about seven yards on the first play. On the first three plays, we lost something like twelve or fourteen yards. We punted. The details are no longer clear to me, but they had a young man named Harry Gilmer, who was supposed to be sick that day. He did not look sick. He either brought that punt back all the way or pretty close to it. They led 7-0. They scored a couple more times in the first quarter. They gave us a real shellacking, scoring sixty points to our nineteen. We scored more points on them than any team that year, if there is any consolation in that.

Shive decided at the end of the year that he did not want any more of that. He had won two and lost eight. It was one of the most badly organized football seasons we ever had at the university. I did not blame Shive for giving it up. Criticism was heaped on him severely. He was a great football player, no doubt about that, and had coached nicely under Gamage. But after having been out of the sport for some time, he just could not get his hand in again, especially with that bunch of wartime 4-F's and immature freshmen that he inherited. Shive inherited a group of boys that just simply could not play big time football. Shive knew football and, as I have mentioned before, was All-American himself. But I don't think that anyone could have had a better record with the material that he had on hand. Once again, I told him the solution to our problem in football was to get an established coach with a reputation that would attract players to the university.

The Board decided to go big time. They looked around and learned of a young fellow named Paul Bryant, who was doing a fine job at the University of Maryland. Paul had coached the naval unit at North Carolina, where he had everyone who could play football at his disposal. He got them in the navy and kept them there. When he went to Maryland, he took a lot of those boys with him and turned out a whiz-bang of a football team. The people in Lexington got to thinking there was the brains of everything. They called Bryant down and hired him. I didn't think they'd get him; in doing so, they got the finest football coach I think America has developed in recent years. When the record of football is written, he will be among the great coaches of all time.

Paul was at Kentucky eight years. He won 60, lost 23, and tied five for .710 percent, which is good enough. He won our only conference championship in football and defeated Oklahoma, 13-7, in the Sugar Bowl. We played in the Sugar Bowl basketball tournament that year. He sat on my bench during our game, and I sat on his bench during his game. Soon as the football game was over and everyone was slapping him on the back, he turned to me and said, "Adolph, get a cab and get in here and get me, and let's you and I get out of here." I got a cab, and we went to his hotel rooms away from the "angry" mob. At his party that night, we celebrated the victory, which was a great thing because that was the first time Oklahoma had been beaten in 32 straight games.

The year prior to that, Paul got beat by Santa Clara in the Orange Bowl. He told me many times the mistake he made was getting down there too early. He spent about 10 or 12 days getting his team ready in that southern heat and wore them out. The following year he didn't do that in New Orleans. He just went down there a couple days early. The next year Paul beat Texas Christian in the Cotton Bowl. He had a wonderful record at Kentucky.

Now, Paul and I have been good friends down through the years. Whenever he comes to Lexington, the first thing he does is pick up the telephone and call me. When I went to Tuscaloosa to play basketball, he always invited me out to his home. One year Mrs. Rupp went down there with us and Mrs. Bryant had Mrs. Rupp out for the day at her home. She brought Mrs. Rupp to the basketball game that night. We've all been friends down through the years. I don't think anybody could have gotten along nicer. How two high-strung fellows like us wouldn't clash somewhere along the line is indeed a mystery, but not once did he say a harsh word to me or did I say anything to him. He took me on a lot of trips with him. I always

Bear Bryant at Millersburg in 1952.

invited him to go with us, but all we had in basketball was a DC-3 and he always laughed. His friends had planes to take him places.

I didn't think the fellow would ever leave Kentucky. He had things going good. He wasn't afraid of basketball. A lot of people said he left because of Rupp, or because he couldn't stand to see basketball a prominent sport. If that were true, why did he build a 15,500-seat basketball facility—the finest auditorium in the nation—in which to play basketball at the University of Alabama? Why did he give his basketball coach, C. M. Newton, the same number of scholarships as we have here? Why does he show this interest in basketball if he wasn't interested in it at Kentucky?

I'll tell you one reason he left. He wanted to be athletic director. The football coaches at most other conference schools were also the athletic directors. Whenever they had an athletic directors' meeting, Paul sat on the outside. It kinda rankled him a little. However, when Texas A&M offered him the position of football coach and athletic director, I didn't think he'd go down there, although it was a stepping stone. They promised him everything, and I think he got everything. Don't think those farmers down there in Texas don't have any money. They've got plenty of it, almost as much as they have at the University of Texas, which has all that oil money, but we won't go into that.

Now, when all the farmers get back of a school like they do at Texas A&M, they can make things move. They got back of Paul. They furnished him planes. They furnished him everything he needed and, by George, just like I predicted to a big bunch of coaches at a clinic in Texas when he first went there, he built a conference championship team and was in the Cotton Bowl.

Well, I was almost sure Paul wasn't going there because I saw him at noon the day they were going to announce the new coach. After I got home that evening, I heard on the radio that he was down at College Station for a huge pep rally. They'd flown him down there, and all those Aggies and everybody had turned out for the pep rally. Don't you think they're not organized in their cheering. Every student on that campus stands up at the beginning of a football game, and they cheer until the game is over. Again, I didn't think Paul would leave Texas A&M, but his "alma momma" called him—he said, "Mother called,"—and, of course his wife wanted to go back home. Her parents lived in Birmingham.

Mrs. Bryant found that Bryan, Texas, isn't much of a place to live when compared to Lexington. You're pretty well isolated down there. I don't think you've got much of a shopping area unless you go a couple hundred miles until you get to a good-sized town. Paul, of course, had a chance to be head football coach and athletic director at the University of Alabama, and some people like to come home and be connected with their home school. I see him quite frequently, and we're still good friends.

When the University of Kentucky played Alabama at Birmingham several years ago, he invited Mrs. Rupp and myself down for the game. He said, "If the university doesn't bring you along with the team, I'll send a private plane along to pick you up." When word of that leaked out, I was immediately invited to make the trip on the University of Kentucky's chartered plane. I was then at Memphis. My wife called me and told me that Mr. Ham had called her the day before to make sure that I would be here to accompany the team. I told her that I'd be here, although I had a chance to fly in a private plane from Memphis to Birmingham with a group of my friends. However, I came home only to find the day before that I had been canceled off for the trip to Birmingham. I called C. M. Newton, the basketball coach, and told him that I would not be on the plane when it arrived although he had agreed to meet me there. Even at that late hour he said that they would fly a private plane up to Lexington to pick us up, as Paul wanted me there for the game. I naturally did not make the trip, but it shows the friendship that we have for each other regardless of what the critics often write.

That brought in Blanton Collier, who was also a good friend of mine. He was coach at Paris, Kentucky, and if I say so myself, probably a better basketball coach than a football coach. At least he was in high school. He had one of the best-coached basketball teams that I have ever seen. If anything, they were too mechanical, but they could surely operate. He met Paul Brown during the war at Great Lakes and helped him with the football team there; then he was an assistant to Brown with the Cleveland Browns.

Both Mr. and Mrs. Collier's folks lived at Paris. I think they wanted to come back home, as did Paul and Mrs. Bryant. When Blanton came back to Kentucky, everybody realized he had some hard shoes to fill. But they felt he could do it. He was a fine coach and don't let anybody tell you any different. He had one weakness: he didn't have the courage to fire some of his assistants that were not capable. I think that hurt him worse than anything. I'd tell him that, and I think he knows that as well as anybody. When he hired a man, he hated to walk in later and say, "Here's your pink slip." The first thing some of these coaches do if they don't win is fire an assistant. If they don't win the next year, they fire other assistants. Then, maybe, the third year they get fired.

Blanton had very fine teams, but for some reason or another, they deteriorated at the close. His last year was a bad year. He coached here eight years, same length of time as Bryant, and won 41, lost 36 and tied three for .531, which is not a bad percentage. He had a contract, and they paid him $51,000 for the last three years that he didn't coach. I was very much surprised that they let him go. I've always regretted that I didn't have more influence on Blanton because I didn't think that he ever entertained the thought of leaving here. He immediately went back to the Cleveland Browns, where he proved to all those "doubting Thomases" in Kentucky that he was a fine coach. He not only won the league championship year after year, but I think he won what they call the world's championship. I don't know who they played. In baseball they call those things "World Series," and I don't know who they play in the world except maybe Baltimore plays New York, which isn't exactly out of this world.

Blanton was a gentleman; if anything, he was too much of a gentleman. You wouldn't want to meet a nicer fellow. He took me on a lot of trips with him. He was never too communicative, because on a trip there was only one subject that he wanted to talk about. That was the particular game of football that was going to be played. I had no knowledge of that at all, so I couldn't communicate with him. The only thing I could say afterwards was, "Your boys played a nice game," or, "I'm sorry we didn't win," or something like that, language that he could understand and that I could speak.

Blanton was succeeded by Charlie Bradshaw, another one of our boys at the university. Charlie also was a high-grade gentleman, as fine a man as you would want to meet. Unlike Blanton he was a great visitor. He came here and got a good sendoff. Charlie had a weakness, also, I think, in that he had trouble getting rid of some of his assistants that were not capable of coaching college football. I think

Adolph Rupp prescribes aspirin and other medications for new football coach Blanton Collier during a reception in 1954.

he knew that, but he kept them on because he felt that since he hired them and took them out of their jobs, he ought to keep them on his staff.

Charlie had some colorful teams that won some very fine games for us. I call him my friend, and I'm sure he calls me his friend. He took me on trips with him, and I took him on trips with us. I always enjoyed visiting his home and he in mine. We were just the best of friends; never an unkind word was ever said from Collier, to Bradshaw, to Bryant, or any of these men; the only one that I had any trouble with at all was the man that I mentioned, and I won't mention him again.

Bradshaw was at UK seven years. He won 25, lost 41, and tied four for .379, and then, of course, they had a shakeup that brings us to John Ray, who wrote the book, *How to Influence People*. And then there's another book, *The Power of Positive Thinking*, that he wrote: someone else put it out 25 or 30 years ago, but John Ray wrote that book when he was in the cradle. You talk about a guy that was a positive thinker? We got along fine. He hollered as loud as anyone can up and down the hall.

Ray believed that he could do anything and he had a way of getting this across to people. I've heard him say many times, "We're gonna win and you can bet on that!" He really believed it. He came to my office almost every day or I came to his. A more friendly man has never existed. I tried to tell him at times that he didn't have a chance to win a certain game. Before I left his office, I was not only convinced that we would win but by a decisive margin. Let's give the man credit. He ran down the length and the breadth of this Commonwealth telling people that Kentucky would never be a big time football team unless they upgraded their facilities and built a new stadium. He finally convinced the people in authority, and you've got to give him credit because it was his dream, and I think it came true. If anything, it was proved the first year the new stadium opened.

The thing I like about this fellow Fran Curci is that he thinks positive the way I do. The first day he was at the university, he knocked on my door and came in and said he'd like to talk to me, if I had the time. I said, "I've always got time to talk to you." He said that Bryant and Bradshaw and Collier and the other coaches had told him to come in and talk to me because I was the one man at the university that could be trusted. He wanted information in regard to four people, whom I won't mention. I told him there were two that couldn't be trusted. He said he had heard about them.

Curci will tell you what he thinks. I just think he's going to make one of the fine football coaches in the country if they let him run his program. He is a man that just does not overlook anything.

My health has not been too good, but there has never been a time when he didn't find an hour in his day that he would stop by the house for a friendly chat. While his office was here in the Coliseum, he came in every day. He is bringing a new era to Kentucky. While John Ray's dream came true, Curci now has visions that if the financial program of this university is successful the present stadium must be enlarged because it now is already inadequate.

People think differently all over Kentucky than they did years ago. Curci has made friends that are real friends and not the downtown faction that meets every morning to decide on strategy. He will run his own program, and no one will ever doubt that. He knows what he wants, he knows what it takes, and he is positive in what he believes. I've tried to help him in any small way that I can, and he doesn't hesitate to ask me for my help. I have visited with him in homes of prospects, and no man has ever presented a finer, cleaner, or more positive approach to football than this young man has been able to do. We will watch him with a lot of interest, and let's give this man time, something that we have not done to others.

I have tried to evaluate the men that I have worked with here in the football program. I hope that when they read what I have said about them, that they will not think I have been too critical about them. I have tried to present in a fair way my relationships with them. I know that other basketball coaches at other schools also have opinions. I would be interested in reading about their relationships, as I am sure that so many of you will read about mine. I've tried to be fair and honest in what I've said. I hope it may be a guideline to other institutions that may profit about what they have read.

Appendix

KENTUCKY'S BOWL RECORD
(Won 3, Lost 1)

Great Lakes Bowl
(Cleveland, Ohio)

1947	Kentucky	3	0	7	14–24
	Villanova	0	0	0	14–14

(Dec. 6, 1947 – Attendance: 15,000)

Orange Bowl
(Miami, Florida)

1950	Kentucky	0	7	0	6–13
	Santa Clara	0	0	14	7–21

(Jan. 2, 1950 – Attendance: 64,816)

Sugar Bowl
(New Orleans, La.)

1951	Kentucky	7	6	0	0–13
	Oklahoma	0	0	0	7– 7

(Jan. 1, 1951 – Attendance: 82,000)

Cotton Bowl
(Dallas, Texas)

1952	Kentucky	7	6	0	7–20
	Texas Christian	0	0	7	0– 7

(Jan. 1, 1952 – Attendance 75,347)

ALL-SOUTHEASTERN CONFERENCE PLAYERS

(Only first team mention makes the player eligible for listing)

Year	Player	Position
1933	Ralph Kercheval	Back
1934	Bert Johnson	Back
1942	Clyde Johnson	Tackle
1944	Washington Serini	Tackle
1946	Wallace Jones	End
1947	Jay Rhodemyre	Center
1949	Harry Ulinski	Center
1949-50	Bob Gain	Tackle
1950-51	Vito Parilli	Quarterback
1951	Doug Moseley	Center
1951	Gene Donaldson	Guard
1951-52-53	Steve Meilinger	End-QB-HB
1953	Ray Correll	Guard
1954-55	Bob Hardy	Quarterback
1955	Howard Schnellenberger	End
1956-57	Lou Michaels	Tackle
1960-61-62	Tom Hutchinson	End
1962	Junior Hawthorne	Tackle
1963	Herschel Turner	Tackle
1964-65	Rodger Bird	Halfback
1964-65	Rick Kestner	End
1965	Sam Ball	Tackle
1967-68	Dicky Lyons	Back
1969-70	David Roller	Tackle
1971	Joe Federspiel	Linebacker
1973	James McCollum	Noseguard
1973-74	Sonny Collins	Back
1973	Darryl Bishop	Safety
1974	Warren Bryant	OT

ALL-SOUTHERN CONFERENCE (PRE-1933)

1915	C. C. Schrader	Tackle
1915-16	William Rodes	Back
1918	John Heber	End
1920	E. V. Murphree	Tackle
1923	Curtis N. Sanders	Fullback
1930	Floppy Forquer	Guard
1930-31	Shipwreck Kelly	Halfback
1930-31	Babe Wright	Tackle
1932	Joe Rupert	End

1,000-YARD PERFORMERS

Year	Player-Pos.	Runs	Yards	Passes	Yards	Plays	Yards
1965	Rick Norton (QB)	57	−117	214	1823	271	1706
1950	Vito Parilli (QB)	31	54	203	1627	234	1681
1951	Vito Parilli (QB)	30	−161	239	1643	269	1482
1974	Mike Fanuzzi (QB)	179	909	83	438	262	1347
1970	Bernie Scruggs (QB)	99	165	209	1181	308	1346
1964	Rick Norton (QB)	70	−195	202	1514	272	1319
1973	Sonny Collins (OB)	224	1213	11	64	235	1277

1963	Rick Norton (QB)	87	63	182	1177	269	1114
1931	Shipwreck Kelly (OB)	171	1074	–	–	171	1074
1954	Bob Hardy (QB)	91	122	108	887	191	1009
1969	Bernie Scruggs (QB)	116	31	183	969	299	1000

(Norton, with a record high accumulation in 1965, gained the distinction of becoming the first UK player to achieve the coveted mark in three straight years.)

KENTUCKY COACHES THROUGH THE YEARS

Years at UK	Coach–School	Tenure	Won	Lost	Tied	Pct.
1881	Unknown	1	1	2	0	.333
1882-1890	No Competition					
1891	Unknown	1	1	1	0	.500
1892	Prof. A. M. Miller (Princeton)	½	1	2	1	.333
1892-93	John A. Thompson (Purdue)	1½	6	4	1	.600
1894	W. P. Finney (Purdue)	1	5	2	0	.714
1895	Charles Mason (Cornell)	1	4	5	0	.444
1896	Dudley Short (Cornell)	1	3	6	0	.333
1897	Lyman B. Eaton (Cincinnati)	1	2	4	0	.333
1898-99	W. R. Bass (Cincinnati)	2	12	2	2	.813
1900-01	W. H. Kiler (Illinois)	2	6	12	1	.342
1902	E. W. McLeod (Michigan)	1	3	5	1	.375
1903	C. A. Wright (Columbia)	1	7	1	0	.875
1904-05	F. E. Schact (Minnesota)	2	15	4	1	.775
1906-08	J. White Guyn (Kentucky)	3	17	7	1	.687
1909-10,'12	E. R. Sweetland (Cornell)	3	23	5	0	.821
1911	P. P. Douglass (Michigan)	1	7	3	0	.700
1913-14	Alpha Brumage (Kansas)	2	11	5	0	.688
1915-16	J. J. Tigert (Vanderbilt)	2	10	2	3	.733
1917	S. A. Boles (Vanderbilt)	1	3	5	1	.389
1918-19	Andy Gill (Indiana)	2	5	5	1	.500
1920-22	W. J. Juneau (Wisconsin)	3	13	10	2	.560
1923	J. J. Winn (Princeton)	1	4	3	2	.556
1924-26	Fred J. Murphy (Yale)	3	12	14	1	.463
1927-33	Harry Gamage (Illinois)	7	32	25	5	.556
1934-37	C. A. Wynne (Notre Dame)	4	20	19	0	.513
1938-42,'44	A. D. Kirwan (Kentucky)	6	24	28	4	.464
1943	No Team–War Year					
1945	Bernie Shively (Illinois)	1	2	8	0	.200
1946-53	Paul Bryant (Alabama)	8	60	23	5	.710
1954-61	Blanton Collier (Georgetown)	8	41	36	3	.531
1962-68	Charlie Bradshaw (Kentucky)	7	25	41	4	.379
1969-72	John Ray (Olivet)	4	10	33	0	.233
1973-74	Fran Curci (Miami)	2	11	11	0	.500
30 Coaches in 83 Seasons–Record for 759 Games			396	333	39	.543

UNIVERSITY OF KENTUCKY
All–Time Football Record

(79 Seasons–Won 396, Lost 333, Tied 39–.543 Percent)

1881—Won 1, Lost 2.
COACH:
CAPT.: (*The Lexington Press* reported, "The A&M boys were commanded by Capt. Irvine.")
Nov. 12 Kentucky U., KU   7¼   1
Nov. 19 Kentucky U., A&M   1   2
Dec. 3 Kentucky U., KU   2¼   3¾
(Kentucky University is not to be confused with the present day University of Kentucky. U. of K., known in those early days as A&M College, was separated from K.U. in 1878. Transylvania College of Lexington evolved from old K.U. while A&M became Univ. of Ky. During the process, U. of K. carried successive titles of A&M College, Kentucky State College and State University of Kentucky. See footnote A for explanation of scoring in early games.)

1882-1890—No record of competition

1891—Won 1, Lost 1.
MGRS: S. M. Pottinger, I. P. Shelby
CAPT.: John Bryan
Apr. 10 Georgetown, Lexington   8   2
Dec. 12 Kentucky U., KSC   ..   ..
(Game called after one play due to injury to KU player.)
Dec. 19 Centre College, Lexington   0   10

1892—Won 2, Lost 4, Tied 1.
COACH: Prof. A. M. Miller, John A. Thompson
CAPT.: Ed Hobdy
Oct. 29 Kentucky U., KSC   0   0
Nov. 5 Central U., Richmond   6   8
Nov. 12 Central U., Lexington   4   8
Nov. 19 Louisville A.C., Louisville   14   10
Nov. 26 V.M.I., Lexington, Va.   0   34
Dec. 3 Central U., Lexington   6   10
Dec. 10 Kentucky U., KU   10   4

1893—Won 5, Lost 2, Tied 1.
COACH: John A. Thompson
CAPT.: Ulysses Garred
Oct. 14 Georgetown, Lexington   80   0
Oct. 21 Tennessee, Knoxville   56   0
Oct. 28 Centre College, Danville   4   6
Nov. 4 Kentucky U., KSC   28   0
(This contest between KU and KSC was regarded as an exhibition game. It was arranged after rain caused cancellation of scheduled games between KSC and Cincinnati YMCA and KU and Central.)
Nov. 11 Central U., Lexington   36   48
Nov. 18 Cincinnati YMCA, Cincy   14   4
Nov. 25 Kentucky U., KU   38   28
Nov. 30 Indiana, Lexington   24   24

1894—Won 5, Lost 2.
COACH: W.P. Finney
CAPT.: George Carey
Sept. 22 Cincinnati U., Cincinnati   4   32
Oct. 6 Georgetown, Lexington   40   6
Oct. 13 Miami (Ohio), Lexington   28   6
Oct. 20 Jeffersonville A.C., Lex.   64   0
Nov. 10 Kentucky U., KSC   44   0
Nov. 17 Centre College, Lexington   0   67
Nov. 29 Central U., Lexington   38   10
(Kentucky Intercollegiate League Champions)

1895—Won 4, Lost 5.
COACH: Charles Mason
CAPT.: Smith Alford
Oct. 5 Frankfort A.C., Frankfort   10   0
Oct. 12 Purdue, Lafayette   0   32
Oct. 14 DePauw, Greencastle   0   18
Oct. 19 Centre College, Danville   6   0
Oct. 26 Georgetown, Georgetown   0   10
Nov. 3 Kentucky U., KU   26   0
Nov. 15 Ohio State, Lexington   6   8
Nov. 23 Louisville A.C., Lexington   16   10
Nov. 28 Centre College, Lexington   0   16

1896—Won 3, Lost 6.
COACH: Dudley Short
CAPT.: Walter Duncan
Oct. 3 Lexington A.C., Lexington   0   10
Oct. 10 Vanderbilt, Nashville   0   6
Oct. 17 Catlettsburg A.C., C'burg   4   6
Oct. 24 Kentucky U., KSC   36   6
Oct. 31 Centre College, Danville   0   32
Nov. 7 Central U., Lexington   62   0
Nov. 14 Centre College, Lexington   0   44
Nov. 21 Georgetown, Georgetown   16   0
Nov. 26 Louisville A.C., Louisville   4   30

1897—Won 2, Lost 4.
COACH: Lyman B. Eaton
CAPT.: Roscoe Severs
Oct. 2 Kentucky U., Lexington   8   6
Oct. 11 Ky. Wesleyan, Winchester   0   4
Oct. 23 Georgetown, Lexington   20   4
Oct. 30 Vanderbilt, Nashville   0   50
Nov. 6 Central U., Richmond   0   18
Nov. 25 Centre College, Lexington   0   36

1898—Won 7, Lost 0.
COACH: W.R. Bass
CAPT.: Roscoe Severs
Oct. 1 Kentucky U., Lexington   18   0
Oct. 8 Georgetown, Georgetown   28   0
Oct. 15 Co. H. of 8th Mass., Lex.   59   0
Oct. 29 Louisville A.C., Louisville   16   0
Nov. 5 Centre College, Lexington   6   0
Nov. 12 160th Indiana, Lexington   17   0
Nov. 19 Newcastle A.C., Lexington   36   0

Date	Team—Site	Ky.	Op.

1899—Won 5, Lost 2, Tied 2.
COACH: W. R. Bass
CAPT.: A. S. Reece

Date	Team—Site	Ky.	Op.
Oct. 7	Kentucky U., Lexington	23	6
Oct. 18	Miami (Ohio), Lexington	18	5
Oct. 21	Centre College, Danville	11	11
Nov. 4	Tennessee, Knoxville	0	12
Nov. 11	Central U., Lexington	0	5
Nov. 18	Georgetown, Lexington	34	0
Nov. 21	Washington & Lee, Lex.	0	0
Nov. 22	Washington & Lee, Lex.	6	0
Nov. 30	Alumni, Lexington	6	5

1900—Won 4, Lost 6.
COACH: W. H. Kiler
CAPT.: Wellington Scott

Date	Team—Site	Ky.	Op.
Sept. 29	Cincinnati, Cincinnati	6	20
Oct. 6	Louisville YMCA, Lexington	12	6
Oct. 13	Centre College, Danville	0	5
Oct. 20	All-Kentucky, Lexington	0	5
Oct. 27	Central U., Lex. (forfeit)	0	6
Nov. 3	Louisville YMCA, Louisville	12	0
Nov. 10	Avondale A.C., Lexington	5	11
Nov. 17	Georgetown, Lexington	12	0
Nov. 24	Central U., Richmond	0	11
Nov. 29	Kentucky U., Lexington	12	0

1901—Won 2, Lost 6, Tied 1.
COACH: W. H. Kiler
CAPT.: L. W. Martin

Date	Team—Site	Ky.	Op.
Oct. 5	Vanderbilt, Nashville	0	22
Oct. 12	Cincinnati, Lexington	0	0
Oct. 19	Georgetown, Georgetown (between second teams)	17	0
Oct. 26	Kentucky U., Lexington	0	27
Nov. 2	Avondale A.C., Cincinnati	6	17
Nov. 9	Louisville YMCA, Louisville	0	11
Nov. 16	Central U., Lexington	0	5
Nov. 23	Tennessee, Knoxville	0	5
Nov. 28	Cincinnati, Lexington	16	0

1902—Won 3, Lost 5, Tied 1.
COACH: E. N. McLeod
CAPT.: John H. L. Vogt

Date	Team—Site	Ky.	Op.
Sept. 27	Q. and C. R. R., Lexington	22	0
Oct. 4	Miami (Ohio), Lexington	11	5
Oct. 18	Georgetown, Lexington	28	0
Oct. 25	Nashville U., Nashville	0	11
Oct. 27	Mooney School, Murfreesboro, Tenn.	0	23
Nov. 1	Central U., Danville	0	15
Nov. 8	Louisville YMCA, Louisville	0	17
Nov. 15	Cincinnati, Lexington	6	6
Nov. 27	Kentucky U., Lexington	5	6

1903—Won 7, Lost 1.
COACH: C.A. Wright
CAPT.: David Maddox

Date	Team—Site	Ky.	Op.
Sept. 25	Cynthiana, Lexington	39	0
Oct. 3	Xavier, Lexington	21	0
Oct. 10	Berea College, Lexington	17	0
Oct. 17	K.M.I., Lexington	18	0
Oct. 24	Miami (Ohio), Lexington	47	0
Nov. 2	Georgetown, Lexington	51	0
Nov. 7	Marietta, Lexington	11	5
Nov. 26	Kentucky U., Lexington	0	17

1904—Won 9, Lost 1.
COACH: F. E. Schacht
CAPT.: J. White Guyn

Date	Team—Site	Ky.	Op.
Sept. 30	Paris A.C., Lexington	28	0
Oct. 8	Indiana, Bloomington	12	0
Oct. 12	Central U., Danville	40	0
Oct. 15	Berea College, Lexington	42	0
Oct. 18	Bethany (W. Va.), Lex.	6	0
Oct. 22	Cincinnati, Cincinnati	0	11
Nov. 5	K.M.I., Lexington	11	0
Nov. 12	Georgetown, Georgetown	35	0
Nov. 19	Central U., Lexington	81	0
Nov. 24	Kentucky U., Lexington	21	4

1905—Won 6, Lost 3, Tied 1.
COACH: F.E. Schacht
CAPT.: Bill Kemper

Date	Team—Site	Ky.	Op.
Sept. 27	Cynthiana (Indpt.), Lex.	52	0
Sept. 30	Catlettsburg A.C., Lex.	23	0
Oct. 7	Indiana, Bloomington	0	29
Oct. 14	K.M.I., Lexington	12	4
Oct. 28	Berea College, Lexington	46	0
Nov. 2	Marshall Col., Huntington	53	0
Nov. 4	W. Virginia, Morgantown	0	45
Nov. 11	Cumberland, Lexington (Forfeit, See footnote B)	12	0
Nov. 18	St. Louis, St. Louis (UK coach and 1st team stayed home)	0	82
Nov. 25	Central U., Lexington	11	11

1906—Won 4, Lost 3.
COACH: J.White Guyn
CAPT.: Frank Paullin

Date	Team—Site	Ky.	Op.
Oct. 6	Vanderbilt, Nashville	0	28
Oct. 13	Eminence A.C., Lexington	48	0
Oct. 27	K.M.I., Lexington	16	11
Nov. 2	Marietta College, Lexington	0	16
Nov. 10	Tennessee, Lexington	21	0
Nov. 24	Georgetown, Georgetown	19	0
Nov. 29	Centre College, Lexington	6	12

1907—Won 9, Lost 1, Tied 1.
COACH: J.White Guyn
CAPT.: George Adair

Date	Team—Site	Ky.	Op.
Sept. 21	Ky. Wesleyan, Winchester	17	0
Sept. 28	Winchester A.C., Lexington (Forfeit)	6	0
Sept. 28	Louisville Manual Training School, Lexington (Game arranged as replacement forfeited game scheduled with Winchester A. C.)	30	0
Oct. 5	Vanderbilt, Nashville	0	40
Oct. 12	Morris-Harvey, Lexington	29	0
Oct. 21	Hanover, Lexington	40	0
Nov. 9	Tennessee, Knoxville	0	0
Nov. 11	Maryville, Maryville	5	2
Nov. 16	Georgetown, Lexington	38	0
Nov. 28	Centre College, Lexington	11	0
Dec. 5	Kentucky U., Lexington	5	0

1908—Won 4, Lost 3.
COACH: J. White Guyn
CAPT.: George Hendrickson

Date	Team—Site	Ky.	Op.
Oct. 10	Berea College, Lexington	17	0
Oct. 17	Tennessee, Knoxville	0	5
Oct. 19	Maryville, Maryville	18	0
Oct. 31	Sewanee, Lexington	0	12
Nov. 7	Michigan, Ann Arbor	0	62
Nov. 14	Rose Polytechnic, Lexington	12	0
Nov. 26	Centre College, Lexington	40	0

Date	Team—Site	Ky.	Op.
1909—Won 9, Lost 1.			
COACH: E. R. Sweetland			
CAPT.: Dick Barbee			
Sept. 25	Kentucky Wesleyan, Lex.	18	0
Oct. 2	Berea College, Lexington	28	0
Oct. 9	Illinois, Urbana	6	2
Oct. 16	Tennessee, Lexington	17	0
Oct. 22	N. C. A&M, Raleigh	6	15
Oct. 28	Rose Polytechnic, Lex.	43	0
Nov. 3	Georgetown, Georgetown	22	6
Nov. 6	St. Mary's College, Lex.	29	0
Nov. 13	Transylvania, Lexington	77	0
Nov. 25	Centre College, Lexington	15	6
1910—Won 7, Lost 2.			
COACH: E. R. Sweetland			
CAPT.: Dick Webb			
Sept. 24	Ohio U., Lexington	12	0
Oct. 1	Maryville College, Lex.	12	5
Oct. 8	North Carolina, Lexington	11	0
Oct. 15	Ky. Wesleyan, Winchester	42	0
Oct. 22	Georgetown, Lexington	37	0
Oct. 29	Tulane, Lexington	10	3
Nov. 5	Tennessee, Knoxville	10	0
Nov. 12	St. Louis, St. Louis	0	9
Nov. 24	Centre College, Lexington	6	12
1911—Won 7, Lost 3.			
COACH: P. P. Douglass			
CAPT.: Tom Earle			
Sept. 30	Maryville, Lexington	13	0
Oct. 7	Morris-Harvey, Lexington	12	0
Oct. 14	Miami (Ohio), Oxford	12	0
Oct. 21	Lex. High School, Lex.	17	0
Oct. 28	Cincinnati, Lexington	0	6
Nov. 4	Georgetown, Georgetown	18	0
Nov. 11	Vanderbilt, Nashville	0	18
Nov. 18	Transylvania, Lexington	5	12
Nov. 23	Centre College, Lexington	8	5
Nov. 30	Tennessee, Lexington	12	0
1912—Won 7, Lost 2.			
COACH: E. R. Sweetland			
CAPT.: W. C. Harrison			
Sept. 28	Maryville College, Lex.	34	0
Oct. 5	Marshall College, Lex.	13	6
Oct. 12	Miami (Ohio), Lexington	8	13
Oct. 19	Cincinnati, Cincinnati	19	13
Oct. 26	Louisville, Lexington	41	0
Nov. 2	V.M.I., Lexington	2	3
Nov. 9	Hanover, Lexington	64	0
Nov. 16	Tennessee, Knoxville	13	6
Nov. 28	YMI of Cincinnati, Cincy	56	0
1913—Won 6, Lost 2.			
COACH: Alpha Brumage			
CAPT.: Herschel Scott			
Sept. 27	Butler, Lexington	21	7
Oct. 4	Illinois, Urbana	0	21
Oct. 18	Ohio Northern, Lexington	21	0
Oct. 25	Cincinnati, Lexington	27	7
Nov. 1	Earlham, Lexington	28	10
Nov. 8	Wilmington, Lexington	33	0
Nov. 22	Louisville, Louisville	20	0
Nov. 27	Tennessee, Lexington	7	13

Date	Team—Site	Ky.	Op.
1914—Won 5, Lost 3.			
COACH: Alpha Brumage			
CAPT.: Jim Park			
Sept. 26	Wilmington, Lexington	87	0
Oct. 3	Maryville, Lexington	80	0
Oct. 17	Mississippi A&M, Lexington	19	13
Oct. 24	Earlham, Lexington	81	3
Oct. 31	Cincinnati, Cincinnati	7	14
Nov. 7	Purdue, Lafayette, Ind.	6	40
Nov. 14	Louisville, Lexington	42	0
Nov. 26	Tennessee, Knoxville	6	23
1915—Won 6, Lost 1, Tied 1.			
COACH: J. J. Tigert			
CAPT.: Charles Schrader			
Oct. 2	Butler, Lexington	33	0
Oct. 9	Earlham, Lexington	54	13
Oct. 16	Mississippi A&M, Starkville	0	12
Oct. 23	Sewanee, Lexington	7	7
Oct. 30	Cincinnati, Lexington	27	6
Nov. 6	Louisville, Louisville	15	0
Nov. 13	Purdue, Lexington	7	0
Nov. 25	Tennessee, Lexington	6	0
1916—Won 4, Lost 1, Tied 2.			
COACH: J. J. Tigert			
Capt.: Maury Crutcher			
Sept. 30	Butler, Lexington	39	3
Oct. 7	Centre College, Lexington	68	0
Oct. 14	Vanderbilt, Lexington	0	45
Oct. 21	Sewanee, Lexington	0	0
Oct. 28	Cincinnati, Cincinnati	32	0
Nov. 13	Mississippi A&M, Lexington	13	3
Nov. 30	Tennessee, Knoxville	0	0
1917—Won 3, Lost 5, Tied 1.			
COACH: S. A. Boles			
CAPT.: John Brittain			
Sept. 29	Butler, Lexington	33	0
Oct. 6	Maryville, Lexington	19	0
Oct. 13	Miami (Ohio), Lexington	0	0
Oct. 20	Vanderbilt, Lexington	0	5
Oct. 27	Sewanee, Chattanooga	0	7
Nov. 3	Centre College, Danville	0	3
Nov. 10	Mississippi A&M, Starkville	0	14
Nov. 17	Alabama, Lexington	0	27
Nov. 29	Florida, Lexington	52	0
1918—Won 2, Lost 1.			
COACH: Andy Gill			
CAPT.: John G. Heber			
Oct. 5	Indiana, Bloomington	24	7
Nov. 2	Vanderbilt, Nashville	0	33
Nov. 9	Georgetown, Georgetown	21	3
Nov. 30	Centre College, Lexington	—	—
(Cancelled because of flu epidemic in Lexington.)			
1919—Won 3, Lost 4, Tied 1.			
COACH: Andy Gill			
CAPT.: Tony Dishman			
Oct. 4	Georgetown, Lexington	12	0
Oct. 11	Indiana, Lexington	0	24
Oct. 18	Ohio State, Columbus	0	49
Oct. 25	Sewanee, Sewanee	6	0
Nov. 1	Vanderbilt, Lexington	0	0
Nov. 8	Cincinnati, Cincinnati	0	7
Nov. 15	Centre College, Danville	0	56
Nov. 27	Tennessee, Lexington	13	0

Date Team—Site	Ky.	Op.
1920—Won, 3, Lost 4, Tied 1.		
COACH: W. J. Juneau		
Capt.: Eger Murphree		
Oct. 2 S.P.U., Lexington	62	0
Oct 9 Maryville, Lexington	31	0
Oct. 16 Miami (Ohio), Oxford	0	14
Oct. 23 Sewanee, Lexington	6	6
Oct. 30 Vanderbilt, Nashville	0	20
Nov. 6 Cincinnati, Lexington	7	6
Nov. 13 Centre College, Lexington	0	49
Nov. 25 Tennessee, Knoxville	7	14
1921—Won 4, Lost 3, Tied 1.		
COACH: W. J. Juneau		
Capt.: Jim Server		
Oct. 1 Ky. Wesleyan, Lexington	68	0
Oct. 8 Marshall, Lexington	28	0
Oct. 15 Vanderbilt, Lexington	14	21
Oct. 22 Georgetown, Lexington	33	0
Oct. 29 Sewanee, Louisville	0	6
Nov. 5 Centre College, Danville	0	55
Nov. 12 V.M.I., Louisville	14	7
Nov. 24 Tennessee, Lexington	0	0
1922—Won 6, Lost 3.		
COACH: W. J. Juneau		
CAPT.: Birkett Pribble		
Sept. 30 Marshall, Lexington	16	0
Oct. 7 Cincinnati, Lexington	15	0
Oct. 14 Louisville, Lexington	73	0
Oct. 21 Georgetown, Georgetown	40	6
Oct. 28 Sewanee, Lexington	7	0
Nov. 4 Centre College, Lexington	3	27
Nov. 11 Vanderbilt, Nashville	0	9
Nov. 18 Alabama, Lexington	6	0
Nov. 30 Tennessee, Knoxville	7	14
1923—Won 4, Lost 3, Tied 2.		
COACH: J. J. Winn		
CAPT.: Dell Ramsey		
Sept. 29 Marshall, Lexington	41	0
Oct. 6 Cincinnati, Cincinnati	14	0
Oct. 13 Washington & Lee, Lex.	6	6
Oct. 20 Maryville, Lexington	28	0
Oct. 27 Georgetown, Lexington	35	0
Nov. 3 Centre College, Danville	0	10
Nov. 10 Alabama, Tuscaloosa	8	16
Nov. 17 Georgia Tech, Atlanta	3	3
Nov. 29 Tennessee, Lexington	0	18
1924—Won 4, Lost 5.		
COACH: Fred J. Murphy		
CAPT.: Curtis Sanders		
Oct. 4 Louisville, Lexington	29	0
Oct. 11 Georgetown, Lexington	42	0
Oct. 18 Washington & Lee, Lex.	7	10
Oct. 25 Sewanee, Lexington	7	0
Nov. 1 Centre College, Lexington	0	7
Nov. 8 Alabama, Tuscaloosa	7	42
Nov. 15 V.M.I., Lexington	3	10
Nov. 27 Tennessee, Knoxville	27	6
Dec. 6 W. Va. Wes., Charleston	7	24
1925—Won 6, Lost 3.		
COACH: Fred J. Murphy		
CAPT.: Ab Kirwan		
Sept. 26 Maryville, Lexington	13	6
Oct. 3 Chicago, Chicago	0	9
Oct. 10 Clemson, Lexington	19	6
Oct. 17 Washington & Lee, Lex.	0	25
Oct. 24 Sewanee, Lexington	14	0
Oct. 31 Centre College, Danville	16	0
Nov. 7 Alabama, Birmingham	0	31
Nov. 14 V.M.I., Charleston	7	0
Nov. 26 Tennessee, Lexington	23	20
1926—Won 2, Lost 6, Tied 1.		
COACH: Fred J. Murphy		
CAPT.: Frank Smith		
Oct. 2 Maryville, Lexington	25	0
Oct. 9 Indiana, Bloomington	6	14
Oct. 16 Washington & Lee, Lex.	13	14
Oct. 23 Florida, Jacksonville	18	13
Oct. 30 Va. Tech., Lexington	13	13
Nov. 6 Alabama, Birmingham	0	14
Nov. 13 V.M.I., Charleston	9	10
Nov. 20 Centre College, Lexington	0	7
Nov. 25 Tennessee, Knoxville	0	6
1927—Won 3, Lost 6, Tied 1.		
COACH: Harry Gamage		
CAPT.: Charles Wert		
Sept. 24 Maryville, Lexington	6	6
Oct. 1 Indiana, Lexington	0	21
Oct. 8 Ky. Wesleyan, Lexington	13	7
Oct. 15 Florida, Jacksonville	6	27
Oct. 22 Washington & Lee, Lex.	0	25
Oct. 29 Vanderbilt, Nashville	6	34
Nov. 5 Alabama, Birmingham	6	21
Nov. 12 V.M.I., Charleston	25	0
Nov. 19 Centre College, Danville	53	0
Nov. 24 Tennessee, Lexington	0	20
1928—Won 4, Lost 3, Tied 1.		
COACH: Harry Gamage		
CAPT.: Claire Dees		
Oct. 6 Carson-Newman, Lexington	61	0
Oct. 13 Washington & Lee, Lex.	6	6
Oct. 20 Northwestern, Evanston	0	7
Oct. 27 Centre College, Lexington	8	0
Nov. 3 Vanderbilt, Nashville	7	14
Nov. 10 Alabama, Montgomery	0	14
Nov. 17 V.M.I., Lexington	18	6
Nov. 29 Tennessee, Knoxville	0	0
1929—Won 6, Lost 1, Tied 1.		
COACH: Harry Gamage		
CAPT.: Will Ed Covington		
Oct. 5 Maryville, Lexington	40	0
Oct. 12 Washington & Lee, Lex.	20	6
Oct. 19 Carson-Newman, Lexington	58	0
Oct. 26 Centre College, Danville	33	0
Nov. 2 Clemson, Lexington	44	6
Nov. 9 Alabama, Montgomery	13	24
Nov. 16 V.M.I., Lexington, Va.	23	12
Nov. 28 Tennessee, Lexington	6	6
1930—Won 5, Lost 3.		
COACH: Harry Gamage		
CAPT.: L. G. Forquer		
Oct. 4 Sewanee, Lexington	37	0
Oct. 11 Maryville, Lexington	57	0
Oct. 18 Washington & Lee, Lex.	33	14
Oct. 25 Virginia, Lexington	47	0
Nov. 1 Alabama, Lexington	0	19
Nov. 8 Duke, Durham	7	14
Nov. 15 V.M.I., Lexington	26	0
Nov. 27 Tennessee, Knoxville	0	8

Date	Team—Site	Ky.	Op.

1931—Won 5, Lost 2, Tied 2.
COACH: Harry Gamage
CAPT.: Ralph Wright
ALT. CAPT.: John Simms Kelly

Oct. 3	Maryville, Lexington	19	0
Oct. 10	Washington & Lee, Lex.	45	0
Oct. 17	Maryland, College Park	6	6
Oct. 24	Virginia Tech, Lexington	20	6
Oct. 31	Alabama, Tuscaloosa	7	9
Nov. 7	Duke, Lexington	0	7
Nov. 14	V.M.I., Lexington, Va.	20	12
Nov. 26	Tennessee, Lexington	6	6
Dec. 5	Florida, Jacksonville	7	2

1932—Won 4, Lost 5.
COACH: Harry Gamage
CAPT.: Bud Davidson

Sept. 24	V.M.I., Lexington	23	0
Oct. 1	Sewanee, Lexington	18	0
Oct. 8	Georgia Tech, Atlanta	12	6
Oct. 15	Washington & Lee, Lex.	53	7
Oct. 22	Va. Tech, Blacksburg	0	7
Oct. 29	Alabama, Lexington	7	12
Nov. 5	Duke, Durham	0	13
Nov. 12	Tulane, Lexington	3	6
Nov. 24	Tennessee, Knoxville	0	26

1933—Won 5, Lost 5.
COACH: Harry Gamage
CAPT.: Howard Kreuter

Sept. 23	Maryville, Lexington	46	2
Sept. 30	Sewanee, Lexington	7	0
Oct. 7	Georgia Tech, Lexington	7	6
Oct. 14	Cincinnati, Cincinnati	3	0
Oct. 21	Wash. & Lee, Roanoke	0	7
Oct. 28	Duke, Lexington	7	14
Nov. 4	Alabama, Birmingham	0	20
Nov. 11	V.M.I., Lexington	21	6
Nov. 18	Tulane, New Orleans	0	34
Nov. 30	Tennessee, Lexington	0	27

1934—Won 5, Lost 5.
COACH: C. A. Wynne
CAPT.: Joe Rupert

Sept. 22	Maryville, Lexington	26	0
Sept. 29	Washington & Lee, Lex.	0	7
Oct. 6	Cincinnati, Cincinnati	27	0
Oct. 13	Clemson, Lexington	7	0
Oct. 20	N. Carolina, Chapel Hill	0	6
Oct. 27	Auburn, Lexington	9	0
Nov. 3	Alabama, Lexington	14	34
Nov. 10	Southwestern, Memphis	33	0
Nov. 17	Tulane, Lexington	7	20
Nov. 29	Tennessee, Knoxville	0	19

1935—Won 5, Lost 4.
COACH: C. A. Wynne
CAPT.: Jim Long

Sept. 21	Maryville, Lexington	60	0
Sept. 27	Xavier (Ohio), Cincinnati	21	7
Oct. 5	Ohio State, Columbus	6	19
Oct. 12	Georgia Tech, Lexington	25	6
Oct. 19	Auburn, Montgomery	0	23
Nov. 2	Alabama, Birmingham	0	13
Nov. 9	Florida, Lexington	15	6
Nov. 16	Tulane, New Orleans	13	20
Nov. 28	Tennessee, Lexington	27	0

1936—Won 6, Lost 4.
COACH: C. A. Wynne
CAPT.: Stan Nevers
ALT. CAPT.: Gene Myers

Sept. 19	Maryville, Lexington	54	3
Sept. 25	Xavier (Ohio), Cincinnati	21	0
Oct. 3	V.M.I., Lexington	38	0
Oct. 10	Georgia Tech, Atlanta	0	34
Oct. 17	Wash. & Lee. Lex., Va.	39	7
Oct. 24	Florida, Lexington	7	0
Oct. 31	Alabama, Lexington	0	14
Nov. 7	Manhattan, N.Y. City	7	13
Nov. 14	Clemson, Lexington	7	6
Nov. 26	Tennessee, Knoxville	6	7

1937—Won 4, Lost 6.
COACH: C. A. Wynne
CAPT.: Joe Hagan

Sept. 25	Vanderbilt, Nashville	0	12
Oct. 2	Xavier (Ohio), Cincinnati	6	0
Oct. 9	Georgia Tech, Lexington	0	32
Oct. 16	Washington & Lee, Lex.	41	6
Oct. 23	Manhattan, Lexington	19	0
Oct. 30	Alabama, Tuscaloosa	0	41
Nov. 6	South Carolina, Lexington	27	7
Nov. 13	Boston College, Boston	0	13
Nov. 25	Tennessee, Lexington	0	13
Dec. 4	Florida, Gainesville	0	6

1938—Won 2, Lost 7.
COACH: A. D. Kirwan
CAPT.: John S. Hinkebein

Sept. 24	Maryville, Lexington	46	7
Oct. 1	Oglethorpe, Lexington	66	0
Oct. 8	Vanderbilt, Lexington	7	14
Oct. 15	Washington & Lee, Lex.	0	8
Oct. 22	Xavier, (Ohio), Cincinnati	7	26
Oct. 29	Alabama, Lexington	6	26
Nov. 5	Georgia Tech, Atlanta	18	19
Nov. 12	Clemson, Lexington	0	14
Nov. 24	Tennessee, Knoxville	0	46

1939—Won 6, Lost 2, Tied 1.
COACH: A. D. Kirwan
CAPT.: Joe Shepherd

Sept. 30	V.M.I., Lexington	21	0
Oct. 7	Vanderbilt, Nashville	21	13
Oct. 14	Oglethorpe, Lexington	59	0
Oct. 21	Georgia, Louisville	13	6
Oct. 28	Xavier (Ohio), Cincinnati	21	0
Nov. 4	Alabama, Birmingham	7	7
Nov. 11	Georgia Tech, Atlanta	6	13
Nov. 18	W. Virginia, Lexington	13	6
Nov. 30	Tennessee, Lexington	0	19

1940—Won 5, Lost 3, Tied 2.
COACH: A. D. Kirwan
CAPT.: John Eibner

Sept. 21	Baldwin-Wallace, Lexington	59	7
Sept. 27	Xavier (Ohio), Cincinnati	13	0
Oct. 5	Washington & Lee, Lex.	47	12
Oct. 12	Vanderbilt, Nashville	7	7
Oct. 19	George Washington, Lex.	24	0
Oct. 26	Georgia, Athens	7	7
Nov. 2	Alabama, Lexington	0	25
Nov. 9	Georgia Tech, Louisville	26	7
Nov. 16	W. Virginia, Morgantown	7	9
Nov. 23	Tennessee, Knoxville	0	33

Date Team—Site	Ky.	Op.
1941—Won 5, Lost 4.		
COACH: A. D. Kirwan		
CAPT.: None		
Sept. 27 Virginia Tech, Louisville	37	14
Oct. 4 Wash. & Lee, Lex., Va.	7	0
Oct. 11 Vanderbilt, Lexington	15	39
Oct. 18 Xavier (Ohio), Cincinnati	21	6
Oct. 25 W. Virginia, Lexington	18	6
Nov. 1 Alabama, Tuscaloosa	0	30
Nov. 8 Georgia Tech, Atlanta	13	20
Nov. 15 Southwestern, Lexington	33	19
Nov. 22 Tennessee, Lexington	7	20
1942—Won 3, Lost 6, Tied 1.		
COACH: A. D. Kirwan		
CAPT.: Charles Walker		
Sept. 19 Georgia, Louisville	6	7
Sept. 25 Xavier (Ohio), Cincinnati	35	19
Oct. 3 Washington & Lee, Lex	53	0
Oct. 10 Vanderbilt, Lexington	6	7
Oct. 17 Virginia Tech, Roanoke	21	21
Oct. 24 Alabama, Lexington	0	14
Oct. 30 George Washington, D. C.	27	6
Nov. 7 Georgia Tech, Atlanta	7	47
Nov. 14 W. Virginia, Lexington	0	7
Nov. 21 Tennessee, Knoxville	0	26
1943—No team (War Year)		
1944—Won 3, Lost 6.		
COACH: A. D. Kirwan		
CAPT.: Jim Little		
Sept. 23 Mississippi, Lexington	27	7
Sept. 30 Tennessee, Knoxville	13	26
Oct. 7 Michigan State, Lexington	0	2
Oct. 13 Georgia, Athens	12	13
Oct. 21 V.M.I., Lexington	26	2
Oct. 27 Alabama, Montgomery	0	41
Nov. 4 Mississippi State, Memphis	0	26
Nov. 12 West Virginia, Lexington	40	9
Nov. 25 Tennessee, Lexington	7	21
1945—Won 2, Lost 8.		
COACH: Bernie Shively		
CAPT.: Roger Yost		
Sept. 21 Mississippi, Memphis	7	21
Sept. 29 Cincinnati, Lexington	13	7
Oct. 6 Mich. State, E. Lansing	6	7
Oct. 13 Georgia, Lexington	6	48
Oct. 20 Vanderbilt, Nashville	6	19
Oct. 27 Cincinnati, Cincinnati	7	16
Nov. 3 Alabama, Louisville	19	60
Nov. 10 W. Virginia, Morgantown	19	6
Nov. 17 Marquette, Lexington	13	19
Nov. 24 Tennessee, Lexington	0	14
1946—Won 7, Lost 3.		
COACH: Paul Bryant		
HON. CAPT.: Phil Cutchin		
Sept. 21 Mississippi, Lexington	20	7
Sept. 28 Cincinnati, Cincinnati	26	7
Oct. 5 Xavier (Ohio), Lexington	70	0
Oct. 11 Georgia, Athens	13	28
Oct. 19 Vanderbilt, Lexington	10	7
Oct. 26 Alabama, Montgomery	7	21
Nov. 2 Michigan State, Lex.	39	14
Nov. 9 Marquette, Milwaukee	35	0
Nov. 16 W. Virginia, Lexington	13	0
Nov. 23 Tennessee, Knoxville	0	7
1947—Won 8, Lost 3.		
COACH: Paul Bryant		
HON. CAPT.: Bill Moseley		
Sept. 20 Mississippi, Oxford	7	14
Sept. 27 Cincinnati, Lexington	20	0
Oct. 4 Xavier (Ohio), Cincinnati	20	7
Oct. 11 Georgia, Lexington	26	0
Oct. 18 Vanderbilt, Nashville	14	0
Oct. 25 Mich. State, E. Lansing	7	6
Nov. 1 Alabama, Lexington	0	13
Nov. 8 W. Virginia, Morgantown	15	6
Nov. 15 Evansville, Lexington	36	0
Nov. 22 Tennessee, Lexington	6	13
GREAT LAKES BOWL		
(Cleveland, Ohio)		
Dec. 6 Villanova	24	14
1948—Won 5, Lost 3, Tied 2.		
COACH: Paul Bryant		
HON. CAPT.: George Blanda		
Sept. 25 Xavier (Ohio), Lexington	48	7
Oct. 2 Mississippi, Lexington	7	20
Oct. 9 Georgia, Athens	12	35
Oct. 16 Vanderbilt, Lexington	7	26
Oct. 23 Marquette, Milwaukee	25	0
Oct. 30 Cincinnati, Cincinnati	28	7
Nov. 6 Villanova, Lexington	13	13
Nov. 13 Florida, Lexington	34	15
Nov. 20 Tennessee, Knoxville	0	0
Nov. 26 Miami (Fla.), Miami	25	5
1949—Won 9, Lost 3.		
COACH: Paul Bryant		
CAPT.: Harry Ulinski		
ALT. CAPT.: Dick Holway		
Sept. 17 Miss. Southern, Lex.	71	7
Sept. 24 La. State, Baton Rouge	19	0
Oct. 1 Mississippi, Oxford	47	0
Oct. 8 Georgia, Lexington	25	0
Oct. 15 The Citadel, Lexington	44	0
Oct. 22 Sou. Methodist, Dallas	7	20
Oct. 29 Cincinnati, Lexington	14	7
Nov. 5 Xavier (Ohio), Cincinnati	21	7
Nov. 12 Florida, Tampa	35	0
Nov. 19 Tennessee, Lexington	0	6
Nov. 25 Miami (Fla.), Miami	21	6
ORANGE BOWL		
(Miami, Fla.)		
Jan. 2 Santa Clara	13	21
1950—Won 11, Lost 1.		
COACH: Paul Bryant		
CO-CAPS.: Bob Gain, Wilbur Jamerson		
Sept. 16 North Texas State, Lex.	25	0
Sept. 23 La. State, Lexington	14	0
Sept. 30 Mississippi, Lexington	27	0
Oct. 7 Dayton, Lexington	40	0
Oct. 14 Cincinnati, Lexington	41	7
Oct. 21 Villanova, Philadelphia	34	7
Oct. 28 Georgia Tech, Atlanta	28	14
Nov. 4 Florida, Lexington	40	6
Nov. 11 Miss. State, St. College	48	21
Nov. 18 North Dakota, Lexington	83	0
Nov. 25 Tennessee, Knoxville	0	7
SEC CHAMPIONS		
SUGAR BOWL		
(New Orleans, La.)		
Jan. 1 Oklahoma	13	7

Date	Team—Site	Ky.	Op.

1951—Won 8, Lost 4.
COACH: Paul Bryant
CO-CAPTS.: Vito Parilli, Doug Moseley

Date	Team—Site	Ky.	Op.
Sept. 15	Tennessee Tech., Lexington	72	13
Sept. 22	Texas, Austin	6	7
Sept. 29	Mississippi. Oxford	17	21
Oct. 6	Georgia Tech, Lexington	7	13
Oct. 13	Miss. State, Lexington	27	0
Oct. 20	Villanova, Lexington	35	13
Oct. 27	Florida, Gainesville	14	6
Nov. 3	Miami (Fla.), Lexington	32	0
Nov. 10	Tulane, New Orleans	37	0
Nov. 17	George Wash., Lexington	47	13
Nov. 24	Tennessee, Lexington	0	28
	COTTON BOWL (Dallas, Tex.)		
Jan. 1	Texas Christian	20	7

1952—Won 5, Lost 4, Tied 2.
COACH: Paul Bryant
CAPT.: John Griggs
ALT. CAPT.: Bob Fry

Date	Team—Site	Ky.	Op.
Sept. 20	Villanova, Lexington	6	25
Sept. 27	Mississippi, Lexington	13	13
Oct. 4	Texas A&M, College Sta.	10	7
Oct. 11	La. State, Lexington	7	34
Oct. 18	Miss. State, St. College	14	27
Oct. 25	Cincinnati, Cincinnati	14	6
Oct. 31	Miami (Fla.), Miami	29	0
Nov. 8	Tulane, Lexington	27	6
Nov. 15	Clemson, Lexington	27	14
Nov. 22	Tennessee, Knoxville	14	14
Dec. 6	Florida, Gainesville	0	27

1953—Won 7, Lost 2, Tied 1.
COACH: Paul Bryant
CO-CAPTS.: Ray Correll, Tommy Adkins

Date	Team—Site	Ky.	Op.
Sept. 19	Texas A&M, Lexington	6	7
Sept. 26	Mississippi, Oxford	6	22
Oct. 3	Florida, Lexington	26	13
Oct. 10	La. State, Baton Rouge	6	6
Oct. 17	Miss. State, Lexington	32	13
Oct. 24	Villanova, Lexington	19	0
Oct. 31	Rice, Houston	19	13
Nov. 7	Vanderbilt, Nashville	40	14
Nov. 14	Memphis State, Lexington	20	7
Nov. 21	Tennessee, Lexington	27	21

1954—Won 7, Lost 3.
COACH: Blanton Collier
CO-CAPTS.: Harry Kirk, Joe Koch

Date	Team—Site	Ky.	Op.
Sept. 18	Maryland, Lexington	0	20
Sept. 25	Mississippi, Memphis	9	28
Oct. 2	La. State, Lexington	7	6
Oct. 9	Auburn, Lexington	21	14
Oct. 16	Florida, Gainesville	7	21
Oct. 23	Georgia Tech, Atlanta	13	6
Oct. 30	Villanova, Lexington	28	3
Nov. 6	Vanderbilt, Lexington	19	7
Nov. 13	Memphis State, Lexington	33	7
Nov. 20	Tennessee, Knoxville	14	13

1955—Won 6, Lost 3, Tied 1.
COACH: Blanton Collier
CO-CAPTS.: Bob Hardy, Howard Schnellenberger

Date	Team—Site	Ky.	Op.
Sept. 17	La. State, Baton Rouge	7	19
Sept. 24	Mississippi, Lexington	21	14
Oct. 1	Villanova, Lexington	28	0
Oct. 8	Auburn, Birmingham	14	14
Oct. 15	Mississippi State, Lexington	14	20
Oct. 22	Florida, Lexington	10	7
Oct. 29	Rice, Lexington	20	16
Nov. 5	Vanderbilt, Nashville	0	34
Nov. 12	Memphis State, Lexington	41	7
Nov. 19	Tennessee, Lexington	23	0

1956—Won 6, Lost 4.
COACH: Blanton Collier
CO-CAPTS.: Dave Kuhn, Roger Pack

Date	Team—Site	Ky.	Op.
Sept. 22	Georgia Tech, Lexington	6	14
Sept. 29	Mississippi, Memphis	7	37
Oct. 6	Florida, Gainesville	17	8
Oct. 13	Auburn, Lexington	0	13
Oct. 20	La. State, Lexington	14	0
Oct. 27	Georgia, Athens	14	7
Nov. 3	Maryland, College Park	14	0
Nov. 10	Vanderbilt, Lexington	7	6
Nov. 17	Xavier, Lexington	33	0
Nov. 24	Tennessee, Knoxville	7	20

1957—Won 3, Lost 7.
COACH: Blanton Collier
CO-CAPTS: Bob Collier, Kenny Robertson

Date	Team—Site	Ky.	Op.
Sept. 21	Georgia Tech, Atlanta	0	13
Sept. 28	Mississippi, Lexington	0	15
Oct. 5	Florida, Lexington	7	14
Oct. 12	Auburn, Auburn	0	6
Oct. 19	La. State, Baton Rouge	0	21
Oct. 26	Georgia, Lexington	14	33
Nov. 2	Memphis State, Lexington	53	7
Nov. 9	Vanderbilt, Nashville	7	12
Nov. 16	Xavier, Lexington	27	0
Nov. 23	Tennessee, Lexington	20	6

1958—Won 5, Lost 4, Tied 1.
COACH: Blanton Collier
CO-CAPTS.: Bob Lindon, Doug Shively

Date	Team—Site	Ky.	Op.
Sept. 13	Hawaii, Louisville	51	0
Sept. 20	Georgia Tech, Lexington	13	0
Sept. 27	Mississippi, Memphis	6	27
Oct. 11	Auburn, Lexington	0	8
Oct. 18	La. State, Baton Rouge	7	32
Oct. 25	Georgia, Athens	0	28
Nov. 1	Mississippi State, Lexington	33	12
Nov. 8	Vanderbilt, Lexington	0	0
Nov. 15	Xavier, Lexington	20	6
Nov. 22	Tennessee, Knoxville	6	2

1959 Won 4, Lost 6.
COACH: Blanton Collier
CO-CAPTS.: Glenn Shaw, Cullen Wilson

Date	Team—Site	Ky.	Op.
Sept. 19	Georgia Tech., Lexington	12	14
Sept. 26	Mississippi, Lexington	0	16
Oct. 2	Detroit, Detroit	32	7
Oct. 10	Auburn, Auburn	0	33
Oct. 17	La. State, Lexington	0	9
Oct. 24	Georgia, Lexington	7	14
Oct. 30	Miami (Fla.), Miami	22	3
Nov. 7	Vanderbilt, Nashville	6	11
Nov. 14	Xavier, Lexington	41	0
Nov. 21	Tennessee, Lexington	20	0

1960—Won 5, Lost 4, Tied 1.
COACH: Blanton Collier
CO-CAPTS.: Jerry Eisaman, Lloyd Hodge

Date	Team—Site	Ky.	Op.
Sept. 17	Georgia Tech, Atlanta	13	23

Date	Team—Site	Ky.	Op.
Sept. 24	Mississippi, Memphis	6	21
Oct. 1	Auburn, Lexington	7	10
Oct. 8	Marshall, Lexington	55	0
Oct. 15	La. State, Lexington	3	0
Oct. 22	Georgia, Lexington	13	17
Oct. 29	Fla. State, Tallahassee	23	0
Nov. 5	Vanderbilt, Lexington	27	0
Nov. 12	Xavier, Lexington	49	0
Nov. 19	Tennessee, Knoxville	10	10

1961—Won 5, Lost 5.
COACH: Blanton Collier
HON. CAPT.: Irv Goode

Date	Team—Site	Ky.	Op.
Sept. 23	Miami (Fla.), Lexington	7	14
Sept. 30	Mississippi, Lexington	6	20
Oct. 7	Auburn, Auburn	14	12
Oct. 14	Kansas State, Lexington	21	8
Oct. 21	La. State, Baton Rouge	14	24
Oct. 28	Georgia, Athens	15	16
Nov. 4	Florida State, Lexington	20	0
Nov. 11	Vanderbilt, Nashville	16	3
Nov. 18	Xavier, Lexington	9	0
Nov. 25	Tennessee, Lexington	16	26

1962—Won 3, Lost 5, Tied 2.
COACH: Charlie Bradshaw
HON. CAPT.: Tommy Simpson

Date	Team—Site	Ky.	Op.
Sept. 22	Florida State, Lexington	0	0
Sept. 29	Mississippi, Jackson	0	14
Oct. 6	Auburn, Lexington	6	16
Oct. 12	Detroit, Detroit	27	8
Oct. 20	La. State, Lexington	0	7
Oct. 27	Georgia, Athens	7	7
Nov. 2	Miami (Fla.), Miami	17	25
Nov. 10	Vanderbilt, Lexington	7	0
Nov. 17	Xavier, Lexington	9	14
Nov. 24	Tennessee, Knoxville	12	10

1963—Won 3, Lost 6, Tied 1.
COACH: Charlie Bradshaw
HON. CAPT.: Darrell Cox

Date	Team—Site	Ky.	Op.
Sept. 21	Virginia Tech, Lexington	33	14
Sept. 28	Mississippi, Lexington	7	31
Oct. 5	Auburn, Auburn	13	14
Oct. 12	Detroit, Lexington	35	18
Oct. 19	La. State, Baton Rouge	7	28
Oct. 26	Georgia, Lexington	14	17
Nov. 2	Miami (Fla.), Lexington	14	20
Nov. 9	Vanderbilt, Nashville	0	0
Nov. 16	Baylor, Waco	19	7
Nov. 23	Tennessee, Lexington	0	19

1964—Won 5, Lost 5.
COACH: Charlie Bradshaw
HON. CAPTS.: Jim Foley and Bill Jenkins

Date	Team—Site	Ky.	Op.
Sept. 19	Detroit, Lexington	13	6
Sept. 26	Mississippi, Jackson	27	21
Oct. 3	Auburn, Lexington	20	0
Oct. 10	Florida State, Tallahassee	6	48
Oct. 17	Louisana State, Lexington	7	27
Oct. 24	Georgia, Athens	7	21
Oct. 31	West Virginia, Morgantown	21	26
Nov. 7	Vanderbilt, Lex. (HC)	22	21
Nov. 14	Baylor, Lexington	15	17
Nov. 21	Tennessee, Knoxville	12	7

1965—Won 6, Lost 4.
COACH: Charlie Bradshaw
HON. CAPTS.: Rick Norton and Sam Ball

Date	Team—Site	Ky.	Op.
Sept. 18	Missouri, Columbia	7	0
Sept. 25	Mississippi, Lexington	16	7
Oct. 2	Auburn, Auburn	18	23
Oct. 9	Florida State, Lexington	26	24
Oct. 16	L.S.U., Baton Rouge	21	31
Oct. 23	Georgia, Lexington	28	10
Oct. 30	West Virginia, Lex. (HC)	28	8
Nov. 6	Vanderbilt, Nashville	34	0
Nov. 13	Houston, Houston	21	38
Nov. 20	Tennessee, Lex. (K-Day)	3	19

1966—Won 3, Lost 6, Tied 1.
COACH: Charlie Bradshaw
HON. CAPTS.: Rich Machel and Larry Seiple

Date	Team—Site	Ky.	Op.
Sept. 17	North Carolina, Lexington	10	0
Sept. 24	Mississippi, Jackson	0	17
Oct. 1	Auburn, Lexington	17	7
Oct. 8	Virginia Tech, Lexington	0	7
Oct. 15	Louisiana State, Lexington	0	30
Oct. 22	Georgia, Athens	15	27
Oct. 29	West Virginia, Morgantown	14	14
Nov. 5	Vanderbilt, Lexington	14	10
Nov. 12	Houston, Lexington (HC)	18	56
Nov. 19	Tennessee, Knoxville	19	28

1967—Won 2, Lost 8.
COACH: Charlie Bradshaw
HON. CO-CAPTS.: Kerry Curling and Doug Van Meter

Date	Team—Site	Ky.	Op.
Sept. 23	Indiana, Bloomington	10	12
Sept. 30	Mississippi, Lexington	13	26
Oct. 7	Auburn, Auburn	7	48
Oct. 14	V. Tech, Lexington	14	24
Oct. 21	La. State, Baton Rouge	7	30
Oct. 28	Georgia, Lexington	7	31
Nov. 4	W. Virginia, Lexington (HC)	22	7
Nov. 11	Vanderbilt, Nashville	12	7
Nov. 18	Florida, Gainesville	12	28
Nov. 25	Tennessee, Lexington	7	17

1968—Won 3, Lost 7.
COACH: Charlie Bradshaw
CAPT.: Jeff Van Note

Date	Team—Site	Ky.	Op.
Sept. 21	Missouri, Lexington	12	6
Sept. 28	Mississippi, Jackson	14	30
Oct. 5	Auburn, Lexington	7	26
Oct. 12	Oregon State, Lexington	35	34
Oct. 19	Louisiana State, Baton R.	3	13
Oct. 26	Georgia, Lexington	14	35
Nov. 2	West Va., Morgantown	35	16
Nov. 9	Vanderbilt, Lexington	0	6
Nov. 16	Florida, Lexington	14	16
Nov. 23	Tennessee, Knoxville	7	24

1969—Won 2, Lost 8.
COACH: John Ray
CAPTAINS: Wilbur Hackett (Def.) and Bill Duke (Off.)

Date	Team—Site	Ky.	Op.
Sept. 20	Indiana, Lexington	30	58
Sept. 27	Mississippi, Lexington	10	9
Oct. 4	Auburn, Auburn	3	44
Oct. 11	VPI, Blacksburg	7	6
Oct. 18	Louisiana State, Lexington	10	37
Oct. 25	Georgia, Athens	0	30
Nov. 1	West Virginia, Lexington	6	7
Nov. 8	Vanderbilt, Nashville	6	42
Nov. 15	Florida, Gainesville	6	31
Nov. 22	Tennessee, Lexington	26	31

Date	Team—Site	Ky.	Op.
1970—Won 2, Lost 9.			
COACH: John Ray			
CAPTAINS: Game Captains			
Sept. 12	North Carolina, Chapel Hill	10	20
Sept. 19	Kansas State, Lexington	16	3
Sept. 26	Mississippi, Jackson	17	20
Oct. 3	Auburn, Lexington	15	33
Oct. 10	Utah State, Lexington	6	35
Oct. 17	L.S.U., Baton Rouge	7	14
Oct. 24	Georgia, Lexington	3	19
Oct. 31	N.C. State, Lexington	27	2
Nov. 7	Vanderbilt, Lexington	17	18
Nov. 14	Florida, Tampa	13	24
Nov. 21	Tennessee, Knoxville	0	45
1971—Won 3, Lost 8.			
COACH: John Ray			
CAPTAINS: Dan Neal (O),			
Joe Federspiel (D)			
Sept. 11	Clemson, Clemson	13	10
Sept. 18	Indiana, Bloomington	8	26
Sept. 25	Mississippi, Lexington	20	34
Oct. 2	Auburn, Auburn	6	38
Oct. 9	Ohio University, Lexington	6	35
Oct. 16	Louisiana State, Lexington	13	17
Oct. 23	Georgia, Athens	0	34
Oct. 30	V.P.I., Lexington	33	27
Nov. 6	Vanderbilt, Nashville	14	7
Nov. 13	Florida, Gainesville	24	35
Nov. 20	Tennessee, Lexington	7	21
1972—Won 3, Lost 8.			
COACH: John Ray			
CAPTAINS: Dan Neal (O), Earl Swindle (D)			
Sept. 16	Villanova, Lexington	25	7
Sept. 23	Alabama, Birmingham	0	35
Sept. 30	Indiana, Lexington	34	35
Oct. 7	Mississippi State, Lexington	17	13

Date	Team—Site	Ky.	Op.
Oct. 14	North Carolina, Chapel Hill	20	31
Oct. 21	LSU, Baton Rouge	0	10
Oct. 28	Georgia, Lexington	7	13
Nov. 4	Tulane, New Orleans	7	18
Nov. 11	Vanderbilt, Lexington	14	13
Nov. 18	Florida, Gainesville	0	40
Nov. 25	Tennessee, Knoxville	7	17
1973—Won 5, Lost 6.			
COACH: Fran Curci			
CAPTAINS: Ray Barga (O)			
Frank LeMaster (D)			
Sept. 15	Virginia Tech, Lexington	31	26
Sept. 22	Alabama, Lexington	14	28
Sept. 29	Indiana, Bloomington	3	17
Oct. 6	Mississippi St., Starkville	42	14
Oct. 13	North Carolina, Lexington	10	16
Oct. 20	LSU, Baton Rouge	21	28
Oct. 27	Georgia, Athens	12	7
Nov. 3	Tulane, Lexington	34	7
Nov. 10	Vanderbilt, Nashville	27	17
Nov. 17	Florida, Gainesville	18	20
Nov. 24	Tennessee, Lexington	14	16
1974—Won 6, Lost 5.			
COACH: Fran Curci			
CAPTAINS: Mike Fanuzzi (O)			
Tom Ehlers (D)			
Sept. 14	Virginia Tech, Blacksburg	28	7
Sept. 21	West Virginia, Morgantown	3	16
Sept. 28	Indiana, Lexington	28	22
Oct. 5	Miami (O), Lexington	10	14
Oct. 12	Auburn, Auburn	13	31
Oct. 19	LSU, Lexington	20	13
Oct. 26	Georgia, Lexington	20	24
Nov. 2	Tulane, New Orleans	30	7
Nov. 9	Vanderbilt, Lexington	38	12
Nov. 16	Florida, Lexington	41	24
Nov. 23	Tennessee, Knoxville	7	24

Footnote A — Although numerical scoring had not yet been introduced in Rugby football, either here or in Great Britain, when Kentucky and Transylvania (then known as Kentucky University) played their series in 1881, persons in charge of the games obviously had arrived at some sort of agreement assigning values to the various scoring plays. Records never existed and men who played in the games are now deceased. All we can do is accept the scores printed in the newspapers and surmise that a touchdown perhaps counted ¼ point and that a goal or an end-kick (a punt into the modern end zone) counted 1. That seems logical, since in the ratio scoring of that day, a touchdown was worth one-quarter of a goal. The end-kick, a British heritage, undoubtedly was introduced because all realized that green Players would score few goals, if any.

Footnote B — The football rules took no official position on the score of a forfeited game until 1908 when it was pegged at 1-0 to make it different from any other score possible in the game. By common consent, forfeited games prior to that were entered into the records as victories by 6-0 for the offended team—everywhere, that is, except in the Southern Intercollegiate Athletic Association, predecessor of the Southern Conference and the Southeastern Conference. In the S.I.A.A. the 6-0 practice was followed unless the offended team had a greater number of points. In that case, the offended team won by the greater score to nothing. Thus, Kentucky's forfeiture to Central University in 1900 is 6-0, since Kentucky led by 11-0 at the time. Kentucky led Cumberland by 12-11 in 1905 when the Tennesseans forfeited. The Blue and White, under S.I.A.A. rules, gets credit for a 12-0 victory.

WILDCAT ALL-AMERICANS

CLYDE JOHNSON
Tackle—1942

BOB GAIN
Tackle—1949-50

VITO PARILLI
QB—1950-51

DOUG MOSELEY
Center—1951

STEVE MEILINGER
E-QB-HB—1952-53

RAY CORRELL
Guard—1953

HOWARD SCHNELLENBERGER
End—1955

LOU MICHAELS
Tackle—1956-57

IRV GOODE
Center—1961

HERSCHEL TURNER
Tackle—1963

RODGER BIRD
Tailback—1965

RICK NORTON
Quarterback—1965

SAM BALL
Tackle—1965

ELMORE STEVENS
End—1974

RICK NUZUM
Center—1974

KENTUCKY FOOTBALL RECORDS
(Regular Season Only)
TEAM RECORDS

TEAM TOTAL OFFENSE—Season
Most Plays—815 (556 runs, 259 passes in 11 games, 1951)
Most Net Yards—4082 (11 games, 1950)
Highest Per Game Average—371.0 (11 games, 1950)
Most First Downs—202 (11 games, 1950)
Most Penalties Against—79 (11 games, 1949)
Most Yards Penalized—688 (11 games, 1949)
Most First Downs Penalty—13 (10 games, 1964)
Most Fumbles—56 (11 games, 1952)
Most Fumbles Lost—29 (11 games, 1952)

TEAM RUSHING—Season
Most Rushing Plays—632 (11 games, 1974)
Most Net Yards—3124 (11 games, 1974)
Highest Per Game Average—284.0 (11 games, 1974)
Best Average Per Rushing Play—4.9 (11 games, 1974)
Most First Downs Rushing—143 (11 games, 1974)

TEAM PASSING-RECEIVING—Season
Most Passes Attempted—326 (10 games, 1969)
Most Completions—157 (11 games, 1970)
Most Yards Passing—1902 (10 games, 1965)
Highest Per Game Average—190.2 (10 games, 1965)
Highest Completion Percentage—.552 (11 games, 1951)
Most Passes Had Intercepted—33* (10 games, 1967)
Most First Downs Passing—86 (10 games, 1964)
Most Touchdown Passes—27* (11 games, 1950)

TEAM PUNTING-KICKOFFS—Season
Most Punts—101 (10 games, 1933)
Most Yards On Punts—4394 (10 games, 1933)
Highest Punting Average—43.5 (10 games, 1933)
Most Punts Returned—48 (11 games, 1950)
Most Yards Punts Returned—487 (10 games, 1946, on 30 returns)
Most Kickoff Returns—51 (11 games, 1971)
Most Yards Kickoffs Returned—1182 (11 games, 1971)

TEAM SCORING—Season
Most Points—380 (11 games, 1950)
   (Conf. Games Only—157 in 6 games, 1950)
Most Points Per Game—41.0 (328 in 8 games, 1914)
Fewest Points (Modern)—91 (10 games, 1933)
   (Conf. Games Only—0 in 5 games, 1937)
Most Touchdowns—56 (11 games, 1950)
Most Touchdowns Rushing—31 (11 games, 1974)
Most Touchdowns Passing—27* (11 games, 1950)
Most Touchdowns Int. Ret.—6* (11 games, 28 interceptions, 1949)
Most Extra Points, Kicking—44 (on 56 tries in 11 games, 1950)
Most Extra Points, Passing—4 (on 10 attempts, 1965)
Most Extra Points, Running—1 (on 1 attempt, 1964) (on 1 attempt 1973)
Highest Per Game Point Average—34.5 (380 points, 11 games, 1950)
Most Games Held Scoreless—6 (In 1917)
Most Field Goals—11 (11 games, 1974)

TEAM DEFENSE—Season
Total Defense (Per Game Average)—153.8 (11 games, 1949)
Rushing Defense (Per Game Average)—71.6 (11 games, 1949)
Pass Defense (Per Game Average)—47.9 (10 games, 1955)
Fewest Points Allowed—None (Seven games, 1898)
   (Ten game season, modern—52 in 1947)
   (Conf. Games Only—6 in 5 games, 1949)
Most Points Allowed—295 (10 games, 1969)
   (Conf. Games Only—224 in 7 games, 1969)
Most Passes Intercepted—28 (11 games, 1949; 1950)
Most Yards Return Int. Passes—700† (11 games, 1949, on 28 int.)

Most Passes Intercepted For Touchdowns—6* (11 games, 1949)
Most Opponent Fumbles Recovered—24 (11 games, 1951)

TEAM TOTAL OFFENSE—Single Game
Most Plays—90 (63 rushing, 27 passing vs. Tenn. Tech, 1951)
Most Net Yards—646 (Against Tenn. Tech. 1951)
Most First Downs—31 (Against Tenn. Tech, 1951)
Most First Downs Penalty—4 (Against Villanova, 1951; Houston, 1965)
Most Penalties Against—18 (Against Ga. Tech, 1951)
Most Penalties Against Both Teams—25 (Kentucky 10, Mississippi 15—1954)
Most Yards Penalized—148 (Against Miami, 1959)
Most Yards Penalized, Both Teams—305* (Kentucky 123, Mississippi 182—1954)
Most Fumbles—11 (Against Miss. State, 1952)
Most Fumbles, Both Teams—16 (UK 9, Tennessee 7—1950)
Most Fumbles Lost—6 (Against Miss. State, 1952)

TEAM RUSHING—Single Game
Most Rushing Plays—70 (Against Miami, Fla., 1949; Tennessee, 1953)
Most Net Yards Gained—446 (Against Tenn. Tech, 1951)
Fewest Yards Rushing—Minus 9 (Against Virginia Tech, 1966)
Highest Rushing Average—9.1 (34 plays, 303 yards vs. North Dakota, 1950)
Most First Downs Rushing—23 (Against Miami, Fla., 1949)

TEAM PASSING-RECEIVING—Single Game
Most Passes Attempted—46 (Against Tennessee, 1969)
Most Completions—28 (Against Tennessee, 1969)
Most Yards Passing—440 (Against Tennessee, 1969)
Most Passes Had Intercepted—6 (By LSU, 1965), (By W. Va., 1969), (By Florida, 1972)
Most First Downs Passing—20 (Against Tennessee, 1969)
Most Touchdown Passes—8† (Against North Dakota, 1950)

TEAM PUNTING-KICKOFFS—Single Game
Most Punts—36 vs. Washington & Lee (1934)
Most Yards On Punts—1,386 (approx.) vs. Washington & Lee (1934)
Highest Punting Average—52.0 (Against Florida, 1957, on 6 punts)
Most Punts Returned—8 (Against W. Va., 1946; Texas, 1951)
Most Yards Punts Returned—142 (Against West Virginia, 1946)
Most Kickoff Returns—8 (Against Florida State, 1964)
Most Yards Kickoffs Returned—186 (Against Florida State, 1964)

TEAM SCORING—Single Game
Most Points—87 (Against Wilmington, 1914) 81 (Against Centre 1904—TD Counted 5 pts then)
Most Touchdowns—14 (Against Centre, 1904), 12 (Against North Dakota, 1950)
Most Touchdowns, Rushing—9 (Against Tenn. Tech, 1951)
Most Touchdowns, Passing—8† (Against North Dakota, 1950)
Most PAT Attempted (Placement)—12 (Against North Dakota, 1950)
Most PAT Scored (Placement)—11 (Against Centre 11-11, 1904), 11* (Against North Dakota, 1950)
Most PAT Scored, Running—1 (in several games)
Most Field Goals Made—3 (Against Auburn, 1970, Vanderbilt, 1974)
Last Time Held Scoreless—Nov. 21, 1970 (UK 0 Tennessee 45)

TEAM DEFENSE—Single Game
Fewest Net Yards Allowed (Rush-Pass Combined)—1 (vs. The Citadel, 1949)
Fewest Net Passing Yards Allowed—Minus 1 (Against LSU, 1953)
Fewest Net Rushing Yards Allowed—Minus 39 (Against Evansville, 1947)
    (SEC Only—Minus 11 vs. Auburn, 1961)
Most Passes Intercepted—6 (Against Tennessee, 1935; Xavier, 1948; Mississippi, 1949)
Most Yards Return Int. Passes—240† (Against Mississippi, 1949)
Most TDs on Int. Returns—3† (Against Mississippi Oct. 1, 1949; Tulane, 1974)
Last Time Held Opp. Scoreless—Sept. 17, 1966 (N. Carolina 0, UK 10)
Most Plays By Opponent—115 (Tennessee, 1933)
Fewest First Downs Allowed—1 (vs. Xavier, 1946)
Most First Downs Allowed—38 by LSU, Oct. 21, 1967
Longest TD Pass Against UK—83 (B. Stanton-W. Morgan, Miss. State, 1955)

†Also National and Southeastern Conference Record.
*Also Southeastern Conference Record.

Longest TD Run Against UK—95 (Harry Gilmer, Alabama, 1945)
Longest Punt Return Against UK—93 TD (Joel Searles, Kansas State, 1961)
Longest Kickoff Return Against UK—100 (Bill Moreman-T. K. Wetherell (lateral) Florida State, 1965); (100, Willie Shelby, Alabama 1973) 96 (Spec Kelly, LSU, 1955, and Harvin Clark Fla., 1969)
Most Punts By Opponent—34 By Washington & Lee (1934)
Most Yards On Punts By Opponent—1,360 By Washington & Lee (1934)
Longest Interception Return Against UK—100 TD (White Graves, LSU, 1964)
Longest Punt Against UK—83 (Dixie Howell, Alabama, 1933)
Longest Field Goal Against UK—55 (Jack Simcsak, VPI, 1969)
Longest Return Of Fumble Against UK—99 TD, Bauer, Georgetown, 1922
Most Field Goals Against UK—4 (Keith Braswell, Georgia, 1970, John Riley, Auburn, 1968, Chris Gartner, Indiana, 1971)*

TEAM MISCELLANEOUS RECORDS
Best Season Record—7-0 in 1898 (Modern: 11-1 in 1950)
Worst Season Record—2-9 in 1970
Most Ties—2 (Eight different seasons. Last: 1962)
Most Consec. Games Scored TD—19 (Nov. 14, 1908-Nov. 12, 1910)
Most Consecutive Shutouts—7 in 1898
Most Shutouts One Season—9 in 1907 (Modern Record 5 in 1934, 1950, 1960)
Most Consecutive Games 3 or More TD's—8 in 1950
Highest Home Attendance, Season—328,515 (6 games 1974)
Highest Per Game Average Home Attendance—54,752 (1974)
Highest Home Attendance, Single Game—56,535 (LSU, 1974)
Longest Win Streak—12 (Oct. 28, 1909-Nov. 12, 1910; Nov. 25, 1949-Nov. 25, 1950)
Longest Losing Streak—7 (Oct. 8, 1938-Sept. 30, 1939; Nov. 24, 1956-Nov. 2, 1957)
Consecutive Home Wins—14 (Nov. 14, 1908-Nov. 24, 1910)
Consecutive Road Wins—6 (excluding bowl) Oct. 29, 1949-Nov. 11, 1950)
Consecutive Conference Wins—5 (In 1950)
Consecutive Conference Losses—13 (Sept. 27, 1969-Nov. 25, 1970)
Consecutive Wins Non-Conference—17 (Oct. 30, 1954 to Sept. 23, 1961)
Widest Winning Margin—87 (87-0 Against Wilmington, 1914)
Worst Defeat—82 (By St. Louis, 82-0, in 1905)
First Night Game at Lexington—Maryville, Oct. 5, 1929

INDIVIDUAL RECORDS

INDIVIDUAL TOTAL OFFENSE—Season
Most Plays—308 By Bernie Scruggs, 1970 (99 runs, 209 passes)
Most Total Yards—1706 By Rick Norton, 1965 (10 games)
Highest Average Gain Per Play—10.8 By Babe Parilli, 1951 (11 games)
Most Time Played (1955-1963)—555:55 By Lou Michaels, 1956 (10 games)
Most Tackles—157 By Mike McGraw, 1965 (10 games)

INDIVIDUAL RUSHING—Season
Most Times Carried—224 By Sonny Collins, 1973 (11 games)
Most Net Yards—1213 By Sonny Collins, 1973 (11 games)
Best Average Per Carry (over 200)—Sonny Collins, 5.5 (1974)

INDIVIDUAL PASSING-RECEIVING—Season
Most Attempts—239 By Babe Parilli, 1951 (11 games)
Most Completions—136 By Babe Parilli, 1951 (11 games)
Most Yards Passing—1823 By Rick Norton, 1965 (19 games)
Best Completion Percentage—.569 By Babe Parilli, 1951 (136 of 299 in 11 games)
Most Had Intercepted—21 By Dave Bair, 1967 (10 games)
Consecutive Passes Without Interception—68* By Rick Norton, 1963
Most Catches—42 By Rick Kestner, 1964 (10 games)
Most Touchdown Passes—23 By Babe Parilli, 1950 (11 games)
Most TD's By Receiver—10* By Al Bruno, 1950 (11 games)
Most Passes Intercepted—9 By Jerry Claiborne, 1949 (11 games)
Most Yards Return Interceptions—197 By David Hunter, 1968 (10 games)

INDIVIDUAL PUNTING-KICKOFFS—Season
Most Punts—101† By Ralph Kercheval, 1933 (10 games)
Most Yards On Punts—4394† By Ralph Kercheval, 1933 (101 punts in 10 games)
Best Punting Average (Minimum 100)—43.5* By Ralph Kercheval, 1933 (10 games)

†Also National and Southeastern Conference Record.
*Also Southeastern Conference Record.

Most Punts Returned—25 By Dicky Lyons, 1966 (For 419 Yards in 10 games)
Most Yards Punts Returned—419 By Dicky Lyons in 1966 (25 Returns in 10 games)
Most Kickoff Returns—25 By Dave Hunter (11 games, 1970)
Most Yards Kickoffs Returned—589 By Doug Kotar (11 games, 1971)
Best Average On Kickoff Returns—45.0 by Don Phelps (6 for 270 in 6 games, 1946)

INDIVIDUAL SCORING—Season

Most Points—80 By Sonny Collins, 1973 (13 TD's one x-pt)
Most Touchdowns—13 By Rodger Bird, 1965 (12 rushing, 1 catch in 10 games), 13 by Sonny Collins 1973 (13 rushing in 10 games).
Most Touchdown Passes—23 By Babe Parilli, 1950 (11 games)
Most TD's By Receiver—10 By Al Bruno, 1950 (11 games)
Most PAT Attempts (Placement)—41 By Bob Gain, 1950 (11 games)
Most PAT's Made (Placement)—37 By Bob Gain (41 tries, 11 games, 1950)
Most Consecutive PAT's (Placement)—18 by Bobby Jones (10 games, 1968)
PAT Kick Percentage—100% By Delmar Hughes (13 of 13 in 10 games, 1955)
Most TD's Accounted For—28* By Babe Parilli, 1950 (5 rush, 23 pass in 11 games)

INDIVIDUAL TOTAL OFFENSE—Single Game

Most Plays—54 By Bernie Scruggs vs. Florida, 1970
Most Net Yards—363 By Rick Norton vs. Houston, 1965 (373 pass, minus 10 rush)

INDIVIDUAL RUSHING—Single Game

Most Carries—30 By Larry Seiple vs. Auburn, 1966
Most Net Yards—280 by "Shipwreck" Kelly vs. Maryville (1930)
Best Average (5 minimum)—18.7 By Shipwreck Kelly vs. Maryville (1930)
Longest Run From Scrimmage—91 TD By Harry Jones vs. George Washington, 1951
Longest Non-Scoring Run From Scrimmage—88 By Bernie Scruggs vs. Georgia, 1970

INDIVIDUAL PASSING-RECEIVING—Single Game

Most Attempts—41 By Steve Tingle vs. Florida, 1969
Most Completions—25 By Bernie Scruggs vs. Louisiana State, 1970
Most Net Yards—363 By Rick Norton vs. Houston, 1965
Most Consecutive Completions—11 By Bernie Scruggs vs. Tennessee, 1969
Best Completion Average—.750 By Babe Parilli vs. North Dakota, 1950; Bob Hardy vs. Villanova, 1955
Most Touchdown Passes—5 By Jim Park vs. Earlham, 1914; 5* By Babe Parilli vs. Cincinnati, North Dakota, 1950
Most Had Intercepted—6 By Rick Norton vs. Louisiana State, 1965; and Bernie Scruggs vs. West Virginia, 1969
Most Intercepted—3 By Clayton Webb vs. Xavier, 1948; Bradley Mills vs. Tennessee, 1952; Terry Beadles vs. Missouri, 1965
Longest Interception Return—100 TD by Bob Davis vs. Wash. & Lee, 1937; 100 TD by Dave Hunter vs. West Virginia, 1968
Most Passes Caught—10 By Calvin Bird vs. Mississippi, 1958; 10 By Steve Parrish vs. Vanderbilt, 1969
Most Yards By Receiver—185 By Rick Kestner vs. Mississippi, 1964
Most TD's By Receiver—4 By Al Bruno vs. North Dakota, 1950; Floyd Wright vs. Earlham, 1914
Longest Non-Scoring Pass Play—78 Terry Beadles to Larry Seiple vs. Tenn., '66

INDIVIDUAL PUNTING-KICKOFFS—Single Game

Most Punts—30 (approx.) By Bert Johnson vs. Washington & Lee (1934); 17 By Ralph Kercheval vs. Alabama, 1931
Most Yards On Punts—1155 (est.) By Bert Johnson vs. Washington & Lee (1934); 680 By Ralph Kercheval vs. Alabama, 1931
Best Punting Average (10 minimum)—52.0* By Ralph Kercheval vs. Cincinnati, 1933 (10 punts)
Most Punts Returned—6 by Dicky Lyons vs. Georgia, 1968
Most Yards Punts Returned—156 by Phil Cutchin vs. Georgia, 1946 (4 returns)

+Also National and Southeastern Conference Record.
*Also Southeastern Conference Record.

Most Kickoffs Returned—5 by Harry Jones vs. Tennessee, 1951; Dicky Lyons vs. Georgia, 1968
Most Yards Kickoffs Returned—160* By Dicky Lyons vs. LSU, Oct. 21, 1967
Longest Punt—78 By Ralph Kercheval vs. Ga. Tech, 1933
Longest Punt Return—97 TD Dicky Lyons vs. Houston, 1966
Longest Kickoff Returns—98 By Doug Kotar vs. Clemson, 1971; 95 by Noah Mullins vs. Wash. & Lee, 1940; Dicky Lyons vs. LSU, Oct. 21, 1967, Roger Gann vs. Indiana, Sept. 20, 1969; 92 by Don Phelps vs. Mississippi (1946)
Most Yards Kickoffs Returned—166 By Roger Gann vs. Indiana, 1969
Longest Punt Against UK—83 By Dixie Howell, Alabama, 1933
Longest Punt Return Against UK—88 By Lee Nalley, Vanderbilt, 1948
Longest KO Return Against UK—100 By Willie Shelby, Alabama, 1975, 96 By Joe May, LSU, 1965, and Harvin Clark, Florida, 1969.

INDIVIDUAL SCORING—Single Game
Most Points—43 (6 TD, 7 PAT) By William Tuttle vs. Maryville, 1914
Most Touchdowns—6 By William Tuttle vs. Maryville, 1914
Most Touchdowns Running—5 By Jim Park vs. Earlham, 1914
Most TD Passes Caught—4* By Al Bruno vs. North Dakota, 1950; Floyd Wright vs. Earlham, 1914
Most Field Goals—3 By Dick Barbee vs. Central, 1909, Bob Jones vs. Auburn, 1970, John Pierce vs. Vanderbilt, 1974
Longest Field Goal—52 By John Pierce vs. Florida, 1974
Most PAT's Att. (Placement)—10 By Bob Gain vs. North Dakota, 1950
Most PAT's Made (Placement)—10* (consecutive) By Bob Gain vs. N. Dakota, 1950
Most TD's Passing—5 By Jim Park vs. Earlham, 1914; Babe Parilli vs. Cincinnati and North Dakota, 1950
Longest TD Run—91 By Harry Jones vs. George Washington, 1951
Longest Touchdown Pass Play—92 by David Bair to Dicky Lyons vs. Georgia, 1968

INDIVIDUAL CAREER HIGHS (Bowl Games Included)
Total Offense (Yards)—4446 By Babe Parilli, 1949-51 (36 games)
Total Offense (Plays)—823 By Bernie Scruggs, 1969-71 (30 games)
Rushing Attempts—529 By Sonny Collins, 1972-74 (30 games)
Rushing Yards—2,685 By Sonny Collins (1972-74)
Rushing Average (200 minimum)—5.3 By Bill Leskovar, 1949-51
Pass Attempts—634 By Babe Parilli, 1949-51 (36 games)
Pass Completions—354 By Babe Parilli, 1949-51 (36 games)
Passing Yards—4669 By Babe Parilli, 1949-51 (36 games)
Regular Season: 4514 By Rick Norton, 1963-65 (30 games)
Passing Percentage—55.8 By Babe Parilli, 1949-51 (36 games)
Passes Had Intercepted—44 By Rick Norton, 1963-65 (30 games)
Passes Caught—94 By Tom Hutchinson, 1960-62
Yards By Receiver—1422 By Larry Seiple, 1964-66 (30 games)
Points Made—180 By Bob Davis, 1935-37
Touchdowns Scored—30 By Bob Davis, 1935-37
Touchdown Passes—50* By Babe Parilli, 1949-51 (Regular Season) (Bowl Games Included—59)
Extra Point Attempts (Placement)—53 By Bob Gain, 1948-50
Extra Points Scored (Placement)—42 By Bob Gain, 1948-50
Consecutive Extra Points Scored (Placement)—18 by Bobby Jones (10 games, 1968)
PAT Percentage (Placement)—.950 (38 of 40) By Delmar Hughes, 1954-56
Most Points By Kicker—80 By Bob Jones (1968-69-70)
Touchdown Passes Caught—17 By Steve Meilinger, 1951-53
Punts—248 By Dave Hardt, 1968-69-70
Punting Yardage—9737 By Dave Hardt, 1968-69-70 (268 punts)
Punting Average—39.8 By Lou Michaels, 1955-57 (122 punts)
Punt Returns—69 by Dicky Lyons, 1966-68
Yards Punts Returned—1065 by Dicky Lyons, 1966-68
Kickoff Returns—56 by Dicky Lyons, 1966-68
Yards Kickoffs Returned—1188 by Dicky Lyons, 1966-68 (28 games)
Average Gain Per KO Return—21.2* by Dicky Lyons (1966-67-68)
Total Kick Return Yardage—2253† by Dicky Lyons, 1966-68 (28 games)
Most Time Played (Since 1955)—1455:47 By Lou Michaels, 1955-57 (30 games)

†Also National and Southeastern Conference Record
*Also Southeastern Conference Record.

WILDCATS' RECORD AGAINST ALL OPPONENTS

Opponent	First Meeting	Last Meeting	Won	Lost	Tied
Alabama	1917	1973	1	26	1
All-Kentucky	1900	1900	0	1	0
Alumni	1899	1899	1	0	0
Auburn	1934	1974	5	15	1
Avondale A. C.	1900	1901	0	2	0
Baldwin-Wallace	1940	1940	1	0	0
Baylor	1963	1964	1	1	0
Berea College	1903	1909	5	0	0
Bethany	1904	1904	1	0	0
Boston College	1937	1937	0	1	0
Butler College	1913	1917	4	0	0
Carson-Newman	1928	1929	2	0	0
Catlettsburg A.C.	1896	1905	1	1	0
Central U.	1892	1911	3	10	1
Centre	1891	1929	12	18	1
Chicago	1925	1925	0	1	0
Cincinnati	1894	1952	17	7	2
Cincinnati YMCA	1893	1893	2	0	0
Citadel, The	1949	1949	1	0	0
Clemson	1925	1971	6	1	0
Co. H. of 8th Mass.	1898	1898	1	0	0
Cumberland U.	1905	1905	1	0	0
Cynthiana	1903	1905	2	0	0
Dayton	1950	1950	1	0	0
DePauw	1895	1895	0	1	0
Detroit	1959	1964	4	0	0
Duke	1930	1933	0	4	0
Earlham	1913	1915	3	0	0
Eminence A. C.	1906	1906	1	0	0
Evansville	1947	1947	1	0	0
Florida	1917	1974	13	12	0
Florida State	1960	1965	3	1	1
Frankfort A. C.	1895	1895	1	0	0
Georgetown	1891	1924	22	1	0
George Washington	1940	1951	3	0	0
Georgia	1939	1974	6	20	2
Georgia Tech	1923	1960	7	11	1
Hanover	1907	1912	2	0	0
Hawaii	1958	1958	1	0	0
Houston	1965	1966	0	2	0
Illinois	1909	1913	1	1	0
Indiana	1893	1974	3	9	1
160th Indiana	1898	1898	1	0	0
Jeffersonville A. C.	1894	1894	1	0	0
Kansas State	1961	1970	2	0	0
Kentucky Wesleyan	1897	1927	5	1	0
K. M. I.	1903	1906	4	0	0
Lexington A. C.	1895	1896	0	1	0
Lexington H. S.	1911	1911	1	0	0
Louisiana State	1949	1974	6	18	1
Louisville	1912	1924	6	0	0
Louisville A. C.	1892	1898	3	1	0

Louisville YMCA	1900	1902	2	2	0
Manhattan	1936	1937	1	1	0
Manual H. S.	1907	1907	1	0	0
Marietta	1903	1906	1	1	0
Marquette	1945	1948	2	1	0
Marshall College	1905	1960	6	0	0
Maryland	1931	1956	1	1	1
Maryville	1907	1938	19	0	1
Memphis State	1953	1957	4	0	0
Miami (Fla.)	1948	1963	5	3	0
Miami (Ohio)	1894	1974	5	3	1
Michigan	1908	1908	0	1	0
Michigan State	1944	1947	2	2	0
Mississippi	1944	1971	8	19	1
Mississippi Southern	1949	1949	1	0	0
*Mississippi State	1914	1972	8	5	0
Missouri	1965	1968	2	0	0
Mooney School	1902	1902	0	1	0
Morris-Harvey	1907	1911	2	0	0
Nashville U.	1902	1902	0	1	0
Newcastle A.C.	1898	1898	1	0	0
North Carolina	1910	1972	2	4	0
North Carolina State	1909	1970	1	1	0
North Dakota	1950	1950	1	0	0
N. Texas State	1950	1950	1	0	0
Northwestern	1928	1928	0	1	0
Oglethorpe	1938	1939	2	0	0
Ohio Northern	1913	1913	1	0	0
Ohio State	1895	1935	0	3	0
Ohio University	1910	1971	1	1	0
Oklahoma	1951	1951	1	0	0
Oregon State	1968	1968	1	0	0
Paris A. C.	1904	1904	1	0	0
Purdue	1895	1915	1	2	0
Q. & C. RR	1902	1902	1	0	0
Rice	1953	1955	2	0	0
Rose Poly	1908	1909	2	0	0
St. Mary's College	1909	1909	1	0	0
St. Louis U.	1905	1910	0	2	0
Santa Clara	1950	1950	0	1	0
Sewanee	1908	1933	7	3	3
Southwestern Presbyterian	1920	1920	1	0	0
South Carolina	1937	1937	1	0	0
Southern Methodist	1949	1949	0	1	0
Southwestern	1934	1941	3	0	0
Tennessee	1893	1974	19	42	9
Tennessee Tech	1951	1951	1	0	0
Texas	1951	1951	0	1	0
Texas A & M	1952	1953	1	1	0
Texas Christian	1952	1952	1	0	0
**Transylvania	1881	1911	15	5	1
Tulane	1910	1974	5	5	0
Utah State	1970	1970	0	1	0
Vanderbilt	1896	1974	17	26	4
Villanova	1947	1972	7	1	1
Virginia	1930	1930	1	0	0
V. M. I.	1892	1944	12	4	0

Virginia Tech	1926	1974	7	3	2
Washington & Lee	1899	1942	11	7	2
West Virginia	1905	1974	9	6	1
West Virginia Wesleyan	1924	1924	0	1	0
Wilmington	1913	1914	2	0	0
Winchester A. C.	1907	1907	1	0	0
Xavier (Ohio)	1903	1962	18	2	0
YMI of Cincinnati	1912	1912	1	0	0
TOTAL 759 GAMES (118 Opponents)			396	333	39

*Record includes four games (2-2) with Mississippi A & M, which later became known as Mississippi State.

**Record includes 19 games (13-5-1) with Kentucky University, which became known as Transylvania in 1909, and two games (1-1) with Transylvania.

WILDCAT GRID LETTERMEN

— A —

Bob Abbott (67)
Kevin Acheson (74)
George Adair (05, 06, 07)
Tommy Adkins (51, 52, 53)
Paul Alaman (73 Mgr)
Burton Aldridge (30, 32, 33)
Smith Alford (93, 94, 95, 96)
Ermal Allen (39, 40, 41)
Rich Allen (71, 72, 73)
H. C. Anderson (93)
Carl Althaus (41, 42)
Jack Alvarez (71, 72, 73)
Tom Anderson (67)
Ken Andrews (29, 30, 31)
John Andrighetti (63, 64, 65)
Frank Antonini, (64, 65)
Leo Arenstein (44)
Chuck Arnold (66)
Bill Arnsparger (44)
A. J. Asher (97)
G. M. Asher (95)
Letcher Asher (32)
Bob Atkins (09)
Presley Atkins (02, 04, 05)
Clarence Ayers (33, 34, 35)

— B —

Harvey Babb (09, 10, 11)
Jim Babb (46, 47)
August A. Bablitz (10, 11)
Stanley Bach (32, 33)
Stanley Baer (05, 06)
J. Yost (Bill) Bailey (13, 14)
Joe Bailey (38, 39, 40)
John Bailey (52)
Dave Bair (67, 68)
M. Baird (05)
Charles N. Baird (92)
Ray Barga (71, 72, 73)
John Baldwin (50, 51, 52)
Sam Ball (63, 64, 65)
Dick Barbee (07, 08, 09)
Jim Barnett (45)
Tom Bartlett (18)
Bill Bartos (73, 74)
Bob Bassitt (52)
A. L. Bastin (18)
Frank Baugh (21)
Walter Baugh (17, 18)
Bob Baughman (29, 30)
T. Gardner Bayless (24)
Terry Beadles (65, 66, 67)
Dick Beal (44)
T. W. Beard (04)
Dick Beard (68, 69)
Jerry Beatty (54)
Tom Becherer (63, 64, 65)
Norman Beck (42)
Bob Beeler (40, 41)
Mike Beirne (67)
Sylvan Belt (26, 27)
Bob Bennett (54, 55, 56)
Leeman Bennett (58, 59, 60)
Pascal Benson (57, 58, 59)
Charles Bentley (46, 47, 48, 49)
Bob Bezuk (49)
Arthur Bickel (27)
George Bickel (30)
Billy Bird (61)
Calvin Bird (58, 59, 60)
Rodger Bird (63, 64, 65)
Darryl Bishop (71, 72, 73)
Fred Bishop (73, 74)
Arvon Bivin (53)
Billy Black (40)
Harold Black (36, 37, 38)
Marvin Black (05)
Charles Blackburn (67, 68)
Leroy Bland (18)
George Blanda (45, 46, 47, 48)
Jerry Blanton (74)
Ralph Blevins (32)
Dick Blocker (57, 58)
Ken Bocard (61, 62, 63)
Bill Boller (46, 47, 48, 49)
George Boone (57, 58, 59)
Joe Bosse (35, 36, 37)
Bill Boston (37, 39)
M. T. Boswell (93)
Mike Boulware (67, 68, 69)
Cecil Bowens (70, 71)
Jim Bowie (58)
Willet L. Bowling (01)
Berl Boyd (21)
Jim Boyd (10 Mgr.)
Charlie Bradshaw (46, 47, 48, 49)
Joe Brandel (61)
"Brandy" Brandstetner (11)
Ben Bransom, Jr. (73, 74)
Don Branson (05)
Bruce Brewer (04, 05, 06)
Ted Brewer (22)
John Brittain (15, 16, 17)
Donnie Britton (66, 67)
Lafayette Brock (96 Mgr.)
George Brockman (07)
William Bronaugh (98 Mgr.)
Jake Bronston (29, 30)
Bobby Brooks (48, 49)
Bob Brown (62, 63, 64)
Dave Brown (39, 40, 41)
Harry Brown (37, 38)
Herbert W. Brown, Jr. (28)
Jack Brown (71)
Locky Brown (55)
Paul Brown (13)
Charles Browning (46, 47)
Joe Brueck (59)
Al Bruno (48, 49, 50)
Tommy Brush (61)
John Bryan (92, 93, 94)
Charles (Perky) Bryant (61, 62, 63)
Gene Bryant (34)
Thomson Bryant (07 Mgr.)
Warren Bryant (73, 74)
Don Buchanan (57)
Randy Burke (74)
Buzz Burnam (70, 71, 72)
Bill Bushong (70, 71)
Bob Butler (59, 60, 61)
Jack Butler (54, 55, 56)

— C —

Ronnie Cain (57, 58, 59)
Ray Callahan (53, 54, 55)
Jim Cambron (57, 58)
A. B. (Red) Cammack (22 Mgr.)
Jim (J. W.) Cammack (21, 22, 23, 25)
Steve Campassi (72, 73, 74)
J. Campbell (09, 10)
James Campbell (97)
Kenton Campbell (44, 45)
Mark Campbell (71)
Tom Campbell (95, 96)
Walter Campbell (00, 02)
Steve Carboni (73)
Denny Cardwell (63)
J. W. Cardwell (08)
George B. Carey (92, 93, 94)
Clyde Carlig (52, 55)
James W. Carnahan (92, 94, 95)
Wilce Carnes (38, 39)
W. T. Carpenter (97 Mgr.)
Ray Carr (73, 74)
William S. Carrithers (12)
Arvel Carroll, Jr. (70, 71, 72)
Mike Carroll (66, 67 Mgr.)
Don Carson (61)
Ron Cason (74)
Bill Cartwright (66, 67, 68)
Jack Casner (42)
Tom Cassady (32, 33)
Michael E. Cassity (66)
Michael L. Cassity (73, 74)
James (Bud) Cavana (29, 30, 31)
Bill Chambers (44, 45, 46)
J. S. Chambers (09, 10, 11, 12)
Mel Chandler (56, 60, 61)

381

Tom Chapala (65)
Dave Chapman (61)
Dick Charles (57)
O. B. Chisholm (06)
George Claiborne (51)
Jerry Claiborne
 (46, 48, 49)
C. C. Clarke
 (97, 98, 99, 00)
Emery Clark (49, 50, 51)
Terry Clark (64, 65)
W. F. Clark (07, 08)
Tom Clark (70, 71, 72)
Jim Clay (08)
R. S. Clayton (15)
Earle Clements (16)
Lee Clymer (71)
Gary Cochran
 (59, 60, 61)
Sam Coleman (05, 06)
Tommy Coleman (36)
Max Colker (28, 29, 30)
Sonny Collins (72, 73, 74)
Bob Collier (55, 56, 57)
Bill Collins (11)
William (Coley) Colpitts
 (19, 20, 21, 22)
Dick Colvin (41, 42)
W. Combs (02)
Carl (Hoot) Combs
 (38, 39, 40)
John Combs (19)
Bill Conde (49, 50, 51)
Fred Conger (67, 69)
C. R. Conn (26 Mgr.)
H. Cook (06)
Joe Coons (03, 04)
Franklin Corn (14, 15)
John Cornelius
 (55, 56, 57)
Ray Correll (51, 52, 53)
Will Ed Covington
 (27, 28, 29)
Mike Coyle (61 Mgr.)
Darrell Cox (61, 62, 63)
Bill Craig (99, 00)
A. B. Crain (06, 07)
Bobby Cravens
 (56, 57, 58)
J. T. Cravens (01, 02, 03)
Ted Creech (24, 26)
Walter B. Croan
 (14 Mgr.)
Tom Crowe (69, 70, 71)
Maury Crutcher
 (13, 14, 15, 16)
William Culp (19)
Kerry Curling (65, 66, 67)
Duke Curnutte
 (52, 53, 54, 56)
Ivan Curnutte (56, 57)
Larry Curry (27)
Phil Cutchin (41, 42, 46)
Tom Cutler (02)

— D —

Al Dabney (00)
Don Danko (64, 65)
Darrell Darby (30, 31, 32)
Jim Darnaby (32, 34)
F. H. Darnall (04)
O. L. (Bud) Davidson
 (31, 32, 33)
Bob Davis (35, 36, 37)

Dameron Davis
 (36, 37, 38)
Doug Davis (63, 64, 65)
Jerry Davis (65, 66)
Bill Dawson (46, 48, 50)
Sam DeBow (94, 95, 96)
Claire Dees (26, 27, 28)
Denver DeHaven
 (24, 25, 26)
C. F. Dempsey
 (15, 16, 17)
Harry Denham (40)
Frank Derrick (24)
James DeSpain
 (72 Mgr.)
Jerry Dickerson (59, 60, 61)
Joe Dipre (73, 74)
Tony Dishman (18, 19)
Wayne Dixon (60, 61)
Mike Doggendorf
 (70, 71, 72)
Tom Domhoff (71)
Gene Donaldson (50, 51)
A. L. Donan (06 Mgr.)
Pat Donley (73, 74)
Bob Dougherty (55, 56)
Tom Dornbrook (74)
Clay Downing (17)
George Downing (17)
Gibson Downing
 (11, 12, 13, 14)
Dennis Drinnen (67, 68)
Bill (Pete) Drury
 (27, 28, 29)
John Drury (32)
Noah Duff (31, 32)
Tom Duffy (69)
Billy Duke (67, 68, 69)
Dick Duncan (18 Mgr.)
Walter Duncan
 (95, 96)
G. G. Dunlap
 (06, 07, 09, 10)
Howard Dunnebacke
 (61, 62)
Raul Durbin (38 Mgr.)
Ron Durbin (71 Asst. Tr.)
Don Dyer (52)
O. K. Dyer (01, 02, 03)
Bill Dysard (30)

— E —

Tom Earle
 (08, 09, 10, 11)
Charles Eblen (42)
Pat Eckenrod (68, 69, 70)
Adolph Edwards (25, 26)
George Edwards (42)
Tom Ehlers (72, 73, 74)
John Eibner (38, 39, 40)
Jerry Eisaman
 (58, 59, 60)
Jeff Elgin (06, 07)
Russell (Duke) Ellington (35, 36, 37)
Cronley Elliott (00)
Milward Elliott
 (96, 97, 98)
Byrne Ellis (09)
Ray Ellis (25, 26, 27)
Robert Ellison (37 Mgr.)
Mike Emanuel (73, 74)
Nick Englisis (44, 45)
George Ewell (00, 01)

Tom Ewing (42)

— F —

B. O. Falconer (19)
Mike Fanuzzi (71, 73, 74)
Bill Farley (50, 51)
Tom Farmer (72, 73, 74)
Bob Farrell (61)
Jack Farris (46, 47)
John Farris (34)
B. O. Faulconer (19)
J. V. Faulkner (92, 93)
Dan Featherston (70)
Loyd Featherson
 (33 Mgr.)
Joe Federspiel (69, 70, 71)
Tom Fee (64, 66, 67)
Allen Felch (51, 52)
Tom Ferguson (67)
Walter Ferguson (21, 22)
Doc Ferrell
 (44, 46, 47, 48)
Fred Ferris, (44)
Fred Fest (20, 21, 22)
Tom Fillion (51, 52, 53)
Al Fish (69, 70)
Bill Fish (33)
Jim Fisher (59, 60)
W. (Slugs) Fleahman
 (21)
Jim Foley (62, 63, 64)
Roy Ford (48)
Warner Ford (27, 28, 29)
L. G. (Floppy) Forquer
 (28, 29, 30)
Stan Forston (68, 69, 70)
John Foster (10)
Mike Foster (74)
Dan Fowler (74)
Don Frampton (48, 49)
J. T. Frankenberger
 (54, 55, 56)
Jim Franklin (73)
Mark Franklin (26)
Joe Frazer (95)
Jack Freeman (56)
Bob Freibert (66, 68)
Eddie Fritz (39, 40)
Rick Fromm (72, 74)
Bob Fry (50, 51, 52)
John Frye (32, 33)
Dom Fucci (48, 49, 50)
Bruce Fuller
 (19, 20, 21, 22)
Frank Fuller (50, 51, 52)
Ken Fuller (72)

— G —

Winston Gaffron
 (71 Mgr.)
Bob Gain (47, 48, 49, 50)
Jake Gaiser (09, 10, 11)
Jack Gallagher (57)
Howard Galloway (06)
 (11 Mgr.)
Roger Gann (67, 68, 69)
Eugene Ganucheau (72, 73)
John Gardner (93, 94)
Larry Garland (36, 37)
Ulysses Garred (92, 93)
Bill Gary (00)
Dave Gash (60, 61, 62)
Augustus Gay (16)

Pete Gemmill (74)
Carl Genito (46, 48)
Ralph Genito (47, 48, 49)
Tony Gentile (30)
Ed Gholson (38)
Frank Gibson (31, 32)
Elmer Gilb (26, 27, 28)
John Gilbert (00)
Jim Giltner (10)
Al Godwin (68, 70)
Carl Goins (58 Mgr.)
Homer Goins (65, 66)
Irvin Goode (60, 61)
William Goodwin
 (03, 04)
Steve Graban (41)
Earl Grabfelder (15, 16)
W. H. Grady (02, 03, 04)
J. H. Graham (98, 99)
Hartford Granitz (45)
Jesse Grant (62)
Jim Grant (69, 70, 71)
Tony Gray (73, 74)
G. B. L. Green (19)
Phil Greer (67, 68)
Roger Greer (69)
Turner Gregg (22, 24)
Jim Gresham (66)
Bill Griffin (42, 46, 47)
John Griggs (50, 51, 52)
Bunky Gruner (51)
Carroll Gullion (01, 02)
George Gumbert (14, 15)
Thomas Gunn (93)
Ed Gusky (72)
J. White Guyn
 (01, 02, 03, 04, 05)
Les Guyn (11)

— H —

Gene Haas (44, 45, 46)
Wilbur Hackett
 (68, 69, 70)
Joe Hagan (36, 37)
G. W. Halcomb (94)
Bob Hall (37)
James Hall (10)
Fred Hamberg (71, 73)
Allen Hamilton
 (46, 48, 49, 50)
Ed Hamilton (49, 50, 51)
L. L. Hamilton (97)
Claude Hammond (41)
Jack Hanley (52, 53, 54)
Dave Hanson (68, 69, 70)
Bill Harbold (24)
Jim Hardin (38, 39, 40)
Dave Hardt (68, 69, 70)
Bob Hardy (53, 54, 55)
Tom Harper (52, 53)
Roger Harrington (56)
John Harris (66)
Wayne Harris (45 Mgr.)
W. C. Harrison
 (10, 11, 12)
Rodger Hart (66, 67)
Junior Hawthorne
 (60, 61, 62)
Langan Hay (34, 35)
Charles Haydon (15, 16)
Chastain Haynes (04)
Terry Haynes (73, 74)
John Heber
 (16, 17, 18, 19, 20)

Henry Hedges (12)
Jimmy Hedges (13, 14)
"Shorty" Heick (15, 16)
Ben Heinzinger (46)
Foster Helm (95)
George Hendrickson
 (07, 08, 09,)
Larry Hennessey
 (51, 52, 53, 54)
Dick Hensley (45, 46, 47)
Bob Herbert (40, 41, 42)
Woody Herzog (56, 56, 57)
Dick Hewling (36)
Broadus Hickerson (16)
Jim Hill (60, 61, 62)
Walter Hillenmeyer (09)
Sherman Hinkebein
 (35, 37, 38)
Paul Hite (12, 13, 14)
William (Ed) Hobdy
 (92, 93)
Lloyd Hodge
 (58, 59, 60)
Walter Hodge (36, 37)
Houston Hogg, Jr.
 (69, 70)
Sam Hogg (97, 98, 99)
Don Holland (67, 68, 69)
David Holliday
 (44 Mgr.)
Carney Hollowell (22)
Bobby Holt (53 Mgr.,
 (55 Mgr., 56 Mgr.)
Dick Holway (47, 48, 49)
Hayden Hooper
 (52, 54, 55)
Elmer Hopkins
 (16 Mgr.)
Calloway Hoskins
 (30 Mgr.)
Jim Hovey (71, 72, 73)
Ledger Howard
 (57, 58, 59)
Jim Howe (44, 48, 49)
Eric Hoyer (42)
Joe Huddleston
 (34, 35, 36)
Charles (Turkey)
 Hughes (23, 24)
Delmar Hughes
 (53, 54, 55, 56)
Lowell Hughes
 (57, 58, 59)
W. N. Hughes (01)
S. T. Hughes (02, 03)
Sam Hulette (39, 40, 41)
Claude Humphreys
 (97, 98, 99, 00)
Tom Hundley (59, 60)
Bob Hunt (58, 59, 60)
Herbie Hunt (51, 52, 53)
David Hunter (68, 69, 70)
John Hurst (42)
F. M. Hutcheson (00)
Tom Hutchinson
 (60, 61, 62)

— I —

John Ignarski (49, 50, 51)
John Ilari (55)
Charles Ishmael
 (38, 39, 40)

— J —

Ralph Jackowski
 (37, 38)
Elmer Jackson (62)
Bill Jacobs (33)
Ed Jacobs (38, 39, 40)
Joe Jacobs (67, 69)
Wilbur Jamerson
 (47, 48, 49, 50)
Pat James (48, 49, 50)
Ernest Janes (32, 33, 34)
Bill Jansen (66)
Jack Jean (33)
A. L. Jenkins (05)
Bill Jenkins (62, 63, 64)
Paul Jenkins (25, 26, 27)
Charles Jett (00, 01)
Don Jirschele (51)
Bill Jobe (33, 34)
Jimmy Johns (57, 58, 59)
Bert Johnson
 (34, 35, 36)
Clyde Johnson
 (40, 41, 42)
Dick Johnson (92)
Ellis Johnson (30, 31, 32)
Harry Johnson (61)
J. E. C. Johnson
 (04, 10, 11, 12)
J. P. Johnson (00)
Jack Johnson (97)
Marshall Johnson
 (62 Mgr.)
Marius Johnson
 (99 Mgr.)
Oliver (Ollie) Johnson
 (28, 29, 30)
Percy (Duke) Johnson
 (31 Mgr.)
Wm. T. Johnston (08, 09)
J. B. Jolly (93, 94)
Bob Jones (68, 69, 70)
Charles (Junior) Jones
 (39, 40, 41)
Harry Jones (50, 51, 52)
Larry Jones (50, 51, 52)
Paul Jones (49, 51)
Roscoe (Hut) Jones
 (42, 46, 47)
Tom Jones (99)
Wallace (Wah Wah)
 Jones (45, 46, 47, 48)
Marty Joyce (67, 68)
Jon Jurgens (60, 61)

— K —

Paul Karem (72)
Lou Karibo (52, 53 Mgr.)
George Katzenbach
 (66, 67, 68)
John Kehoe
 (98, 99, 00, 01)
E. E. Kelly (15, 18, 19)
Henry Kelly (33)
John (Shipwreck) Kelly
 (29, 30, 31)
Tom Kelly (95, 96)
Priest Kemper
 (03, 04, 05)
Jim Kennard (46)
George Kent (44)
Ralph Kercheval
 (31, 32, 33)
Felix Kerrick (95 Mgr.)

383

Rick Kestner (63, 64, 65)
Howard Keyes (64, 65)
A. S. Kidd (96)
Steve Kiefer (54, 55)
Bill Kincer (41)
Doyle King (67, 68, 69)
Kenneth King
  (21, 24, 25)
Kenny King (70, 71, 72)
Lawson King (55)
T. E. King (96)
Vic King (67, 68)
Howard Kinne (15, 16)
Bob Kipping (30, 31)
Harry Kirk
  (51, 52, 53, 54)
Tom Kirk (71)
Jim Kirkendall (27)
Ted Kirn (51)
Frank Kirschner (70, 71)
Ab Kirwan (23, 24, 25)
Norman Klein
  (44, 46, 47, 48)
Sam Klein (44)
Gary Knutson
  (70, 71, 72)
Joe Koch (52, 53, 54)
Jim Komara (62, 63, 65)
Steve Koon (67, 68)
Bob Kosid (62, 63)
Doug Kotar (71, 72, 73)
Jim Kovach (74)
Howard Kreuter
  (31, 32, 33)
Charlie Kuhn (41, 42)
Dave Kuhn
  (53, 54, 55, 56)
Dennis Kunkle (58)
Pete Kurachek (37)
Mike Kypriss (73)

— L —

Matt Lair (46, 47)
W. A. Lassiter (95)
Robert Laufer Jr.
  (28 Mgr.)
Bobby Lavin (19, 20, 21)
Cliff Lawson (49, 50, 51)
Bobby Lee (61)
Frank LeMaster (71, 72, 73)
Bill Leskovar
  (49, 50, 51)
Jim Lett (70)
Ernie Lewis (72, 73, 74)
Jim Lewis (07)
Ned Lidvall (72, 73, 74)
Jeff Lightcap (74)
Bob Lindon (57, 58)
Luke Lindon (37, 39)
Dwight Little (65, 66, 67)
Jim Little (44)
Tom Little (44)
Bill Livings (56, 57, 58)
Emmett Logan (06)
Dick Lombard
  (58 Mgr.)
Jim Long (34, 35)
Pat Looney (66 Mgr.)
Neil Lowry (52, 53, 54)
R. A. Lowry (09 Mgr.)
Chet Lukawski (50, 51)
Bill Luther (31, 32)
Ken Lutz (55)
Ernest Lyle (98, 99)

Joel Lyle
  (93, 94 Mgr., 95)
Dicky Lyons (66, 67, 68)
Les Lyons (70)

— M —

Dick Mabry (57)
Rich Machel (64, 65, 66)
Jim Mackenzie
  (49, 50, 51)
F. M. Maddox (02, 03)
Roy Maddox (98)
F. C. Mahan (04, 05)
Raynard Makin
  (68, 69, 70)
William Maloney (25)
Tony Manzonelli (64, 65)
Dave Margavage (71, 72, 73)
Dave Markem (69)
Marty Marks (72, 73)
Dick Martin
  (47, 48, 49, 50)
Givens (Doc) Martin
  (22, 23)
Jack Martin (57 Mgr.)
John Martin (59)
L. Wynn Martin
  (97, 98, 99, 00, 01)
Paul Martin (68, 69, 70)
Chester Mason (38)
Max Mason (51)
Albert Mathers (07)
Jack Mathews (68, 69)
A. M. Matthews (07)
R. E. Mattingly
  (12 Mgr.)
Clarkie Mayfield
  (60, 61, 62)
Jim Mayo (52)
Gates McCauley
  (35 Mgr.)
George McClellan (67)
Charlie McClendon
  (49, 50)
Ulysses A. McClure (01)
Charles McClurg
  (34, 35)
Jim McCollum (71, 72, 73)
Frank McCool (34, 35)
Henry McCorum
  (34 Mgr.)
Bill McCubbin
  (37, 38, 39)
Jesse McCune (44)
Lloyd McDermott
  (47, 48, 49)
Louis McDonald (44, 45)
Otho McElroy (29)
Bill McFarland (23)
Hilton McGee (02, 03)
Lawrence McGinnis (30)
Mike McGraw (64, 65, 66)
Ernest McIlvaine
  (15, 16)
James McKay (72)
N. T. McKee (01)
Walter McKinney
  (04, 05, 06)
Grandison McLean
  (24 Mgr.)
Norris (Double O)
McMillan (33, 34, 35)
Gilcin Meadors (11)
Mike Meck (70, 71)

Gene Meeks (42, 46)
Hilton Megill (03 Mgr.)
Johnny Meihaus (48)
Steve Meilinger
  (51, 52, 53)
John N. Menifee (03)
Vernon (Bo) Meyer
  (29, 30, 32)
Lou Michaels (55, 56, 57)
Frank Milburn (99, 00)
Jim Miles (64, 65)
Jim Miller (32)
J. F. Miller III (57, 58)
Leonard Miller (27)
Bradley Mills
  (52, 53, 54, 55)
Jerry Mingus (52)
Bill Mitchell (41)
Billy Mitchell
  (54, 55, 56)
Dick Mitchell (52, 53, 54)
Jim Mitchell (69, 69, 70)
Tony Moffett (71)
Gayle Mohney
  (25, 26, 27)
Dick Moloney
  (52, 53, 54, 55)
Bob Montgomery
  (31, 32)
George Montgomery
  (03, 04, 05)
Robert Montgomery (24)
Don Moore (57)
Roger Moore (18)
Joe Moraja (61)
George Morgan (95 Mgr.)
Tom Morris (69, 70, 71)
Waymond Morris
  (57, 58)
Bill Moseley (42, 46, 47)
Doug Moseley
  (49, 50, 51)
Dickie Mueller
  (58, 59, 60)
Rick Muench (60, 70, 71)
Basil Mullins (63, 65, 66)
Noah Mullins (40, 41)
Steve Murgita (72, 73, 74)
Eger V. Murphree
  (16, 17, 18, 19, 20)
Gerard Murphy
  (63, 64, 65)
O. B. Murphy (32, 33)
Robert Murray (73)
John Mutchler (60, 61)
Albert Muth (19)
Art Myers (72, 73, 74)
Gene Myers (34, 35, 36)

— N —

Dan Neal (71, 72)
J. C. Nesbit
  (04 Mgr., 05 Mgr.)
Don Netoskie
  (53, 54, 55, 56)
John Netoskie
  (49, 50, 51)
Stanley Nevers
  (34, 35, 36)
Homer Nicholas (36)
John Nicholson (71 Mgr.)
John Nochta (73, 74)
Rick Norton (63, 64, 65)

Orval Kowack (28)
Don Nuerge (59, 60)
John Nuttall (94)
Rick Nuzum (72, 73, 74)

— O —

Doug O'Brien (61)
Nick Odlivak (47, 48, 49)
Arperd Olah (33, 35)
Ken O'Leary (71, 72)
Joe Orr (35)
Isaac Ott (26)
Oweney Owen (79 Mgr.)
Dallas Owens (74)

— P —

Roger Pack (54, 55, 56)
Greg Page (67)
Bob Palmer (38, 39, 40)
Dick Palmer (67, 68, 69)
Ralph Paolone (52, 53)
Alex Parda (37)
Vito (Babe) Parilli
 (49, 50, 51)
Jim Park (11, 13, 14)
Smith Park (19 Mgr.)
Sam Parker (00)
Steve Parker (72, 73, 74)
Frank Parks (42 Mgr.)
Allen Parr (40, 41, 42)
Doug Parrish (32, 33)
Steve Parrish (69, 70)
Jim Parrott (44)
Henry Paul (44, 45)
Frank Paullin (05, 06)
Bernie Pavlovich (45)
J. Hamilton Payne (07)
Bart Peak (15)
Jim Pence (25, 26, 27)
W. H. Perkins (00 Mgr.)
Wally Pesuit (73, 74)
Charles Petrie (14)
Al Phaneuf (66, 67)
Don Phelps (46, 47, 49)
Bob Phillips (54, 55)
Hal Phillips (45)
Randy Phillips (38)
Steve Phillips (72)
O. E. Philpot (54, 55)
Frank Phipps (25, 26, 27)
Jack Phipps (29, 30, 31)
Tom Phipps (29, 30)
Phil Pickett (62)
John Pierce (74)
Joe Platt (52, 53)
George Plummer (09)
Bob Pope (48, 49, 50)
Ray Porter (47, 48, 49)
Don Porterfield
 (68, 69, 70)
Al Portwood (26, 27, 28)
Bill Portwood (41)
Henry Portwood (24, 26)
Shelby Post (08)
Derek Potter (66, 67)
Lexie Potter (35, 36)
Sam Potter (34, 35)
Sam Pottinger (92 Mgr.)
Archie Powers
 (55, 56, 57)
Jimmy Poynter (59, 60)
Leonard Preston (46, 47)
Birkett Pribble
 (19, 20, 21, 22)

Holton Pribble (32, 34)
J. T. Pride (02, 03)
Bob Pritchard
 (33, 34, 36)
Jim Proffitt (51, 52, 53)
John Puntillo (71)
Dave Pursell (68, 69, 70)

— R —

John Rampulla (61)
Dell Ramsey
 (20, 21, 22, 23)
Tom Ranicri (72, 74)
Bill Ransdell (59, 60, 61)
Clark Ratcliffe (52)
Babe Ray (45)
Keith Raynor (67)
Jim Reader (59, 60)
Harry Redmond (93)
Jim Reed (70, 71, 72)
Tom Reed (72 Mgr.)
A. S. Reese
 (96, 97, 98, 99)
Chester Reichle
 (39 Mgr.)
Walter Reid (38, 39, 40)
Kent Reyes (73)
Jay Rhodemyre
 (42, 46, 47)
Dan Rhyne (59 Mgr.)
Chuck Rice (20, 22, 23)
Dennis Rice (46)
Guy Rice (99)
William H. Rice
 (22, 24, 25)
Dick Richards
 (29, 30, 31)
Clyde Richardson (62, 63)
Ches Riddle, (73)
Craig Riddle (17, 18)
Don Ridge (46, 47)
Dan Riveiro (61)
Ronnie Roberts (65, 66, 67)
H. B. Roberts (93)
Kenny Robertson
 (55, 56, 57)
Tom Robinson (13 Mgr.)
Vincent (Dick) Robin-
 son (35, 36, 37)
J. W. Rodes (04, 05)
Pete Rodes (07, 08)
Wm. (Black Doc) Rodes
 (15, 16)
Wm. (Red Doc) Rodes
 (09, 11, 12)
Tom Rodgers (58, 59, 60)
Harry Rogers (49, 50)
David Roller (68, 69, 70)
Conrad Rose, (28, 29, 30)
John Ross (25, 26)
Abe Roth (12, 13, 14)
Tony Rotunno (44)
G. C. Routt (07, 08, 09)
Frank Rucks (68, 69)
Gerald Rueff (68 Mgr.)
Joe Rupert (32, 33, 34)
Leonard Rush (66, 68)
Dick Rushing
 (52, 53, 54)
James R. Russell
 (21, 22, 23)

— S —

Frank Sadler
 (46 Mgr., 47 Mgr.)

Harold Salsbery
 (70 Mgr.)
Curtis Sanders Jr.
 (45 Mgr.)
Curtis Sanders
 (21, 22, 23, 24)
Curtis Sauer (23, 24)
Bruce Sauerbry (70, 71)
Francis Saunders (44)
Hugh Saunders (03)
Unis Saylor
 (48 Mgr., 49 Mgr.)
Bill Schaffnit
 (48, 49, 50)
Jim Schenk (52, 53)
Charles Schifler (41)
F. A. Schilling (12)
George Schlegel (41)
Howie Schnellenberger
 (52, 53, 54, 55)
Steve Schoenbaechler (72)
Frank Schollett
 (57, 58, 59)
Herman Scholtz
 (98, 00, 01, 02)
John Schornick (65)
C. C. Schrader
 (12, 13, 14, 15)
Dennis Schrecker (61)
Ray Schrecker (59)
Wilbur Schu (44)
Ray Schulte (25, 26)
Bill Scott (60)
George Scott (93)
Herschel Scott
 (12, 13, 14)
John Scott (93)
Phil Scott (38, 39, 40)
Steve Scott (69)
Wellington Scott
 (99, 00, 01)
William Paul Scott (26)
Bernie Scruggs
 (69, 70, 71)
Frank Seale (30, 31, 32)
Tom Searcy (72)
Larry Seiple (64, 65, 66)
Vince Semary (62, 63)
George Sengel
 (42, 46, 47)
Wash Serini
 (44, 45, 46, 47)
Jim Server
 (15, 19, 20, 21)
Ed Settle (64)
Barry Settles (72 Mgr.)
Pat Settles (70 Mgr.)
Roscoe Severs (97, 98)
Doug Sexton (72)
Cary Shahid (67, 68, 69)
Arthur Shanklin
 (17, 18, 19, 20)
Eugene Shanklin (33)
George Shanklin
 (07, 08, 09, 10)
Hugh Shannon (44, 45)
Dick Shatto (53)
Fred Shaw (20 Mgr.)
Glenn Shaw (57, 58, 59)
Joe Shelby (08, 09)
F. M. Sheldon (05)
John Shelton (24)
Joe Shepherd
 (37, 38, 39)
Bob Sherman (37)

Doug Shively (56, 57, 58)
J. Cleves Short (94, 95)
Mike Siganos (74)
Clay Simpson (15, 16)
Elmore Simpson
  (35, 36, 37)
Tommy Simpson
  (60, 61, 62)
Ed Singleton (73, 74)
Don Sinor (58, 59, 60)
Wendell Skaggs
  (35, 36, 37)
George Skinner
  (30, 31, 32)
D. D. Slade (97)
Paul Slaton (36 Mgr.)
Paul Sloan (57)
Calvin Smith (51)
D. P. Smith (92)
Ed Smith (63)
Frank Smith (24, 25, 26)
George Smith (14)
Giles Smith
  (64, 65 Mgr.)
Jim Smith (70, 72 Mgr.)
Joe David Smith (64, 66)
S. J. Smith (98)
Ed Smolder (74)
Frank Smotherman (47)
Dan Spanish (64, 65, 66)
W. A. Spanton (01, 02)
Howell Spears (11)
Larry Spears (38, 39, 40)
B. W. Spencer (02, 03)
Howell Spencer (01, 02)
H. A. Speyer (06)
Bill (Bud) Spicer (58)
Carey Spicer (28, 29, 30)
Tom Spickard (38, 39)
Paul Sponheimer (71, 73, 74)
C. P. St. John (03)
Jim Stacey (99)
Ed Stanko (64, 65)
Dick Steckler (59 Mgr.)
Ron Steele (73)
Sherman Steely (93)
Joe Stephan (69, 70, 71)
Elmore Stephens (71, 73, 74)
E. A. Stephenson (23)
Gary Steward (60, 61, 62)
Art Still (74)
R. T. Stofer (08)
Richard C. Stoll (93, 94)
Earl Stone (06)
Neville Stone (06, 07)
B. E. W. Stout (08 Mgr.)
Leo Strange (53, 54, 55)
Charles L. Straus
  (97, 98)
Jack Strother (32 Mgr.)
Joe Stuart (54)
Charles Sturgeon
  (58, 59, 60)
George Summers (27)
G. Sumner (06)
John Sutak (44)
Jim Swart (64, 65, 66)
Earl Swindle (70, 71, 72)
Harvey Sword (71, 72, 73)
Joe Sydnor (37)

– T –

Bob Talamini
  (57, 58, 59)

John Tatterson (72, 73, 74)
Harry Taylor (41, 42)
Jim Taylor (41 Mgr.)
N. S. Taylor (08)
Flanery Terrill (28)
Bill Thiesing (09)
Ben Thomas (72, 73, 74)
Hobart Thomas (44)
Smith Thomas (03)
J. J. Thompson (02)
Jim Thompson
  (13, 14, 15)
Joe Thompson
  (28, 29)
Mark Thompson (61)
Phil Thompson
  (67, 68, 69)
W. T. Thompson (19, 20)
David Thornton (20)
Polk Threlkeld (09, 10)
Bill Tichenor (33)
Steve Tingle (69)
Talbott Todd (63, 64, 65)
Louis Toth (28, 29, 30)
Fay Townes (15 Mgr.)
Bill Tracy (37)
Len Tracy (23, 24, 25)
Cliff Tribble (56, 57, 58)
Pete Triplett (42)
Lee Truman (47, 48, 49)
Rich Tucci (63, 64, 65)
Jesse Tunstill (42, 45, 46)
Herschel Turner (61, 62, 63)
J. M. Turner (05)
James D. Turner
  (94, 95, 98)
William Tuttle
  (11, 12, 13, 14)

– U –

Harry Ulinski
  (46, 47, 48, 49)
Cecil Urbaniak
  (29, 30, 31)
Jim Urbaniak
  (55, 56, 57)

– V –

Wendell Vance (49, 50)
Ben VanMeter
  (93 Mgr., 94 Mgr.)
Dave Van Meter
  (69, 70, 71)
Doug Van Meter (65, 66, 67)
Emanuel Van Meter
  (24, 26, 27)
Jeff Van Note
  (66, 67, 68)
Russell Vanzant
  (23 Mgr.)
Charles Vaughn (59)
Pete Vires (37, 38)
John Vogt
  (99, 00, 01, 02)

– W –

Beverly Waddell (26)
Jim Wadlington (35, 37)
Sheldon Wagner (33, 34)
Harry Wagner (32)
Bobby Walker
  (54, 55, 56)

Charlie Bill Walker
  (41, 42, 46)
H. L. Walker (07)
Harry Walker
  (32, 33, 34)
W. G. Walker (17, 19)
Tom Walters (27, 28, 29)
Roger Walz (65, 66)
Bill Wannamaker
  (48, 49, 50)
A. F. Ward (96)
Paul Ward (96)
Leo Warring (68, 69 Mgr.)
C. Wathen (21)
George C. (Possum)
  Watkins (10, 11)
Cova Watson (21 Mgr.)
Rufus Weaver (93)
Clayton Webb
  (48, 49, 50)
Dick Webb (07, 09, 10)
Al Weinman
  (50 Mgr., 51 Mgr.)
John T. Welch (97)
David Weld (67)
Charles Wert (25, 26, 27)
E. C. Whayne (97, 98)
Bill Wheeler (53, 54, 55)
H. R. Whittinghill
  (02 Mgr.)
R. T. Whittinghill (00)
Bill Wilburn (42)
Newell Wilder (31)
Ed Wiley (20)
Jim Wilhelm (17, 20)
Miles Wilard (51, 53)
Charles Williams
  (40 Mgr.)
Delon Williams (11)
Fred Williams (74)
Howard Williams
  (28, 29, 30)
James Williams
  (29 Mgr.)
John Williams (98)
Ken Williams (53)
W. C. Willim (98)
Emmett Willoughby
  (38, 39, 40)
Cullen Wilson
  (57, 58, 59)
James M. Wilson (06, 07)
W. B. Wilson (10)
Murray Wilson (06)
Dick Wilson
  (98, 01 Mgr.)
S. E. Wilson (96)
Bob Windsor (65, 66)
Bob Winkel (74)
Calvin Withrow
  (64, 65, 66)
Bob Wixson, Jr.
  (69, 70, 71)
Bob Wodtke (48)
Louis Wolf (66, 67, 68)
Rod Wolfe (69)
Clark Wood (40, 41, 42)
Hugh Wood
  (00, 02, 03, 04)
Kenny Wood (67)
Jeff Woodcock (71, 72, 73)
Harold Wooddell (49, 50)
Greg Woods (73, 74)
John Woods (93, 94, 95)

Harry Woodson
  (11, 12, 13)
Jeff Woodcock (71, 72, 73)
Jerry Woolum
  (60, 61, 62)
Floyd Wright (13)
Ralph Wright
  (29, 30, 31)
Rich Wright (57, 58, 59)

Ed C. Wurtele (02)

— Y —

Leo Yarutis (42, 46, 47)
George Yates (29, 30, 31)
Roger Yost (44, 45)
Walter Young (60 Mgr.)
Walt Yowarsky
  (48, 49, 50)

— Z —

Al Zampino (51, 53, 56)
Ben Zaranka
  (47, 48, 49, 50)
George Zerfoss (19)
Karl Zerfoss (13, 14, 15)
Tom Zerfoss (13)
Tommy Zinn (41)
Dave Zoeller (38, 39, 40)